# Cultural Mythology and Global Leadership

## Dedication

To my beloved sons, Jacob and Daniel, whose childhood pasts planted the seeds for this book and whose adult futures will (hopefully) reap the benefits of its germination. – EHK

To the legacies of my grandmothers, Chung How Mah and King Fong Louie, whose lives carried forth the wisdoms of ancestors through to my mother, Quen Kui Wong, and to our children, Quentin and Maya. – DJW

# Cultural Mythology and Global Leadership

*Edited by*

Eric H. Kessler

*Pace University, New York, USA*

and

Diana J. Wong-MingJi

*Eastern Michigan University, Ypsilanti, USA*

**Edward Elgar**
Cheltenham, UK • Northampton, MA, USA

Published by
Edward Elgar Publishing Limited
The Lypiatts
15 Lansdown Road
Cheltenham
Glos GL50 2JA
UK

Edward Elgar Publishing, Inc.
William Pratt House
9 Dewey Court
Northampton
Massachusetts 01060
USA

Paperback edition 2010
Paperback edition reprinted 2013, 2016

A catalogue record for this book
is available from the British Library

**Library of Congress Control Number: 2008943829**

Printed on elemental chlorine free (ECF)
recycled paper containing 30% Post-Consumer Waste

ISBN   978 1 84720 403 5 (cased)
       978 1 84980 180 5 (paperback)

Typeset by Cambrian Typesetters, Camberley, Surrey
Printed and bound in the USA

# Contents

*Editor biographies*                                                    vii
*List of contributors*                                                   ix

Introduction to cultural mythology and global leadership                  1
*Eric H. Kessler and Diana J. Wong-MingJi*

## PART I   THE AMERICAS

1.  Cultural mythology and global leadership in the United States        31
    *Eric H. Kessler*
2.  Cultural mythology and global leadership in Canada                   49
    *Nina D. Cole and Rhona G. Berengut*
3.  Cultural mythology and global leadership in the
    Caribbean islands                                                    65
    *Betty Jane Punnett and Dion Greenidge*
4.  Cultural mythology and global leadership in Argentina                79
    *Patricia Friedrich, Andrés Hatum and Luiz Mesquita*
5.  Cultural mythology and global leadership in Brazil                   93
    *Adriana V. Garibaldi de Hilal*

## PART II   EUROPE

6.  Cultural mythology and global leadership in Greece                  111
    *Theodore Peridis*
7.  Cultural mythology and global leadership in Germany                 127
    *Sonja A. Sackmann*
8.  Cultural mythology and global leadership in England                 145
    *Romie Frederick Littrell*
9.  Cultural mythology and global leadership in Sweden                  166
    *Lena Zander and Udo Zander*
10. Cultural mythology and global leadership in Poland                  187
    *Christopher Ziemnowicz and John Spillan*

PART III   AFRICA AND THE MIDDLE EAST

11.   Cultural mythology and global leadership in South Africa          209
      *David N. Abdulai*
12.   Cultural mythology and global leadership in Kenya                 225
      *Fred O. Walumbwa and George O. Ndege*
13.   Cultural mythology and global leadership in Iran                  242
      *Afsaneh Nahavandi*
14.   Cultural mythology and global leadership in Egypt                 257
      *Mohamed M. Mostafa and Diana J. Wong-MingJi*
15.   Cultural mythology and global leadership in Israel                270
      *Shay S. Tzafrir, Aviv Barhom-Kidron and Yehuda Baruch*

PART IV   ASIA AND THE PACIFIC RIM

16.   Cultural mythology and global leadership in China                 289
      *Diana J. Wong-MingJi*
17.   Cultural mythology and global leadership in India                 306
      *Shanthi Gopalakrishnan and Rajender Kaur*
18.   Cultural mythology and global leadership in Russia                325
      *Stanislav V. Shekshnia, Sheila M. Puffer and Daniel J. McCarthy*
19.   Cultural mythology and global leadership in Japan                 343
      *Tomoatsu Shibata and Mitsuru Kodama*
20.   Cultural mythology and global leadership in Australia             359
      *David Lamond*

*Index*                                                                 375

# Editor biographies

 **Eric H. Kessler**, Ph.D. is a senior Professor of Management at Pace University in New York City and founding Director of the Lubin Leaders and Scholars Program, which prepares students for careers in global business leadership. He is a Fellow and past President of the Eastern Academy of Management, the northeastern United States association of business management scholars, and during that time organized a symposium on cultural mythology and leadership at the EAM-International conference in Cape Town, South Africa that formed the foundation for this book. He has served on several editorial boards and as the guest editor for a number of professional journals, as well as on review panels with the US National Security Education Program. Dr Kessler has published or presented over 100 scholarly papers in top academic outlets and conferences, won numerous research and teaching awards, and is the author or editor of several additional books including *Handbook of Organizational and Managerial Wisdom* (2007, Sage Publications) and *Management Theory in Action* (forthcoming, Palgrave Macmillan). He is a member of Phi Beta Kappa and has been inducted into national and international honour societies in Business, Economics, Forensics, and Psychology. Professor Kessler instructs courses on the doctoral, masters, and bachelors levels, has led several international field studies, and has worked as an executive educator, policy analyst, and business consultant for public and private organizations. His professional travels have taken him across the six continents represented in this volume. Eric is an avid reader of history and philosophy, a sports and puzzle junkie, as well as the spinner of many a bad pun. He lives with his best friend/wife, two terrific sons, and faithful Black Labrador.

**Diana J. Wong-MingJi,** Ph.D., is an Associate Professor of Strategy and Entrepreneurship at Eastern Michigan University. She also teaches international management, leadership, and organization development and change. Her research examines how strategic alliances evolve through different competitive conditions and the related development of leadership competencies to manage change. In particular, Diana is interested in organizational change processes related to globalization. Her international experiences include studying indigenous communities while attending the University of Oslo in Norway, working with negotiating teams on subsidies for the US-Canada Free Trade Agreement and later NAFTA; teaching in Papua New Guinea and China; and launching an international education agreement between Eastern Michigan University and Osmania University in India. Her professional activities include contributing to the internationalization of organizations, serving as President of the American Society of Training and Development's Ann Arbor chapter, and consulting through her practice, Sensei Change Associates. Currently, Diana resides in Ann Arbor, MI with her family and spends most summers in Vancouver, Canada.

# Contributors

**David N. Abdulai** is currently the CEO/Executive Director of the Graduate School of Business Leadership at the University of South Africa. He holds graduate degrees from the Graduate School of International Studies from the University of Denver, and the School of International Services at the American University in Washington, DC. His undergraduate degree was obtained at Howard University in Washington, DC. His has written widely in the areas of culture, leadership as well as on development issues pertaining to Africa.

**Yehuda Baruch** is Professor of Management at UEA Norwich UK and formerly held visiting positions at the University of Texas at Arlington, and London Business School. He published extensively in the areas of Global and Strategic HRM, Careers, and Technology Management, including over 80 refereed papers, in journals including *Human Resource Management, Organizational Dynamics, Journal of Vocational Behavior, Human Relations* and *Organization Studies* and over 20 books and book chapters, including *Managing Career: Theory and Practice* and co-edited *Winning Reviews: A Guide for Evaluating Scholarly Writing* and *Opening the Black Box of Editorship.* Editor of *Group & Organization Management* and former Chair, Careers Division, Academy of Management.

**Rhona G. Berengut**, MBA, is a Lecturer in Organizational Behaviour at the Ted Rogers School of Business Management, Ryerson University in Toronto, Canada. She is a founding partner of SIGMA Strategic Solutions Inc. where she works with organizations to align people, performance and strategic purpose. In her practice, Rhona works with organizations to understand their culture and the impact of culture on organization dynamics and performance. Her areas of specialization include: Leading Sustainable Strategic Change, Critical Thinking and Innovation Skills, Interpersonal Effectiveness, and Strategic Analysis. Rhona is a Certified Facilitator and Strategic Planner, Executive and EQ Coach.

**Nina D. Cole**, Ph.D., is Associate Professor of organizational behaviour and human resource management at the Ted Rogers School of Business Management, Ryerson University in Toronto, Canada. She is a past president of the Administrative Sciences Association of Canada and a member of the

Academy of Management and the Academy of International Business. She has lectured on leadership to classes in Canada, Australia, Cambodia and the Philippines. Her past programme of research on applying organizational justice theories to human resource management activities has become more global and her current research focuses on cross-cultural organizational justice and management of expatriate employees.

**Patricia Friedrich** is an Assistant Professor in the Department of Language, Cultures and History at Arizona State University. A trained Sociolinguist, Dr Friedrich's research focuses on the social, political and economic impact of the spread of languages throughout the world and on issues of intercultural communication especially at the firm level. She is the author of *Language, Negotiation and Peace: the Role of English in Conflict Resolution* (Continuum Books, 2007) and the editor of *Teaching Academic Writing* (Continuum Books, 2008). Her work has appeared in such journals as *Harvard Business Review*, *Management Research*, *World Englishes* and the *International Journal of Applied Linguistics*. She is a member of the editorial board of the *International Multilingual Research Journal*.

**Adriana Victoria Garibaldi de Hilal**, Doctor in Business Administration with focus in International Business (Federal University of Rio de Janeiro – COPPEAD). Has a post-doctorate at IRIC (Institute for the Research on Intercultural Cooperation) – Tilburg University – Netherlands, where she held the position of Hofstede Fellow. She is a full time Associate Professor of Organizations and International Business at COPPEAD/ UFRJ. She has also been involved in cross-cultural research with Professor Hofstede (Netherlands); writes articles and books, which have been published internationally and in Brazil, and works as a consultant. She has participated in several projects dealing with organizational culture/ national culture, leadership and change, focusing on takeovers, mergers, acquisitions and the internationalization of companies.

**Shanthi Gopalakrishnan** is a Professor and Associate Dean at the School of Management, at NJIT, New Jersey. She received her Ph.D. in Organization Management from Rutgers University. Prior to her Ph.D. she did her MBA and worked in Sales and Product Management for a diversified consumer and industrial products company. Her research interests are in the area of innovation management, strategic management of technology, strategic alliances and cross-cultural leadership issues. She has published over 20 articles on these topics in the top management journals. Dr Gopalakrishnan is a member of the Academy of Management and was the Past President of Eastern Academy of Management. She sits on the Editorial Board of several management journals.

**Dion Greenridge** holds a BA (Honours) in Psychology (UWI) and an MSc in Work and Organisational Psychology (University of Nottingham). He is currently completing his PhD at Nottingham, and is an instructor with the Department of Management Studies, University of West Indies in Barbados. He has been involved in a number of academic and industry-related research projects and has presented work at regional and international conferences, and published in well-established journals. His research interests are the structure and measurement of personality and other individual difference variables, and employee job performance constructs – task performance, contextual performance, and counterproductive work behaviours.

**Andrés Hatum** is Associate Professor of Human Resource Management at IAE Business School at Austral University (Argentina). He received his Ph.D. in Management and Organization from Warwick Business School at the University of Warwick (UK). His research interests include flexibility in organizations, management across cultures in Latin American countries, the study and dilemmas of careers and talent management in firms in the region. Andrés Hatum has published papers and books in English and Spanish. His latest book is *Adaptation or Exploration in Family Firms: determinants of organizational flexibility in emerging economies* (Edward Elgar, 2007).

**Rajender Kaur** is Assistant Professor of English at William Paterson University, NJ, where she teaches courses in Postcolonial Studies and World Literatures. Her primary research has been on the Literature of the Bengal Famine of 1943 and she also works on social justice and the environment, gender and culture in South Asia, and South Asian Literatures. Currently she is working on a book project, *South Asians in North America: A Documentary History* to be published by Rutgers UP in 2009.

**Eric H. Kessler**, Ph.D. is a senior Professor of Management at Pace University in New York City and founding Director of the Lubin Leaders and Scholars Program, which prepares students for careers in global business leadership. He is a Fellow and past President of the Eastern Academy of Management, the northeastern United States association of business management scholars, and during that time organized a symposium on cultural mythology and leadership at the EAM-International conference in Cape Town, South Africa that formed the foundation for this book. He has served on several editorial boards and as the guest editor for a number of professional journals, as well as on review panels with the US National Security Education Program. Dr Kessler has published or presented over 100 scholarly papers in top academic outlets and conferences, won numerous research and teaching awards, and is the author or editor of several additional books including *Handbook of Organizational and Managerial*

*Wisdom* (2007, Sage Publications) and *Management Theory in Action* (forth-coming, Palgrave Macmillan). He is a member of Phi Beta Kappa and has been inducted into national and international honour societies in Business, Economics, Forensics, and Psychology. Professor Kessler instructs courses on the doctoral, masters, and bachelors levels, has led several international field studies, and has worked as an executive educator, policy analyst, and business consultant for public and private organizations. His professional travels have taken him across the six continents represented in this volume. Eric is an avid reader of history and philosophy, a sports and puzzle junkie, as well as the spinner of many a bad pun. He lives with his best friend/wife, two terrific sons, and faithful Black Labrador.

**Aviv Barhom-Kidron** is a doctorate candidate in the Graduate School of Management at the University of Haifa. She received her MA in organizational sociology from Bar-Ilan University. She also teaches as instructor at the Open University of Israel. Her current research interest includes human resource management integration and leadership. Her articles have been published in *The Journal of Applied Behavioral Science*.

**Mitsuru Kodama** is a Professor of Information and Management in the College of Commerce and Graduate School of Business Administration at Nihon University. His research papers have been published in *Long Range Planning*, *Organization Studies*, *Technovation*, and *Research-Technology Management,* among others. He published three books: *The Strategic Community-Based Firm* (Palgrave Macmillan, 2007), *Knowledge Innovation – Strategic Management As Practice* (Edward Elgar Publishing, 2007), *Project-Based Organization In The Knowledge-Based Society* (Imperial College Press, 2007).

**David Lamond**, during the time his chapter was being written, was Founding Dean of the Kochi International Business School (KiBS) in India, where he was living out Gandhi's injunction to be the change he wished to see in the world. His doctoral degree, from Macquarie University, was focused on person and situation antecedents of managerial behaviour. David has worked in many countries and regions – India, China, Singapore, Sri Lanka, Malaysia and the UK – drawing on his insights from those experiences and his migrant Celt background to inform the analysis in the current chapter. Currently, David serves as the Associate Dean at the Nottingham Business School and the Editor-in-Chief for the *Journal of Management History*.

**Romie F. Littrell**, BA, MBA, PhD, FIAIR, is Associate Professor of International Business at Auckland University of Technology in New Zealand,

and has been involved in academic teaching and research for 12 years in the USA, China, Switzerland, Germany and New Zealand, and as a visiting professor in China, India and Turkey. He is facilitator of the Centre for Cross-Cultural Comparisons and of the Leadership and Management Studies in Sub-Sahara Africa biennial conferences. Industry experience includes management and marketing in the USA, England, the Caribbean and Latin America, and China. His research interests are leadership and management across cultures.

**Daniel J. McCarthy** is the Alan S. McKim and Richard A. D'Amore Distinguished Professor of Global Management and Innovation at Northeastern University, and a Fellow at the Davis Center for Russian Studies at Harvard University. His research and publications centre on strategic management, entrepreneurship, and corporate governance, particularly in Russia's transitioning economy. He has more than 85 publications, including numerous journal articles, four editions of *Business Policy and Strategy*, *Business and Management in Russia*, *The Russian Capitalist Experiment*, and *Corporate Governance in Russia*. He earned his AB and MBA degrees from Dartmouth College and his DBA from Harvard University.

**Luiz Mesquita** is Assistant Professor of Strategy and International Management, at the School of Global Management and Leadership, Arizona State University. He has published on alliance management, networks of SMEs, cross-cultural management and business groups in emerging economies in academic journals such as the *Academy of Management Review*, *Strategic Management Journal*, *Academy of Management Journal*, *Harvard Business Review*, *Journal of Business Studies* and *Management Research*, among others. He is also the co-editor of *Can Latin American Firms Compete?* (Oxford University Press), as well as *Entrepreneurial Strategies: New Technologies and Emerging Markets* (Blackwell).

**Mohamed M. Mostafa**, Ph.D. University of Manchester UK is a Visiting Professor of Marketing at Auburn University, AL, USA, having previously been employed at universities in Egypt, Cyprus, Jordan, United Arab Emirates, and Kuwait. His research has appeared in several leading academic peer reviewed journals, including *Psychology and Marketing*, *Journal of Managerial Psychology*, *International Journal of Consumer Studies*, *International Journal of Health Care Quality Assurance*, *Journal of International Consumer Marketing*, *Cross-Cultural Management*, *International Journal of Productivity and Performance Management*, *International Journal of Business Performance Management* and *Journal of Economic Studies*. He has also presented numerous papers at professional conferences worldwide.

**Afsaneh Nahavandi** is a professor of Public Administration and associate dean of the College of Public Programs at Arizona State University. Her areas of speciality are leadership, culture, ethics and teams. She has published articles about these topics in journals such as the *Academy of Management Review,* the *Journal of Management Studies,* the *Journal of Business Ethics,* and the *Academy of Management Executive.* Her article about teams won the *Academy of Management Executive*'s 1994 Best Article award. She has written books about culture and mergers and organizational behaviour and is the author of *The Art and Science of Leadership* now in its fifth edition.

**George O. Ndege** is currently an associate professor of History at Saint Louis University. He has previously taught at Maseno and Moi Universities in Kenya. His research focuses on state and society in colonial and postcolonial Africa. Ndege is the author of *Health, State, and Society in Kenya* (2001), and *Culture and Customs of Mozambique* (2007). He has many articles in journals, books, and encyclopedias, most recently in the *Journal of Development Alternatives and Area Studies, Economic History of Kenya, Ethnicity, Nationalism and Democracy in Africa* and the *Encyclopedia of African History.*

**Theodore Peridis,** B.Sc., MA, M.Phil., Ph.D, is a professor of Strategic Management at the Schulich School of Business, in Toronto, Canada and the Director of the Global Leadership Program. He has taught at universities in Europe, North America, Asia, and the Middle East. He has worked with many companies and government committees on industrial policy and has acted as special consultant on issues of acquisitions and alliances. His work and leisurely pursuits have taken him to six continents and over 50 countries but he still can't find his way around his own back yard. He was named Best in Class by the *Canadian Business* magazine and Professor of the Yearby the Kellogg/Schulich EMBA programme.

**Sheila M. Puffer** is Walsh Research Professor and Cherry Family Senior Fellow of International Business at Northeastern University, and a Fellow at the Davis Center for Russian Studies at Harvard University. She has more than 150 publications, including eight books such as *The Russian Management Revolution, Business and Management in Russia, The Russian Capitalist Experiment* and *Corporate Governance in Russia.* She is a former editor of *The Academy of Management Executive.* She holds BA and MBA degrees from the University of Ottawa (Canada), a Ph.D. from the University of California, Berkeley, and a diploma from the Plekhanov Institute of the National Economy (Moscow).

**Betty Jane Punnett**, Ph.D. International Business, New York University, is a native of St. Vincent and the Grenadines. Professor of International Business/ Management, Cave Hill Campus, University of the West Indies, she has published over 50 academic papers in an array of international journals. Recent books are *The Handbook for International Management Research*, *International Perspectives on Organizational Behavior and Human Resource Management*, *Experiencing International Business and Management* and *Successful Professional Women of the Americas*. Her research interests are culture and management, and Caribbean issues in management and global competitiveness. Professor Punnett recently completed a Fulbright Fellowship with Wayne State University.

**Sonja A. Sackmann** has a chair in Organizational Behaviour at the University of Munich and is Director of the Institute of Human Resources and Organization Studies. She has taught at the Graduate Schools of Management at UCLA, USA; St Gallen, Switzerland; Constance and EBS European Business School, Germany; Vienna, Austria and Jiao Tong University, Shanghai, China. She has developed and delivered numerous leadership programmes for managers and executives of international and global firms. Her areas of specialization are leadership, culture, team- and organizational development. She received her BS and MS in Psychology from the Karl-Ruprecht University, Heidelberg and her Ph.D. in Management from the Graduate School of Management, UCLA. She has published several books and numerous articles.

**Stanislav Shekshnia** brings a perspective of a business executive and an academic. He is an Affiliate Professor of Entrepreneurship and a Program Director at the Global Leadership Center at INSEAD where he concentrates on executive development and coaching. Earlier, his experience included a decade of top-level positions in Russia, Eastern Europe, and France. In 2002 he co-founded the international consultancy, Zest Leadership, which provides personal coaching and leadership development services to business owners and corporate executives. Dr Shekshnia is the author or editor of seven books and over 50 articles. He has an MBA from Northeastern University and a Ph.D. from Moscow State University.

**Tomoatsu Shibata** is a Professor of Technology Management, Graduate School of Management, Kagawa University. His research papers have been published in *Research Policy, International Journal of Innovation Management, Business Strategy Series*, among others.

**John Spillan**, MBA and Ph.D. in Business and Management, serves as

Associate Professor of Business Administration at The Pennsylvania State University – DuBois Campus. His research interests centre on Crisis Management, International Marketing, Entrepreneurship and International Business with specific interest in Latin America and Eastern Europe. His articles have appeared in the *International Journal of Marketing and Marketing Research, Journal of Business in Developing Nations, Southern Business Review, Journal of East West Business, European Management Journal, Journal of Teaching in International Business, Journal of Small Business Strategy, International Small Business Journal, Journal of Crisis and Contingency Management, Journal of Small Business Management, Journal of Marketing Theory and Practice, Journal of World Business* among others.

**Shay S. Tzafrir** is a senior lecturer in the Department of Human Services at the University of Haifa. He received his Ph.D. in behavioural science from the Technion – Israel Institute of Technology. He serves as associate editor of *Journal of Managerial Psychology*. His current research interest includes the role trust plays in various organizational factors such as strategic human resource management, leadership, organizational performance, emotion, and service quality. His articles have been published in journals such as *Industrial Relations, Human Resource Management, International Journal of Human Resource Management,* and others.

**Fred O. Walumbwa**, PhD, The University of Illinois at Urbana-Champaign is an assistant professor of management at Arizona State University. His research interests include leadership development, organizational culture/identity, organizational justice, cross-cultural research, business ethics and multilevel issues in research. He currently serves on the editorial review boards of *Organizational Behavior and Human Decision Processes, Journal of Management* and *Leadership Quarterly*. He is also a member of the 'Distinguished Science Advisory Council' of Gallup Organization as a Senior Scientist. His latest book (with W. L. Gardner and B. J. Avolio) is titled, *Authentic Leadership Theory and Practice: Origins, Effects and Development* (Volume 3) (Oxford, UK: Elsevier Science, 2005).

**Diana J. Wong-MingJi**, Ph.D., is an Associate Professor of Strategy and Entrepreneurship at Eastern Michigan University. She also teaches international management, leadership, and organization development and change. Her research examines how strategic alliances evolve through different competitive conditions and the related development of leadership competencies to manage change. In particular, Diana is interested in organizational change processes related to globalization. Her international experiences include studying indigenous communities while attending the University of Oslo in Norway, working with negotiating teams on subsidies for the US-Canada Free Trade Agreement and later NAFTA; teaching in Papua New Guinea and China; and launching an international education agreement between Eastern Michigan University and Osmania University in India. Her professional activities include contributing to the internationalization of organizations, serving as President of the American Society of Training and Development's Ann Arbor chapter, and consulting through her practice, Sensei Change Associates. Currently, Diana resides in Ann Arbor, MI with her family and spends most summers in Vancouver, Canada.

**Lena Zander** is Associate Professor at the Institute of International Business, Stockholm School of Economics (SSE), Sweden, and currently Visiting Professor at Victoria University of Wellington, NZ. Her academic background includes studies at the SSE and visiting scholarships at Stanford University and the Wharton School, University of Pennsylvania. She is a member of the *Journal of International Business Studies*, and the *International Journal of Cross-Cultural Management*'s (IJCCM) editorial review boards. Following Lena's multiple awarded Ph. D. dissertation she has published chapters and articles in international books and academic journals, edited books and special issues of IJCCM and *International Studies of Management and Organization*.

**Udo Zander** is Professor and Director of the Institute of International Business, Stockholm School of Economics (SSE), Sweden, and currently Visiting Professor at Victoria University of Wellington, NZ. His academic background includes studies at SSE, UC Berkeley, Stanford University, as well as visiting professorships at the Wharton School, University of Pennsylvania, and Stanford. Udo is a Fellow of the Academy of International Business, Member of the Royal Swedish Academy of Engineering Sciences, and the Royal Swedish Academy of Sciences. He has published in journals such as *American Sociological Review*, *European Management Review*, *Journal of International Business Studies*, *Management Science* and *Organization Science*.

**Christopher Ziemnowicz** is Professor of Business at the University of North Carolina at Pembroke, and Chair of the Management, Marketing, and International Business Department. His bachelor degree is from George Mason University and MBA from American University in Washington, DC. While at Virginia Polytechnic Institute and State University (Virginia Tech) he facilitated faculty exchanges with the Social Sciences and Economics Institute at the Warsaw University of Technology (Politechnika Warszawska PW). He then earned a Ph.D. at PW in Poland. He has taught at Susquehanna University, College of Saint Rose and Concord University. An extensive traveller, his teaching and research interests include international business and entrepreneurship.

# Introduction to cultural mythology and global leadership

## Eric H. Kessler and Diana J. Wong-MingJi

We live in an age of critical albeit curious confluences ... and the stakes have never been higher. On the one hand, the forces of globalization bring together peoples and practices at a level unprecedented in human history. Cultures are simultaneously blending and battling, ushering in an intermingling seemingly omnipresent dynamic of connections and collisions. As a result, effective global leaders and leadership practices are of preeminent importance be it in business, political, or social realms. Yet on the other hand our age is also marked by superficial analyses, quick-fixes, limited and ill-focused attention spans, sound bytes and Internet summaries, educational and intellectual approximations, increasingly sophisticated yet bounded technological heuristics, and a proliferation of elaborate yet surface training fads and fashions. Thus it should be of no surprise that the daily press is replete with tales of lost leadership opportunities and colossal management systems failures in both public and private domains, the latter including cases such as the collapse of Barings Bank in England, Enron in the US, Société Générale in France, Guangdong International Trust and Investment Corporation in China, and Toshoku Ltd in Japan. This combination of a heightened demand for globally competent leaders and endemic threats to its supply is simply not sustainable.

The world is complex. Leadership is critical. We need a depth of analysis that appreciates these challenges by addressing foundational issues. This project of international collaboration focuses on a central concept at the intersection of these forces – mythology. Specifically, we focus squarely on the dizzying diversity of myths that underlie societal values and visions ... and trace their significant impact on global leadership.

Renowned anthropologist Joseph Campbell (1988) described, perhaps better than no other, the penetrating explanatory and normative power of myth. First, invoking his insights, we must recognize that myths are sacred stories passed down within a society that, at their essence, are about communicating core principles, morals, and meanings. They serve as validations of individual and societal significance. They represent clues to the spiritual. They can be seen as logical and emotional road maps to the experience of being alive. Second, myths are contextual. They support and validate a particular social order. They evolve with the societal changes to reinforce the desired norms and institutionalize what should take people beyond the present reality. They communicate wisdom to help untangle conundrums of life according to specific prescribed principles. 'In a culture … there are a number of understood, unwritten rules by which people live. There is an ethos there, there is a mode … an unstated mythology, you might say' (1988: 9). Indeed this is consistent with the observations of noted anthropological scholars such as Bronislaw Malinowski, who considered myths to be validations of established practices and institutions, and A. R. Radcliffe-Brown, who found myths to emphasize and reiterate the beliefs, behaviors, and feelings of people about their society (Columbia Encyclopedia, 2007). We extend this mode of insight to examine the seminal influence of myths on core aspects of leadership in the age of globalization. Our central premise is that leadership is inexorably intertwined with culture, and that mythology provides one of the most important keys for understanding the nature, manifestation, and dynamics of global leadership both within and across cultures. If indeed culture is the 'software of our minds' (as per Hofstede and Hofstede, 2005) and this collective programming is primarily learned rather than inherited, then myth needs to be understood as the deep architecture of this programming that reveals fundamental patterns of thinking and acting and thus critical criteria in leading.

A perusal of the business literature reveals that among the business topics generating the greatest interest, and critical to success, are globalization, culture and leadership. There is much written on each subject but little that actually integrates the three in a meaningful or useful manner. Moreover, an application of mythology is practically ignored in terms of its relevance to the practice of global leadership and its ability to bridge all three domains. This is the very subject of our book. Some potentially provocative ideas that emerge from this mode of thinking are: Leaders are socialized from early childhood onward and develop their approaches within a culture; mythology both captures (static/snapshot) and evolves (dynamic/cinema) to reflect essential elements of this; there are areas of commonality and divergence between culture's leadership styles; there are both intercultural acumen and potentially problematic predilections and biases within any culture's leadership styles; and that a knowledge of these issues is essential for effective development of leaders in an increasingly complex global context.

This project brings together management thinkers and practitioners from around the globe to explore the integration of cultural mythology and global leadership. It speaks to the international scholar engaged in research and education, the corporate leader formulating their organization's strategic course, the businessperson trying to navigate the complexities of the international marketplace, the public persona or political office-holder charged with shepherding globally relevant causes, and to anyone trying to gain a better understanding of how their personal and professional lives relate to these modern day forces. The ubiquitous reach of globalization and the transnational development of organizations require current and future leaders to shift from a traditional international management approach with learning about one country and its culture at one time to learning about managing multiple cultures at the same time (Adler and Bartholomew, 1992). The challenges are exponentially more complex which in turn require access not just to norms and beliefs of different cultures but also a sense of the dynamic cultural contexts within historical trajectories. The common base of mythology is particularly functional for facilitating such an understanding.

In this overview we will address the importance of the focal subject, sketch its relationship with a body of core concepts and ideas, preview the 20 content analyses which literally span the six inhabited continental regions of the world, and finally offer some of our own insights into the potential syntheses and implications of these considerations.

## THE IMPORTANCE OF MAKING THE CONNECTIONS

In September 2005, the Danish newspaper *Jyllands-Posten* published 12 cartoons depicting the prophet Mohammed. The incident led to a crisis reverberating around the world resulting in riots across the Muslim world; numerous death threats and over 100 related deaths; escalation of the controversy with reprints of the cartoons in over 50 Western newspapers; and calls for economic boycotts of Western companies from Muslim countries. The Prime Minister of Denmark described it as the worst international crisis since World War II. Scandinavian retail operations in the Middle East experienced overnight vertical drops in sales. The editors who published the 12 cartoons probably did not expect the resulting firestorm. But if one understood how violating what is most sacred in others, one may possibly make a different decision and take a different course of action, or not. For the scores of Western publications that subsequently published the story with the cartoons, an intentional decision was made to exercise their own sacred value of freedom of speech. While not possibly on the same level of intensity, other examples of such cultural controversies in the global arena can be expected.

The future development of globalization will most likely continue to perpetuate encounters between what is held sacred between different cultures. Hopefully, they will not be on the scale sparked by the *Jyllands-Posten*'s cartoons. Most international incidents related to cultural differences fall into the realms of discomfort, embarrassment, puzzlement, or amusement with some leaving a wake of insurmountable conflicts. Some are seriously offensive and may be quite controversial as well as possible deal breakers in otherwise viable economically rational business relationships.

Briefly, a few other examples are as follows: in the 2006 G8 Summit meeting, the US President George Bush's friendly massage of the German Chancellor Angela Merkel created an awkward unwelcome moment of discomfort that did not reflect well on him. In another example, different standards of hygiene in France versus US based McDonalds led to years of litigation when the French partner did not comply accordingly, especially when many US tourists were expecting to find the same restaurant experience as they experienced in the US franchises. In a separate incident, the Governor of Kentucky presented a US flag to Japanese leaders in an opening ceremony of a Hitachi subsidiary and then the Japanese carelessly let the flag drag on the ground which offended many of those present. Many Americans have a patriotic reverence for their flag relative to the Japanese who like many others do not hold flags with as much reverence as Americans. Even successful business relationships may be strained by cross-cultural difficulties like the economic success of Northwest Airline and KLM Dutch Airline which is often referred to as a 'marriage from hell'.

Cultural faux pas also happen within domestic borders as well as beyond them. An inappropriate marketing promotion compared a luxury hotel opening in New York to the Taj Mahal which is a mausoleum. In another example, a US company tried to sell a brand of cooking oil in the South American market with Spanish translation that meant 'jackass oil'. Or another gaffe that advertised an automobile named 'Nova' which is a bright star, but also translates as 'does not go' in Spanish and Italian speaking countries. Cultural difficulties also added to challenges that confounded a US air courier's international expansion and resulted in $1.2 billion losses and closure of 100 European operations. In addition to these examples of cross-cultural faux pas, David Ricks (1999) offers a large collection of stories in all facets of business which impact and impede the ability of businesses to succeed in the global marketplace. Stories of cultural blunders create amusing cocktail stories after the fact but their impacts can be quite serious and far ranging.

Leaders can potentially prevent and/or mitigate cross-cultural challenges by developing a requisite portfolio of knowledge and skills. As organizations move through different stages of international development from a domestic business to an international one to a multinational operation and to a transnational organization, the need for transnationally competent leaders increases. In order to achieve this, it is important to have a global perspective and work with multiple cultures simultaneously, both of which depend on learning 'about many foreign cultures' perspectives, tastes, trends, technologies, and approaches to conducting business' (Adler and Bartholomew, 1992: 53). The demands on global leaders will likely grow more intense with growing potential for more cultural gaffes. The challenge that lies before us is how to reconcile the complex range of cultural differences to develop synergistic pathways from the diverse range of cultural richness.

As suggested previously, the purpose of this project is to go deeper beyond the stories of cross-cultural faux pas and their associated perfunctory or mischaracterized simplistic explanations to address the need for more transnationally competent leaders. We use cultural mythology as a vehicle to appreciate the richness of traditions and cultural heritages that enable leaders to navigate an increasingly interdependent global context. More importantly, gaining a contextually informed understanding of cultural values and norms provides a foundation to move organizations toward what Adler (1991) refers to as cultural synergy that combines multiple cultures into a unique organizational culture. The following collection of writings on cultural mythology and global leadership extends a conversation that started in a symposium of the same nature at the International Eastern Academy of Management (EAM-I) 2005 Conference in Cape Town, South Africa. Organized by the then EAM President Eric Kessler, the original panel of six focused on the United States, Canada, Greece, Guyana, China and South Africa to discuss how cultural mythologies from their respective countries provide models for leadership behavior, attitudes and values in a global context.

The format of an edited volume made possible the luxury of a forum for broader inclusion from the original six to 20 different countries. They include the United States, Canada, the Caribbean, Brazil and Argentina from the Americas; Greece, Sweden, England, Germany and Poland from Europe; South Africa, Kenya, Iran, Egypt and Israel from the Middle East and Africa; Russia, Japan, China, India and Australia from Asia and the Pacific. The contributors are highly accomplished researchers and practitioners who often straddle multiple cultural boundaries at the same time. Most write as cultural insiders to host the reader and introduce him/her to their cultural contexts and histories in order to situate leadership theories in a sense making forum. While the collection of mythologies from any country is quite vast, we requested that the authors focus on the prominent myths related to leadership. Reflections are also drawn from current practicing global leaders who are working in the respective countries. As a result, the reader hears from the essential voices of cultural insiders who are often missing from many international business writings.

While many studies have explored underlying relationships of cross-cultural interactions in international business, there is often a significant challenge in achieving a common reality and shared understanding to achieve what Adler (1991) terms as 'cultural synergy'. Challenges stem from what things are similar and what things may differ as well as sometimes misconstruing one for the other. For example, a taken for granted business value around the world is high quality customer service. But the means of delivering and receiving such service may significantly differ across cultures. Thus, in order to have shared meaning, cultural context is very important and in particular, a historical perspective that provides insights into the formative influences of the present.

## THE NEXUS OF THREE IDEAS

The three key interrelated ideas in this book are globalization, cultural mythology, and leadership. The current trends of globalization create a context for more cross-cultural interactions that are often spearheaded by leaders of organizations. First, increasing globalization and its accompanying backlashes create an increasingly complex environment for organizations to conduct business (Friedman, 2005). International business opportunities are driven by many factors. General factors include free trade agreements, advances in computer technology to support internet telecommunication and information processing, and subsequently, growth of international business relations. More complex issues often refer to sourcing of cheap labor, outsourcing organizational functions, violation of human rights, labor migration from poor to wealthier economies, refugees from political conflicts, global competition, environmental sustainability, international cyber crimes, counterfeit goods, terrorism, migration of disease among many others, and domino impacts of economic decline in larger economies reverberating around the world.

A significant tension with rising globalization is the collision between what is considered global versus local. The global is often seen as a homogenization of the local. Terms such as McDonaldization, Disneyfication, or the WalMart phenomenon are used to convey the idea of displacing local businesses with

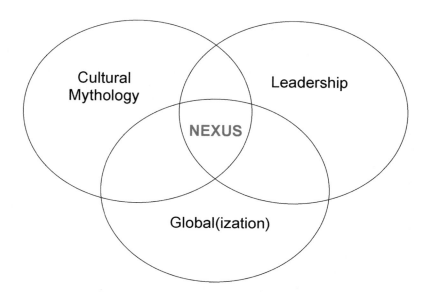

*Figure I.1    The nexus of cultural mythology, globalization, and leadership*

global entities that are essentially indistinguishable from one location to another around the world. Experiences and products become replicated around the global to the detriment of small businesses and local diversity. Eating at a McDonalds in the US is relatively the same as the experience of eating at a McDonalds in any other country. Menus may differ somewhat among McDonalds in different countries but the experience is similar *vis-à-vis* dining at a US McDonalds versus a franchise in Lebanon. Consequently, authenticity of what is local is subsumed under the global.

At the same time, the picture is a little more complicated because cross-cultural dynamics are rarely a one way phenomenon. Thus, McDonald's US leaders must also learn to adapt to business conditions in Lebanon. Any business going global needs to go through a process of 'how to do business in' whether the process is proactively planned with cross-cultural training or reactively learnt in the moment through cross-cultural interactions. The adaptation process of global organizations to local conditions circles back to demise of the local. But collective active local resistance may also fend off the global and/or reconstruct the terms of engagement. In sum, globalization eventually leads to cross-cultural relationships that require intentional and thoughtful considerations for all parties involved.

Second, culture is an integral concern in globalization. At the epicenter of the local lies culture. Over the last several decades, numerous researchers from different disciplines have built a body of research examining the phenomenon of culture. Some highlights include Benedict's (1934) *Patterns of Culture*, Hall's (1976) cultural contexts, Hofstede's (1980; 2001) cultural dimensions, Kroeber and Kluckhohn's (1963) review of definitions of culture, the GLOBE comparative studies of 62 societies (House *et al.*, 2004). A current trend in international management research addresses cultural intelligence and cross-cultural competencies which focus on the need for more knowledge, skills and abilities to enable more effective leadership operating on a global scale. There are important implications of these issues that lead to the cultural dimensions of globalization which entails a complex flow of ideas, knowledge and cultural practices (Prasad and Prasad, 2007). Thus, we offer a vehicle for accessing the multiple facets of different cultures by using their core mythology. It offers a means of accessing and learning about a culture with a contextual, integrative and dynamic approach for future considerations in directions such as sustaining traditional heritages that underlie local rights, cultural globalization for convergence versus divergence, and daily organizational practices in cross-cultural interactions.

Before moving on we do need to address an integral phenomenon of culture by surfacing the particular nature of myths and mythology. Grasping mythology is like reaching up into the clouds to capture the droplets of rain. There is nothing and something at one and the same time. In the moment you think you grasp it, it dissipates again. In many ways, the description also captures the dynamic characteristics of culture as well as myths. Many of the authors in this project also refer to the multi-dimensional, paradoxical and dualistic nature of myth from their respective cultures. A myth from the perspective of science or business often refers to a fabrication unveiled and deconstructed whereas in philosophy and the humanities, myths capture essential truths and construct sacred rituals that inspire human beings to overcome adversities, fears and tragedies in life.

Studying cultural mythology is the aspirations, dreams, and desires of many scholars through the ages and from fields as far ranging as philosophy, religion, literature, anthropology, sociology, psychology, linguistics, education, history, gender and feminist studies and the sciences. Many luminaries like E. B. Tylor, Bronislaw Malinowski, Karl Popper, Max Muller, Claude Levi-Strauss, Rudolf Bultmann, Jane Harrison, Sigmund Freud, Carl Jung, Mircea Eliade, and Joseph Campbell have all reached up into the clouds. Each one retrieved insights into mythology but often their grasp of insights are like moist dews that may evaporate with the onset of a paradigm shift. Furthermore, contemporary expressions of myths proliferate a broad eclectic range of cultural practices such as story telling and traditional celebrations of heritage and cultural industries such as education, mass media, tourism, music, entertainment and consumer products.

We stand on the shoulders of many giants in our attempt to bring forth cultural mythology that can help illuminate the journey for global leaders who travel to distant lands and need to gain a greater understanding of others. An increasing need with the diffusion of globalization is to bridge multiple cultural boundaries, often at the same time. While transportation and telecommunication technologies facilitate greater ease in transcending time and space, the human ability to effectively work and relate to each other across cultures remains an enduring challenge. The notion of a competent global leader may remain as a mirage unless one accesses deeper cultural insights into norms, beliefs and historical contexts.

Technology offers little to prevent international business blunders or resolve communication and relationship challenges which are rooted in human foibles. More likely, the solution lies in global leaders learning to develop effective relationships. The following collection of writings offers global leaders a bridge with cultural mythology into both the predominant characteristics of a culture and the historical contextual trajectories that help to make meaning over time.

The importance of cultural mythology centers on its role of bridging across generations whereby culture is passed down from one generation to the next. 'The word *myth* comes from the Greek word *mythos*, which means "word", "speech", "tale", or "story", and that is essentially what a myth is: a story'

(Morford and Lenardon, 2003: 3). For the purpose of this project, we use a general approach to myth that includes saga, legends, folktales and fairytales while leaving the distinctive differences to discussions among experts who engage in much deeper debates about these matters. Our focus is on how myths are significant from the earliest socialization to shape cultural values, norms and behaviors. Often childhood experiences include listening to stories that are passed down from one generation to the next. Various family members and community members often draw the myths from their childhood memories to illustrate important life lessons and emphasize what are appropriate or ideal behaviors, attitudes, and logics.

The major premise of social learning theory (Bandura, 1977; 1985) is that we can learn by observing others. Thus mythologies may serve as important sources of values and behaviors. Social learning theory is of course a general theory of human behavior, but Bandura and others have also used it specifically to explain media effects, warning that 'children and adults acquire attitudes, emotional responses, and new styles of conduct through filmed and televised modeling' (1977: 39). As mythological stories are passed down from generation to generation, as well as retold in broader brushstrokes through literature and the modern media, they serve as potentially powerful sources of attitudes, emotional responses, and styles of conduct. A generation socialized on mythological heroes and villains who connote certain values and styles are the future designers and leaders of organizations, those very same people responsible for organizational structure, strategy, operations, and the like. Therefore, there is a dynamic link to organizations because myths may have had an influence on the people in them over time. Additionally, leaders may be exposed to these influences even in their adult lives vicariously through their children (as were the editors of this book) or through educators and consultants that apply analogy and metaphor-related learning tools to show how an organization should work (see Weber, 1947) and really does work (see Adams, 1996).

Our journey into cultural mythology focuses primarily on examining the myths that significantly shape the collective expectations and characteristics of their leaders. We recognize that cultural communities often transcend current nation state boundaries and that multiple cultural groups exist within sovereign borders along with more localized regional versions of prevailing myths. These features contribute to the multiplicity layers in many cultural identities and their dynamic cultural evolution. Yet cultural myths provide a stabilizing constant for the transmission of culture from one generation to the next. At the same time, myths may be adapted to institutionalize new cultural ideals.

For example, the Chinese Communist regime rejected and suppressed the worship of deities including the myth of the Yellow Emperor for almost 30 years during the Cultural Revolution. Then the mythical figure and stories were resurrected as the ideal of one patriarch for all Chinese people everywhere. By holding up the Yellow Emperor as the origin and Father of Chinese civilization, the government reasoned that Taiwan should return to the fold of the family because Chinese people belong together. Hence, myths may ebb and flow from the consciousness of a community as the needs arise to reach beyond the realm of rational reasoning into the realm of imagination and spirits.

Last, leadership makes up the third domain of concern in this book. Global leaders are at the tip of the spear to advance the interests of both the global and the local. The essence of their work requires straddling multiple cultures to initiate and respond to strategies that sustain the momentum for increasing globalization. But leaders are first and foremost a product of their own culture. By entering into another culture, leaders often become sharply aware of their own cultural identity as contrasting differences unfold.

Developing effective leadership characteristics, knowledge, skills, and abilities is a lifetime pursuit for many. The four eras of leadership theory began with the image of the Great Man and his associated traits. Then rational management unfolded with behavioral and contingency models. Subsequently, shifts in flattening of organizations and increased use of teams required leaders who can empower others and achieve quality goals with cross-functional groups.

The current era of leadership thinking focuses on the importance of facilitating shared visions, alignment, and unlocking high performance potentials of those around the leader. In addition, current needs for learning organization also require leaders to manage change quickly in dynamic complex environments. Recent leadership ideas include primal leadership with emotional intelligence (Goleman *et al.*, 2002), Level 7 leadership to move organizations from good to great (Collins, 2001), and appreciative inquiry for building positive organizations (Cooperrider *et al.*, 2005). Indeed the globalization of business has magnified the complexity and dynamism of these leadership challenges.

Today's global leaders – be they in the business, political, economic, or social spheres – need to have all the qualities identified above as well as capabilities for understanding different languages, religion, attitudes, social organization, education, and business infrastructure in multiple cultures at the same time. This is the recipe for what has been termed the globally or transnationally competent leader. Leaders need cross-cultural competence to build networks of partnering organizations that effectively leverage disparate resources from diverse markets. Moreover, knowledge of geopolitical forces, socio-cultural forces, and cultural communication differences provides a foundation for global leaders who are confronted by more logistical challenges that involve time zone differences, geographical distance and mediating between different business systems. Developing cross-cultural competencies would enable global leaders to improve their chances for success, and that of their organizations, with the ever-expanding range of complex challenges.

## ROADMAP FOR OUR JOURNEY

*Cultural Mythology and Global Leadership* encompasses 20 national contexts within four geographic regions of the Americas, Europe, Africa and the Middle East and Asia and the Pacific Rim (see Figure I.2 for a content map of specific locations). These original analyses bring exciting perspectives and penetrating insights to the practitioner as well as scholars of leadership and international management. For the purpose of overview, we preview these chapters with the intention of stimulating interest in the reader to experience them directly.

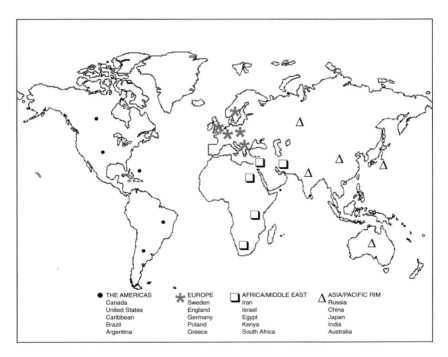

| ● THE AMERICAS | ✳ EUROPE | ☐ AFRICA/MIDDLE EAST | △ ASIA/PACIFIC RIM |
|---|---|---|---|
| Canada | Sweden | Iran | Russia |
| United States | England | Israel | China |
| Caribbean | Germany | Egypt | Japan |
| Brazil | Poland | Kenya | India |
| Argentina | Greece | South Africa | Australia |

*Figure I.2    Cultural mythology and global leadership from 20 countries*

**The Americas**

Cultural mythologies from the Americas were drawn from the US, Canada, the Caribbean, Argentina and Brazil. The geography spans across nine time zones and extends from the far north of the Arctic Circle to the southern reaches toward Antarctica. Many of the cultural mythologies reflect relatively recent historical trajectories relative to other regions of the world.

In Chapter 1, Eric Kessler examines cultural mythology and leadership in the United States. The primary myth developed is the comic-book superhero. From campfire tales to children's cartoons to blockbuster cinematic characters and their mass marketed paraphernalia, American leadership is frequently conveyed through larger-than-life individuals whose styles are idealized and idolized. Through a discussion of ten representative comic-book superheroes and their leadership lessons, a prototypical American 'superhero leader' profile is derived – they fight for noble personal and societal goals, are strong, fast, brave, and nimble, leverage cutting-edge technology and physical resources, creatively develop and exploit unique advantage, are self-reliant yet compassionate, actively manage reputation and image, and self-reflect on identity and purpose. In the corporate and public arenas these American Supermen and Wonder-Women receive much fame and fortune for their heroic individual and performance-driven exploits. Kessler points out that this mythology spans multiple domains, differs from other cultural depictions, is grounded in historical and ethical foundations, and is constantly evolving to reflect changes in the broader social context. He concludes with a discussion of a more collaborative 'post-heroic' leadership style and the need to balance these two approaches to create true and enduring organizational greatness.

In Chapter 2, Nina Cole and Rhona Berengut examine cultural mythology and leadership in Canada. They first discuss myths of the land that literally as well as figuratively shape Canadian leadership. Harsh weather and open spaces spawn small communities and esteem for communicative and connective mediums. They then transition to myths of the cultural fabric that binds these communities. Recounting imagery from early settlers and natives, the authors describe artistic mediums that propagate stories of railroad and frontier travel. Subsequent myths of the winter and sport focus on ice hockey and the legendary status of its superstars. Taken together these myths connote values of resiliency, cooperation, and acceptance that underlie the vast Canadian mosaic and, even though they might agree on very little (except that they are not Americans, as per the Canadian 'anti-heroism sentiment' in contrast to the preceding chapter), shape a leadership paradigm emphasizing contingency and accommodation, socialized power and justice, and fundamentally transformational and participatory approaches. Examples from politics, business, sports, and the social conscience reinforce these claims, perhaps most interestingly in the winner of a 'Greatest Canadian' poll – Medicare father Tommy Douglas. Cole and Berengut emphasize pluralistic cooperation and team building in Canadian leadership that, despite misconceptions of simplicity and potential shortcomings in proactive and aggressive styles, are seen as well positioned to adapt to the complex, pluralistic global business context.

In Chapter 3, Betty Jane Punnett and Dion Greenidge examine cultural mythology and leadership found in the Caribbean. While not a single country, many of the small nation-states in the Caribbean display much variety yet, as the authors contend, share many factors that shape a common cultural foundation. Punnett and Greenidge begin by providing historical context and, from this analysis, focus on two of the region's fundamental mythologies. First, they discuss the unique mix of African magical beliefs with traditional Christian influence. Voodoo and Obeah, which include active supernatural powers that can be brought to bear through spells and other practices, are seen to convey the importance of leadership-related factors such as information, access, and centralization. Second, mythical stories of Anancy are described that paint a picture of the 'trickster spider' that is able to upend larger and more powerful foes. This mythological image suggests a means for balancing power through informal methods. Examples of leadership within business and political contexts reinforce the manifestation of these myths within the give and take of modern practice. The authors then suggest practical considerations for leaders to accommodate these myths such as through greater transparency and participation, the promotion of trust and a sense of security, and achieving fit with and proactively affecting positive change.

In Chapter 4, Patricia Friedrich, Andres Hatum and Luiz Mesquita examine cultural mythology and leadership in Argentina. The authors anchor their discussion by presenting three central Argentine mythological figures: Evita Peron, Che Guevara and the iconic gaucho. They then trace the influence of these mythologies through modern public and business leaders. Insofar as myths reveal collective value systems and central characteristics, these Argentine myths have acquired symbolic meaning as representatives of the collective identity. The authors' analysis reveals that the three focal myths draw out inherent contradictions in the Argentine fabric, such as exhibiting simultaneous glamor and suffering á la Peron, acting as both rebel and savior á la Che, and representing the national spirit as well as irrelevant outsider á la the gaucho. Digging deeper, these contradictions reveal the crux of an 'Argentine paradox' and requisite leadership style which is, at the same time, charismatic and team oriented, willing to listen but a take charge personality, high power distance but egalitarian oriented, and self-acclaiming while socially devoted. Friedrich *et al.* build from their analysis to offer insights into effective leadership within Argentina and ways of navigating its 'muddy road' of social/business indivisibility, linguistic indirectness, and highly interactive trust-building dynamics.

In Chapter 5, Adriana Garibaldi de Hilal examines cultural mythology and leadership in Brazil. In Brazil, Western and non-Western cultures have mingled for centuries creating what is termed the 'Brazilian Dilemma' – a unique dynamic when things run both through a personal egalitarian code as well as a traditional hierarchical system. Brazilian myths have thus developed as special kinds of narratives, traditions in their own right which in many ways mirror the society, and reveal deeper levels of consciousness that mediate between modes of existence. They are seen to include the carnival rite – myth of equality versus hierarchy; the home and the street – myth of the dual social domains; 'Do you know who you are talking to' – myth of the conflict-averse society; myth of the worker versus the adventurer; myth of the cordial man; and the myth that 'foreign is better'. These mythological frameworks in turn underlie deep-seeded cultural values that are exhibited in manifest public expressions such as the collective, almost spiritual passion for *fútbol* as well as the famous Brazilian 'jeitinho' or art of bending rules. Combining these insights with empirical research findings, Garibaldi de Hilal extends her analysis to offer several guidelines for motivating, communicating, and leading successfully in and with Brazil.

## Europe

From Europe, Greece, Germany, England, Sweden and Poland provide a broad array of cultural mythologies many of which are the roots of Western civilization. Hofstede (2007: 412) traced the origin of the word Europe to Phoenician sailors from 3000 years ago who 'oriented themselves between *esch* and *ereb*, that is dawn and dusk, or East and West; and this became Asia and Europa'. Over time the name also became linked to Europa, a Phoenician princess of Greek mythology. In addition to Greece, cultural mythologies extending back to early times from different countries also contribute to form a collective European identity and culture.

In Chapter 6, Theodore Peridis examines cultural mythology and leadership in Greece. Peridis rightly observes that some of the greatest stories of heroes and quests ever told have been handed down from the ancient Greeks, and the word 'myth' itself is of Greek origin. The chapter offers three clusters of Greek myths that center on common themes and, together, illustrate the nature of Greek worldview and subsequent leadership style. First, we see king of the gods Zeus rule from the highest position and legendary Agamemnon with a focused and ambitious drive, yet even in their strength they both struggle with inherent limits in the power, both internal and external, to impose their will. Second, stories of mighty Hercules and brave Achilles recount almost superhuman deeds yet they are often characterized as arrogant and befallen by an overly emotional, or perhaps, ultimately human, nature. Third, the epic tales of the intrepid Odysseus exhibit a remarkable resourcefulness in his adventures yet their recounting also reveals that the journey might be more important than any of its eventual outcomes (or lack thereof). Together Peridis employs these Greek myths to paint a picture of the noble but tragic nature of leadership, a conception of a contingent and almost capricious sense of justice, a portrayal of the hero as both noble yet flawed, and a broadly conceived leadership mission with a tolerance, indeed some might say a charge, for fluid and malleable execution.

In Chapter 7, Sonja Sackmann examines cultural mythology and leadership in Germany. She focuses on four aspects of Germanic mythology and history: The medieval saga 'Nibelungenlied', which includes the story of Siegfried and lessons that power must be supplemented with a greater sense of wisdom; Prussian Virtues, including legendary exploits of Frederick the Great; the Hanseatic League, retelling the honor and pride in being a merchant; and post-World War II democratization following the dictatorial system of the National Socialists, which sought to distance itself from a 'führer' (German translation of the word 'leader') in order to establish more participatory and collective mechanisms for governance. Sackmann then considers the core values that these mythologies implanted in modern German leadership as well as the popular, often outmoded stereotypes that too frequently obscure them. Discussed are characteristics such as team orientation and participation, charisma and inspiration, as well as hard work and performance/humane orientation. Chancellor Angela Merkel and Allianz Group CEO Michael Diekmann are presented to illustrate the cultural dynamic and socialization processes emergent from these mythological traditions. Projecting forward, Sackmann sees the 'hard' side of leadership giving way to a more team-based approach of younger leaders, especially in high-tech industries, and as such she suggests that an evolving German mythology be appreciated accordingly.

In Chapter 8, Romie Littrell examines cultural mythology and leadership in England. He brackets his analysis with reflections by Primrose and Rhodes, which express the view that England is destined to lead the world and that this is indeed for its betterment. Littrell traces the evolution of Britannia and the British Empire, describing various larger-than-life figures such as William the Conqueror and Queen Elizabeth I. English mythology is held up as a looking glass upon this history to highlight core values and themes. Included in these are the indomitable but prudent Beowulf, multifarious Romano-Celtic deities, legendary King Arthur, and rebellious Robin Hood. These latter two merit special attention from the author insofar as they are seen as divergent yet complementary elements which help define the essential English identity. From King Arthur emerge a warrior spirit and dedicated defense of the nation, a just and generous outlook, a courtly and noble demeanor, and the fundamental rules of chivalrous behavior and knighthood. These attributes are complemented by Robin Hood's romantic, common-man, outlaw struggle against oppressive and unjust structures. When Sir Francis Drake's jaunty, daring attitude in the face of danger (that is, stiff upper-lip) is added to the equation the portrait becomes clear. Modern English leadership is seen by Littrell as embodying these aspects and this is reinforced through reference to scholarly research and current practice.

In Chapter 9, Lena and Udo Zander examine cultural mythology and leadership in Sweden. The Zanders offer a longitudinal, probing analysis of the Swedish leadership paradigm, hailed by some studies as among the best in the world. From a starting point of Swedish and Norse mythology the authors recount colorful stories of mythological deities including Oden, who bargained health and hardiness for but a sip of wisdom and a taste of knowledge; and his son Tor, who with his mighty hammer and aggressive temperament battled giants to bring order from chaos. Also discussed are folk tales and the myths of 'potential' helpers Tomte and Will-o-the-wisp, who can be of great help if treated well but equally mischievous if treated poorly. From these foundations the authors deduce five emergent Swedish leadership themes: practical knowledge and action-orientation, social individualism and teamwork/consensus, respectful egalitarianism and empowerment, fairness and logical universalism, and an engaged walking around. Seen as embodying these ancient mythological-derived characteristics are modern leaders as ICA Ahold AB's Kenneth Bengtsson, ABB's Percy Barnevik, SAS's Jan Carlzon, and IKEA's Ingvar Kamprad. The authors conclude by examining some leadership strengths, challenges, as well as changes in the Swedish paradigm and in turn offer suggestions for their effective engagement.

In Chapter 10, Christopher Ziemnowicz and John Spillan examine cultural mythology and leadership in Poland. The authors describe myths such as legendary Prince Krakus, King Boleslaw and outlaw Jerzy Janosik and trace these through to two examples of historical memory deeply rooted in Polish cultural heritage: the Polish Nation's Anthem and Warsaw Uprising. First, the former lyrics are characterized as symbols of perseverance and hope that inspire Poles through times of difficulty. Second, the later uprising is seen to represent atrocities befallen the Polish peoples that put down, but did not keep down, the country and its inhabitants. Ziemnowicz and Spillan then point to the conception of a Polish 'before', preceding Nazi and communist occupation, which continues to guide and motivate. They also emphasize the particularly insidious influence of imposed communist systems that created an attitude of passivity and helplessness, an 'it is not mine so I do not care' worldview institutionalized in economic and educational structures. Eventually overcome in solidarity movements and new 'can-do' mythological figures such as Lech Walesa, as well as larger market reforms, the dynamic Polish environment is embodied in leaders such as Geofizyka Torun CEO Stanislaw Zon who are promoting progressive leadership approaches. The authors conclude with an analysis of old versus new Polish leadership as well as a comparison with American style, a profile of the modern Polish manager, and suggestions for succeeding in Poland's rapidly evolving context.

## Africa and the Middle East

The third geographical region, Africa and the Middle East, offers an extensive and diverse range of cultural mythologies from South Africa, Kenya, Egypt, Iran and Israel. Each offers an extensive cornucopia collection of myths that extends back to ancient times with multiple cultural layers formed by dramatic historical disruptions. Yet, the cultural myths endure and continue to shape contemporary leaders.

In Chapter 11, David Abdulai examines cultural mythology and leadership in South Africa. Abdulai focuses on ancestral veneration among the people of sub-Saharan Africa with a specific focus on the Zulus of South Africa. A frequently misunderstood practice by non-native scholars, ancestral veneration resides at the core of the culture and cosmology of the African, serving as a bridge between the living and spiritual domains, and as such highlights the critical role that ancestors play in the lives, principles and leadership of the local peoples. The author describes different native conceptions of the creator and conditions of ancestors as well as the various practices in which veneration is expressed. Notwithstanding the area's considerable development and modernization, many of the contemporary business practices can still be seen to reflect this core mythology. For example, ritualistic ceremonies for honoring ancestors are shown to reinforce deeply-held societal values and form a critical part of the African family and kinship system. These in turn are manifested in the Zulu idea of 'Umuntu Umuntu ngabantu', South African concept of '*Ubuntu*', and a subsequent compassion-based leadership approach. Abdulai suggests that an accurate appreciation of the special relationship between the mythology surrounding ancestral veneration and subsequent leadership paradigms would reduce lingering prejudice and, from a leadership perspective, facilitate more effective cross-cultural partnerships, policy decisions, conflict interventions, business communications, and relationship management.

In Chapter 12, Fred Walumbwa and George Ndege examine cultural mythology and leadership in Kenya. They set the tone for their chapter by pointing out that, despite its natural wealth and Western aid, Africa is still home to the world's most impoverished people and thus has a need to improve the quality and capacity of leadership. Focusing specifically on Kenya,

Walumbwa and Ndege provide a brief overview of its colonial history and makeup – it is made up of 43 ethnic groups each with its own myths and subsequent rituals and social practices. These include mythological traditions based on the Kikuyu's belief in common ancestor Gikuyu as well as the Maasai's belief in creator and guardian Enkai. The authors appropriately focus on the subcultures or 'microcultures' within Kenya to propose two frameworks – transformational and authentic leadership – that, although on the surface might appear incongruous with the context, they believe are particularly applicable to the challenges facing the country. Due to the complex forces that shape Kenyan business systems and society, Walumbwa and Ndege advance the notion that these somewhat idealized notions of leadership are indeed compatible with indigenous modes of behavior in Kenya. They are seen as promising leadership approaches which build from mythological foundations and thus are apt to engender receptivity and positive results by breaking down misconceptions and mistrust, motivating diverse work groups, and moderating widespread concerns of corruption and ethics.

In Chapter 13, Afsaneh Nahavandi examines cultural mythology and leadership in Iran. Tracing its roots back thousands of years, Nahavandi focuses on the rich collection of Iranian mythology as conveyed in the Shahnemeh (Book of Kings), which is a collection of verses several times longer than Western epics such as the Iliad and Odyssey. The Shahnemeh, the author describes, is a highly patriotic glorification of Iran which is omnipresent in the schools, streets, and literature of the country and that focuses on the essential yet complex role of the leader-hero as the guardian and savior of the nation. Colorful stories abound in the recounting of such figures as King Bahram Gur, Rostam, Kaveh, Nushin-Raven and Hormozd. These mythological foundations are seen to reveal a core Iranian identity through their emphasis of values such as integrity, humility, loyalty, fairness, kindness, moderation, courage, forgiveness, wisdom, and patriotism. The author also considers the Shahnemeh in light of the historical as well as contemporary relationship between religion and state in Iran. In terms of business in Iran, several practical leadership guidelines are suggested that revolve around the issues of people, relationships, and responsibilities. Nahavandi underscores the enduring strength and survival of these leadership themes in Iranian mythology and, as a result, the importance of their understanding for succeeding with and within its cultural context.

In Chapter 14, Mohamed Mostafa and Diana Wong-MingJi examine cultural mythology and leadership in Egypt. Going back thousands of years and spanning a broad temporal as well as geographic spectrum, the authors discuss four of the most important figures among the Egyptian pantheon of mythologies both in local reverence and relevance toward leadership. Presented are Set (root of Satan), with his accompanying chaos and destruction, Isis, icon of motherly devotion and healing, Osiris, representing resurrection and the mythical judge/protector, and Horus, brave conqueror as well as unifier. These characters are linked to the styles of Egyptian leaders such as Cleopatra, Saladin, Mohammad Ali Pashta, Nasser, Sadat, Mubarak and prominent business leaders such as Talaat Pasha Harb and Osman Ahmed Osman. In addition, the authors forge linkages with scholarly research models of culture and the distinct embedded characteristics within the local domain. The authors then extract several core values that can be seen to both span the many eras of Egyptian life, for example family and service, as well as manifest in dynamic tensions, for example authoritarian versus consultative approaches, and draw attention to emergent guidelines for leading within the Egyptian context.

In Chapter 15 Shay Tzafrir, Aviv Barhom-Kidron and Daniel McCarthy examine cultural mythology and leadership in Israel. The authors begin by describing the historical, geographic, and religious contexts in which Israeli mythology is based, painting a vivid picture of the unique characteristics that underlie its worldview. Biblical stories are recounted highlighting Abraham's *chutzpa*, Moses' vision, King David's unification battles, and King Solomon's wisdom. In addition, the authors describe more recent mythical narratives that emerged from such critical events as the courageous stand at Masada, victorious Maccabee liberation movement, inspired Warsaw ghetto rebellion, and self-sacrifices of Yosef Trumpeldor. From these Tzafrir, Barhom-Kidron, and Baruch derive and discuss four common characteristics of Israeli mythology: The struggle of the few against the many, the conception of genius, a pioneering vision and spirit, and a guiding principle of justice. These mythological-based roots are in turn seen to explain and even drive the styles of such renowned political leaders as Golda Meir and Yitzhak Rabin as well as such respected business leaders as Eli Horvitz and Gil Schwed. In addition the authors reconcile Israeli myths with cultural frameworks described by Hofstede, including potential shifts in values, and then conclude with lessons for global leadership that can be learned from such an analysis.

## Asia and the Pacific Rim

The fourth and final set of chapters considers Asia and the Pacific Rim with cultural mythologies drawn from China, Russia, India, Japan and Australia. The region is at the center of globalization dynamics as leaders criss-cross the east-west divide. The various mythologies from the five countries offer a bridge to access critical insights and entry into a deeper understanding of the cultures that at times mystify outsiders.

In Chapter 16, Diana J. Wong-MingJi examines cultural mythology ('*shenhua*', or holy narratives) and leadership in China. China is among the most ancient of civilizations and boasts over 150 deities. Wong-MingJi focuses on five that illustrate some of the core elements of its culture: the Yellow Emperor, a legendary sage king; the First Emperor Qin Shi Huang, who established China as a nation; the Queen Mother of the West, who created the Eight Immortals that represent the various factors of life; the Monkey King, a powerful but defiant spirit; and Kuan Yin, the caring Goddess of Mercy. She then systematically derives common themes which can be seen to run through these myths, and which map onto core Chinese values, including: a holistic orientation, ingenuity, hierarchy, compassion, balance, family and Confucian values. The author traces the influence of the mythologies and projects them into contemporary times, profiling their influence on Chinese business leaders including Zhang Ruimin, Sir Li Ka-Shing and Cheung Yan. Wong-MingJi points to the importance of related leadership concepts such as establishing integrity, managing social networks and *guanxi*, and adopting a long-term view which are considered essential for understanding and successfully interacting within the Chinese context.

In Chapter 17, Shanthi Gopalakrishnan and Rajender Kaur examine cultural mythology and leadership in India. The authors describe India as a kaleidoscope of many cultures, languages, and religions, and observe that permeating this societal amalgamation is an especially close relationship with myth. The predominant religion of India, Hinduism, is one of the oldest in the world. From its central trinity, two of Vishnu's incarnations Rama and Krishna are immortalized in epic narratives and oral tales. The authors discuss the myths of Rama as embodying a selfless and humane idealism rich in righteousness, humility and tradition. Mahatma Gandhi is held as an embodiment of a Rama-like struggle as well as demonstrating the ability to mobilize people by understanding the tremendous power of symbols and mythology. Similarly the myths of Krishna portray a leader of farsightedness, cleverness, and pragmatic effectiveness. His counsels have been passed down in the *Bhagavad Gita* and emphasize the disinterested execution of one's dharma or duty. Moreover the *Gita* discusses various relationship dyads which define the worldview of leaders and offer guidelines for different leadership situations. Gopalakrishnan and Kaur link modern cultural scholarship and political developments to these core mythologies. Several Indian leaders are presented who demonstrate the principles as set forth by Rama and Krishna, including Infosys founder Narayana Murthy, Tata founder Ratan Tata, and father of the Indian space program Vikram Sarabhai. The authors conclude by considering several emergent values of Indian leadership and their implementation.

In Chapter 18, Stanislav Shekshnia, Sheila M. Puffer and Daniel McCarthy examine cultural mythology and leadership in Russia. The authors take the reader on a journey through traditional Russian folklore, state-sponsored stories, and modern-day political and business myths to illustrate perennial leadership themes of: delivering extraordinary results, demonstrating superior ability, being exempt from the normal rules, serving as caregiver to the common people and acting assertively. On display in their chapter are the Protoslavic mythical Perun, a heavenly god of thunder and lightning; Oleg the Visionary, a king of exceptional abilities and deeds; the mythical Stalin, a seemingly divine-like defender and father figure; president Vladimir Putin, symbolic reification of storied Peter the Great; and modern CEO legend Dmitry Zimin. Of particular interest is the authors' portrayal of the Russian leader through supernatural miracle-worker and benevolent patriot/warrior mythologies, which connote the necessity to appear able to overcome any hardship and deliver highly successful or symbolic outcomes for their people, as well as the proactive predilection of leaders in creating their own mythological images that may or may not reflect objective reality. Shekshnia *et al.* distill these insights into practical implications for doing business with Russian leaders and conclude with a warning that leadership myths are a powerful tool that can be used more or less effectively and for positive or negative ends.

In Chapter 19, Tomoatsu Shibata and Mitsuru Kodama examine cultural mythology and leadership in Japan. They begin by examining Shinto and Buddhist teachings, which were integrated to form the 'backbone of Japanese consciousness' by communicating values such as balance and harmony, community and commitment, as well as moderation and application. These in turn are seen to underlie Japanese work styles, business models, and company cultures that are translated to their employees through stories, traditions, and unique corporate myths. The authors describe Shinto influenced 'resonating leadership' and Buddhist influenced 'practical knowledge leadership' to characterize a Japanese style of value-based and dialectical leadership which, through mutual trust and dialog, enables the simultaneous pursuit of efficiency and creativity. The authors illustrate this with examples from several companies including Toyota, Honda, Matsushita and Fanuc. Fanuc, originally an in-house venture of Fujitsu and now a leader in the factory automation sector, is profiled in detail and its rich description in this chapter brings forth the mythological foundations and traditional values of the Japanese culture which similarly characterize modern day business leadership.

In Chapter 20, David Lamond examines cultural mythology and leadership in Australia. Lamond describes this geographically isolated and dispersed culture through popular macho images of the Man from Snowy River and Crocodile Dundee as well as Wary Dunlop, who summoned the energy to fight for the lives and wellbeing of his compatriots even in the most horrific of conditions. Probing deeper, the author distills the core Australian mythology as embodied in the stories of three groups: 'Bushies' (early settlers), 'mates' (people who stand together in the midst of hardship and adversity), and 'ANZACS' (soldiers who displayed selfless courage and sacrifice). The inherent values conveyed within these mythologies reflect a tough-minded leadership style that, in the business world, can be characterized as a self-reliant and command-and-control style. Notwithstanding, the author suggests it might occasionally be handicapped by a lesser emphasis on softer leadership skills and a people-orientation. This notion is illustrated in the chapter through public comments by Rupert Murdoch and Kerry Packer. Given the historical mythological roots of the task oriented ethic and its emphasis on efficiency, Lamond posits that an increasingly diverse Australian social and business context might very well sow some seeds of cultural and hence leadership changes.

## SYNTHESES AND CENTRAL INSIGHTS

The journey through 20 nation-states' cultural mythology and leadership offers a myriad of insights and, we humbly submit, guideposts emerging from the preceding commentary. Neither comprehensive nor indisputable, we offer the following distillation of six core insights for the reader's consideration.

First, given the rich lineages traced in this volume and the clear connections that were time and time again established between cultural mythology and leadership, we postulate that leadership is firmly grounded in the mythology of its cultural context. This debunks the idea that leadership styles, predilections, and competencies are merely modern manifestations that can be understood outside of these roots. This is clearly false. Any analysis of leadership which does not take into account the ingrained socialization processes down through the generations, communicated values and worldviews of both leaders and followers, and subsequently the rich models for behavior and practical behavior which are ingrained in mythological histories and trajectories, is unavoidably surface and incomplete. The fundamental implication of this proposition is that leaders, and those who study leadership, must understand cultural mythology to understand the fundamental nature of the phenomena. As a result, a more profound appreciation of the cultural mythology roots would facilitate a deeper approach to global leadership.

Formally stated:

*Core Insight 1: Leadership is grounded in the mythology of its cultural context.*

Second, we draw on the significant overlap of analyses as well as their dizzying divergences to postulate that there are both universal and unique aspects of cultural mythology, and hence of leadership. This debunks the idea that leadership is universal across cultural contexts as well as the countervailing but equally misguided assumption that leaderships are completely different. Any analysis of leadership which does not take this into account will overlook critical overlaps and consistency (miss the synergies) and/or be blindsided by complex peculiarities and uniqueness (miss the idiosyncrasies) – a double whammy indeed! The fundamental implication of this proposition is that leaders, and those who study leadership, must work hard to differentiate as well as demonstrate competency in mastering both the common and unique aspects of the phenomena. Stated in other terms, we conclude that leadership has both emic and etic properties (see Earley and Offermann, 2007). Leadership, or components thereof, would be considered purely 'emic' if its meaning and effectiveness are defined only within a specific culture and differs substantially from that of other cultures. Alternatively, leadership would be considered purely 'etic' if its meaning and practical execution were universally consistent across cultures. The various analyses throughout this volume have suggested that indeed leadership blends both properties into a complex web of general principles (for example, in the nature of heroes, morals, and themes) and specific ideas and applications. And these are not always predictable. For example, although there are critical differences between mythologies and subsequent leadership paradigms in the United States and Iran, there are also deep-seated similarities which represent real opportunities for meaningful convergence. As a result, a more discriminating analysis of cultural mythologies would facilitate a finer-grained approach to global leadership.

Formally stated:

*Core Insight 2: Both universal and unique characteristics are present in cultural mythology, and hence in leadership.*

Third, a collective appreciation of the chapters' analyses leads us to postulate that cultural mythology manifests both intercultural acumen (some might call these 'strengths') and potentially problematic cultural biases (some might call these 'vulnerabilities'), and hence does its manifest leadership. This debunks the idea that there is any ideal or best leadership paradigm. Any analysis of leadership which does not take this into account will sub-optimize, be challenged to learn and self-enhance. The fundamental implication of this proposition is that leaders, and those who study leadership, must strategically simultaneously draw from and blend strengths while at the same time mitigate potential contingencies and constraints in order to succeed (a) within any one context as well as (b) across multiple contexts. For instance, where some mythologies emphasize the attainment of extraordinary individual achievement others are more adept at the equally critical leadership dimension of forging close bonds and fostering feelings of teamwork and community. Popularized in the business literature in the concepts of Individualism and Collectivism, in this particular example the analyses of mythologies shed new light on the roots, perpetuation, and nuanced characteristics thereof. Moreover it points to prospectively problematic predilections and cultural biases as well as opportunities for development and synergistic cross-cultural management. Borrowing from Perlmutter (1969), taking an integrative geocentric attitude to the issue at hand would open greater opportunity for leveraging collaborative capabilities. As a result, a more balanced accounting of cultural mythologies would facilitate an enhanced potential for global leadership.

Formally stated:

> *Core Insight 3: Cultural mythology manifests both intercultural acumen and potentially problematic predilections and biases, and hence does leadership.*

Fourth, and building on the previous suggestions, we postulate that globalization demands global leadership. This debunks the idea that myopic, ethnocentric, or egocentric approaches to leadership can succeed to any meaningful degree for any significant length of time. Any analysis of leadership which does not take this into account will engender a host of barriers, among them root defensiveness and disconfirmation, that inhibit the scope of leadership paradigms. As the beginning of this introduction suggests, there are critical implications of leading without a global mindset established firmly in the mythological foundations of cultural contexts. The fundamental implication of this proposition is that leaders, and those who study leadership, must demonstrate a depth of appreciation and sophistication by incorporating the roots, not just the behavioral expressions, of cultural contexts. This would reinforce the functionality of a type of 'cultural intelligence' (Thomas & Inkson, 2004), cosmopolitan leadership style (Kanter, 2006), transnational competence (Adler & Bartholomew, 1992), transnational mindset (Bartlett & Ghoshal, 1998), etc … but oriented toward deeply-ingrained, foundational cultural mythologies. It would also prompt a precursory review of local heroes and legends to develop a fuller sense of the business context and leadership expectations. As a result, a more broad-based adoption of cultural mythologies would facilitate an enhanced and even enlightened execution of global leadership.

Formally stated:

*Core Insight 4: Globalization demands global leadership.*

Fifth, expressing optimism and hope, we postulate that learning and leveraging cultural mythology promote global leadership development. This debunks the idea that leadership is hopelessly foreign or irreconcilably impenetrable. Cultural mythology acts as a torch, and we submit a rather bright one at that, for illuminating the proverbial black box or dark caverns of global leadership. Evoking yet a different metaphor, any analysis of leadership which does not take the lessons of cultural mythology into account will never be able to master the beast that has slain many a narrow-minded expatriate, ill-prepared executive, or insensitive principal. The fundamental implication of this proposition is that leaders, and those who study leadership, must become masters of cultural mythology in order to master their craft. This demands cognitive, affective, and behavioral training and development to fully understand and execute the expectations of cultural mythology in the practice of global leadership. The chapters in this volume suggest that this is possible. As a result, within a culture's heroes and villains, its sacred stories, its legends and lore, can be found its core values and central paradigms for global leadership effectiveness. To discover, deploy, or develop them is then a matter of mustering the will and delineating the way.

Formally stated:

*Core Insight 5: Global leadership can be developed by learning and leveraging cultural mythology.*

Sixth and finally, we describe the nexus of these three ideas as a forum for cultural evolution in which reciprocal dynamics unfold between global leaders and dynamics of globalization. This debunks the idea that culture or leadership is static and can be understood simply in snapshot. Leaders carry their cultural identities when they spearhead global engagements, and this may create an entry for the evolution of one's own culture as well as a heightened awareness and reflective thinking process that bears on decisions regarding one's cultural trajectory. Any analysis of leadership which does not take into account the reciprocal evolution will necessarily be a prisoner of past paradigms as opposed to the sage adventurer who appreciates both the depth of the oceans on which they sail as well as the undercurrent of elements and interactions that foretell, or even enable, waves of change. Cultures are not static and their evolutions are both an underappreciated and under-studied phenomenon (Tung, 2008); we propose that these shifts are often reflected in gradually morphing mythologies. The fundamental implication of this proposition is that leaders, and those who study leadership, must consistently venture into this nexus and synergistically engage its forces if they are to understand the evolution of the context, proactively confront and address ethnocentric or nationalistic biases (Adler, 1991), and ultimately shape and succeed in its manifest dance. This is reflected in the hero's return from the journey into lands beyond, from Joseph Campbell's (1949) comparative study of mythology in the *Hero With a Thousand Faces*, or in modern vernacular the accumulative transmigration of expatriates, third country nationals, and professional global managers that is both effected by and affects the interacted systems. The mere exposure to radically different ways of being as a leader creates changes in oneself that can be fed back into one's own cultural system for its development into the future. At the same time, the rise of contemporary globalization of culture takes place through multiple channels of interactions in both organizations and the larger community. As a result, a conversation uniting cultural mythology, globalization, and leadership would facilitate each in its own evolution and character.

Formally stated:

> *Core Insight 6: The nexus of cultural mythology, globalization, and leadership is a dynamic space where interactions between global leaders enable cultural evolutions.*

All in all, in this age of dynamic confluence and contradiction, our project of international collaboration seeks to help reconcile the unsustainable imbalance between the supply and demand for global leadership acumen. We focus on fundamental mythologies which underlie cultural contexts by examining how their core characteristics both manifest and shape leadership predilections and competencies (or lack thereof) and analyzing their practical lessons for modern day business. It is this type of deep consideration and comparative analysis, we believe, that will enable a more fundamental understanding, appreciation, and practical application of these phenomena. As such, and as suggested by the preceding discussion of core insights, we propose that a mastery of cultural mythology will facilitate leadership in the global arena by: (a) contextualizing analyses and perspectives; (b) bridging similarities and reconciling differences; (c) applying unique strengths and managing latent exposures; (d) broadening paradigms and capability portfolios; (e) illuminating and leveraging deep-seeded insights; and (f) evolving a reflective dialog of learning and continuous development. In short, applying the lens of cultural mythology enables a more effective and potentially successful approach for addressing the wonderful opportunities and preeminent challenges of global leadership.

## REFERENCES

Adams, S. (1996), *The Dilbert Principle*, New York: HarperCollins.

Adler, N. J. (1991), *International Dimensions of Organizational Behavior* (2nd edn), Boston, MA: PWS Kent.

Adler, N. J. and Bartholomew, S. (1992), Managing globally competent people, *Academy of Management Executive*, **6**(3): 52–65.

Armstrong, K. (2005), *A Short History of Myth*, Edinburgh, Scotland and New York: Canongate Books Ltd.

Bandura, A. (1977), *Social Learning Theory*, Englewood Cliffs, NJ: Prentice Hall.

Bandura, A. (1985), *Social Foundations of Thought and Action: A Social Cognitive Theory*, New York: Prentice Hall.

Bartlett, C. A. and Ghoshal, S. (1998), *Managing Across Borders: The Transnational Solution*, Cambridge, MA: Harvard Business School Press.

Benedict, R. (1934), *Patterns of Culture*, Boston, MA: Houghton-Mifflin.

Bidney, D. (1955), Myth, symbolism, and truth, in Thomas A. Sebeok (ed.), *Myth: A Symposium, Bibliographical and Special Series of the American Folklore Society Volume 5*, reprinted in Bloomington, IN: Indiana University Press, Midland Book Edition MBS3 (1970), Third printing, pp. 3–24.

Bierlein, J. F. (1994), *Parallel Myths*, New York and Toronto, Canada: Random House.

Campbell, J. (1949), *The Hero with a Thousand Faces*, Princeton, NJ: Princeton University Press, Third Printing (1973).

Campbell, J. with B. Moyers (1988), *The Power of Myth*, New York: Doubleday.

Collins, J. (2001), *Good to Great: Why Some Companies Make the Leap . . . and Others Don't*, New York: HarperCollins Publishers Limited.

The Columbia Encyclopedia (2007), Columbia University Press, www.cc.columbia.edu/cu/cup/

Cooperrider, D. L., P. F. Sorenson, Jr., T. Y. and Whitney, D. (2005), *Appreciative Inquiry: Foundations in Positive Organization Development*, Champaign, IL: Stipes Pub. Llc.

Earley, P. C. and Offermann, L. R. (2007), Interpersonal epistemology: Wisdom, culture, and organizations, in E. H. Kessler and J. R. Bailey (eds) *Handbook of Organizational and Managerial Wisdom*, Thousand Oaks, CA: Sage Publications.

Friedman, T. L. (2005), *The World Is Flat: A Brief History of the Twenty-first Century*, New York: Farrar, Straus and Giroux.

Goleman, D., McKee, A. and Boyatzis, R. E. (2002), *Primal Leadership: Realizing the Power of Emotional Intelligence*, Boston, MA: Harvard Business School Press.

Hall, E. T. (1976), *Beyond Culture*, New York: Anchor Books/Doubleday.

Hofstede, G. (1980), *Culture's Consequences: International Differences in Work-Related Values*, Beverly Hills, CA: Sage Publications.

Hofstede, G. (2001), *Culture's Consequences: Comparing Values, Behaviors, Institutions and Organizations Across Nations* (2nd edn), Beverly Hills, CA: Sage Publications.

Hofstede, G. (2007), Asian management in the 21st century, *Asian Pacific Journal of Management*, **24**(4): 411–20.

Hofstede, G. and Hofstede, G. J. (2005), *Cultures and Organizations: Software of the Mind* (2nd edn), New York: McGraw Hill.

House, R. J., Hanges, P. J., Javidan, M., Dorfman, P. W., and Gupta, V. (2004), *Culture, Leadership and Organizations: The GLOBE Study of 62 Societies*, Thousand Oaks, CA: Sage Publications.

Kanter, R. M. (2006), How cosmopolitan leaders inspire confidence, *Leader to Leader*, **41**: 55.

Kirk, G. S. (1970), *Myth: Its Meaning and Functions in Ancient and Other Cultures*, London: Cambridge University Press and Berkely, CA and Los Angeles, CA: University of California Press.

Kroeber, A. L. and Kluckhohn, Clyde (1963), *Culture: a Critical Review of Concepts and Definitions*, Cambridge, MA: Harvard University Press.

Morford, M. and Lenardon, R. J. (2003), *Classical Mythology*, Oxford and New York: Oxford University Press.

Perlmutter, H. V. (1969), The tortuous evolution of the multinational corporation, *Columbia Journal of World Business* (**January/February**): 9–18.

Prasad, A. and Prasad, P. (2007), Mix, flux, and flows: The globalization of culture and its implications for management and organizations, *Journal of Global Business Issues*, **1**(2): 11–20.

Ricks, D. A. (1999), *Blunders in International Business*, Malden, MA and Oxford: Blackwell Publishing.

Segal, R. A. (2004), *Myth: A Very Short Introduction* (3rd edn), Oxford and New York: Oxford University Press.

Thomas, D. C. and Inkson, K. (2004), *Cultural Intelligence: People Skills for Global Business*, San Francisco, CA: Berrett-Koehler Publishers.

Tung, R. (2008), The cross-cultural research imperative: the need to balance cross-national and intra-national diversity, *Journal of International Business Studies*, **39**: 41–6.

Weber, M. (1947), *The Theory of Social and Economic Organization*, tr. A. M. Henderson and T. Parsons, New York: Oxford University Press.

PART I

The Americas

# 1. Cultural mythology and global leadership in the United States

## Eric H. Kessler

### INTRODUCTION

Imagine that your organization is interviewing several well-known leadership gurus with the hope of improving business performance. Person A speaks about how to utilize cutting-edge technology to produce results. Person B wants you to leverage your competencies in a more effective and socially responsible manner. Person C emphasizes the challenges and opportunities of diversity, recounting how a capable woman can make good in a world dominated by men. Person D talks about boundary management and emphasizes how an outsider can adapt and contribute to an organizational culture. Team E focuses on uniting young diverse talent into an empowered work group.

Sound like typical CEO talking points? Or a management consulting firm's pitch? Perhaps derivative of a standard MBA curriculum?

Leadership guru A is Batman, his show on cable television, using his fancy gadgets to battle the evil Riddler and Two-Face. Leadership guru B is Spiderman, his blockbuster movie at the local cinema, who strives to find his core identity. Leadership guru C is Wonder Woman, her comic book at the local bookstore, trying to balance personal and professional callings. Leadership guru D is Superman, his action figure sold on the Internet, dedicated to fighting for individual freedom and justice in his new home. Leadership gurus E are the X-men, their like-named candy products at the corner drug store, seeking to manage diverse talents and personalities toward a common goal.

The central premise of this chapter is that United States leadership style, if such a heterogeneous culture can be boiled down so simply, might be at its core akin to acting like and creating the image of the mythological super-hero.

Classic US mythology is centered on the heroic nature of a leader in a wide variety of life situations (see, http://www.americanfolklore.net, http://www.rabbitears.com). These myths pervade US folklore, emphasizing rugged individualism and super-human spirit, as per: Casey Jones, heroic railroad engineer who always brought the train in on time; Davey Crocket, brave

31

woodsman and defender of the Alamo; Ethan Allen, gruff but gallant leader of the Green Mountain Boys; John Henry, mighty steel-driver who outperformed the machine; Johnny Appleseed, benevolent naturalist who sowed the Earth and spread goodwill; Paul Bunyan, 'big as a mountain and strong as a grizzly bear' lumberjack; Pecos Bill, the original cowboy hero of the wild-west; Annie Oakley, guns-blazing angel with sharp-shooter exploits; and Brer Rabbit, clever defender of the village who outsmarts Boss Lion.

In this modern age of high-technology, US myths are now played out on the big screen in Hollywood movie productions. As such, the American Film Institute's (AFI) list of top 'heroes' can be seen to exemplify superhero-like characteristics, for instance the idealistic Atticus Finch, resourceful Indiana Jones, clever Rick Blain, macho John Wayne, indomitable Rocky Balboa, noble George Bailey and courageous Ellen Ripley. These images are magnified when set against a similar list of AFI villains, suggesting an ongoing battle with evil (Darth Vader), cunning (Hannibal Lecter), manipulative (Nurse Ratched) and exploitative (Mr Potter) forces. Jumping to the business context, the prototypical American CEO heroes exhibit a similarly superhuman and charismatic, yet also entrepreneurial, drive akin to those of folklore and film but clad in business suits and set inside the corner office. These heroic icons have reached mythological larger-than-life status and are easily recognizable by single-word monikers such as …Walton, Disney, Ford, Sloan, Rockefeller, Watson, Hewlett, Turner, Welch and Jobs. A pictorial in *Business Week* (2002) made this argument explicit, actually depicting famous American CEOs such as Bill Gates, Michael Dell and Meg Whitman as cartoon superheroes.

All in all, the superhero is a foundational US leadership mythology. Superheroes are among the most popular and durable cultural stalwarts as portrayed in books, comics, film, television, consumer products and toys (Poniewozik *et al.*, 2002). Thus they are readily accessible potential role models for values and behaviors, especially in the early life socialization of children – that is, future leaders. Superheroes connote distinct values, ideas, methods of play, genres of experiences, and diverse cognitive structures to their impressionable audiences that, as proposed here, manifest themselves into behavioral and leadership styles. They may even be seen to express the 'American Dream' (Bischoff, 2007). The superhero concept is therefore interesting and useful in studying global leadership in at least two respects: (a) Descriptive – how has superhero mythology influenced US leaders?; and (b) prescriptive – is it beneficial to act like a superhero? First, the metaphor speaks to the issue of socialization – superheroes affect leaders in terms of who they become and how they behave. They are stories, read by children and adults alike, which serve as vehicles for transferring esteemed values and modes of behavior (Bandura, 1977; 1985). Second, it allows us to look at the more and less desirable aspects of superhero leadership in terms of its relative functionality. It can highlight preferred styles, as well as their strengths and blind-spots, and ultimately the establishment of competitive advantage both within and across cultural contexts. So this is just what I propose to examine in the remaining sections of this chapter.

## OVERVIEW OF USA AND SUPERHEROES

Although the 'hero journey' is a somewhat universal mythology that permeates nearly all corners of the globe (Campbell, 1968), the US superhero is a rather distinctive manifestation of the lone individualist calling up super powers to overcome evil and rescue the powerless (Faludi, 2007). US business, political, athletic and related folklore has consistently emphasized larger than life leaders who are said to stand above their peers and perform superhuman feats (Shamir, 2006). Lawrence and Jewett (2002: 6) contend that 'Americans have not moved beyond mythical consciousness ... in the distinctive pattern of what we call here the American monomyth', which echoes the theme of a lone superhero coming to rescue a threatened community. Thus superheroes are both a contributing factor to and a reflection of cultural contexts insofar as they represent a distinct art form (Bongco and Philipzig, 2000; Saltzberg, 2002). Indeed this conception of superhero leader is consistent with studies (for example, Hofstede, 1980; Javidan, *et al.*, 2006) characterizing the US culture as highly individualistic, assertive, and performance oriented.

Moreover, although hero idolization per se is not particular to the US context, Kamm (2001) observes 'what is new is the degree to which their values are impacting the rest of the culture'. Superheroes have been part of the social fabric for some time and are a major presence in the US market (Coville, 2002). Sales for action figures and accessories, a category that includes the superhero toys, has been estimated to exceed $1.3 billion (Ebenkamp, 2006). Total gross receipts for superhero motion pictures is enormous, with combined revenue for just the Superman, Batman, Spiderman, and X-Men movie franchises topping $4.5 billion (www.boxofficemojo.com, 2007). Alliances between comic book hero and consumer products purveyors take the mythology to another level. For example, a deal between Kraft Post, Warner Bros. Inc. and DC Comics Inc. enabled superheroes' collectible trading cards to jump out of 15 million kids' cereal boxes (Reyes, 2004). A recent Zogby poll shows that people in the US are actually more familiar with Superman than with current events and world leaders, emphasizing 'how much more effective popular culture information is communicated and retained by citizens than many of the messages that come from government, educational institutions and the media' (Harper, 2006). The devotion to superhero myths has even been described as akin to 'worship', and their glamorous motion picture manifestations certainly maintain this image (Postrel, 2006).

Models of leadership are rooted in a social framework and, as such, comic book heroes can be understood as a visualization of US oral folk history (Fletcher, 2004; Scott, 2006). Perhaps the first genuine US 'superhero' was George Washington, whose image was important in inspiring colonial troops in the battle for national independence (McCullough, 2005). The ubiquitous penetration of like myths has since permeated all facets of the culture. The US Postal Service issued sheets of classic superhero characters from DC and Marvel Comics. US television featured network shows based on superheroes as well as the modern breakout drama 'Heroes' and popular cartoon 'Ben-10'. Disney pop icon Hannah Montana has been described as 'the superman for tween girls: she's got the secret identity, a more relevant superpower and a blond wig instead of a cape' (Poniewozik, 2007). Superheroes are also trendy on college campuses (Hertz, 2005). The Economist (2003) likened bosses to supermen. Clergy have been described, or at least viewed, as possessing super-hero status (Crowe, 2005). Taylor and Greve (2006) have utilized the super-hero metaphor in evaluating individual (superman) versus group (Fantastic Four) performance. All in all, in multiple arenas, we see that 'the American century produced scores of larger-than-life people with enduring legacies' (Hunt, 1999). Combined with comic book and film heroes, this offers 'further proof of American popular culture's extreme devotion to the ... superhero myth' (Patterson, 2007).

## MAJOR AMERICAN SUPERHEROES AND LEADERSHIP STYLE

Our central thesis is that superheroes are a valuable tool for understanding how US leaders and their organizations have acquired values and behavioral propinquities and what they might teach us about understanding the dynamic. In a general sense, we might look at the classic US superhero myth as suggesting that leaders should strive to be larger than life – super-brave, super-strong, super-smart, with super technology, doing super deeds, and so on; an individual that towers above everyone else. This aligns with what has been termed by Kamm (2001) as a 'superman syndrome', described as the 'active glorification of speed and toughness' and is so pervasive that 'anyone not wishing to be part of this hyperactive-interactive world is in danger of being labeled an outcast, slow, irrelevant, or depressed'. Let us now consider ten representative US-style superheroes, how they might act as CEOs, and some potential 'lessons' for understanding and modeling leadership styles (see Table 1.1).

*Table 1.1    Select American-style superhero myths and leadership*

| Hero/myth | Advises leaders to leverage … | Advises leaders to avoid … |
| --- | --- | --- |
| Aquaman | Diversity, communication, domain | Straying from core, poorly-transferable competencies, overextended resources |
| Batman | Innovation/ technology, creativity, judgment under uncertainty | Dark side, greed, overly emotional responses |
| Captain America | Courage, identity, commitment, loyalty | Self-doubt, rigidity |
| Fantastic Four | Diverse talents, synergy | Ill-managed transformations, disharmony, self-loathing, trappings of celebrity |
| Flash | Speed, first mover advantages | Going too fast, poor advanced planning, losing control |
| Incredible Hulk | Power, physical resources | Rage, in-your-face competition, poor self monitoring, low emotional intelligence |
| Spiderman | Learning, intuition, flexibility, social responsibility | Ego-orientation, loss of public sentiment, stress/angst, confused identity |
| Superman | Strength, moral code, resiliency, vision | Rigidities, blind spots, over-confidence |
| Wonder Woman | Wisdom, strength, beauty, stealth | Base prejudice and bias, uneven work-life balance, poor alliance and relationship strategies |
| X-Men | Transformations, core values, teamwork, youthful energy | Public mistrust, negative motivation, ineffective image management, indiscretion |

## Aquaman

(First Appearance: November 1941 – *More Fun* #73), alter ego Arthur Curry, also known as King of the Seven Seas and Marine Marvel, was born of Tom Curry (ex-sailor) and a woman from Atlantis. Aquaman can live underwater, perform great marine feats, and communicate with sea creatures. However, he cannot survive more than one hour without some contact with water. Because of his superior performance within a limited domain, he recalls Porter's (1980) ideas of niche strategy and competitive advantage. His interaction and synergistic coordination sea denizens invoke ideas on diversity management and cross-cultural communication. CEO Aquaman, the proverbial king of his realm, might emphasize these ideals to his organization while warning against straying too far from one's core domain, lest one suffer suffocating over-extensions of capacity and poorly-transferable practices. A leadership lesson: Strength in one area does not guarantee universal generalizability.

## Batman

(First Appearance: May 1939 – *Detective Comics* #27), alter ego millionaire socialite Bruce Wayne, also known as the Caped Crusader and Masked Manhunter, was 'created' when witnessing his parents' murder and thus swearing an oath to prevent this tragedy from happening to others. Batman is a master scientist and creative criminologist/detective, of impressive physical prowess, owner of state-of-the-art technology (Waid, 1990), and aided by sidekick Robin. However, he is constantly struggling against his 'dark side' and inner daemons. These characteristics relate to leadership and technology, the functionality of personal reflection and introspection, and the need for strategic flexibility and adaptive decision making under uncertainty. CEO Batman might emphasize practical innovation, combined with sound yet malleable judgment, while warning against the lure of greed and overly emotional responses to wrongdoing (see similar manifestations in popular media, including the *Star Wars* franchise). A leadership lesson: Technology is not panacea, and logic does not always rule emotion.

## Captain America

(First Appearance: March 1941 – *Captain America* #1), alter ego World War II army Private Steve Rogers, is a symbol of patriotism and was once displayed as punching Adolph Hitler. Also known as Cap and the Star-Spangled Avenger, his powers genesis from a secret government experiment with a special serum to build the body and brain. Captain America is distinguished by his athleticism, intelligence, and especially strong shield. However, he is haunted by doubts about hero persona (re: public sentiment during the US-Vietnam War). Cap prompts one to consider leadership interventions oriented toward organizational loyalty, courage and commitment, as well as approaches to conflict (for example, competition versus collaboration). CEO Cap might leverage these attributes while working to understand and manage genuine questions of self, values and identity. It is interesting to note that in 2007 Cap was 'killed off' in the comics, executed amid a modern chaos of shifting alliances and deep internal divisions when he refused to betray old-school values and unmask. A leadership lesson: There are many layers, and chapters, to competitive dynamics and conflict resolution.

**The Fantastic Four**

(Or F4, First Appearance: November 1961 – *Fantastic Four* #1) is a team of superheroes. They consist of Mr Fantastic (a.k.a. Reed Richards), Invisible Girl (Sue Storm), the Human Torch (Sue's brother Johnny Storm) and Thing (Benjamin Grimm). The F4 gained their powers when a test pilots' ship was penetrated by cosmic rays. Modeled after the four classic Greek elements, they have the unique abilities of elasticity, invisibility, fire and strength. Sometimes they cannot control their collective infighting or personal transformations to and from their alter-egos, especially the hotheaded Torch and short-fused Thing. Thing's self-loathing and self-pity are reminiscent of the success-trap executives sometimes find themselves in. Leadership issues such as team management, flexibility, diversity management, and emotions relate to these characters. Their celebrity status also speaks to the leadership mystique. Top management team F4 might emphasize teamwork and synergy while seeking to increase control over one's environment (see Pfeffer and Salancik, 1978), as well as deal more effectively with their heroic status and public persona. A leadership lesson, as per President Lincoln: A house (that is, individual or collective) divided against itself cannot stand.

**Flash**

(First Appearance: January 1940 – *Flash Comics* #1), alter ego police scientist Barry Allen, also known as the Scarlet Speedster and Sultan of Speed, gained his abilities from a lightning-induced explosion at a chemical lab. Flash is an incredibly fast runner, with a top velocity estimated at 10x light (or faster than the speed of thought, perhaps suggesting act > think?), and has a good sense of humor, yet can sometimes operate too fast and lose control of a situation. Flash maps quite well with leadership issues relating to speed, time manage-ment and accelerated practices. CEO Flash might lead his organization toward a speed-based paradigm (see Kessler and Chakrabarti, 1996) and possible first-mover or fast-follower strategic orientation. He would hopefully remain vigilant against going too quickly, outpacing one's strategy and structural capabilities, not planning ahead sufficiently and losing control. A leadership lesson: Speed kills ... but faster is not always better.

## The Incredible Hulk

(First Appearance: May 1962 – *Incredible Hulk* #1), alter ego nuclear scientist Dr Bruce Banner, also known as the Green Goliath and Jolly Green Giant, emerged from Dr Banner when he was exposed to a gamma-bomb weapon while saving a teenager at its test site. Hulk is renowned for his brutal, awesome strength but at the same time is held prisoner by his rage-induced transformations, so much so that he cannot risk revealing it in his daily relationships. This superhero gains his advantage as well as handicap from areas overlapping the issues of power, personality, and (lack of) emotional intelligence or EI (Goleman, 1995), specifically that related to anger management. CEO hulk might be well served to mitigate his focus on in-your-face competition with training in self-monitoring, emotional intelligence and self-control. A leadership lesson: Physical resources are but tools that must be properly managed.

## Spiderman

(First Appearance: August 1962 – *Amazing Fantasy* #15), alter ego high school student Peter Parker, also known as Spidey and Web-Head, transformed after the combined events of being bitten by radioactive spider and realizing that his misuse of this power contributed to his uncle's death. This superhero is distinguished by such spider-like attributes as climbing, leaping, web-slinging, and a special sense-of-danger. However, he is constrained by a misunderstood public sentiment, personal ego, identity crises, and human angst. There are many links between the Spiderman character and leadership issues such as the learning organization, strategic flexibility, intuitive decision making, and the call for greater corporate responsibility. CEO Spiderman might lead a flexible and socially oriented enterprise, but must also reconcile personal doubt and stress, better deal with the 'burden of leadership', and buttress this with initiatives in external relations and image management. A leadership lesson, as per the Spiderman theme song: 'With great power comes great responsibility'.

## Superman

(First Appearance: June 1938 – *Action Comics* #1), alter ego newspaper reporter Clark Kent is the oldest of the considered superheroes and the recognized usher of the 'golden age of comics'. Also known as the Man of Steel and Man of Tomorrow, this character escaped to earth from the destroyed planet Krypton. Despite his mild mannered appearance, he boasts amazing strength, the ability of flight, impenetrable skin, and x-ray vision. However, his powers are compromised by exposure to home planet elements such as Kryptonite or a red sun. His steel, flight, and strength map well onto issues such as resiliency, resource-based competition and power and influence. CEO superman might enjoy the fruits of these awesome advantages but keep an eye towards fundamental strategic vulnerabilities and blind spots and perhaps incorporate some form of sound contingency planning, lest his 'strategic kryptonites' get the best of him. Even the most powerful leaders and organizations are not omnipotent. A leadership lesson (or two): Do not judge a book by its cover; and too much confidence can be dangerous.

**Wonder Woman**

(First Appearance: December 1941 – *All Star Comics* #8), alter ego army major Diana Prince, is our sole female representative on the list. Also known as the Amazing Amazon, she was born when the Goddess Aphrodite brought a statue to life on the Amazon people's Paradise Island. She is known to be as strong as Hercules, swift as Mercury, wise as Athena, and beautiful as Aphrodite. Wrapped in the US flag, Wonder Woman wields an invisible robot plane, magic lasso, and bullet-resistant feminium (yes – 'feminine-idiom') bracelets. She is also hampered by her rather ineffectual boyfriend, Steve Trevor, and the widespread and rather villainous negative stereotyping of women. One can see numerous desirable characteristics in her stealth (plane), corporate intelligence (rope), and form/function (bracelets) tools. CEO Wonder Woman might easily combine her godlike attributes and cutting-edge technology to forge supernormal rents but she must at the same time be weary of energy-draining alliances, personal responsibilities and relationships, and base prejudice that might mitigate her successful completion of her missions. A leadership lesson: The playing field is neither level nor insurmountable.

**The X-Men**

(First Appearance: September 1963 – *X Men* #1) consist of The Beast (a.k.a. Hank McCoy), Iceman (Bobby Drake), Cyclops (Scott Summers), the Angel (Warren Worthington III) and Marvel Girl (Jean Grey). These youngsters are mutated teenagers with extra powers, the proverbial next step in the evolutionary chain, who were recruited and gathered into a team by Professor X – note the prominent role of a professor in superhero lore! They leverage the diverse abilities of apelike attributes, freezing, eye-laser, wings, and teleportation. They also are on constant guard against the trappings of youth as well as public distrust and potentially evil mutants' motivations. We can see the issues of stakeholder relationships, teamwork and synergy, team leadership, values and social responsibility mirrored and developed in the X-Men saga. Top management team X-Men might do well to combine a focus on continuous professional development and the management of complex relationships with a better reconciliation with perception and public sentiment. After all, the constructed schema (by employees, customers, competitors, and so on) is ultimately the foundation for action – that is, image is everything. A leadership lesson: Perception, both of self and others, is the practically important reality.

All in all, we can glean several themes from these classic US-style superheroes. On the macro level, they reinforce the notions of developing and leveraging competitive advantage (through unique, valuable, and difficult-to- replicate powers), the pitfalls of poorly managed relationships and networks (coordination among diverse individuals is key, *á la* the Fantastic Four, X-men), the virtues of ambidexterity and contingency (through their changing forms), and skepticism toward wholehearted reliance on public institutions (resembling a free market, capitalistic, and in some senses Darwinian view of competition). On the meso level they reinforce the potential of power, creativity, speed and technology (gadgets and gizmos) as well as the balancing of individual forces (win-win partnerships, image management, and supportive infrastructure). At the micro level they speak to ethical distinctions of good versus evil and the importance of self-reflection and finding one's place in the world.

Delving deeper, we might extract from the proceeding a profile of the prototypical US 'superhero leader' who seeks to:

- fight for noble personal and societal goals;
- be strong, fast, brave, and nimble;
- leverage cutting-edge technology and physical resources;
- creatively develop and exploit unique advantage;
- be self-reliant yet compassionate;
- manage reputation and image; and
- self-reflect on identity and purpose.

Further, as the superheroes are inherently and thus inevitably human, they do not always approximate these metrics. Goals are not always met and character is often tested. As per Poniewozik and colleagues (2002), US superheroes, though possessing amazing powers, are particularly 'human' insofar as they reflect our anxieties, embody our weaknesses, and are basically normal and flawed. Indeed as these characters illustrate, even heroes struggle with internal conflicts, external challenges and complex contingencies in their enactment of values and their pursuit of ideals. Thus the prototype is unevenly pursued and imperfectly realized. Notwithstanding, its idealistic lure remains a perennial benchmark.

## GLOBAL IMPLICATIONS

We have thus far considered the US superhero myth in somewhat of a vacuum, largely immune from cultural and other relevant contingencies such as history, genre, and the like. Here, let us at least partly take up the challenge and consider three particularly interesting ones – culture, domain, generation – as well as a particularly critical pitfall of the superhero lens.

**Culture**

Comic book superheroes are among the most globally recognized fictional characters. Batman and Superman images can be found on T-shirts and in toy boxes across the four corners of the earth. Notwithstanding, the native super-hero is often differentially portrayed between cultures as illustrated by the following examples (Mayfield *et al.*, 2001). In France, comics appeal to all age groups via genres of humor, fantasy, adventure, erotica and psychological drama. The Italian comic book industry focuses mainly on national norms and historical works, crime stories, erotic and even classical literature adaptations. The Japanese comic book industry is both the oldest and most successful in the world, leveraging animation (anime) to create highly popular and trans-portable characters such as Pokèmon and Power Rangers. Mexican comics show a strong national character in their humorous works involving historical protagonists and cultural icons. There is also a rich history of superhero lore in China, including the Monkey King, White Snake, and Ghosts and Fox Spirits. Take for example the Monkey King, a 400 plus year old allegorical rendition of a shape-shifting master of magic tricks and kung-fu. Or recently developed 'Soccer Boy', about a group of children who succeed only by obey-ing their coach's authority and working together (http://www.gospelcom.net).

In total, one might see in these examples some cultural divergences (for example, collectivist versus individualist, high versus low power distance – see Hofstede, 1980) from 'traditional' US-based superheroes. These in turn might be attributed to deep-seated mythologies and ultimately manifest in organizational approaches and personal predilections. It also suggests that there might be more than one best way to lead. Consider the following ques-tion: Should Superman engage issues differently depending on where in the world he is called (or assigned)? This speaks to the need to develop diagnos-tic acumen and behavioral flexibility required for global leadership success, and on the flip side, the frequent difficulties encountered by 'ugly American' supermen who do not consider these nuanced relationships.

## Domain

There are of course a plethora of rich fields in religion, history, literature, and the like from which to draw similar superhero comparisons. Insofar as US culture was traditionally conceptualized in relation to the Judeo-Christian ethic, consider for example the following link between Superman and the religious figure of Moses (Saltzberg, 2002):

> His people faced destruction. They sent out a baby boy, placing him in a box, to ensure his survival. He grew up to be a hero, a savior, able to achieve feats that no ordinary man could do. Moses? Or Superman? It could be either. Superman was drawn by two Jewish boys, Jerry Siegel and Joe Shuster, and was based on Moses. It is reported that the Superman comics were never drawn on Thursday night, as Mrs. Siegel needed her breadboard to knead her loaves of bread for Shabbat!

For a more recent blending of biblical 'superheroes' and modern media, see for example Jones' (1995) discussion of Jesus as CEO or the children's cartoons based on Bill Bennett's virtues (1996) and 'Veggie Tales' series. These latter vegetable-based heroes include superman-like Larry Boy, a caped cucumber who along with his vegetable character friends battle the evil Weed (spreads rumors about people), Big Gourd (tells lies and gets others to fib), and star in adventures such as 'Leggo My Ego'. Upshot – One should not underestimate the myths and leadership values embedded in religious traditions and lore. Similarly, one should not view superheroes as divorced from their spiritual and ethical context.

## Generation

It is our contention that the superhero mythology is both snapshot and cinema insofar as it is useful in describing general values and characteristics as well as shifting trends and evolving affinities in the culture. Superheroes are not static, and their meaning and influence cannot be wholly captured cross-sectionally. This is to say; in addition to the prototype's functionality as a conceptual overlay, the superhero genre is also reflective of social changes in a culture (Grossman, 2005). For instance, compare the do-gooder Batman of the 1970s with the darker, more introspective character in the 1990s. Indeed, the United States comic book industry has adapted to many social and political issues in its narratives through the years (Palmer-Mehta and Hay, 2005). Societal tensions are even on display, as Stanley (2005) argues that there is a general poor US response to female superhero films, reflecting a 'glass ceiling' effect. Although the classic US superhero is often portrayed in a consistent manner – attractive, powerful, and dynamic in character (Huey, 1994) – some degree of change is afoot, as modern depictions of classic superheroes include formerly Caucasian male characters now shown as minorities and women. From the simple themes of the 1930–40s to more complex, even cynical attitudes toward institutions and actors, the evolving nature of these metaphors underlines the analogy between superheroes and America itself (Bischoff, 2007).

Insofar as superheroes are mirrors of their societies, we can expect the mythology to keep adapting to reflect widespread values and conditions which bear upon US leadership styles. For instance, the toy industry has recently created 'business' action figures such as MoneyMan, BossMan, and IT-based GeekMan (Trancos, 2005). Disney has launched a film and products franchise based on a seemingly normal but secretly superhero family called the 'Incredibles'. This trend begs the question; just as Captain America led the charge against the Nazis, can superheroes address today's challenge of unconventional war against terror? Or compete in a context of rapidly advancing technology and constantly shifting markets? To the former point, Poniewozik (2001) wonders if Superman could defeat global terrorist networks and argues that, in a post-9/11 world, it is ordinary citizens that embody the true nature of heroism. This was reinforced by a young boy, whose father worked near the former World Trade Center, who identified firefighters and police officers as superheroes (Kessler, 2002). As such, superhero myths, and by extension their leadership implications, must be appreciated as a constantly evolving genre that reflects an equally dynamic cultural context.

## Potential Pitfall

It is important that we do not come across as being exclusively positive on the superhero myth. One particularly important blind-spot is raised by what has been termed (and this certainly is no coincidence) 'post-heroic leadership'. The argument is that collaborative, or post-heroic models of leadership, may be more congruent with post-industrial society than 'classic' models emphasizing the great individualist, partly because single individuals simply cannot unite all the multifarious expertise needed and process all the contingencies required to succeed in the modern business context (Dentico, 1999) – see Commentary box below. In a post-heroic paradigm, leaders are less towering figures and more akin to coaches or partners, sharing power and addressing challenges through open collaboration and teamwork (Bradford and Cohen, 1998). It counters what has been labeled the 'romance of leadership' (Meindl *et al.*, 1985), the tendency to idealize leaders and to attribute to them much greater influence on outcomes than they actually have. Post-heroic leadership embodies a different way of looking at the world, which admits limitations and delegates true power. Thus Dutton (1996) asks us:

> Are you a hero? If you answer 'no', you are probably a better leader than those who said 'yes'. Heroic leaders – those who have all the answers, make all the decisions and are totally responsible for their departments' or companies' fates – are being swept away by a business environment that requires leaders to share responsibility, implement a tangible vision and encourage a sense of ownership among employees at all levels of their organizations – and accept criticism well.

Indeed, creating a sense of collaboration (or post-heroic leadership) is seen by many as a necessity for the modern organization to succeed. As such leaders must relent in their attitudes toward centralized control and purely individualized competency (Roth, 1994). Wonderful examples of US post-heroic leadership are embodied in the practices of its plethora of high-technology and entrepreneurial juggernauts (for example, Google, Microsoft, Apple, HP, 3M) as well as W. L. Gore and Associates, which has enjoyed profitable growth for over three decades due in large part to a leadership philosophy of no hierarchy, no titles, and no permanent team leaders (Dutton, 1996). This and other post-heroic companies work from a strong set of core values and a dedication to flexible and collaborative leadership. Thus merging these two spheres of myth – heroic and post-heroic – may help approximate enduringly successful, perhaps even wise, leadership in organizations (Kessler and Bailey, 2007). The resultant framework would recognize the extraordinary intellectual prowess and principled objectives endemic in an individual leader but also their synergistic orientation, inherent humility, and essential interconnectedness with organizational actors and stakeholders.

## COMMENTARY BOX:

### President of Consulting Firm and Former CEO/COO of Major US Corporations

I had the personal experience of following a 'superhero' into a job … He was an autocrat who prided himself on his knowledge of the industry, the market, technology, with very visible stature in the business community. He took steps to flatten the organization, removing the layer of leadership below him, ostensibly to speed decision making, but in practice to consolidate power and decision making. All strategic decisions were made by him alone, and he was constantly deferred to with any questions or issues, and no one openly disagreed with him.

**USAF Lt Col (retired) and Senior VP Finance for Major US Corporation**

I have worked with and for individuals who had the 'superhero' or 'Lone Ranger' complex ... I see them more on Wall Street than in the military ... Superheroes tend to be rewarded with bonuses, raises and promotions – which feeds their belief in the value of the superhero approach to work ... The people I've seen engage in this behavior are very competitive, and seem to believe that for them to win others must lose. They think this is the path to success in terms of compensation and prestige ... If successful, they tend to work long hours and get a lot done ... Some super-heroes tend to be disruptive inside an organization, and cause low morale and increased turnover in their wake. Long-term orga-nizational effectiveness can be diminished by a superhero leader who is not developing a strong bench.

## SUMMARY AND CONCLUSIONS

In this chapter we have considered the United States superhero mythology and its implications for understanding leadership style, including its origins, strengths and blind spots, as well as applications to modern challenges. The prototypical US superhero leader develops and leverages unique competitive advantage, esteems strength and speed, competes vigorously, embraces flexi-bility and contingency, actively manages reputation and image, does not rely on public institutions, develops cutting-edge tools and technology, constantly explores moral and ethical issues, and self-reflects on power and purpose. This ideal might be more or less closely approximated and is accompanied by both advantages and potential pitfalls. Ten popular superheroes were discussed that illustrate these cultural characteristics and project lessons for global leader-ship.

Throughout its history, US superhero mythology has evolved throughout frontier lore, cultural conglomeration, industrial and mass-media develop-ment, and geopolitical expansion. It has been revealed in campfire stories, cinematic productions, and perhaps most unabashedly through comic book idols. Although such a heterogeneous and complex culture is difficult to capture with a single metaphor, understanding the US superhero mentality, including the core values and behavioral dynamics that it connotes, is a useful vehicle for making sense of manifest leadership. And more than this, perhaps harmonizing this mentality with more distinctly collaborative attributes is the next step in its engagement within an increasingly interconnected global area. Superman, Batman, Aquaman, and others did in fact work together within the rubric of the 'Justice League' to synergistically leverage their diverse personal attributes across multiple domains in pursuit of a greater good. Perhaps it is also the wise leader – and as per the chapter's opening vignette the wise CEO, consultant or educator – who can creatively blend heroic and post-heroic characteristics to create true and enduring organizational greatness.

# REFERENCES

Adams, S. (1996), *The Dilbert Principle*, New York: HarperCollins.
Ahn, M. J., Adamson, J. S., and Dornbusch, D. (2004), From leaders to leadership: Managing change, *Journal of Leadership & Organizational Studies*, **10** (4), 112–23.
Bandura, A. (1977), *Social Learning Theory*, Englewood Cliffs, NJ: Prentice Hall.
Bandura, A. (1985), *Social Foundations of Thought and Action: A Social Cognitive Theory*, New York: Prentice Hall.
Bennett, W. J. (1996), *Book of Virtues: A Treasury of Great Moral Stories*, New York: Simon and Schuster Childrens Publishing.
Benton, M. (1991), *Superhero Comics of the Silver Age: An Illustrated History*, Dallas, TX: Taylor Publishing Company.
Birken, M. and Coon, A. C. (2001), *The Pedagogical and Epistemological Uses of Analogy in Poetry and Mathematics*, http://www.aber.ac.uk/tfts/journal/archive/birken-coon.html.
Bischoff, D. (2007), *Apocalypse POW: Exhibition Unmasks America's Comic Book Tradition*, The Star Ledger, July 15, Section 4, p. 1 and p. 6.
Bongco, M. and Philipzig, J. (2000), *Reading Comics: Language, Culture, and the Concept of the Superhero in Comic Books*, New York and London: Garland Publishing.
Bradford, D. L. and Cohen, A. R. (1998), *Power Up: Transforming Organizations through Shared Leadership*, John Wiley & Sons.
Bruning, R. H., Schraw, G. J. and Ronning, R. R. (1999), *Cognitive Psychology and Instruction* (3rd edn), Englewood Cliffs, NJ: Merrill.
*Business Week* (2002), 25 November, 88–9.
Campbell, J. (1968), *The Hero with a Thousand Faces*, New York: World Publishing.
Coville, J. K. (2002), *The History of Superhero Comic Books*, http://www.geocities.com/Athens/8580/menu.html
Crowe, J. M. (2005), Brother Martin or pastor superstar?, *Clergy Journal*, **82** (1), 33–4.
Dentico, J. P. (1999), Games leaders play: using process simulations to develop collaborative leadership practices for a knowledge-based society, *Career Development International*, **4** (3), 175–82.
Dutton, G. (1996), Leadership in a post-heroic age, *Management Review*, **85** (10), 7.
Ebenkamp, B. (2006), Heroes (and Bratz) to save the day, *Brandweek*, **47** (25), S62.
Faludi, (2007), Post 9/11, a more macho America, *US News and World Report*, 22 October: 30.
Fletcher, J. K. (2004), The paradox of post heroic leadership: An essay on gender, power, and transformational change, *Leadership Quarterly*, **15** (5), 647–61.
Gardenswartz, L. and Rowe, A. (1993), *Managing Diversity: A Complete Desk Reference and Planning Guide*, Homewood, IL: Irwin.

Goleman, D. (1995), *Emotional Intelligence*, New York: Bantam Books.

Grossman, C. L. (2000), *Bam! Zap! Comic Book Newcomers bring New Attitude to Old Genre*, http://detnews.com/2000/entertainment/0414/comic/comic.htm.

Grossman, L. (2005), The geek shall inherit the earth, *Time*, 3 October: 98.

Harper, J. (2006), Superman tops supremes, *Washington Times*, 15 August.

Hertz, R. (2005), Why do we need superheroes?, *Campus Life*, **63** (9), 50.

Hofstede, G. (1980), *Culture's Consequences: International Differences in Work-related Values*, Beverly Hills, CA: Sage.

http://www.americanfolklore.net

http://www.boxofficemojo.com.

http://www.gospelcom.net/rox35media/Quote01a.html

http://www.indiana.edu/~chasso.monkey.html

http://www.majorpowerkidsclub.org/watts/ddn011002.htm

http://www.rabbitears.com

http://www.superherostuff.com/

Huey, J. (1994), The new post-heroic leadership, *Fortune*, 21 February, 42–50.

Hunt, A. R. (1999), The century's larger-than-life leaders, *Wall Street Journal*, December 30, A-13: 3.

Javidan, M., Dorfman, P. W., Sully de Luque, M. and House, R. J. (2006), In the eye of the beholder: Cross cultural lessons from Project GLOBE, *Academy of Management Perspective*, **20** (1), 67–90.

Johnson, S. (1998), *Who Moved My Cheese?: An Amazing Way to Deal with Change in Your Work and in Your Life*, New York: Putnam Publishing.

Jones, L. B. (1995), *Jesus, CEO: Using Ancient Wisdom for Visionary Leadership*, New York: Hyperion Press.

Kamm, R.H. (2001), The superman syndrome, *Journal for Quality and Participation*, **24** (2), 38–40.

Kane, E. J. (1999), Implications of superhero metaphors for the issue of banking powers, *Journal of Banking and Finance*, **23** (2), 663–73.

Kanter, R. (1989), *Teaching Elephants to Dance*, New York: Simon & Schuster.

Kao, J. (1996), *Jamming: The Art and Discipline of Business Creativity*, New York: Harper Business.

Kessler, E. H. (2001), The idols of organizational theory: From Francis Bacon to the Dilbert Principle, *Journal of Management Inquiry*, **10** (4), 285–97.

Kessler, E. H. and Bailey, J. R. (2007), *Handbook of Organizational and Managerial Wisdom*, Thousand Oaks, CA: Sage Publications.

Kessler, E. and Chakrabarti, A. (1996), Innovation speed: A conceptual model of context, antecedents, and outcomes, *Academy of Management Review*, **21** (4), 1143–91.

Kessler, E. H., Bierly, P. E., and Gopalakrishnan, S. (2001), Vasa-syndrome: insights for product development, *Academy of Management Executive*, **15** (3), 80–91.

Kessler, J. F. (2002), Personal interview, 4 September.

Lawrence, J. S. and Jewett, R. (2002), *The Myth of the American Superhero*, Grand Rapids, MI: William B. Eerdmans Publishing Company.

Makay, H. (1988), *Swim with the Sharks Without Being Eaten Alive: Outsell, Outmanage, Outmotivate and Outnegotiate Your Competition*, New York: Ballantine Books.

Mayfield, M., Mayfield, J. and Genestre, A. D. (2001), Strategic insights from the international comic book industry: A comparison of France, Italy, Japan, Mexico, and the USA, *American Business Review*, **19** (2), 82–92.

McCullough, D. (2005), *1776*, New York: Simon and Schuster.

Meindl, J. R., Ehrlich, S. D. and Dukerich, J. M. (1985), The romance of leadership, *Administrative Science Quarterley*, **30** (1), 78–102.

Morgan, G. (1986), *Images of Organization*, Beverly Hills, CA: Sage.

Palmer-Mehta, V. and Hay, K. (2005), A superhero for gays?: Gay masculinity and Green Lantern, *Journal of American Culture*, **28** (4), 390–404.

Patterson, J. (2007), A time for heroes, *The Guardian*, 17 February, 10.

Pfeffer, J. and Salancik, J. R. (1978), *The External Control of Organizations: A Resource Dependence Perspective*, New York: Harper & Row.

Poniewozik, J. (2001), Super human strength, *Time*, 22 October, 77.

Poniewozik, J. (2007), Hurricane Hannah, *Time*, 29 October, 64.

Poniewozik, J., Arnold, A., Nugent, B. and Tesoriero, H. W. (2002), Superhero nation, *Time South Pacific*, 20 May, 57.

Porter, M. E. (1980), *Competitive Strategy*, New York: The Free Press.

Postrel, V. (2006), Superhero worship, *Atlantic Monthly*, **298** (3), 140–4.

Reyes, S. (2004), Post, DC comics unite to cereal-ize superheroes, *Brandweek*, **45** (6), 9.

Rosa, J. (2002), *Superhero to the Rescue*, http://www.destination crm.com/

Roth, T. (1994), 'How the post-heroic leader scores, *Management Development Review*, **7** (6,) 4–6.

Saltzberg, D. (2002), *Leaders and Superheroes*, http://www.aish.com/literacy/concepts/Leaders_and_superheros,asp

Scott, B. A. (2006), Superpower vs. supernatural: Black superheroes and the quest for a mutant reality, *Journal of Visual Culture*, **5** (3), 295–314.

Shamir, B. (2006), Review of 'In Their Time: The Greatest Business Leaders of the Twentieth Century', *Academy of Management Review*, **31**(3), 760–3.

Stanley, T. L. (2005), Super heroines fly into glass ceiling, *Advertising Age*, **76** (50), 3–33.

Taylor, A. and Greve, H. R. (2006), Superman or the Fantastic Four: knowledge combination and experience in innovative teams, *Academy of Management Review*, **39** (4), 723–40.

The Economist (2003), The boss as Superman, *The Economist*, 11 January, 366 (8306), 58.

Trancoso, Y. (2005), Finally, some hero worship, *CA Magazine,* **138** (1), 9.

Waid, M. (1990), *Who's Who In The DC Universe #5*, New York: DC Comics Inc.

Weber, M. (1947), *The Theory of Social and Economic Organization*, tr. A. M. Henderson and T. Parsons, New York: Oxford University Press.

Zimbalist, A. and Driggs, L. (1998), *Developing Heroic Characters: A Language Arts Lesson Plan*, Nytimes.com/learning/teachers/lessons

# 2. Cultural mythology and global leadership in Canada

## Nina D. Cole and Rhona G. Berengut

## INTRODUCTION

The mythologies of Canada emanate from three fundamental aspects of Canadian life: its northern geography, its three founding cultures and its complex democracy. The physical geography of Canada covers six time zones, and includes flat, rolling prairies, soaring mountain peaks and the frozen north. English, French, and First Nations peoples joined together to unite the land from sea to sea to sea. The peaceful democracy of Canada has endured despite, or perhaps due to, its constitutional complexity. Together, these three historical realities have shaped a national culture characterized by accommodation of differences. These mythologies of Canada will now be further explored.

## OVERVIEW OF CANADIAN MYTHOLOGIES

### Mythologies of the Land that Shapes it

Canada is a vast and often inhospitable land, abundantly rich in geographic variety. Bounded by three oceans, it stretches from a southern boundary that shares latitude with Northern California, to a northern boundary above the Arctic Circle. Perhaps nothing has shaped the Canadian psyche as much as the challenges of living within its physical realities.

### Myths of the land

Canada is a land whose character has been shaped by the vastness of distance, the harshness of weather, and the compromises that both require in order to survive. Early European explorers, rather than trying to conquer the terrain, learned from the First Nations peoples their ways of travel and life. The Voyageurs explored the waterways and paved the way for the Hudson's Bay Company, one of the world's oldest commercial enterprises. It was incorporated in 1670 and granted monopoly over the Indian Trade – more specifically the fur trade, in the region watered by all rivers and streams flowing into Hudson Bay. From the Cree, the traders learned that the best fur country was north and west of Lake Superior and the frozen sea of Hudson's Bay. The interaction between the Voyageurs and the First Nation fur traders is central to understanding much of what is the Canadian legacy in the west and north of the country.

Canada is settled along the southern stretch of highway known as the Trans Canada that provides one continuous ribbon of connection from the Atlantic to the Pacific and stretches itself generally just north of the 49th parallel though the border does dip as far south as the 45th parallel in Ontario. Keeping in mind that the most northerly of the contiguous United States is the most southern of Canada's geography, one can begin to understand the challenge of settling in a country where harsh winters deterred all but the hardiest of pioneers.

The sheer size and harsh climate of Canada have combined to create small clusters of community isolated by vast spaces between. Thus Canadians have always been obsessed with the need to create communication links. In their time, both the railway (the original was known as the Canadian Pacific Railway) and the Trans Canada Highway have served the dual purposes of not only facilitating movement, but literally tying together the country. It is also not surprising therefore, that both have been immortalized in the culture that reflects the nation's heritage.

## Mythologies of the Culture that Binds it

Canadian culture reflects the reality of learning to compromise in order to live in an uncompromising space – themes of isolation and environmental adaptation are prominent. In a physical space that does not invite change, but requires compliance, Canadians have survived by learning to adapt, compromise, and innovate.

### Myths of the settlers

The two founding European heritages – English and French – preserved in legislation, set the stage for what is now a multicultural society. The Québec Act of 1774 allowed francophone culture to survive and thrive within Canada, and the British North America Act of 1867 further paved the path toward multiculturalism in an effort to avoid the tensions of the bloody Civil War experience to the south. The continued constitutional accommodation of francophone culture has fostered a patchwork of regional cultures and an inclusive society that in recent years has extended to accept gay and lesbian culture and same-sex marriage.

## Myths of the natives

The complexity of the Canadian identity and culture extends beyond the recent immigrant groups from Asia. The land that the French and English settled in was already home to First Nations peoples and the Inuit. The First Nations, of which there are dozens of cultural groups, are identified through their biological and geographical location. For example, west coast cultures were centered on ocean and river fishing while interior and plains cultures were centered on hunting and gathering. The extent of diversity of these First Nations has historically been overlooked, and efforts to rectify this oversight have led to the creation of the Museum of Civilization in Ottawa, and the Museum of Anthropology at the University of British Columbia, both of which have extensive exhibits dedicated to understanding the life and culture of both the First Nations and Inuit.

The Inuit (meaning 'the people') are Aboriginal people of the Arctic. They were traditionally hunters and fishermen, existing on the Arctic animal life. The harshness and isolation of the Arctic posed governance problems for the federal government in Ottawa, and resulted in program after program that attempted to govern by removing the Inuit from their homeland and either resettling them or educating them in the south.

While isolation necessitated programs to move the Inuit south for educational purposes, the isolation also had a way of protecting the culture from assimilation. However, technological intrusion – communication, transportation – and lifestyle changes have created a threat to the Inuit within their own community, as they find the south migrating north via these highways. In recent years, particularly with the creation of Nunavut (a northern territory governed by the Inuit), the Inuit have taken an active role to preserve their language, culture and way of life.

## Myths in art, song and story

Canadian cultural artifacts reflect the experience of a diverse people coping with the challenging realities of land, sea, language and weather. Song and literature reflect the settling of the land, the building of the railroad, and the Prairie hinterland. Art and sculpture reflect the Aboriginal cultures; their symbols and materials distinctly reflect their geography and lifework.

In literature, Pierre Berton's (2001) *The Last Spike* reconstructs the incredible story of how some 2000 miles of steel crossed the continent in just five years – exactly half the time stipulated in the contract. Berton recreates the adventures that were part of this vast undertaking: the railway on the brink of bankruptcy, with one hour between it and ruin; the extraordinary land boom of Winnipeg in 1881–1882 as the railway opened the west to eastern settlers; and the epic tale of how a half-finished railway was used to move 3000 troops to quash an Aboriginal rebellion.

Although the completion of the railway was historic in that it created the possibility of nationhood, it is the building of the railway that is immortalized in Canadian cultural mythology. More than 7000 Chinese workers toiled and died in the canyons of the Fraser Valley; and many other people – land sharks, construction geniuses, politicians, and entrepreneurs – played a role in the founding of the new Canada west of Ontario.

Whereas folk music in the US chronicles the stories of the blacks, the indigent, and working class, Canadian folk music chronicles life on the land. In the *Canadian Railroad Trilogy* Gordon Lightfoot sings of the 'navvies who worked upon the railway' and remembers 'There was a time in this fair land when the railroad did not run; when the wild majestic mountains stood alone against the sun'. In the song *Four Strong Winds* Ian and Sylvia sang of 'Four strong winds that blow lonely … think I'll go out to Alberta; weather's good there in the fall … '

In a country as large and diverse as Canada, perhaps it is fitting that the iconic nation building institution would be its public broadcaster. The Canadian Broadcasting Corporation (CBC) is the one common element that touches Canadians on a day-to-day basis. From its earliest days, CBC has had a mandate to inform, enlighten and entertain in a distinctly Canadian voice, to reflect Canada and its regions to national and regional audiences. CBC broadcasts in English, French and eight Aboriginal languages.

### Myths of winter and sport

A country dominated by winter, Canada's athletic heroes come from winter sports. Perhaps no single cultural icon captures Canada better than ice hockey. Saturday night is *Hockey Night in Canada*, and one would be hard pressed to find a bar or club in the land where the television was tuned to anything other than hockey. They may not know the name of every current world leader, but Canadians can tell you, in detail, of Wayne Gretzky, Jean Beliveau, Rocket Richard and Gordie Howe. Stomping Tom Connors sang 'Oh the good old hockey game is the best game in the land'. Canadians know that Don Cherry and Ron MacLean are the Saturday night pundits of hockey, and no game is complete until Don Cherry in his custom-tailored glory has spoken. Hockey rivalries are legendary: the Leafs and Canadiens, or the Flames and the Oilers, are match-ups guaranteed to fill the arena.

Passion for hockey extends to anything hockey – even if that means coffee at Tim Horton's. Canadians are often asked what is so special about Tim Horton's, and whether the coffee is really that good. While Americans line up at Starbucks for sophisticated Grande Mocha Lattes, unpretentious Canadians line up for a 'double double' coffee with double milk and double sugar and Timbits doughnut holes!

Ice plays large in another sport – curling. Curling arrived in Canada in the

1800s. With the completion of the railway and Scottish immigration to the prairies, it became quickly entrenched as the game seemed to capture the character and spirit of self-discipline, persistence and cooperation – the very qualities required to survive in those years.

The indomitable climate and vastness of space shape every aspect of the Canadian psyche. The harsh realities of climate and the loneliness of space created a people who learned to live with adversity, to adapt through cooperation, and to seek common solutions. Despite their many differences, Canadians have agreed on important social questions regarding race, justice and language. The country has one of the world's oldest constitutions and no history of the civil strife and violence that have occurred in so many other nations. This legacy shapes Canada's reputation as a peaceful nation, and a peacekeeping nation.

**Mythologies of the Mosaic that Defines it**

Perhaps nothing reflects the Canadian identity more than its physical and cultural divisions. East versus West, English versus French, rural versus urban – these tensions continue to shape Canadian experience. Canadians agree, seemingly, on little. The national food – poutine? maple syrup? perogies? lobster? The national drink – Newfie Screech? Molson Canadian? The best show on earth – Calgary Stampede? Pacific National Exhibition? Canadian National Exhibition? The best hockey team – the Leafs or the Canadiens? the Flames or the Oilers?

The sheer size of the country means that British Columbia and Alberta turn on the television when the polls close on election night, to discover the government has already been elected by Canadians in the eastern time zones. If you are not born in the Maritimes, no matter how long you may live there you are 'from away'. The national symbol – the maple leaf – grows on trees found only in eastern Canada.

**A confluence of mythologies**

These broad-ranging divisions reflect the complexity that is Canada. Founded by three cultures – English, French and Aboriginal – the struggle for existence has created a continuing balancing act between the needs of the country and the needs of the regions. Although Canada was created in 1867, it was only in the 1980s that the constitution moved from Britain to Ottawa. The refusal of the French to abandon their culture created the foundation for linguistic and cultural differences that became manifest in regional differences. The British North America Act of 1867 provided the provinces with economic power based on natural resources that rivaled the federal government's economic power. This duality has created vigorous debate over the national agenda, as the ten provinces, the federal government, and the three territories attempt to govern when there is no one leader to set the agenda.

### But ... Canadians are not Americans

One thing Canadians do agree on is that they are not Americans. Americans are motivated by the notion of individual achievement (life, liberty, pursuit of happiness) while Canadians balance individual autonomy with a sense of collective responsibility (peace, order, good government). Thus Americans experience a high standard of living while Canadians enjoy high quality of life. Despite the two countries' profound economic integration and the ubiquity of American popular culture in Canada, the two countries increasingly view the world differently (Adams, 2003). In the last quarter century, it has been suggested that Canadians have become the true revolutionaries, at the forefront of a fascinating social experiment. Canadians are coming to define a new sociological post-modernity, characterized by multiple, flexible roles and identities, which will establish the future cultural context for leadership by Canadians and of Canadians.

### Conclusion

Thus it is perhaps no surprise that Canadians are an inclusive and peace seeking people. Shaped by land, distance, weather and constitutional complexity, Canada is a democracy with vigorous attention paid at all levels of society to the fashioning of the public agenda. It is also no surprise then that Canadians face a never ending quest to define themselves.

Recently, the CBC held a competition to identify Canada's 'Seven Wonders'. They reflect physical (Niagara Falls, prairie skies and the Rockies), accommodation (canoes and igloos) and settlement (Old Quebec City and the Pier 21 immigration site in Halifax) realities that reflect Canada. The contest, initially scoffed at, generated a huge grassroots movement. At times the website was inaccessible – everyone wanted a say. *Mais oui, c'est* nation building Canadian style!

## OVERVIEW OF CANADIAN LEADERSHIP

> To be Prime Minister of Canada, you need the hide of a rhinoceros, the morals of St. Francis, the patience of Job, the wisdom of Solomon, the strength of Hercules, the leadership of Napoleon, the magnetism of a Beatle, and the subtlety of Machiavelli. (Pearson, 1964)

Canadian leaders cannot be easily categorized into typical leadership styles. The complexity and diversity of the Canadian experience have produced effective leaders exhibiting many different leadership styles. From environmental expert

David Suzuki to hockey legend Wayne Gretzky and socialist politician Tommy Douglas, a diverse group of successful Canadian leaders has emerged.

## Contingent Leadership

The constant adaptation involved in contingent leadership (Evans, 1996) is second nature to Canadians reared on the constant and unpredictable movement in ice hockey. The complex and changing socio-political balancing acts that enable peaceful unity amidst regional, linguistic and cultural variation demand such an approach to leadership.

Contingency approaches to leadership in Canada have been built on a foundation of cooperation and accommodation established by the Fathers of Confederation in 1867. Accommodation was used in agreeing to two official languages (French and English) and two separate school systems (Protestant and Catholic). Cooperation was exemplified when communication with the Northwest Territories and the development of trade between the West and the Eastern provinces were specified as being of the highest importance. These historical facts are consistent with research findings that successful heterogeneous teams compensate for their differences by developing norms of cooperation (Chatman and Flynn, 2001).

Pragmatism is another Canadian characteristic often involved in contingent approaches to leadership. Sir John A. MacDonald, Canada's first prime minister, is credited with the idea of joining provinces and territories together as a pragmatic solution to economic problems facing each one (CBC, 2006a). The invention of the telephone by Alexander Graham Bell in 1876 was a pragmatic solution to communication across the vast distances between Canadian communities. More recently the invention of the Blackberry wireless email device by Canadian high tech firm Research in Motion revolutionized communication as the world entered the twenty-first century (Stone, 2005).

## Socialized Power

Canada's history of cooperation between the three founding minorities and the ensuing peaceful addition of dozens more minorities has resulted in a strong focus on inclusiveness and human rights. For example, current Governor-General Michaëlle Jean is a Haitian immigrant with a distinguished career in journalism. As a result of this heritage, Canadian leaders have typically exhibited socialized power, the desire to have a positive influence on others and make a difference in the world, as opposed to personalized power, meaning a need for status and recognition (Henein and Morissette, 2007). The Inuit have a similar concept known as 'isuma', meaning intelligence that includes knowledge of one's responsibility towards society (Saul, 1998).

Prime Minister Lester Pearson exemplified socialized power when he introduced universal health care and the Canada Pension Plan in the 1960s. His
groundbreaking work in peacekeeping at the UN earned him the 1957 Nobel
Peace Prize (CBC, 2006b). The use of socialized power by Canadians has
continued. Stephen Lewis displayed a passion for humanitarianism and human
rights that led to his work at UNICEF in the 1990s and his subsequent appointment as the UN Secretary-General's Special Envoy for HIV/AIDS in Africa
from 2001 to 2006. His unrelenting attacks on first world nations standing by
as millions died were a highly visible example of socialized power (Reinhart,
2005).

**Transformational Leadership**

Canadian leaders are more likely to exhibit the characteristics of transformational leadership (inspiring followers and empowering them to enact change)
rather than transactional (reward and punish) or charismatic leadership. One
study even showed that for Canadians, transactional leadership had no relationship with effectiveness (Bass, 1997)! Another study showed that the
Canadian characteristics of high levels of pragmatism and nurturance and low
levels of aggression and criticism are associated with transformational leadership (Ross and Offerman, 1997).

Cross-cultural leadership studies have shown that ideal leadership across
many countries, including Canada, includes transformational elements (Bass,
1997). Transformational leadership involves a complex set of behaviors –
inspirational motivation, idealized influence, intellectual stimulation and individual consideration – that are consistent with Canadian culture (Casimir,
2001). Canadian leaders provide inspirational motivation based on articulating
an appealing vision. Prime Minister Brian Mulroney's vision of free trade with
the US resulted in his party winning a majority in the 1988 federal election,
and the Canada–US Free Trade Agreement became a reality (CBC Archives,
1988).

Prime Minister Pierre Trudeau exhibited idealized influence by taking a
firm stand on the issue of terrorist acts by Québec separatists. He invoked the
War Measures Act in 1970 when two people were kidnapped and one was
killed – actions that were supported by 87 percent of Canadians (Centre for
Canadian Studies, 2001).

Canadian business leaders provide intellectual stimulation to their well-
educated workforce that is receptive to new ideas and ready for empowerment.
For the first time since the invention of the automobile, more cars were manu-
factured in 2005 and 2006 in Ontario than in Michigan (Keenan, 2006).
Foreign car makers prefer the education and work ethic of the Canadian workforce over American workers.

Canadian leaders are comfortable with providing individualized consideration to motivate followers because they are at ease with diversity. One of the
ways this consideration is demonstrated is through flexibility in work arrangements such as flexible work schedules (Comfort *et al.*, 2003).

## Participative Leadership

The Canadian tradition of inclusiveness in its longstanding history as a pluralist democracy makes participative leadership an instinctive approach for its
leaders and mitigates against the emergence of leaders with a high need for
control in favor of those who can work together with others. His Highness the
Aga Khan, world leader of the Shia Ismaili Muslim community, established
the Global Centre for Pluralism in Ottawa so that Canadian leaders could share
their experience in governing a pluralist society with leaders in the developing
world. Canadian leaders provide an example of how pluralist societies succeed
due to choices requiring enlightened education and continuous investments by
governments, civil societies and individual citizens in celebrating their own
diversity (Global Centre for Pluralism, 2006).

Participative leaders realize that the most effective types of power they can
use are based on the respect of followers. For example, David Suzuki,
Canada's foremost environmental conscience for over three decades, says 'I
believe in the power of reason to alter human behavior' (Suzuki, 1990). As a
broadcaster, he has issued frank warnings on climate change and influenced
vast numbers of Canadians to take action to protect the environment (Pooley,
2005).

Canadian teams often display the collaborative individualism style of
balance between individualism and team focus (Limerick, 1990). Individual
team members, such as hockey star Wayne Gretzky, are not limited by the
boundaries of their team. They maintain their personal internal motivation,
network with outsiders, and will not hesitate to transform the group in its own
best interest, but simultaneously cooperate with other team members and are
tolerant of differences of opinion (Falla, 1998).

Further comfort with participative leadership comes from the anti-heroism
sentiment of Canadians, who willingly respect heroes but distrust the domination and imposition that can result from hero worship. The humility and
modesty of Wayne Gretzky were clearly shown in his statement 'the highest
compliment that you can pay me is to say that I work hard every day, that I
never dog it' (*The Hockey News*, 1998).

Other examples of very successful Canadian leaders who are decidedly
non-heroic and very unpretentious abound. Mike Lazaridis and Jim Balsillie,
co-CEOs of the successful high-tech firm Research in Motion, have not moved
the company from its roots in humble Waterloo, Ontario, and have maintained

their focus on technological innovation by donating generously to scientific research institutes (Seife, 2003). Isadore Sharpe, founder of Four Seasons Hotel and Resorts, is quiet, unassuming, and understated. He has also accomplished something quite remarkable in that Arab businessmen are willing to work with Sharpe, who is Jewish, as he establishes hotels in the Middle East (Newman, 2007).

### Canadians' Choice

A CBC special event in 2006 asked Canadians to name 'The Greatest Canadian.' The winner was Tommy Douglas, a feisty Saskatchewan politician known as the 'Father of Medicare.' Originally branded as a socialist radical for his idea that all Canadians, not just the wealthy, were entitled to quality health care, Douglas and his ideas eventually gained mainstream acceptance. Clearly, his legacy lives on in the hearts and values of Canadians (CBC, 2006c).


## GLOBAL IMPLICATIONS

Cultural myths can both inform and misinform our understanding of leadership in Canada. Consistent with the preceding cultural overview, a recent study found that the two main trademarks of Canadian leadership are an emphasis on inclusion and good process skills such as team building, negotiation and building consensus (Henein and Morissette, 2007). Pillars of Canadian leadership include a strong sense of principle representing Canadian values, professionalism, diversity and peace. Canadians understand that peace based on integration rather than domination is a condition for prosperity.

These characteristics have positioned Canadians well for leadership positions in the global economy. Canada's history of alliances and interdependence, as well as the pragmatic nature of the culture, further enhance the potential of Canadian leaders to assume positions involving complex global business dealings. And indeed, Canadian executives are proving to be particularly strong as global leaders. *Canadian Business* magazine proclaimed that, 'With a reputation for combining North American-style business smarts with sensitivity toward cultural diversity and language differences, Canadians are one hot commodity' (Olijnyk and Gagne, 2006). For example, one Canadian who is leveraging a diverse cultural background into leadership success is Huynh Thanh Phong, who is managing director of Prudential Financial's Vietnam, Thailand and India operations (Olijnyk *et al.*, 2005).

Consistent with the egalitarian nature and anti-heroism sentiments of their culture, Canadian leaders are not usually charismatic, paternalistic or heroic, and do not generally seek out the spotlight. They are more comfortable with a participative approach than with transactional command and control leadership styles, and with respect but not hero worship. Michael Rapino, president and CEO of Live Nation in Beverley Hills, the world's largest concert promotion business, says he takes a humble approach to growing Live Nation. He attributes this humility to his Canadian background as a blue collar teenager from northern Ontario who sat on a bus for 16 hours to see his first live concert in Toronto (Olijnyk and Gagne, 2006).

On the other hand, it is possible to be misinformed by Canadian cultural mythology. The stereotypical nice, unpretentious Canadian from a country with a history of reconciliation and non-violence may be perceived as not aggressive enough, not confident enough, or not strong enough to be an effective leader. Characterizations suggesting that caring is weakness, compromise is betrayal, and moderation is boredom have plagued the Canadian approach to leadership from the beginning (Saul, 1998). Yet Canada has prospered under this form of leadership that does not pretend to resolve or eliminate the complexity of their country. Ken Thomson was for many years the richest man in Canada (*Canadian Business*, 2006). Thomson was very unpretentious, unfailingly courteous and polite. He said that 'in London, I'm Lord Thomson; in Toronto, I'm Ken'. His down to earth lifestyle included eating at neighborhood restaurants and even buying his suits off the rack despite his wealth (CBC News Online, 2006a, 2006b).

Canadian leaders have relied on their heritage of adaptability to become successful transformational leaders in dealing with change. Robert Booth, executive director of Emaar Properties, is overseeing the world's largest construction project in Dubai. He says that success as a global leader requires people with an open mind who accept change in their lives as they learn a different culture, business dynamic and decision making process. Scott Beattie, chairman and CEO of Elizabeth Arden, says that Canadians have a more outward looking perspective in terms of understanding and adapting to markets around the world (Olijnyk and Gagne, 2006).

Misinformation about Canadian leaders may also arise from the perception of Canada as a relatively simple, straightforward country because it has never experienced major internal conflicts. Canadian leaders may thus be perceived as not capable of dealing with difficult business situations. In reality, the Canadian cultural experience involves many complexities such as multiculturalism and regional power struggles. Internally, the country has displayed success in negotiating compromises amongst a culturally and linguistically varied population.

Canadian leaders, both men and women, are in fact dealing with very complex business issues in some of the biggest companies in the world – see Commentary box. Consider General Motors (GM), where ongoing changes in the world auto industry are seriously threatening its very survival. Former GM chairman and CEO Rick Wagoner once joked that Canadians were taking over the place. He was referring to Ray Young, head of GM Brazil, Simon Boag, who ran operations in Argentina, Paraguay and Uruguay, and their boss, Maureen Kempston Darkes, one of just four General Motors regional presidents (Olijnyk *et al.*, 2005).

---

## COMMENTARY BOX

Growing numbers of Canadian women are proving to be effective leaders in global settings. Patricia Arnold credits the bilingualism and multiculturalism of her home country, and especially rural Québec, for giving her an advantage abroad. 'We try to integrate,' she says. When working in largely Muslim Sudan she wore long sleeves and long skirts, and while in Switzerland she's been reading a two-volume book on local history. Barbara Kovacs, vice-president and managing director for Tiffany & Co. in London, says that executives who want to work internationally have to want to be part of another culture and another environment, and must be willing to immerse themselves in it. Adaptability is the key, according to Marie-Josée Lamothe, international marketing director for L'Oréal in Paris. She says 'If you are interested in working abroad, you have to love the idea of being in a situation that is a bit unsettling. The best way to adapt is to get right in there' (from Olijnyk *et al.*, 2005).

Roberta Bondar now guides business leaders navigating uncharted territory by sharing knowledge about the pitfalls in moving from a known environment to one that is constantly changing. Analysis of the organization's culture, process and group dynamics is used to plan how to meet challenges head on. By sharing wisdom from scientific enquiry relevant to business, she energizes the need to think and change (from Bondar, 2007).

---

### Blindspots

A background in the Canadian cultural context can also create certain leadership blindspots. For example, Canadians may not be effective with followers who want a paternalistic and directive leader. This need to be controlled on the part of followers is antithetical to Canadian culture.

Canadian leaders can also be unprepared for the evil that exists in the world, the cruelty that it spawns, and the abdication of responsibility to the affected people and societies by the developed world. In 1994, Canadian General Roméo Dallaire was assigned to lead a UN peacekeeping force in Rwanda. Once on the ground, Dallaire learned that a massacre was imminent and warned UN leaders. Although ordered by the UN Security Council to pull out of Rwanda, he stood his ground during the ensuing genocide because of his deep Canadian sense of moral and ethical responsibility to the 30 000 Rwandans under his direct protection. He later said that Western nations must intervene to stop genocide in other countries whether or not there is an economic payoff and that he blamed the UN for aiding and abetting the perpetrators of the genocide (Dallaire, 2003; McKibbon, 2007). Dallaire subsequently suffered major post-traumatic stress disorder that ended his military career (Dineen, 2000).

More recently, Stephen Lewis was enraged by the inhumanity of the world that largely ignored the AIDS pandemic in sub-Saharan Africa. He found the indifference of the international community to be unconscionable, and became more and more critical of governments who were slow to act or did not follow through on commitments to the fight against AIDS. His concern with the human imperative did not play well with his UN colleagues. 'He seems to get quite worked up,' said one senior UN officer (Nolen, 2003).

## PRACTICAL APPLICATIONS

There are a number of practical applications of these insights into Canadian leadership styles. In most cases, it is not difficult to work and engage effectively with Canadian leaders, as they are unassuming, moderate, and comfortable dealing with people from diverse backgrounds. Canadians can be expected to seek solutions based on cooperation, compromise, or even accommodation, which may lead to disagreement with those who prefer to use coercion or violence to force their point of view. It is possible that Canadian leaders may be underestimated because of these qualities.

People from cultures where leaders are expected to be paternalistic or heroic may find it uncomfortable dealing with Canadian leaders who display humility and prefer empowerment rather than dominance. The expectation that influence over others can be based on position power or transactional approaches would be quite unusual for a Canadian leader. They are more likely to motivate others at an intellectual level. It would also be unusual to meet a highly charismatic Canadian leader who bases his or her influence on an emotional connection with followers.

It may become common to meet Canadian leaders in global executive positions and in organizational situations involving change. They are likely to excel at dealing with multicultural workforces. Canadians can be expected to be team players while at the same time retaining their individuality, without finding this balancing act to be unusual or difficult.

The most likely situation in which to expect disagreement or conflict when dealing with a Canadian leader is one involving moral or ethical issues relating to other human beings. Particularly strong views can be expected on human rights issues in the workplace.

## CONCLUSION

Canadian mythologies relating to its harsh land, three founding cultures and complex mosaic of people and laws enlighten our understanding of its inclusive, peace seeking and accommodating people. The complexity and pluralism of the Canadian experience had produced leaders with a strong focus on socialized power who are adaptable, participative and transformational. Although unlikely to be comfortable in situations where paternalistic approaches to leadership are expected, Canadian leaders are proving to be particularly suited to global leadership challenges involving complex business issues in a multicultural context.

## REFERENCES

Adams M. H. (2003), *Fire and Ice: The United States, Canada and the Myth of Converging Values*, Toronto: Penguin Canada.

Bass B. M. (1997), Does the transactional-transformational leadership paradigm transcend organizational and national boundaries?, *American Psychologist*, **52** (2), 130–9.

Berton P. (2001), *The Last Spike: The Great Railway, 1881–1885*, East Mississauga, ON: Random House of Canada.

Bondar R. (2007), *Navigating Uncharted Territory*, http://www.robertabondar.com/executive_development.php 3, December 2007.

*Canadian Business* (2006), *Canada's 100 Wealthiest People*, Winter 2006/2007, 38.

Casimir C. (2001), Combinative aspects of leadership style: The ordering and temporal spacing of leadership behaviors, *Leadership Quarterly*, **12** (3), 245–78.

CBC (2006a), Top ten greatest Canadians: Sir John A. Macdonald, www.cbc.ca/greatest/top_ten/, 15 June 2007.

CBC (2006b), Top ten greatest Canadians: Lester B. Pearson, www.cbc.ca/greatest/top_ten/, 15 June 2007.

CBC (2006c), Top ten greatest Canadians: Tommy Douglas, www.cbc.ca/greatest/top_ten/, 20 June 2007.

CBC Archives (1988), Betting on free trade, http://archives.cbc.ca/IDC-1-73-1469-9807/politics_economy/brian_mulroney/clip8, 29 June 1997.

CBC News Online (2006a), Ken Thomson, Canada's richest man, dies, 13 June, www.cbc.ca/money/story/2006/06/12/thomson.html, 29 June 2007.

CBC News Online (2006b), Ken Thomson: The bashful billionaire, 12 June, www.cbc.ca/news/background/thomson-ken/, 20 June 2007.

Centre for Canadian Studies (2001), *About Canada Online Publications – Great Canadian Debates: The War Measures Act*, New Brunswick: Mount Allison University, www.mta.ca/faculty/arts/canadian_studies/english/about/index.html, 29 June 2007.

Chatman J. A. and Flynn F. J. (2001), The influence of demographic heterogeneity on the emergence and consequences of cooperative norms in work teams, *Academy of Management Journal*, **44** (5), 956–74.

Comfort D., Johnson K. and Wallace D. (2003), Part-time work and family-friendly practices in Canadian workplaces, *The Evolving Workplace Series*, Ottawa: Human Resources Development Canada.

Dallaire R. (2003), *Shake Hands with the Devil: The Failure of Humanity in Rwanda*, Toronto: Random House Canada.

Dineen T. (2000), The solitary, tortured nobility of Roméo Dallaire, *Ottawa Citizen*, 13 July, A15.

Evans M. G. (1996), R. J. House's 'A path-goal theory of leader effectiveness', *Leadership Quarterly*, **7** (3), 305–9.

Falla J. (1998), Wayne Gretzky: greatness ascendant, in D. Diamond, J. Duplacey, R. Dinger and I. Kuperman, *Total Hockey: The Official Encyclopedia of the National Hockey League*, Kingston NY: Total Sports, pp. 123–5.

Global Centre for Pluralism (2006), Global Centre for Pluralism. www.pluralism.ca/backgrounder.shtml, 26 June 2007.

Henein A. and Morissette F. (2007), *Made in Canada Leadership: Wisdom from the Nation's Best and Brightest on the Art and Practice of Leadership*, Toronto: Jossey Bass.

Keenan G. (2006), The most valuable car part? People, *Globe and Mail*, 22 May, B1.

Limerick D. C. (1990), Managers of meaning: from Bob Geldof's Band Aid to Australian CEOs, *Organizational Dynamics*, **18** (4), 22–33.

McKibbon S. (2007), Dallaire urges genocide action: West must put economics aside, *Ottawa Sun*, 16 April, 18.

Newman P. C. (2007), Out like a lamb, *Macleans*, 23 April, 30.

Nolen S. (2003), Stephen Lewis has one word for us: Help, *Globe and Mail*, 4 January, F1.

Olijnyk Z. and Gagne C. (2006), Taking on the world, *Canadian Business*, 20 November–3 December, 42.

Olijnyk Z., Brown M., Holloway A., Leung C., Mlynek A., Pooley E., Sanford J., Wahl A. and Watson T. (2005), Canada's global leaders, *Canadian Business*, 28 March–10 April, 36.

Pearson L. B. (1964), Leading Canada, Ottawa: library and archives Canada, www.collectionscanada.ca/2/4/h4-2200-e.html, 20 June 2007.

Pooley E. (2005), David Suzuki, *Canadian Business*, **17** (30) (January), 78.

Reinhart A. (2005), Awakening the world to Africa's AIDS plight, *Globe and Mail*, 28 December, A3.

Ross S. M. and Offerman L. R. (1997), Transformational leaders: Measurement of personality attributes and work group performance, *Personality and Social Psychology Bulletin*, **23**, 1078–86.

Saul J. R. (1998), *Reflections of a Siamese twin: Canada at the end of the Twentieth Century*, Toronto: Penguin Books.

Seife C. (2003), At Canada's Perimeter Institute, Waterloo means Shangri-La, *Science*, **302** (5), 1650–2.

Stone B. (2005), Blackberry: bring it on!, *Newsweek*, 26 September, 38.

Suzuki D. (1990), *Inventing the Future: Reflections on Science, Technology and Nature*, Toronto: Allen & Unwin.

*The Hockey News* (1998), The greatest hockey player of all time, 23 January, 1.

# 3. Cultural mythology and global leadership in the Caribbean islands

## Betty Jane Punnett and Dion Greenidge

### INTRODUCTION

This chapter examines mythology and leadership in the islands of the Caribbean. The focus is largely on the Commonwealth Caribbean; that is, the former British colonies, where English is the usual language. Although the focus is on the English-speaking islands, much of the discussion is relevant to the French, Dutch and Spanish islands as well, as all the islands share a similar history. In order to understand the Caribbean today, and to understand its mythology and leadership, one needs to reflect on the history of the Caribbean. This chapter begins with a brief historical overview of the Caribbean. Then, the chapter looks at two aspects of mythology in the region – first, the mix of African magical beliefs with traditional Christian beliefs, and second the African Ananci stories that have metamorphosed into a Caribbean tradition. Later sections of the chapter consider what we know about management and leadership in the Caribbean, and how management and leadership in the Caribbean relate to the history and mythology, as well as how this information can provide practical insights for managers, especially in today's global business environment.

The Caribbean is a region of variety and contrast, and there is substantial variation across the countries of the region. Many people would argue, on the basis of casual observations, that patterns of behavior differ from one island to another, and that cultures differ. At the same time, the islands share many of the factors that are believed to shape cultures – history, geography, language, religion, and so on, and there are many similarities across the region. This chapter focuses on the similarities across the region, rather than the differences.

### HISTORICAL BACKGROUND OF THE CARIBBEAN ISLANDS FROM COLUMBUS TO THE PRESENT[1]

The Caribbean islands are in some ways unique in terms of their people. The majority of the people in almost all the islands are of African descent, and were brought to the Caribbean against their will, due to the slave trade. A small minority of the people are descended from Europeans who came to the islands as colonizers, with the army or to establish plantations. There are a substantial number of people of Indian descent as well (especially in Trinidad and Guyana) whose forebears were brought to the islands as indentured servants, following the abolition of slavery, and there is a smaller number of Chinese who are also descended from indentured servants. There are virtually no descendants of the original inhabitants. The culture of the Caribbean is thus heavily influenced by African beliefs, but in the context of European domination, which sought to suppress or eliminate these beliefs and enforce European ideals, including Christianity. This may have led to a conflicted sense of beliefs in the Caribbean.

Before Columbus came to the Caribbean in 1492, the native people of the Caribbean were the Ciboney, the Arawak and the Caribs. These indigenous peoples were related ethnically and linguistically to present-day tropical forest people in the northern regions of South America. Unfortunately, these indigenous people were essentially wiped out during the eighteenth century by the arrival of the Europeans. The Caribs were a warrior tribe and resisted European conquest and assimilation, and some groups still survive today, but their numbers are very small. Some words and customs of these original people have survived, but their influence is difficult to identify in the present Caribbean. Of course, their habit of smoking tobacco has spread worldwide and had a major impact around the globe!

European conquest and settlement of the Caribbean began with Columbus' four voyages between 1492 and 1502, but the first major settlement was in Santa Domingo where 2500 Spanish colonists settled in 1502. From this base the Spanish moved through the region, settling in Jamaica in 1509 and Trinidad in 1510. In the Eastern Caribbean the Caribs resisted the European penetration until the late 1600s. The Spanish dominated the Caribbean for over a century, but in the 1600s, the Dutch, the English and the French all established colonies in the Caribbean. By this time, the indigenous populations had dwindled, and the Spanish had started the practice of importing African slaves to provide labor.

By the middle of the seventeenth century the Caribbean had become a plantation society based on slave labor. This resulted in a switch from small farms to large land holdings devoted to sugar. The change is quite dramatic – for example, in Barbados in 1640 there were 10 000 settlers, predominantly white, and virtually all were land owners; by 1680, the wealthiest 175 planters owned 54 per cent of the land and there were 38 000 African slaves, and 2000 English servants who owned no land. This formed the basis of a class system that persists to some extent even today.

As sugarcane production grew and spread throughout the islands, the need for African slaves in the Caribbean also grew. The import of slaves grew from 2000 a year in 1600 to 13 000 a year in 1700, and was at its height in 1810, when 55 000 slaves were brought to the Caribbean. The slave trade was extremely important to the development of the Caribbean. Of course, it made the European colonists rich and started a social system of a small wealthy elite, largely based on color. Equally important was the African cultural influence that the slaves brought with them, which influenced all of the people of the region. For example, note this influence in the 'creole dialect' that is spoken in each island where the structures and some words are based on grammatical forms of African languages.

Although the white population would continue to maintain their superior social position, even after slavery was abolished, the white population was a minority throughout the region. By the early nineteenth century, less than 5 percent of the total population in many of the islands was white (Jamaica, Grenada, Nevis, St Vincent, Tobago), and in most others less than 10 percent was white. Only in Barbados, the Bahamas and Trinidad was the white population greater than 10 percent.

The abolition of slave trading in the mid-1800s (a law passed by the British Parliament in 1834 abolished slavery in the empire) was a major event for the Caribbean. A large proportion of ex-slaves settled in free villages, and formed the basis of an energetic, dynamic peasantry. Emancipation was however a 'landless emancipation' (Beckles, 2004a, b) for many, and while freedom meant the ability to own property, this became a focus for many former slaves and their descendants. Even today this is an important goal of people of the Caribbean.

Following the abolition of slavery, the Caribbean islands still needed labor. Indentured Chinese and Indian immigrants now provided this labor. They brought greater heterogeneity to the region, and contributed to the current mixed population. In spite of these developments, the white elite remained the upper class, and color remained an important factor in social life. Although the populations in the islands have intermarried, and the people represent a range of colors, the remnants of the plantation system have not disappeared entirely, even today.

The Caribbean islands remained colonies after emancipation, governed by an Administrator appointed by the colonial power. The British colonial governors were responsible to the Secretary of State for the Colonies in London. Not surprisingly the dominant views of the local legislators were those of the planter classes. Equally unsurprising, these views did not favor the majority of the population (African descendants), and increasingly in the 1900s these views were being challenged, both violently and philosophically. Slowly political democratization occurred throughout the Caribbean, culminating in independence for most states from the 1950s on.

Today, at the beginning of the twenty-first century, the Caribbean island states are independent, middle income developing countries, many of which rate relatively highly on the United Nations' Human Development Index. The population is primarily African derived, but the different races and ethnic groups have mixed and intermarried. The region has produced scholars of note, Nobel laureates, sports greats, world-class artists and the music of the region – reggae, calypso, steelband … has captivated listeners around the globe. Nevertheless, the Caribbean countries face an uncertain future as a global economy and business means that these small island states need to find ways to compete effectively with larger countries and companies. One potential competitive advantage is leadership. In this chapter a variety of influences on management and leadership are considered, and these are used to explore current practices and their effectiveness.

In the following section, the chapter looks at some specific aspects of the culture that can be considered as part of the mythology of the region. This section examines aspects of traditional African magical beliefs which sometimes fuse African beliefs with Christianity, and also looks at a particular mythical figure, Anancy, the trickster spider, whose stories are still today told by the old to the young.

## OVERVIEW OF CARIBBEAN MYTHOLOGY

Understanding mythology in any location is helpful in understanding the wider culture, and its influence on behavior, including leadership. The Caribbean mythology is largely based on its African roots, but circumscribed by European influences.

### African Traditional Magical Beliefs

According to Olmos and Paravisin-Gebert (2003: vii) the 'creole religions' of the islands of the Caribbean 'are quite unique and dynamic'. These religious traditions are based on beliefs brought with African slaves to the Caribbean. The amazing reality is that these beliefs survived in spite of European attempts to suppress or erase them. Two of the best known of these beliefs are Voodoo (known mainly in Haiti) and Obeah (known in much of the English-speaking Caribbean). Olmos and Paravisin-Gebert tell the following story to illustrate the pervasion of these beliefs:

> Desmond and Earl, young Jamaicans living in Toronto, have engaged in a series of robberies involving small suburban banks. They are assiduous clients of an Obeahman from whom they seek the ritual cleansings and massages that they believe will protect them from arrest and punishment. (p. 2).

As a child, one author remembers the following incident:

> My mother was annoyed because the oranges on our orange trees were constantly being stolen, so my father summoned the Obeahman, who put a 'spell' on the trees so that only he (the Obeahman) could pick the oranges; he hung small bottles and coffins in the trees to make the spell work. Shortly after, my father realized that he had to pay the Obeahman to come and pick the oranges if we wanted any, because we were also not allowed to pick them because of the nature of the spell!

Both of these stories illustrate the reality of these practices in the current environment of the Caribbean. People of the Caribbean still believe in the efficacy of these practices – essentially a 'belief in an active, supernatural, mysterious power that can be invested in objects  ...  in turn linked to animistic beliefs in other spirits'; these beliefs include 'contact or mediation between humans and the spirit world', 'the practice of magic in the form of spells, conjurations, an ethno-magical medicine-healing' as well as 'a central symbol or focus' (Olmos and Paravisine-Gebert, 2003: 9–10).

Voodoo, Obeah and other African practices were outlawed by the European colonists, but they survived, and continue to be reported. In more formal religious practices the African beliefs have often been incorporated into Christian practices – for example, a belief in a Supreme Being, creator of the universe, 'complemented by a belief in a pantheon of deities' (Olmos and Paravisine-Gebert, 2003: 9). Typically, in our experience, when someone is buried in St Vincent, the burial will be Christian, but rum must also be poured into the grave site to placate the spirits, so that they will let the dead person rest. Many of the formal churches in the Caribbean have a unique mix of African and Christian beliefs. Some, such as the Spiritual Baptists were outlawed at one time, because the Europeans felt that their singing, praying, baptism, dress, and so on, was 'too African', and that their practices bordered on magic. Now legal, the Spiritual Baptists and other 'fringe' religions (from a mainstream perspective) have large followings.

The practice of both Voodoo and Obeah depends on a belief in the world being essentially magical, and the important Voodoo priest or the Obeah man or woman, who has access to that magical world and can use this magic, often for good (for example, healing the sick, improving someone's fortune, helping find love), but also for more sinister purposes (for example, revenge on an enemy or former lover, making someone lose power, taking someone's possessions, and, in the case of Voodoo, creating zombies). In these belief systems, someone powerful, with specialized knowledge, can help those with less power, who do not share in the knowledge, to achieve what they want; but their power must be maintained by keeping knowledge secret.

Such a belief system if translated to leadership would imply powerful managers who would depend on their secret information base to maintain control. Subordinates would have little power and would rely on the favor of their bosses for benefits. There would likely be an 'in group' of subordinates who would receive disproportionate favors and more information, and an 'out group' who would receive little, and possibly suffer negative effects. This leadership system, which fits with the African traditional magical beliefs, would also fit with the plantation and colonial systems, therefore the historical development of the Caribbean, combined with traditional beliefs, could be expected to result in a top-down, hierarchical leadership system, with little trust, information sharing or empowerment of subordinates.

In addition to the magical beliefs that the Africans brought to the Caribbean, they also brought stories of Anancy (also spelled Anansi, and sometimes known in the Caribbean simply as Nancy), a trickster spider, and his adventures. These are outlined in the following section.

**Mythical Stories of Anancy**

Surprisingly, and unfortunately, there is a dearth of academic literature dealing with the Anancy stories. The discussion of these stories here is, consequently, based on personal interpretations of Anancy and the meaning of the stories.

One of the authors says: 'As a child I remember sitting on the back steps of our house where my nanny would tell us children "nancy stories", as we called them. I didn't always understand the stories, but I felt part of some greater heritage, especially when Nanny would sing parts of the stories – "Ah see me Nancy coming down" is a sung line that remains in my head some 50 years after I heard it, showing its power to shape beliefs'. The author continues that much later I learned that these stories had traveled from West Africa with the African slaves, and had been told and retold down many generations, keeping the African culture alive in a new land, and spreading African beliefs to new peoples.

Nancy, as I knew him, was in fact Anancy, or Anansi, an Ashanti word meaning spider. McDermott (1972) describes Anansi the spider as 'one of the great folk heroes of the world'. He continues that 'Anansi is a rogue, a mischief-maker, and a wise, loveable creature who triumphs over larger foes'. Anancy in the stories I heard as a child, was a trickster who nobody trusted, but everybody loved, because he could always find a way out of any conundrum. Pelton (1989) warns against simplistic explanations of Anancy and other tricksters because 'the trickster can change form as easily as he can tell lies' (p. 224) so explanations in this chapter should be taken in this context as rather simplistic interpretations.

The Anancy stories share their roots with the Brer Rabbit and Brer Fox stories, but the spider stories took root in the Caribbean, while the rabbit and fox stories were popular in the southern USA. Presumably this resulted from the differences between those Africans who ended up in the Caribbean and those who ended up in the USA, or because of the different environments in which they lived. Sometimes in current day children's books the characters (spider, fox, rabbit) are together, but I do not remember this in the early stories – Anancy was, however, sometimes called Brer Anancy, illustrating the common roots.

Imagine the trickster spider in the context of the top-down leadership structure described as emanating from traditional magical beliefs. Anancy is, in fact, the great leveler – through his tricks, he brings those more powerful than himself to their downfall, and gets his rewards this way. For example, if Anancy meets a powerful and vain elephant, he does not confront him directly, but leads him to the water and persuades him that the beautiful elephant in the water is waiting for him … when the elephant enters the water, Anancy is off to the tree tops carrying the elephant's bag of riches that was left on the river bank. Similarly, in a leadership system which is dependent on power at the top and information hoarding, subordinates will focus on 'tricking' those in power, either to become one of the 'in-group', to portray those in the 'in-group' in a negative light, or to find alternative ways of achieving the rewards they believe they deserve. Again, this is supported by the practices of the plantation and the colonies. Slaves, servants, and colonial underlings were in positions where their best route to rewards was through misinformation and 'trickery'. For the powerless in the plantation, colonial system Anancy provided evidence that ingenuity could succeed against power, and thus could provide a powerful positive image for the powerless.

## OVERVIEW OF CARIBBEAN LEADERSHIP

According to Punnett (2001, 2006) the colonial heritage of the Caribbean has influenced management and leadership practices in a number of ways. Colonies were in subordinate positions and instructed by the 'colonial masters' (as the European powers were called) in matters of government, economics and business. A top-down decision-making style was enforced and accepted. Decisions were made at the master level, with little input from the local level, and these decisions were not questioned. Information was not shared and it was assumed that 'London' knew what was best for the colonies. The remnants in leadership style in many companies in the Caribbean are that information is not shared and those at higher levels do not trust those at lower levels – power is centralized and hierarchy is important.

This leadership style in North America is labeled 'Theory X'. It is essentially top-down, with leaders in tight control. This style is described in textbooks as ineffective; however, it may be that under certain cultural conditions, employees accept this style, and therefore it may work. While leadership is autocratic in nature, it may also be seen as somewhat benevolent – that is, the leader is expected to look after subordinates (as a father is expected to look after the family) and in return for this, employees are loyal and obedient to the leader.

Political leaders in the Caribbean are a good example of the power attributed to leaders, and they are generally seen as 'all powerful'. One current leader makes decisions at such a micro-level that individual road repair decisions must be sanctioned by the Prime Minister. This clearly contributes to the 'in group' versus 'out group' thinking – that is, if you are one of the in group you get your road fixed; if you are one of the out group, you do not.

This leadership style can certainly be related to the traditional beliefs and stories of the Caribbean. The traditional beliefs relied on an important, learned person who had information that others did not have, and could use this either for benefit or harm. Much in the same way, powerful managers have access to information, which is not shared, and which allows them to make decisions and take actions, which can affect their subordinates in both positive and negative ways. In Caribbean leadership today, both those in powerful positions and their subordinates believe that this system is acceptable, perhaps because it reflects traditional beliefs. This leadership style and management approach may be accepted, but whether it is effective is open to debate.

In the next section, research results on cultural values in the Caribbean are presented, and the relationship of these values to effective leadership explored.

**Research on Cultural Values in the English-speaking Caribbean**

Some recent research in the Caribbean (Punnett, 2002, 2006) has been based on Hofstede's (1984) cultural model. This research has examined aspects of individualism, hierarchy, and certainty. Briefly, these dimensions can be described as follows:

- individualism/collectivism indicates the degree to which people in a society prefer individual decisions, actions, and so on to group decisions, actions, and so on;
- hierarchy refers to the degree to which people in a society believe in and accept differences in power; and
- certainty suggests the degree to which people in a society accept uncertainty or seek out certainty.

The research in the Caribbean identified the following cultural characteristics based on a variety of projects in several of the countries (Barbados, Jamaica, Trinidad and Tobago, St Vincent and the Grenadines):

- High on both individualism and collectivism, comfortable with both individual and group interactions, resulting in a moderate individualism score using the Hofstede cultural value model.
- Low on hierarchy, preferring equality to power distinctions, resulting in a low score on power distance using the Hofstede cultural value model.
- Preferring certainty and wanting to think things through before acting, resulting in a high score on uncertainty avoidance using the Hofstede cultural value model.

It was a surprising finding that the Caribbean countries were low on power distance. As noted throughout this chapter, the history of colonialism and plantation economies has left the Caribbean with a legacy of top-down leadership, which many people feel is acceptable and accepted, and which is supported by the traditional beliefs. For example, this would lead one to expect a high power distance score. The reported low score on this cultural value may be especially pertinent in thinking about effective leadership in the Caribbean.

The trickster spider's reaction to power is interesting in this context. Anancy played tricks, and usually got what he wanted. Anancy did not accept that because you were powerful you should be able to dictate to others. In fact Anancy assumes that he can 'out trick' the powerful because of his resourcefulness. Anancy is anti-hierarchy and anti-power and may partially explain the low power distance in the Caribbean. Of course, there are other explanations; namely, freedom after having been enslaved, and independence after being colonized both encourage values of equality and low power distance – see Commentary box.

---

## COMMENTARY BOX

### Colin Morrison, President of Business Fit International

In the facilitation of a national program in St Lucia the leadership practice developed was congruent with the top-down hierarchical leadership system with little information sharing or empowerment of subordinates. This style emerged in spite of efforts on the part of the consultants to flatten the hierarchy and share the power. It appeared that leaders and subordinates supported and felt more comfortable with the clearly defined hierarchy. A significant factor was the personality of the manager which made the style more palatable for everyone. This comfort is not present with a Caribbean manager in my Canadian company. In St Lucia this style worked because it was accepted. In Canada it is not working and tricksters continually tried to undermine the manager's authority. The more this happens the less she trusts them and accordingly her dictatorial stance increases. We are currently initiating training and mentoring for this manager and team and this article will be helpful in increasing the manager's understanding of the issues, their origins and hopefully point the way to a successful shift in style. Perhaps the increased awareness generated by this chapter will set her free from what appear to be deeply un-inculcated beliefs of how to maintain control as a leader.

In terms of leadership, it may be appropriate for managers to pay more attention to this aspect of Caribbean culture, and move to a more inclusive and participative style. Of course, the 'trickster' nature of Anancy reinforces the lack of trust that leaders have for subordinates, and vice versa, so that changing the existing system of leadership in the Caribbean is not easy.

In the next section the cultural value profile of the English-speaking Caribbean, previously outlined, is explored in terms of effective leadership.

## PRACTICAL APPLICATIONS

The cultural value profile identified can be related to leadership practices in a wide variety of situations. Briefly, we consider each of the dimensions, and what they suggest about leadership practices.

### Collectivism/Individualism

A moderate score on this dimension (or possibly a score that can be interpreted as high on both) suggests people who should be able to work effectively in a variety of situations. They should be good team players, but they should also be able to contribute individually. They will be comfortable in group discussions and seeking consensus, but they will also be willing to take individual decisions, under appropriate conditions. Effective managers will draw on both the individualism and collectivism that are important to these employees. Of course, the trickster concept in the Caribbean can undermine teamwork and trust, and this has to be considered in effective leadership.

### Uncertainty Avoidance

A relatively high score on this dimension suggests that people are more comfortable with a degree of certainty and security. They should react well to secure jobs and a sense of organizational stability. They will welcome clear policies and procedures. They will value transparency and consistency in employee practices. Effective managers will find ways to ensure that these employees know what is expected of them, and what they can expect of their managers and the organization. The trickster character introduces an element of uncertainty into any situation, and may provide a helpful model for encouraging creativity and entrepreneurial activity.

**Power Distance**

A relatively low score on this dimension suggests that people value equality and are uncomfortable with the differences in power and status that are an integral part of hierarchies. They should react well to delegation and participation in decision making, and a flattening of organizational structures. They will value open communication and trust. They want to feel that their input is valued. Effective managers will learn to delegate successfully, to seek and accept input from their subordinates, to share information and communicate openly, and to create a climate of trust. The trickster's aim is to trick the powerful and achieve his own aims, so managers need to find ways to finesse this characteristic for the good of the organization.

The typical organization in the English-speaking Caribbean earlier described is hierarchical, with top-down leadership, little trust, and information guarded to maintain positions of power. This is reinforced by Punnett *et al.* (2006) who reported that managers said of themselves that they delegated, communicated openly and trusted subordinates, but when asked to describe other managers, they said that others were authoritarian, lacked trust and did not communicate. The authors suggest that this discrepancy likely indicates that the managers may have 'read the right books' and 'taken the right courses', so they know what 'good leadership' should be, but these 'good leadership' practices are likely not to be the reality.

A top-down, authoritarian leadership style, exhibiting little trust in or communication with employees, is not just incongruent with, but actually antithetical to a low power distance culture. In other words, it is not neutral, but actively negative. This leadership style not only does not motivate, it actively de-motivates, it does not encourage attendance, it actually encourages absenteeism, it does not simply lead to average productivity, it leads to poor productivity, and encourages the formation of unions. The negative outcomes cover a wide range, and can include strikes and sabotage at the dramatic end, to staying home or working little at the more benign end. These outcomes have very negative consequences for firms, and dramatically decrease their ability to be competitive. Further this style encourages the 'trickster' behavior of Anancy.

It is very common for managers to attribute these negative outcomes to poor worker attitudes, but what is critical for managers to recognize, is that poor worker attitudes arise because of poor leadership. Carter's (1997) book *Why Workers Won't Work* demonstrated this in the Jamaican context. If Caribbean companies are to prosper in today's competitive environment, changes in leadership may provide a stimulus for managers and their subordinates. If managers in the region want to embrace change, the cultural profile described here provides the context in which to design change.

Managers need to recognize that the congruence, or fit, between leadership style and practices and the cultural values and preferences of subordinates is critical to success. Achieving a fit will mean that employees are highly motivated and committed. In turn, this will result in higher levels of productivity, lower costs, lower levels of absenteeism, fewer labor disputes, more innovation, and a host of other positive organizational outcomes. Managers, therefore, need to make a conscious effort to change their own attitudes and behaviors.

It is not easy for employees, however, in spite of their cultural values, to accept and deal with new and possibly unexpected attitudes and behaviors on the part of their managers. For example, if employees are accustomed to a lack of trust in the workplace, and a manager seeks to establish a climate of trust, employees may well react with suspicion and fear. If employees are accustomed to close supervision, and a manager wants to increase delegation, employees may not accept the delegated tasks, because they are unsure what the outcomes will be. The manager who really wants to change the organization will have to find ways to foster the desired attitudes and behaviors among peers and subordinates. Consistency will be key to success, because of the preference for certainty.

Achieving congruence between cultural values and leadership style and practice can pay off. Conversely, dissonance between cultural values and leadership style can create negative outcomes, such as high absenteeism, labor disputes, high costs, and low morale and productivity. If we consider the English-speaking Caribbean cultural value profile, described in this chapter, relative to the traditional approach to leadership in the region, and ask 'is there congruence between leadership style and culture?', an answer might be that there is reasonable congruence in relation to collectivism/individualism and uncertainty avoidance, but that there is incongruence in relation to power distance.

The discussion in this chapter focused on the most important of the traditional beliefs in the Caribbean, and the historical consequences of the plantation economy and colonialism, which indicate support for existing patterns of leadership in the Caribbean. Nevertheless, there is need for change. One important question for managers in the region is whether these practices can change, given the context. A second question is how to change the practices, given the context. This chapter has suggested that change can occur, although not easily, and it has provided information on culture in the Caribbean that can serve as a basis for achieving change.

## NOTE

1.  Much of this discussion is based on Meditz and Hanratty (1989).

## REFERENCES

Andrews, J. B. (1880), Ananci stories, *The Folk-Lore Record*, **3** (1), 53–5.

Beckles, H. M. (2004a), *Chattel House Blues Kingston*, Jamaica: Ian Randle Publishers.

Beckles, H. M. (2004b), *Great House Rules Kingston*, Jamaica: Ian Randle Publishers.

Boswell,T. D. and Conway, D. (1992), *The Caribbean Islands: Endless Geographic Diversity*, New Brunswick, NJ: Rutgers University Press.

Budwhar, P. and Debrah, Y. (2005), International HRM in developing countries, in H. Scullion and M. Linehan (eds), *International Human Resource Management*, London: Palgrave, pp. 259–80.

Carter, K. (1997), *Why Workers Won't Work*, London: Macmillan Publishers Ltd.

Hofstede, G. (1984), *Culture's Consequences: International Differences in Work-Related Values*, Beverly Hills, CA: Sage Publications.

McDermott, G. (1972), *Anansi the Spider: A Tale from the Ashanti*, New York: Henry Holt.

Meditz, S. W. and Hanratty, D. M. (1989), *Islands of the Commonwealth Caribbean: A Regional Study*, Washington, DC, Library of Congress, accessed at lcweb2.loc.gov 8/26/2007 – temporary site.

Nurse, L. and Punnett, B. J. (2002), Management research on the English-speaking Caribbean: toward a research agenda, *Journal of Eastern Caribbean Studies*, **27**, 1–37.

Olmos, M. F. and Paravisini-Gebert, L. (2003), *Creole Religions of the Caribbean*, NY: New York University Press.

Pelton, R. D. (1989), *The Trickster in West Africa: A Study of Mythic Irony and Sacred Delight*, Berkeley, CA: University of California Press.

Prasad, A. (ed.) (2003), *Postcolonial Theory and Organizational Analysis: A Critical Reader*, London: Palgrave.

Punnett, B. J. (2001), Caribbean management, in M. Warner (ed.), *IEBM Regional Set Management in the Americas*, London: International Thomson Publishing (2nd edn), pp. 333–41.

Punnett, B. J. (2002), Culture and management in the English speaking Caribbean, *International Western Academy of Management Proceedings*, July.

Punnett, B. J. (2006), Culture and management in the English speaking Caribbean: some empirical evidence, *Journal of Eastern Caribbean Studies*, **31**, 31–54.

Punnett, B. J. (2008), Management in developing countries, in C. Wankel (ed.), *21st Century Management*, Thousand Oaks, CA: Sage Publications.

Punnett, B. J., Dick-Forde, E. and Robinson, J. (2006), Culture and management in the English speaking Caribbean, *Journal of Eastern Caribbean Studies*, **31**, 44–71.

Roberts, P. A. (1988), The misinterpretations of Brer Anancy, *Folklore*, **99** (1), 98–101.

Wake, C. S. (1883), Ananci stories, *The Folk-Lore Journal*, **1** (9), 280–92.

# 4. Cultural mythology and global leadership in Argentina

## Patricia Friedrich, Andrés Hatum and Luiz Mesquita

### INTRODUCTION

Since ancient times, human beings have relied on myths to try and understand/explain the world around them. According to the *Britannica Concise Encyclopedia*, a myth is a 'traditional story of ostensibly historical events that serves to unfold part of the worldview of a people or explain a practice, belief, or natural phenomenon'. As such a myth can be argued to have an extensive potential to help us discover the significance of past events, figures and times in hopes of forging a future of accomplishment and success.

One common understanding of myth is that it refers to an ages-old, sacred (in the strict sense of the word) or often fictitious story which oftentimes provides explanations to the potentially unexplainable (for example the origin of the universe, the nature of love, and so on). A myth can also secondarily mean a lie which is nevertheless generally considered to be true, as expressed in the well known quote by Warren Bennis which goes:

> The most dangerous leadership myth is that leaders are born – that there is a genetic factor to leadership. This myth asserts that people simply either have certain charismatic qualities or not. That's nonsense; in fact, the opposite is true. Leaders are made rather than born.

In this chapter, however, we take a broader conceptualization of the myth as the story of individuals or the individuals themselves who have come to symbolize aspects of collective value systems and beliefs, aspects which help us understand what a people, a historical moment, or a cultural membership is all about.

Many such figures inhabit our cultural universe – Ghandi has come to symbolize pacific civil disobedience and the plight for human rights; Marilyn Monroe epitomizes the glamour and femininity of old Hollywood; Freud possesses the title of the father of psychoanalysis and Cleopatra has endured throughout the centuries believed to have been a seductress and strong political figure. After an individual ascends to a position of myth, the veracity of their accomplishments becomes a relative factor in the maintenance of their legendary status, for they acquire new symbolic meanings as representatives of a collectivity and its values.

## OVERVIEW OF ARGENTINE MYTHOLOGY

Three figures, two of famous Argentines elevated to mythological status and one representative of the collective self of this country, come to mind when one tries to decipher what it means to be Argentine and, as a consequence, what it means to lead in Argentina. Evita Perón, Che Guevara and the mythological gaucho are these three legendary icons; they give away the complexity of a people sometimes divided by their Latin-American membership and their worldwide ambition, by the pride of being who they are and the frustration of wanting to be more. These three figures are not less conflicted; they create in our collective consciousness images of rebellion, of afflicted souls, torn between righteousness and passion, pain and glory, melancholy and impatience, the very spirit of the nation itself best sung and danced in tango, the national rhythm. Passion and conflict are the nouns that arguably best describe the Argentine essence. Marcos Aguinis (2001) may have captured it better than anyone else. He called his book, a social analysis of the Argentine at the turn of the twenty-first century, *El Atroz Encanto de Ser Argentinos* (roughly, 'the atrocious charm of being Argentine'), a title which contains a fortunate and clever oxymoron, so emblematic of the contradictions of Argentina. The question then is, in a country self-analyzed to contain such paradoxes, what does it take to be a leader?

### Evita

The first legendary figure described here is full of contradictions. She embodied grace but also strength, a seemingly secondary role (that is that of First Lady) but an arguable powerful influence over the president's decisions, a body that gave way after only 33 years but a spirit that has endured the passing of time. Evita Perón was born in 1919 and died prematurely in 1952. From the announcement of her death by the Subsecretariat of Information, one can gather the extent of reverence she commanded in Argentina; the words were, 'It is our sad duty to inform the people of the Republic that Eva Perón, the Spiritual Leader of the Nation, died at 8:25 P.M.' (*To be Evita*, 2007).

Evita was the second wife of President Juan Perón and a naturally charismatic person. She was well known for her charitable work and for having elevated the status of women. She organized women voters, for example, into a national power around the time of Perón's re-election, the first time women had been allowed to vote. She pursued not only the cause of women, but also of children, of the elderly and of the poor. Not having borne any children herself, Evita became a symbolic mother of the country.

Eva Perón seemed unrelenting, an Argentine martyr who stood by her husband and in front of the nation even when her fragile body was being battered by the cancer which would ultimately kill her. Her death elevated her to the level of myth; she had the right combination of beauty, glamour but also suffering and pain, just like tango.

While in life Evita received great support from the working class, she was disliked by the country's elites and the military for her social work and involvement with the masses. After her death and the fall of Perón, as Fraser and Navarro (1980) explain, the press which had been inhibited during the Perón government took it in its hands to revert the image of Evita. They explain:

> Sometimes the attacks on Evita would have an almost religious character and would depict her as a sort of fiend, evil beyond rational explanation; but more usually their frame of reference was secular and drawn from the conventions of yellow journalism, pulp fiction or bad movies. (179)

For at least 15 years, such attacks became common as part of an attempt to repress *Peronismo*. It was only in the 1970s, with new political changes, that the myth of Evita was revived. Since then many works have been written about her. Besides book biographies, the musical *Evita* has arguably been the most successful attempt at telling her story, or at least a side of it. The film version of the musical, with Madonna and Antonio Banderas, helped continue the legacy which has ultimately made Eva Perón not only an Argentine myth but also an international and contentious pop icon.

## El Che

The second myth is not only an Argentine legend, but he is also one of the most controversial figures in recent history. His biography is so complex and so great is the lack of agreement on what he means and where he stands that this brief note on his life story can certainly do no more than scratch the surface. However, for our purposes, what is important to highlight is his charisma as a leader (it is beyond the scope of this chapter to argue for or against his actions and/or the different versions of Che which are propagated in different countries) and the mystique of yet another Argentine whose profile defies fast conclusions and whose complex personality points to inevitable highs and lows along his path.

Ernesto 'Che' Guevara was born in 1928. During his formative years, he traveled extensively through South America. It was during this time that, many believe, the medical student saw such impoverished conditions and such blatant inequality across the region that he decided that the only path to change was revolution. Guevara joined Fidel Castro's revolutionary forces in 1956. The movement would ultimately upturn the government of dictator General Fulgencio Batista in 1959. Guevara was given posts in the new Cuban government before he moved on to encouraging revolutions in Africa and Bolivia. He was ultimately captured and executed in Bolivia in 1967.

When McLaren (2000: 7) writes of the myth of Che, he creates a picture that in many ways reminds us of the extreme interpretations that Evita was subjected to. He contends that:

> The discovery of Che's remains metonymically activated a series of interlinked associations – rebel, martyr, rogue character from a picaresque adventure, savior, renegade, extremist – in which there were no fixed divides among them.

The Che Guevara myth has been maintained the way many have; part of the myth results from the impact El Che had on social and political dynamics in Latin America and the way in which his life called attention to great economic disparities. The other part of the myth is kept by the fact that he died young and under violent and still disputed circumstances. Because upon his death Che Guevara was elevated to pop culture icon (sadly to many, including McLaren, who see his depiction on t-shirts and the like as standing in extreme contrast to all he believed in), his story took on larger-than-life proportions. His profile demonstrates the power that attempts at social transformation have on the collective consciousness of people. His saga also reinforces the controversies and the drama of being an Argentine icon.

## The Gaucho

Our third myth, differently from the other two is not a person. Rather, it is a type both revered and questioned and also identified with Argentine folklore. The gaucho is without a doubt yet another controversial figure. Mestizo or criollo, he is a symbol of 'Argentineness' and also a reminder against the Europeanization of the country. It was arguably literature which made an icon out of the gaucho. In his romanticized version, the gaucho 'became a symbol of the national spirit and of national achievement' (Nichols, 1968: 62).

The origin of the word gaucho is traced by some to mean vagabond or outlaw, a man who is fair in his heart but also rough in his manners – a mostly lonely and quiet individual who is also capable of violence if provoked. He has been both revered and rebuffed as emblematic of Argentina because, while he is brave and adventurous on the one hand, he is unrefined, uneducated and not

at all suave on the other. Lehman (2005) explains that the gaucho 'was originally an illiterate, landless rural horseman, often a cattle rustler and frontier
dweller' (152). However, she also argues, 'social economists analyze the ways
in which the gaucho was coerced into shifting from his preferred nomadic
lifestyle into working as an itinerant ranch-hand, finally setting into the more
permanent agricultural labor force that would bring wealth to the nation'
(150). While the gaucho plays an important role as leader of the pampas and
is as such an important reference in the formative years of the country, his
figure is all the more controversial because, as Lehman also explains, the more
urban the population of Argentina became, the more its people wanted to be
associated with Europe and unrelated to the gaucho. Additionally, what was
once seen as one of his virtues, his manliness and masculinity so desirable in
war and the wilderness of the pampas, became a kind of liability for some, or
as Lehman puts it, 'problematical' as a national icon, as 'he does not "represent" women, urban workers, upper or middle classes, or indigenous peoples'
(154). In the end, in tandem with the iconic figures portrayed in this chapter,
the gaucho has all the makings of an Argentine myth; no agreement exists
about his place in the culture and one will see Argentines both singing his
praises and denying his relevance.

## OVERVIEW OF ARGENTINE LEADERSHIP

Besides providing clues to the values and character of Argentina, investigating
the country's myths has the additional benefit of setting this nation apart from
its neighboring countries, a task that is not always met with seriousness by
those researching the region. It is often the case that one will find in the literature (instead of the Brazilian leadership style or the Argentine cultural
profile) references to Latin American business management, Latin American
culture, Latin American food, the Hispanics and other generalizations which
yield the wrong perception that within Latin America there is a coincidence of
beliefs, values, cultural manifestations and, as a consequence, ways of doing
business (we have addressed this misconception in Friedrich *et al.* (2006)
which along with the GLOBE study of House *et al.* (2004) is frequently cited
in the next few sections). In reality, this is not so. The Argentine businessperson has his/her unique characteristics, a consequence of their unique history,
the challenges they face in their leadership efforts, and the current political and
economic reality of the country. Among such defining aspects of Argentine
identity, we can find a history that reinforces the elements represented by the
myths above. There are the times of wealth and tranquility during the beginning of the twentieth century, the uncertainties and problems generated by
alternating periods of militarism and democratic leadership during most of the

twentieth century, the attempt to reproduce the relative calmness of times past by pegging the local economy to the dollar in the 1990s, a crumbling economy that followed at the turn of the twenty-first century, and the current attempt at economic reconstruction.

This is the formative background of the Argentine leader, a background that once again evidences the polarizing events and the conflicting feelings which define these people. The Argentines have been dubbed polite but sometimes proud, elegant but at times indifferent, friendly but a bit self-important, making it hard for the novice to pin them down. Evidently, the Argentine is a complex type, just like his/her icons, and the Argentine leader can initially be a puzzle for his/her business partners.

Since we have been writing about paradoxes in Argentina, it seems only appropriate to choose two local leaders for analysis who themselves represent opposing styles of leadership but who also have enough similarities to make them representative of a collectivity. Although both come from families known for their businesses and have followed their parents in leadership roles, they display different managerial styles, which are apparent everywhere, from their strategic decisions to their manner of dress.

The first such leader is Mauricio Macri, president of Boca Juniors (that is the famed soccer team) and now mayor of the city of Buenos Aires. Mauricio is the eldest son of Franco Macri, one of the richest and most influential businessmen in Argentina. The family business includes such companies as Socma, Sideco and Sevel. Macri is a conservative man, controversial in some of his commentaries, sexist in the account of some, arguably a representative of what has been dubbed the *neo machismo* (some may be reminded of the image of the gaucho). He has openly spoken of the role of women in the home. Yet, his supporters portray him as a good listener and a sympathetic leader, qualities which have been highlighted by researchers as admirable in Argentina (House *et al.*, 2004). For example, in a profile in *La Nacion* (6-25-07) those close to Macri described his managerial style as follows:

> Since taking over the presidency of Boca ten years ago, Macri has turned out to be a leader who delegates a lot of administrative power to those hierarchically below him; he makes good use of the knowledge displayed by others, learns from them and lets all that are by his side participate. (our translation)

The newspaper article continues,

> Always, in the meetings of the board, even in face of the hardest disagreements and most complex conflicts, Mauricio tries to assimilate the arguments of others while he looks for the positive aspects of the discussion, rather than its confrontation potential. (our translation)

Whereas some of Macri's critics may point out that some of his more direct commentaries can result in confrontation, his appeal as a leader seems at this point undeniable; since his election as mayor of Buenos Aires, Macri has been flooded with questions about a possible future presidential candidacy, questions which he so far has been answering in the negative.

The second leader is Luis Pagani, CEO of Arcor, the largest candy producer in the world and the only Argentine multinational within the food industry to still be a family firm. Under Pagani's leadership Arcor has spread its presence to countries such as Brazil, Peru and the United States and has exported its products to about 120 countries. Pagani agrees with Macri when the topic is the ability to delegate responsibility to those around him. When asked if times of crisis (such as the one experienced by Argentina since 2001) turned a leader into a more autocratic individual, Pagani explained that with him it was quite the opposite. In an interview with WinRed.com (2003), he explained that the first thing the company did at that time was 'put together a "crisis committee" with executives from all areas with whom we were able sit down and analyze the upcoming client and provider deadlines'. Pagani believes in leadership with employee participation and in solidarity and social responsibility (remember that likewise the Argentine myths we described were in life greatly concerned with social issues). Under Pagani's guidance, Arcor has reaffirmed its commitment to sustainable development and conservation. Moreover, the group guided by him believes in the development of the employees as individuals, individuals who will then take the values and ethics acquired into their respective communities. That employees develop not only professionally but also and especially as human beings is a recurrent theme for Argentines and, as a consequence, a leader who is willing to pursue such a goal will be respected for his/her commitment.

The acknowledgment that one's profession and personal selves are inseparable is frequent in Argentina. The need for self-analysis is too. Indicative of this desire to grow as a person is the fact that Buenos Aires concentrates more psychoanalysts per inhabitant than any other city in the world. Macri, for one, has in interviews referred to being in therapy since the early 1990s. Contrary to therapy in the United States, for example, where short treatment for specific problems is the norm, in Argentina therapy in general and psychoanalysis in particular are seen as paths to self-knowledge and personal growth. The successful Argentine leader is one who recognizes and fosters self-knowledge and self-development in his/her team.

## GLOBAL IMPLICATIONS

In the GLOBE study of 62 societies, their cultural traits, and their leadership styles (House *et al.*, 2004: 14), the researchers have found that in Argentina charismatic/value based leadership and team-oriented leadership are usually endorsed as good leader behaviors. The first dimension has to do with the 'ability to inspire, to motivate and to expect high performance outcomes based on firmly held values' while the second pertains to 'effective team building and implementation of a common purpose or goal among team members.' Granted the former was universally endorsed by all cultures surveyed, in Argentina it received a high score of 5.98 out of a possible 7 points. Team-oriented leadership was equally highly rated at 5.99. Figures such as Evita Perón and Che Guevara become myths in Argentina to a great extent because of their leadership style; while on the one hand they inspire because of their personal charisma, on the other, they display goals which unite the people around a universal purpose. By the same token, political and business leaders such as Macri and Pagani become successful because they are capable of analogous feats (scale aside) within their realm of influence: they unite and inspire, and they display a discourse and a plan which ultimately point to social change.

In the same GLOBE study, Argentina received the second lowest score for the dimension of future orientation, that is, the level to which a society prizes and motivates its members to pursue future-oriented actions including delaying rewards and planning (House *et al.*, 1999). The volatile Argentine environment which displays frequent economic and political changes has made long term planning difficult and delayed gratification risky. Nevertheless, Argentina scores amongst the high rating countries in future orientation as a laudable societal value. The desire for stability and long range planning stands in stark opposition to the perceived reality. In that context a leader who manages to plan for the future and provide relative stability in an unstable environment is greatly appreciated. Pagani is an example of such a leader. While his leadership is standing the test of time, Arcor is a company capable of drawing a longer term plan.

The study of the myths who survived the passing of time in Argentina can greatly help us understand the social and business environment of the country. The differences between what is and what people perceive relations should be also help fulfill such a goal. While some of the strengths displayed by the myths described herein and the business leaders who embed some of the same traits point to charisma, poise, flair and a consequent obedience by devotees (myths) and employees (business leaders), some of the weaknesses include a need to be acknowledged, revered, and to maintain high power distance besides a tendency to see power as a goal in itself – see Commentary box.

---

## COMMENTARY BOX

### Manuel Estruga, Planning Director, Exiros SA

Unfortunately in Argentina leadership has lately been carried out in a feudal and individualistic style. We lack a strategic plan which will yield leaders able to carry out their leadership. If you take a book definition of leadership and test it against our current political leaders, for example, you see that such definition, along with the skills and values presented with it, differ significantly from those of our government, and so on. These forms of leadership in Argentina have been about centralizing power, arriving at unilateral decisions, denying dialogue, and lacking a strategic plan, a mission, and values. It is regrettable that to become a cultural icon in our country, the path to be taken is more associated with figures from the past than with the leaders we would like to have in the future. In our history, icons such as Perón and Evita are very strong especially among the working class.

---

We now discuss some aspects of this claim. In a 2003 interview with Luiz Mesquita, former presidential candidate Lopez Murphy explained that:

> Contrary to the image that the international community might have of us Argentines, we are not a prodigious self-confident people. It is true we have bragged about our self-worth many times, even in ways that have gone beyond reality, mostly to massage our egos. (46)

Murphy's insightful quote gets to what we believe is the crux of the Argentine paradox. While in some developing nations a fear of not measuring up to international partners/competitors/peers may result in a constant degrading of one's own resources and abilities, in Argentina this same fear takes the shape of a certain self-acclamation. In the end, self-congratulation does not have the intent of only convincing the others of someone's worth but also of convincing oneself that they fit in. Perhaps the attempt to 'massage one's ego', as Murphy puts it, can explain some of the weakness so to speak, that international travelers may find among Argentine leaders (granted that we are making a judgment call when it comes to their non-desirability). In that respect, the need to massage the ego may at times take the form of seemingly great assertiveness.

Assertiveness, or the degree to which people are motivated by a society to be assertive, tough and forceful in relationships (House *et al.*, 1999), is largely present but not always revered in Argentina. Argentines seem to prefer a leader who is able to listen while still showing who is in charge. This ability may have played a part in Evita's ascent to leadership as she was perceived as able to listen to the plight of the masses and act to address their problems.

Similar inferences can be made about Power Distance. Establishing high levels of Power Distance between those who lead and those who follow can be a way of reaffirming one's leadership and also signaling status to those around. In the GLOBE, Argentina was one of the highest scoring countries for Power Distance at 5.64 of a possible 7 points. Such findings are corroborated by our own empirical study (Friedrich *et al.*, 2006) where Argentina scored the highest of the five Latin American countries for Power Distance (3.67 out of a possible 5). However, in the GLOBE study, managers also indicated that they wished such distance was much smaller. In our study (Friedrich *et al.*, 2006), when we asked managers if they thought that those in leadership positions seemed motivated by having power more than by achieving results, we again obtained for Argentina the highest score of the group (2.72 compared to a much smaller 2.09 for Brazil). Given the difference between what is and what employees report it should be, we can infer that a leader in Argentina will be appreciated for bringing hierarchical differences to a more equalitarian level. As the discussion on Macri and Pagani above shows, these are two leaders who are perceived to be able to do so.

Finally the great ability that Argentines have developed to survive uncertain business environments stands in contrast to greater difficulty in dealing with stability. According to Marcelo Arguelles, chairman of Sidus Pharmaceuticals, quoted in Fracchia and Mesquita (2006: 54), 'Argentines work well on "muddy roads", but when it comes to working on the "highway" they do not perform as well.' This commentary, which makes us once more think of the gaucho in the untamed pampas, correlates with the finding by the GLOBE project that when it comes to uncertainty avoidance, Argentina rates low. Because of the instability of the environment, Argentines have learned to remain composed in face of unpredictable situations.

It is not unusual, however, that clashes occur with international partners who might not fully understand the motivation and rationale for Argentine leadership preferences. Those international partners, for example, who are not adept of the 'play by ear' philosophy may feel puzzled by the lack of or relative emphasis on long term plans. Likewise, those international partners who see the need for tight formal contracts might be unaware of the fact that because the legal system will not always work as a fast mediator/enforcer, Argentines have developed other mechanisms for successful partnership (for example trust). Finally, in uncertain business environments, certainty seeking may be very elusive; the international partner may be mystified by the Argentine attitude toward vagueness. To avoid such clashes, a great leader in Argentina will know how to close the distance between the need for long range planning, formal contract signing and certainty seeking expressed by certain international partners and the more focused-on-the-moment Argentine mentality.

## PRACTICAL APPLICATIONS

Several practical ideas can be drawn from the leadership profile we delineated above and hopefully they will help newcomers and international travelers interact with Argentine leaders. The first such idea relates to the more blurred lines between professional and personal life that one will find in this country. This characteristic is very common in countries deemed to have a collectivist culture (Hofstede, 1980). In our own study (Friedrich *et al.*, 2006: 65), the results obtained for questions which proxy the construct 'privacy and personal relations', confirmed that Argentines display 'leniency toward personal questions and the roles of different forms of casual and jovial conversation between business dealings'. The score for Argentina was the second highest at 3.05 (and the difference between it and the highest score of Chile was statistically insignificant). Because Argentines tend to see the person behind the employee (for example Pagani has spoken often of the need to foster the development of his employees as people), it is important to allow for social interaction to flourish. Hurried and timed interactions are bound to fail. The international manager can expect to be invited to social events, dinner parties, or even a tango presentation in the city before any further business talks can take place. The Argentine leader may also ask the visitor personal questions about family and life back in his/her country. These questions are not seen as invasion of privacy, but rather as a way to integrate one's personal and business selves. Trompenaars and Hampden-Turner (1997) offer an example of the importance of devoting time to social interaction. They describe how a European company was able to beat an American competitor by scheduling a trip that allowed enough time for personal interaction and even for a fishing trip. In Argentina, having a superior product or a lower price are not guarantees of deal making if the company in question is not willing to give interaction its proper attention.

Connected to the above issue is the establishment of trust. Besides allowing for a personal/professional relationship to thrive, lengthier interactions allow for trust to be established. In an environment where formal contracts mean less than personal trust (because enforcing a contract through legal means is complicated and not always effective), it is not surprising that a leader would choose to get to know his/her partners more extensively before engaging in business dealings. Therefore, personal interactions may have an important dual intent – to get to know a prospective partner better while furthering one's personal relations.

In 1966, Robert Kaplan designed a now ubiquitous table in which he presented the rhetorical style of different discourse communities; for him, while linguistic groups such as the Anglo-Saxon presented a direct style of communication, those individuals with a Romance language background tended to incur in digressions and winding dialogue paths before arriving at the point they wanted to make. Although Kaplan's hypothesis has been revised, amended and otherwise critiqued over the last forty years, his work became seminal in the then newborn field of Contrastive Rhetoric because it pointed to, although in a simplified manner, differences in discourse patterns which could result in clashes in communication. Even if the knowledge we gained from Kaplan's framework does not help us tell Brazilians, Italians and Argentines linguistically apart, it help us understand why an American businessperson might leave Argentina thinking that a business partnership has no future while the Argentine counterpart might remain positive about the next step in negotiations. An illustrative example of this kind of potential miscommunication can be found in the case study *An American Gaucho in Argentina* by Charles A. Rarick (2003). In it, an American businessman travels to Argentina to present a business plan in hopes of establishing a partnership with an Argentine meat producing company. This is what happens at the end of the visit:

> The evening with Jorge and Eduardo was filled with great food, wine, and song. Peter enjoyed the company of the two men and he was able to again discuss his proposal with them. The two men seemed genuinely interested in the ideas, but they stopped short of offering any advice or assessments. Finally Peter asked Eduardo directly why it appeared that the proposal was not being accepted. Eduardo said that there was really not any big problem with the proposal, and that he thought the two companies could in fact work together in the future. Eduardo suggested that he come to Iowa and visit Great Plains and discuss further the prospects for cooperation. While agreeing with Eduardo about the idea of the visit, Peter felt that the business trip was not a success, and that there was little chance that the partnership would materialize. (7)

This excerpt from the case demonstrates several of the communicative patterns discussed in this chapter – the social/business indivisibility, the directness of the American and the indirectness of the Argentine, the short time span necessary for the American to feel comfortable enough to close a deal as opposed to the need for extended contact by the Argentine. As the case shows, in Argentina bluntness and directness will often times be replaced with indirectness and caution in a rhetorical style which often matches the expectations of lengthy interactions before business dealings can take place. Not willing to engage in these interactions can be even seen as an offense; it is as if the person does not deem the relationship important enough to devote time to it. In the end, business interactions as much as social ones are much about context.

In context-oriented cultures such as the Argentine, how you say something is equally important to what you say. On the other hand, not all messages by the leader will be communicated verbally. The person who decides to interact with an Argentine leader might learn about leadership styles through non-verbal statements as well. In an environment where Power Distance is large, one of the ways of asserting leadership is being seemingly unavailable – at least for a while.

Finally, in a country whose citizens take pride in their accomplishments and like to 'massage [...] egos' as Murphy puts it, it is important to recognize not only the achievements of the leaders themselves, but also the beauty and majesty of the country. Those who arrive with some historical and geographical knowledge, who are familiar with aspects of the culture, and who are willing to pay heartfelt compliments to cities such as Buenos Aires, the food, or the music will carve themselves a much greater competitive edge than the ones that are not. And there is certainly much to compliment, from the natural beauty of the land, to the character of the people, a people who surely display a complex nature and who make the adventure of getting to know them really interesting.

## REFERENCES

Aguinis, M. (2001), *El Atroz Encanto de Ser Argentinos*, Editorial Planeta.

Entrevista al Cdor. Luis Pagani, presidente de ARCOR. (2004), Retrieved 07/07, from http://www.undp.org.ar/boletines/Junio2004/notas/nota14.htm

Entrevista a Luis Pagani: Seamos más competitivos para vender (2003), Retrieved 07/07, from http://winred.com/entrevistas/seamos-mas-competitivos-para-vender/gmx-niv100-con2019.htm

Fracchia, E. and Mesquita, L. (2006), Corporate strategy of business groups in the wake of competitive shocks: Lessons from Argentina, *Management Research*, **42**, 81–98.

Fraser, N. and Navarro, M. (1980), *Eva Perón*, New York: W. W. Norton and Company.

Friedrich, P., Mesquita, L. and Hatum, A. (2006), The meaning of difference: Beyond cultural and managerial stereotypes of Latin America, *Management Research*, **41**, 53–71.

Hofstede, G. (1980), *Culture's Consequences: International Differences in Work-Related Values*, Newbury Park, CA: Sage Publications.

House, R. J., Hanges, P. J., Ruiz-Quintanilla, S. A., Dorfman, P. W., Javidan, M., Dickson, M., Gupta, V., *et al.* (1999), Cultural influences on leadership and organizations: Project GLOBE, In W. Mobley, J. Gessner and V. Arnold (eds), *Advances in Global Leadership*, **1**, 171–234. Greenwich, CT: JAI.

House, R. J., Hanges, P. J., Javidan, M., Dorfman, P. W. and Gupta, V. (eds) (2004), *Culture, Leadership, and Organizations: The GLOBE Study of 62 Societies*, Thousand Oaks, CA: Sage Publications.

Kaplan, R. (1966), Cultural thought patters in intercultural education, *Language Learning*, **16**, 1–20.

La Nacion (2007a), Macri delega la gestión y desconoce los ardides, *La Nacion*, online edition, 6-25-07. Retrieved 06/07 http://www.lanacion.com.ar/archivo/nota.asp?nota_id=920368&origen=relacionadas

La Nacion (2007b), Mauricio Macri: Mas alla de la politica, *La Nacion*, online edition, 5-09-07. Retrieved 05/30, 2007, from http://www.lanacion.com.ar/Archivo/nota.asp?nota_id=906842

Lehman, K. (2005), The gaucho as contested national icon in Argentina, In M. E. Geisler (ed), *National Symbols, Fractured Identities: Contesting the National Narrative*, pp. 149–171, Hanover and London: University Press of New England.

McLaren, P. (2000), *Che Guevara, Paulo Freire, and the Pedagogy of Revolution*, New York: Rowman and Littlefield Publishers.

Mesquita, L. (2003), Former Argentine presidential candidate Ricardo Lopez Murphy on rationality as the basis for a new institutional environment, *Academy of Management Executive*, **173**, 45–50.

Murphy, M. (2007), Profile: Mauricio Macri, Retrieved 6/2007, 2007, from http://news.bbc.co.uk/1/hi/world/americas/6222126.stm

Nichols, M. W. (1968), *The Gaucho*, New York: Gordian Press.

Plotkin, M. B. (2003), *Argentina on the Couch: Psychiatry, State, and Society, 1880 to the Present*, Albuquerque, NM: University of New Mexico Press.

Rarick, C. A. (2003), *An American Gaucho in Argentina*, Miami, FL: Barry University.

*To be Evita* (2007), Evita Perón historical research foundation. Retrieved 06/2007 http://www.evitaperon.org/Principal.htm

Todo sobre Arcor (2007), Retrieved May/07, 2007, from http://www.arcor.com.ar/front/App/institucional/tpl_quienes.asp?snpt=t_historia.html

Trompenaars, F. and Hampden-Turner, C. (1997), *Riding the Waves of Culture: Understanding Diversity in Global Business* (2nd ed), New York: McGraw-Hill.

# 5. Cultural mythology and global leadership in Brazil

## Adriana V. Garibaldi de Hilal

### INTRODUCTION

Brazil is the only country in the Western hemisphere that has the continental proportions, the regional contrasts and the demographic diversity that can be compared to the US and Canada.

According to Hess (1995), Brazil, in spite of its Western-like institutions, is a country where Western culture has mixed and mingled with non-Western cultures for centuries. This mixture of Western and non-Western, as well as modern and traditional is what DaMatta (1997a) has called the 'Brazilian dilemma', or what Brazilians call the Brazilian reality. Brazil is a country where institutions operate through personal relationships as much as general rules. Diversity is not the best word for describing Brazil and Brazilians; mixture is better. Brazil is a nation of the mixing of races (miscegenation), religions (syncretism) and cultures (diasporas, borderlands).

In cultural anthropology and studies of Brazilian national culture, DaMatta (1997a; 1997b) has influenced a number of scholars (such as, David Hess, 1995; Livia Neves Barbosa, 1995; Rosane Prado, 1995; Martha de Ulhoa Carvalho, 1995; and Roberto Kant de Lima, 1995) with his framework for interpreting Brazilian culture.

Hess (1995) describes Brazil as the product of a particular colonial legacy that includes a class of wealthy landowners who supported a highly centralized Portuguese state. In turn, the state implanted a *latifundia* or plantation agricultural system in Brazil, where plantations were controlled by patriarchs who exercised a nearly absolute authority over their dominions. According to Buarque de Holanda (1995), the colonial legacy also includes the origins of the traditional Latin American *personalism,* the lack of social cohesion and the looseness of the institutions. Additionally, the Tocquevillian legacy of comparative analysis influenced a number of twentieth-century thinkers such as Louis Dumont (1980). Dumont's comparative studies focused on two key dimensions for comparing values and patterns of social relations across societies: 'hierarchy and equality', and 'holism and individualism'.

In the ascribed form of hierarchy used by Dumont, one's social position is assigned at birth or is limited by one's family position. In a traditional hierarchical society, laws apply differently to different groups of people. Of course, there are remnants of the ascribed kind of hierarchy even in the most modern of societies, but the legal recognition of such hierarchy is considered an affront to the fundamental value of equality.

The concepts of holism and individualism are closely related to those of hierarchy and equality. In a hierarchical society everyone occupies a definite position in the whole, and people's identity is rooted in their association with a particular position in society.

DaMatta's approach to Brazilian culture departs from these key concepts as developed by Dumont. DaMatta uses the term 'persons' to describe the category of identity, in which one is defined by one's position in the family or in a hierarchically ordered social group. In contrast, in an individualistic society identity is rooted in one's own life history and choices and people are individuals linked by the rules of the game, which are assumed to apply equally to all (or universally). Although in an individualistic society people certainly have personalistic loyalties, one's identity as an individual rather than as a person tends to prevail. Likewise, in a personalistic or relational society, there are domains of society that operate according to individualistic and egalitarian principles, but in general, personal loyalties tend to prevail.

DaMatta argues that Brazil is somewhere between the two ideal polar extremes (hierarchical and holistic, and egalitarian and individualistic). He rejects the model of two Brazils, in which a traditional culture located in the lower classes of the cities and in the rural areas is opposed to a modern Brazil in the upper classes and in the big cities, showing how in societies like Brazil, Dumont's distinctions can be applied simultaneously throughout the society. Instead of working with an 'either or' model, he opted for a 'both and' model, as both tendencies are present in any number of social groups, institutions and practices. Thus, Brazilians are constantly negotiating between a modern, egalitarian code and a traditional one. In some situations, modern practices predominate. However, frequently, hierarchical and personalistic/relational practices encompass modern ones.

Thus, Brazil is neither modern nor traditional but both, as in Brazil there is a tendency to move toward a middle ground of mediation and ambiguity, where myths make the transition between apparently different or even contradictory worlds. For example, the injustices of the Brazilian authoritarian and hierarchical system are blunted by the existence of a number of mediating institutions: extended kin networks, nepotism, the famous Brazilian *jeitinho* (the art of bending rules), and all sorts of social practices that would appear corrupt in North America and Western Europe. In short, personal relationships form the flip side of official hierarchies. Personalism is more than a cultural system that gives people a social address in the hierarchical society; it is also a resource that people can use to get around the official rules of the hierarchical society. Of course, personalism does not work the same way for everyone. The networks of the weak are usually smaller and less influential. As a result, although personalism can be used as a resource to subvert hierarchy, as an overall system it ends up reproducing the general hierarchical order (Hess, 1995).

## OVERVIEW OF BRAZILIAN CULTURE MYTHS

A myth, like a parable or an allegory, is a traditional story that embodies popular belief or phenomena. Like dreams, myths have the ability to resolve ambiguities and conflicts; they encourage rites and ritual. Indeed, myth is to ritual as music is to dance (Furnham, 1996).

Myths are one of the ways in which a society mirrors its contradictions, expresses its paradoxes and doubts. They can be considered as a possibility to reflect about existence or about social relationships. Myths are diffuse and multiple. They mean many things, represent several ideas and can be used in different contexts (Rocha, 1985).

But, myths are not any kind of narrative. They are a special kind of narrative, one that is a tradition in itself. Myths are not objective; they hide something, something without reality, or, in other words, a lie. Nevertheless, myths operate at the social level. Consequently, their truth should be found in another level, even in another logic. Myths have to be interpreted; myths are part of existence (Rocha, 1985).

In Brazil, mediation myths become sites for the conflict of values and the encompassment of the modern by the traditional.

### Myth of Equality (Versus Hierarchy): the Carnival Rite (DaMatta, 1997b)

Carnival, a three day long yearly rite, is perceived as being the property of everybody, as a moment when a hierarchically traditional society decentralizes. In a hierarchically ordered society, such as Brazilian society, when hierarchy is suspended, the myth of equality materializes in the parade of the samba schools, mixing the poor and millionaires, football and TV stars. The parade is an exotic symbol of luxury as it is anchored in an aristocratic and mythical period, as perceived by the members of the dominated classes (the poor, usually Negroes and *Mulatos*). Carnival shows an inversion between the poor who take part in the parade, and the mythical figures they represent (kings, nobles, heroes), with the direct or indirect participation of all society.

In this controlled popular rite, the rich (dominating classes) are not seen as rich (with money, status symbols and power), but as nobles, with the aristocratic virtues of nobility. The social positions of everyday life are neutralized or inverted giving the myth of equality a semblance of reality.

Carnival costumes create a social field for encounter, for mediation, where the frontiers that separate groups, categories and people are suspended. There is a place for all kinds of people, characters and groups, for all values. It is an open social field situated out of the hierarchical reality; it is a world of metaphor where everyday social rules are temporarily suspended.

Carnival invents its own social space, with its own rules and logic. That space is an inverted image of the 'real world' and basically confirms it. However, it also represents an alternative model for collective behavior, mainly because it is the arena where new avenues of social relationship, normally conceived as mythical utopias, are tested.

### Myth of the Dual Social Domains: the Home and the Street (DaMatta, 1997a)

The space of the home is identified with the hierarchical and relational/personalistic moral world, whereas that of the street is egalitarian and individualistic. Of course, in Brazil, the two worlds of home and street interact considerably.

As a social space, the home, and institutions modeled on the home, such as the workplace, is a place where relations among family members and servants or among superiors and subordinates institute hierarchies of race, class, age and gender. The home is the place of the in group, of family and friends.

The street is a different sort of place where those hierarchies are suspended. The street is the place where the egalitarian and individualistic principles of the marketplace or legal system are in operation. The street is a semi-unknown domain where danger prevails, where there are no precise contractual relations.

The home is the place where people find their identity, while the street is the place of individual anonymity. In certain situations the home encompasses the street and all matters are treated in a personal, familiar domestic way; in others, the street encompasses the home: the domain of personal relations is totally submersed and the axis of impersonal laws and rules prevails. There is, therefore, a double-edged ethic that operates simultaneously and that determines different behaviors that apply to the street (where behavior is free of the sense of loyalty, free of the meaning of us, ruled by the criteria of individualism, by laws and by the rules of the market) and to the home (where behavior is ruled by personal relations, the sense of loyalty and emotions, by reciprocity and friendship).

In brief, in a dynamic sense, behaviors continually oscillate in Brazil:

people can express apparently different or even contradictory opinions and behaviors depending on whether they position themselves in the street or in the home.

## Myth of the Conflict Averse Society: the 'Do You Know who You are Talking to?' Rite (DaMatta, 1997b)

The 'Do you know who you are talking to?' rite implies a radical authoritarian separation of two real social positions. It places Brazilians on the side of hierarchical scales that they think should not be externalized, as 'everyone should know their place'. The 'Do you know who you are talking to?' expression is considered part of the real world, a resource activated in the domain of the street.

The 'Do you know who you are talking to?' expression, usually followed by: I am so and so; or the wife of so and so; or the son of so and so; or even the friend of so and so, is not exclusive of any social segment or class. On the contrary, the expression seems to allow identification by means of social projection, when a subordinate uses it to take the place of his superior, acting in certain circumstances as if he was the superior himself, and thus placing another individual, who would normally be his equal, in a situation of inferiority.

That authoritarian expression always indicates a conflictive situation, and Brazilian society perceives itself as conflict averse. It does not mean that such perception eliminates conflict; on the contrary, like all hierarchical societies, Brazilian society has a high level of conflict and crises. But, between the existence of conflict and its acknowledgement there is a great distance. In Brazil, conflict tends to be perceived as 'the end of the world' and as weakness. Thus, historically, dominant groups always adopt a perspective of solidarity, while the dominated ones systematically defend the position of revealing the conflict in the system. Actually, in a world that has to move according to a hierarchy that has to be perceived as natural, conflict tends to be considered an irregularity. The world has to move in terms of absolute harmony, fruit of a system dominated by hierarchy that leads to a profound agreement between the strong and the weak (Dumont, 1980).

In such an environment, conflict cannot be considered as a critical symptom of the system, but as revolt that has to be repressed. Thus, conflict is personally circumscribed and the system is maintained.

## Myth of the Worker (Versus the Adventurer) (Buarque de Holanda, 1995)

In the forms of collective life there are two principles that regulate in different ways the activities of men and that are represented by the worker and the adventurer. The ideal of the adventurer is to collect the fruit without having to plant the tree. The worker, on the other hand, is the one who first sees the difficulties to be overcome, not the prize to win.

There is an ethic of work and one of adventure. Thus, the worker will only attribute positive moral value to the actions he feels the will to practice, and will consider immoral the qualities of the adventurer (audacity, improvidence, irresponsibility, instability). On the other hand, the energy and effort invested to have immediate reward are valued by the adventurer, while, for him, nothing is more senseless than the ideal of the worker. Both types exist in multiple combinations, although, in their pure state they do not exist out of the world of ideas.

In the colonization of Brazil, the worker had a very limited role, almost null. The desire for prosperity without cost, for easily acquired wealth, characteristic of Portuguese people are clear traits of the adventurer. Thus, those same traits favored the adaptation and flexibility that were necessary conditions during the colonization period, with intensive use of slave labor, latifundia and monoculture.

## Myth of the Cordial Man (Buarque de Holanda, 1995)

Wherever the idea of family lies on a solid basis, and mainly, where the patriarchal type of family predominates, the formation and evolution of society according to modern concepts tend to be precarious and face strong restrictions. The adaptation crisis of individuals to the social mechanism is, thus, especially sensitive due to the triumph of certain antifamily virtues, such as those based on the spirit of personal initiative and of competition among individuals.

In Brazil, where, since ancient times, the primitive type of patriarchal family has prevailed, the development of urbanization (that does not exclusively derive from the growth of cities, but also from the expansion of means of communication, attracting vast rural areas to the sphere of influence of cities) produced strong social disequilibrium.

In Brazil, only exceptionally has there been an administrative system and a body of public officers dedicated only to objective interests. On the contrary, history shows us the constant predominance of particular interests fostered in closed circles not really adequate to impersonal ordination. Among those circles, the family was, undoubtedly, the one with stronger expression in Brazilian society. The family, in Brazil, is the unquestionable sphere of primary contacts, of blood bonds and of the heart. The relationships created in domestic life always provided the obligatory model of any social composition. This happens even where democratic institutions, based on neutral and abstract principles, try to establish a society built according to anti-particularistic rules.

The cordial man, where hospitality and generosity are virtues recognized by the foreigners who visit Brazil, represents a clear trait of Brazilian character that denotes the ancestral influence of social patterns derived from the patriarchal culture.

The standardization of external forms of cordiality is equivalent to a disguise that allows individuals to protect their sensibility and emotions. In general, Brazilians accept reverence formulas with a superior, but only while they do not completely suppress the possibility of a more familiar relationship.

The ignorance of any kind of relationship that is not ruled by an emotionally based ethic represents an aspect of Brazilian life that few foreigners can easily grasp.

### Myth 'Foreign is Better' (Caldas, 1997)

The myth that foreign is better and that the solution comes from abroad is strongly set in Brazilian culture. With the flexibility and adaptability that they possess, Brazilians first privileged Lisbon, to then change it for Paris and London, and finally, for the United States. Brazilians tend to look for solutions abroad, importing concepts without much adaptation or resistance, without stopping to seriously consider local reality and specificities, as if this behavior was an unavoidable sign of modernity.

For Wood Jr. (1997), Brazilians appear to feel an ancestral need to have somebody to guide them, to decide for them. According to Caligaris (1993), this need for external or paternal references indicates that Brazilians need something that tells them where to go, and at the same time, something that allows them to disobey such indication, something that they can despise and blame when their actions demand a reason for failure. The myth of foreign is better serves this purpose of both cult and repulse and, if it can be considered as an archetypical construction of Brazilian imaginary, it is undoubtedly a convenient one.

## OVERVIEW OF BRAZILIAN LEADERSHIP

The study of how culture affects organizational behavior has been the focus of recent research (Hofstede, 1980; Laurent, 1981 among others) and considerable difference has been found in the values, attitudes and behaviors of individuals in the work environment. The behaviors of leaders and workers are based on beliefs, attitudes and values that are strongly influenced by their national cultures (Prestes Motta, 1997).

The study by Geert Hofstede (1980; 2001) initially involved 40 countries and then was expanded to 60 to include both oriental and occidental cultures. Hofstede, as well as Laurent, found significant differences in the behavior and attitudes of executives and workers of different countries, and those differences have proved to be consistent in time. Hofstede's most important finding resides in the importance of national culture to explain differences in attitudes and work related values. He identified four independent dimensions of culture differences: power distance, uncertainty avoidance, individualism versus collectivism and masculinity versus femininity.

According to Hofstede (2001), an unequal distribution of power over members is the essence of organizations, as such inequality is essential for control and for temporarily overcoming the law of entropy, which states that disorder will increase (Cotta, 1976). In most utilitarian organizations the distribution of power is formalized in hierarchies. In the relationship between leader and subordinate both objective and subjective factors play roles.

Organizations, according to Hofstede (2001), use technology, rules and rituals to cope with uncertainty. Rules are the way in which organizations reduce the internal uncertainty caused by the unpredictability of their members' and stakeholders' behavior. Rules are semirational: they try to make the behavior of people predictable, and as people are both rational and nonrational, rules should take account of both aspects. The authority of rules is something different from the authority of persons. The first relates conceptually to uncertainty avoidance; the second to power distance. Rituals serve social as well as uncertainty avoidance purposes. The former keep people together; the latter try to control the future.

The norm prevalent in a given society as to the degree of individualism or collectivism expected from its members will strongly affect the nature of the relationship between a person and the organization to which he or she belongs. More collectivistic societies call for greater emotional dependence of members on their organizations. The level of individualism or collectivism in society will affect the organization's members' reasons for complying with organizational requirements. The level of individualism or collectivism in a society will also affect the types of persons (locals versus cosmopolitans) who will be admitted into positions of leadership in organizations. The local type is largely preoccupied with problems inside the organization and is most influential in a collectivistic culture. The cosmopolitan type is more influential in organizations with an individualistic culture and considers him or herself an integral part of the world outside it (Hofstede, 2001).

National culture differences along the masculinity/femininity dimension affect the meaning of work in people's lives. Between the two poles of living in order to work and working in order to live, masculine cultures are closer to the first and feminine cultures are closer to the second. The concerns for relationships and life quality in feminine cultures and for material rewards, performance and competition in masculine cultures are carried over from the family and school to the work environment. Masculine and feminine cultures create different leader types. The masculine leader is assertive, decisive and aggressive (only in masculine societies does this word carry a positive connotation). The leader in a feminine culture is less visible, intuitive rather than decisive, and accustomed to seeking consensus (Hofstede, 2001).

According to Hofstede (2001), Brazil is a collectivistic society, although its ranking does not place it among the most collectivistic, which happens to be Guatemala. Brazil also ranks among the nations where uncertainty avoidance and power distance are higher. In terms of the masculinity/femininity dimension, Brazil can be classified as feminine although quite close to the masculine side of the continuum, which in fact indicates a not very clear position in this dimension.

Another way of looking at Brazilian culture is through the lens of football. DaMatta (1994) draws a parallel between football and Brazilian culture and leadership. Football, for Brazilians, is a synonym of passion; a kind of passion that cannot be verbally explained, but that belongs to the universe of things that are related to the spirit. Football reveals many of the characteristics of Brazilian culture, such as the tendency to carnivalization, with the temporary suppression of hierarchy where mainly Negroes and *Mulatos* are heroes. It also contributes to the idea of exclusive collectivity, such as the home or the family, in a modern dimension where, on one hand, there is a sense of collectivity (the home, the team) and, on the other hand, there are individuals with universal rules (the street, the football rules). The Brazilian people see themselves in football; they learn lessons of democracy, of equality and of respect for rules. In contrast, Brazilian football also openly institutionalized the Brazilian *jeitinho* as the art of surviving and as the national style (DaMatta, 1994). In this sense, the *jeitinho* represents Brazilian warmth and flexibility even as it exerts a corrupting force on Brazil's modern institutions (Neves Barbosa, 1995).

According to Sevcenko (1994) football is one of the main vehicles, in Brazil, of the popular manifestation of affection and passion. The cordial man, product of the contradiction of the patriarchal society with modern capitalism, found in football the ideal base to express its extremely rich emotional side; a side that conflicts with the bureaucratic impersonality of organizational structures and, in many ways, defines the Brazilian leadership style.

Brazilian research (Arruda, s.d., no date; Prestes Motta, 1997; Garibaldi de Hilal, 2006; among others) indicates that in Brazilian organizations, leaders are usually actively involved in the decision process, which requires intense social interaction. Brazilian leaders are generally considered autocratic with traits of paternalism. Hierarchical authority, as well as the intensive communication that takes place at work or after work, seems to guarantee the agility and speed of the decision process, although research also suggests that leaders tend to decide based on the information at hand, even if the content is poor.

Brazilian organizations generally denote such high power distance that it reminds us of the Brazilian inequality in terms of income distribution and of its slave labor past. The core of Brazilian culture was the sugar plantation, where plantations were controlled by patriarchs who exercised a nearly absolute authority over their dominions. In such an environment, social distance was the counterpart of physical proximity and the ambiguity of the social relations was inevitable (Freyre, 1981). Nepotism is a common practice in Brazilian organizations (Prestes Motta, 1997) and Brazilian leaders represent a society that is not close to the universalistic and entrepreneurial society of Talcott Parsons (1964).

Brazilian leaders tend to treat their followers based on masculine type controls, on the use of authority as well as on feminine type controls, on the use of seduction (Prestes Motta, 1997). In general, democratic values are not very strong in Brazilian organizations. However, if it is not democracy, it is not autocracy either, but something in between, ambiguous, as many Brazilian cultural traits.

In Brazil, ambiguity favors alternative leadership options that include creativity and innovation, but also perpetuate the figure of the godfather (or protector within the organization based not on meritocracy but on personal bonds), the preference for informal social relationships, the famous Brazilian *jeitinho* (the art of bending rules) and the intense expression of emotions. Brazil is a land of contrasts, where leadership reflects both sides of this contradictory world: the characteristics of individualism, rationality and capitalism on one side, and the characteristics of a patriarchal culture with its tradition, affection and personalism, on the other.

Garibaldi de Hilal (2002) studied a large Brazilian bank with international operations. Results suggested that leadership was based on hierarchical authority supported by a set of clearly defined norms and rules, but where the authority of the leaders prevailed over the rules. Garibaldi de Hilal (2002) identified two apparently contradictory aspects that legitimize leadership in Brazil: the relational aspect and the Caxias aspect (Caxias was a Brazilian general known for his efficiency, dedication and commitment to work). The relational aspect would be supported by the myth of the home (DaMatta, 1997a), while the Caxias aspect would privilege commitment, efficiency and meritocracy. This paradox would symbolize a potential source of conflict that embodies the difficulties faced by Brazilian leaders in order to develop practices sanctioned by all, as they would frequently be led to violate one of the two aspects that legitimize Brazilian leadership. Moreover, in the Brazilian chain of social relationships, there is the belief according to which, once people are positioned in the network of personal bonds, they are automatically treated as friends and become a potential source of power for social and political manipulation by means of favor (DaMatta, 1997a).

The quotations in the Commentary box illustrate Brazilian views about the role of the leader.

---

## COMMENTARY BOX

### Top Manager of a Large Brazilian Bank with International Operations

The role of the leader, in Brazil, is an ambiguous one. It is the role of socialized autocracy with strong traits of paternalism, where the leader is also hostage of the group as he only becomes legitimate in his relationship with the group.

### President of a Large Energy Distribution Company

If a leader is openly authoritarian he is hated; if he is paternalistic he can be loved. We have participative rituals, but that is relative. Participative rituals are necessary because, although nobody dares contradict the leader, without them the leader cannot implement anything and has to deal with great resistance to change.

### Director of a Large Brazilian State Owned Company

Conflicts are not managed in this company. Conflict resolution can lead to opposing factions in the group. The role of the leader is that of a peacemaker so things are never clearly defined … The leader has simultaneously to command and seduce.

### Superintendent of a Large Brazilian State Owned Company

In a relational culture such as Brazilian culture, leaders have to consider the expectations of their followers, and one of the relational assumptions is that for the in-group members anything may be possible; while for outsiders the law applies.

---

# PRACTICAL APPLICATIONS

A work of this nature has great risk for oversimplification and generalization for which many exceptions can be found. Nevertheless, keeping in mind the need to avoid stereotyping, the mistake of assuming that every Brazilian leader conforms to the profile presented in this chapter, foreigners can understand behaviors driven by Brazilian culture dimensions and myths and adapt their behaviors to perform effectively in the Brazilian cultural setting.

Most management models and leadership theories have been developed in the United States, and have been conceived in the context of its dominant cultural values. For example, had Frederick Herzberg, in developing his well-known two factor, job-enrichment model, studied Brazilian culture, it is very unlikely that he would have found that personal relationships were not a motivator. In fact, it was this very question of the applicability to other cultures of American management practices that lies at the heart of Hofstede's research (2001).

A leadership style consistent with McGregor's (1960) Theory X is based on assumptions that workers require thorough supervision, explicit direction, and coercion and derive little satisfaction from their work in and of itself but only from the sustenance and security it provides. This authoritarian style would seem clearly out of place in cultures with small power distance (Scarborough, 2001). Conversely, Theory Y assumptions, which hold that workers are motivated best by responsibility, autonomy, trust, and a more open, communicative environment, seem ill-suited for large power distance cultures, such as Brazilian culture. However, Adler (1991) suggests that the Y theory is well suited to those cultures because workers share common interests among themselves and with management and value relationships that are the collectivistic/relational values that often coincide with large power distance. Workers in large power distance cultures would still expect their leaders to make the decisions, clarify expectations, and demonstrate strength and technical proficiency, but, in relational Brazil, *personalism* and ambiguity suggest the applicability of a leadership style also consistent with Theory Y, at least with respect to the leader's assumptions about worker motivation.

In the collectivistic/relational Brazilian culture, leaders have to take into account in-group membership in hiring, promotion and disciplinary decisions as individuals may feel compelled to act in the interests of the group when those interests conflict with those of the employer. In Brazil, leaders have to communicate in ways that do not cause loss of face within the in-group, and shame will be a more effective control device than guilt. In Brazil, relationships are paramount, even at the cost of breaking rules in order to promote and maintain the personal network.

The key to encouraging participation or just greater willingness to speak up, among large power distance subordinates is to build trust (Scarborough,

2001). In Brazil, it is important for a leader to let his subordinates know what is needed from them and why, and there should be an explanation that this is the preferred kind of relationship. Then patience, maintaining a low key, and repeated requests for input will be called for. In relational Brazil, leaders must understand that as Brazilians see themselves as a cordial and conflict averse society, there might be a tendency to accept a problem as is, rather than solve it, in effect denying the need for a decision. The belief in the conflict avoidance and in the cordial man myths may also cause a search for familiar solutions rather than innovative ones.

In terms of cross-cultural management, some personal traits or skills necessary to engage effectively with Brazilian leaders include open-mindedness, patience, flexibility to adapt considering the local reality, humility, consideration and good manners, to search for common ground rather than conflicting positions, the desire to build lasting relationships rather than to merely collect acquaintances and customers, and demonstrating some interest in matters beyond the business at hand and business in general.

Brazilian leaders are expected to be charismatic and value based but are also known for personalism, particularism and paternalism. Rule of law is often moderated by personal connections and the concepts of in-group and out-group are very strong. Temporal, geographical and cultural complexities separate the domestic role of the leader from its global context role. To be effective in the global context Brazilian leaders have to be aware of their cultural foundations, expect to encounter cultural differences, educate themselves about different cultures, be flexible about the existence of other patterns of logic, experience cross-cultural interactions and learn from them.

Human societies are certainly diverse, but once differences are discovered, one must show how one difference can be turned into another, that is, one must go back over the road, retracting it inversely. Otherwise, all that is left is a catalog of mutually inaccessible human experiences. If the concepts of culture, leadership and tradition are not seen as dynamic, they merely freeze differences and screen out an understanding of reality (Da Matta, 1995).

Thus, we can conclude that one's behavior and conduct in a foreign setting are even more important than the ability to speak the host's language; that, if one can manage successfully in one cultural environment, the same is possible in another, provided that one understands the different cultural rules and myths and learns from experience.

# REFERENCES

Adler, N. (1991), *International Dimensions of Organizational Behavior*, Belmont, CA: Wadswoth.

Arruda, C. s.d. (no date), *Bases culturais do processo de decisao estrategica*, Belo Horizonte: Fundação Dom Cabral.

Buarque De Holanda, S. (1995), *Raízes do Brasil*, São Paulo: Companhia das Letras.

Caldas, M. (1997), *Santo de Casa Não Faz Milagre. Em: Cultura organizacional e cultura brasileira*, Sao Paulo: Editora Atlas, pp 73–93.

Caligaris, C. (1993), *Hello Brazil! Notas de um psicanalista europeu viajando ao Brasil*, São Paulo: Escuta.

Cotta, A. (1976), 'An analysis of power processes in organizations', in G. H. Hofstede and M. S. Kassem (eds), *European Contributions to Organization Theory*, Netherlands: Van Gorcum, pp 174–92.

Da Matta, R.. (1994), A antropologia do óbvio, *Revista da USP*, 22 (10-17). Sao Paulo: USP jun/ago 94

Da Matta, R. (1995), For an anthropology of the Brazilian tradition or 'a virtude está no meio', in D. Hess and R. Da Matta (eds), *The Brazilian Puzzle*, New York: Columbia University Press, pp 270–91.

Da Matta, R. (1997a), *A Casa & a Rua: Espaço, Cidadania, Mulher e Morte no Brasil*, Rio de Janeiro: Editora Guanabara.

Da Matta, R. (1997b), *Carnavais, Malandros e Heróis: Para uma Sociologia do Dilema Brasileiro*, Rio de Janeiro: Rocco.

Dumont, L. (1966; 1980), *Homo Hierarchicus: The Caste System and its Implications*, Chicago, IL: The University of Chicago Press.

Etzioni, A. (1975), *A Comparative Analysis of Complex Organizations: On Power, Involvement and their Correlates*, New York: Free Press.

Freyre, G. (1981), *Casa grande e Senzala,* Rio de Janeiro: Jose Olympio.

Furnham, A. (1996), *The Myths of Management*, London: Whurr Publishers.

Garibaldi de Hilal, A. (2002), *Dimensoes e clusters de cultura organizacional de uma empresa brasileira com atuaçao internacional*, Doctoral Dissertation. Rio de Janeiro: Coppead/ Federal University of Rio de Janeiro.

Garibaldi de Hilal, A. (2006), Brazilian national culture, organizational culture and cultural agreement: Findings from a multinational company, *International Journal of Cross Cultural Management*, London: Sage Publications, pp 139–67.

Hess, D. (1995), Introduction, in D. Hess and R. Da Matta (eds), *The Brazilian Puzzle*, New York: Columbia University Press, pp 1–30.

Hofstede, G. (1980 / 2001), *Culture's Consequences* (1st and 2nd edn), London: Sage Publications.

Kant De Lima, R. (1995), Bureaucratic rationality in Brazil and in the United States: criminal justice systems in comparative perspective, in D. Hess and R. Da Matta (eds), *The Brazilian Puzzle*, New York: Columbia University Press, pp 241–69.

Laurent, A. (1981), The cultural diversity of western conceptions of management, *International Studies of Management and Organization*, **13** (1–2), 75–96.

McGregor, D. (1960), *The Human Side of Enterprise*, New York: McGraw-Hill.

Neves Barbosa, L. (1995), The Brazilian jeitinho: an exercise in national identity, in D. Hess and R. Da Matta (eds), *The Brazilian Puzzle,* New York: Columbia University Press, pp 35–48.

Parsons, T. (1964), *The Social System*, New York: Free Press.

Prado, R. (1995), Small town Brazil: heaven and hell of personalism, in D. Hess and R. Da Matta (eds), *The Brazilian Puzzle*, New York: Columbia University Press, pp 59–84.

Prestes Motta, F. (1997), *Cultura e Organizações no Brasil. Em: Cultura organizacional e cultura brasileira*, Sao Paulo: Editora Atlas, pp 27–37.

Prestes Motta, F. and Caldas, M. (1997), *Cultura organizacional e cultura brasileira*, Sao Paulo: Editora Atlas.

Rocha, E. (1985), *O que é mito. Editora,* Sao Paulo: Brasiliense.

Romani, L. and Zander, L. (1998), Individualism and collectivism. A critical review and attempts to refine the concepts with a holistic approach, *IIB*, Stockholm School of Economics.

Scarborough, J. (2001), *The Origin of Cultural Differences and their Impact on Management*, London: Quorum Books.

Sevcenko, N. (1994), Futebol, metrópoles e desatinos, *Revista da USP*, **22**, 30–37. Sao Paulo: USP jun/ago 94.

Triandis, H. (1995), *Individualism and Collectivism*, San Francisco: Westview Press.

Ulhoa Carvalho, M. (1995), Tupi or not Tupi MPB: popular music and identity in Brazil, in D. Hess and R. Da Matta (eds), *The Brazilian Puzzle*, New York: Columbia University Press, pp 159–69.

Wood Jr., T. (1997), 'For the English to see': the importation of managerial technology in late 20th century Brazil, *Organization*, **4**, pp 4–15.

# PART II

# Europe

# 6. Cultural mythology and global leadership in Greece

## Theodore Peridis

## INTRODUCTION

Few would quibble with the assertion that some of the greatest stories ever told of how the world and the creatures in it came to be in their present form, have been handed down to us from the ancient Greeks. The stories of great heroes, who fought overwhelming odds and defeated formidable enemies, slaughtered atrocious monsters and overcame great adversities, have inspired generations of people to pursue laudable goals and achieve greatness. Greeks even gave us the word to describe those ostensibly historical events that capture the imaginary dealings of gods, demigods and legendary heroes. Myths narrate a people's popular view of how practices, events, and phenomena unfolded. Mythology, the telling and re-telling of these traditional stories, as well as the systematic collection, study and interpretation of myths have engaged both literary and historical scholars for centuries, for the myths do reveal a wealth of insights about the people that nurtured those stories.

Greek mythology offers us a tremendously fertile ground of fabulous stories and a fascinating window into the culture and the psychology of the Greeks. The 12 Olympian gods, the demigods, and the innumerable heroes, their deeds, labours, and achievements, their passions and indiscretions, their journeys, battles, and conflicts reveal a people that drew on tremendous imagination and rich artistic genetic material, but also reflect how Greeks come to terms with human pain and suffering, their inability to understand, and a genuine attempt to explain why the world is just 'not fair'.

Myths reflect and are reflected in a society's deep cultural and spiritual values. Myths are shaped to tell how the world came to be, how the gods made choices about the way things unfolded, and how situations influenced momentous events. Myths help explain phenomena that could not be comprehended by the prevailing knowledge and understanding. As such, they describe the unfolding of events in a way that people will not only find palatable, but also accept, which essentially requires that myths reflect people's values and beliefs. At the same time, myths help shape the society's values as they remind people of those in the past that were rewarded and those that were punished, who did well and who did poorly, who was favoured and who was chastised for their actions.

While one can readily allow for such connections between the culture of classical Greece and its mythology, it is easy also to see how those stories are indeed, reflections of the fabric that created both their ancient predecessors and the current inhabitants of that beautiful, sun-drenched land. While the modern Greek may not enjoy the world renown of his ancestors, and some may even challenge the fact that a direct connection could still exist after more than 25 centuries, it is simply stunning to see the similarities that are embedded in the values of the ancient Greek myths and readily manifest themselves in today's Greece, a modern European society.

This mutually reinforcing relationship between myths and the culture that has given rise to them is critical to understanding the insights we can pierce into a society's psychic through the study of its mythology and from reading between the proverbial lines of its oral traditions. Most relevant, since culture shapes the dominant forms of behaviour within a society, one will reasonably expect that the characters of those that lead within any given society, will be heavily coloured by the culture that dominates that society and will be abundantly displayed in its mythology.

Greek myths present innumerable examples of leadership as well as leaders and heroes who commanded such leadership. House *et al.* (2004) define a leader as someone who can influence, motivate and enable others to contribute towards the success of an organization or community of which they are members. Certainly, we can identify with Prometheus, Daidalos, and Theseus[1] as leaders that inspired people to act for the betterment of their communities. Consistent with House's definition, the numerous myths instruct us that gods and heroes exert themselves towards noble goals and use their positions, intelligence, skills and power not only to achieve greatness but to persuade others of the virtue of such labours.

Yet, even the all powerful gods face limits to their powers. Influence, motivation and example are not always sufficient to lead and enable others to contribute to the same cause; more critically, in Greek mythology there is no such thing as absolute control. Mighty Zeus faces the wrath and the machinations of other gods. Frequently, his wishes do not prevail. He often resorts to cajoling humans and gods to work his ways and achieve his aims. Greeks do not have 'superheroes' of the kind one can find in other traditions; their heroes and their leaders even the divine ones, are limited in their capacity to control what happens.

But Greeks also accept the fact that one cannot question the power of those in charge and the decisions, whether capricious or noble, made by those from above. Hofstede (1980; 1991) places Greece at the middle of the pack on the power distance dimension, far below the uncompromising stance towards authority that Israelis and some western Europeans exhibit or those people's confidence in questioning authority and its decisions. Greeks seem to accept and expect that individuals may pose and exercise power, not always in the interest of those below. Moreover, those below may not always be able to influence the decisions and actions of those in charge. Power distance refers to the extent to which the less powerful members of a society accept and expect that power should be distributed unequally. Hofstede notes that this represents inequality defined from below, not from above and reflects the society's acceptance of such unequal distribution of power within institutions and organizations. Power distance relates to acceptance of hierarchy and the resignation to a reality that those above can and will exercise power, whether justified, just and fair or not, over those below them.

These insights illuminate the complexity of the psychology of leadership and the muddled character of the leader within Greek mythology and Greek society. Unlike our contemporary typologies of leadership, which typically demarcate two extremes of the superhero and the toxic leader (see Drucker, 1967; Kets de Vries and Miller, 1985; Kets de Vries, 2004), we see much more complex and conflicting prototypes that defy classification and do not allow us to easily proclaim pure types of leadership. The hero of ancient Greece cannot be easily placed in neat categories, but not just because he exhibits a complex personality. There is much of that undeniably, within every one of the fine specimens of the genre. More so, heroes in Greek mythology are very human, have major flaws, are inconsistent, can be proud and brave in one instance and petty and small in the next.

So, how can one make sense of what leadership meant in ancient Greece and what the myths about those gods, heroes and leaders were supposed to tell, what values were they intended to inspire and what behaviours to encourage? The following sections attempt to answer those questions. Through the next few pages, our intent is to critically but selectively review the Greek mythology with an eye to be instructed by the richness of the personalities it reveals, the complexity of the people it captures and the humanity of the main characters. Put together, they illuminate the intricacies of leadership and speak volumes of how Greeks saw human life and the meaning of our existence.

Before proceeding though, a few words of caution are in order. It is rather difficult to attempt to summarize the vast assortment of myths that the ancient Greeks weaved so extensively into their stories. Sometimes it is difficult to even separate the myths from history, as we have come to realize with the discoveries of archaeological sites where there was supposed to be only a mythical Troy or Mycenae (Boardman *et al.*, 1986). We have found evidence of bull sports in the great palace complexes of Knossos in Crete that gave rise to the myths of the Labyrinth and the Minotaur. Moreover, as one can expect from different accounts of specific myths, not unlike historical events, different reporters and story tellers have chosen to emphasize different perspectives, tell the unfolding of events from a different angle and give different interpretations of what happened (Griffin, 1980). If this is true once for history, it is ten times reflective of any myth. What supposedly happened varies from description to description, likely because the story teller was in a different context, reflected different morals, different situations, and wanted to be heard and applauded by different audiences with very different tastes. Twenty-seven centuries later, Margaret Atwood (1986) said that 'context is all' to remind us that neither history nor truth can be safely considered universal.

Compounding the above, our modern accounts of the ancient Greek myths are at best biased interpretations utilizing multiple filters and lenses, imposing our own values on them and emphasizing what would suit our own accepted wisdom about divinity and heroism (Bulfinch, 1898; Hamilton, 1940; Graves, 1957; as they are contrasted in Lefkowitz, 2003). Our sense of right and wrong and our notions of divinity have influenced how we have come to understand the Greek myths, and how we interpret them. Lefkowitz (2003) for example, articulates the substantively different perspective that arises from our own common accounts of Homer's *Odyssey*, which typically starts with Odysseus departing from the coast of Troy after the destruction of the beautiful city of Ilion at the end of a ten year war. She contrasts it to the original text[2] that begins with Athena imploring Zeus to force Calypso, a minor goddess, to release Odysseus from seven years of captivity and allow him to return to his wife and son. The different narrative reflects different perspectives about the role of gods and mortals in the order of things on this earth and in the heavens and of course, places different individuals on centre stage, critically upsetting our perspective of leadership that arises from within those accounts. Lefkowitz illustrates how our rendition emphasizes the role of humans in the unfolding of events, while Homer reflected a much more god-centric perspective.

Nevertheless, what we can certainly say is that indeed, there were 12 gods, or maybe more[3], residing at the top of Mount Olympus, enjoying nectar and ambrosia, each god with his or her own jurisdiction, pet projects and favourite subjects. They were surrounded by dozens and dozens of demigods, nymphs, and legendary heroes. Within this rich and populous world, different leaders with vastly different characteristics can be sketched among the vast assemblage of gods and heroes.[4] For our purposes, three clusters can capture some of the patterns of leadership that adorn the Greek mythology.

# OVERVIEW OF GREEK MYTHOLOGY AND LEADERSHIP

## Zeus, Agamemnon

The god of gods and the mighty king draw as much power on achievement as on position. They exercise that power to satisfy either higher ends or personal wimps and ambitions. Pedigrees, as much as their own actions, have brought them to their leadership positions. They are driven by justice and righteousness, while their behaviours frequently leave mere mortals to wonder what is right and fair. Even as they might care about seeing that wrongs are corrected and justice prevails, ultimately they care more about gratifying their own desires.

Zeus, the son of Rhea and Cronus, may be a son of the ruler of the entire universe but he is destined to follow his siblings' fate and be swallowed by his father. His mother's determination to stop the injustice on her children and his sheer intelligence ensure that he, among all of Cronus' children, escapes and rises against his evil father to force him out and become the ruler among the immortals. Hesiod's *Theogony* (the genesis of the gods) describes how Zeus enlists the help of all that have been wronged by Cronus in the famous battles against the titans, which Zeus eventually wins with the help of the Cyclopes and his siblings. The thunder, lightning and thunderbolt given to him in gratitude by the liberated Cyclopes ensure his dominance.

Zeus proceeds to divide the world between himself and his two brothers, Poseidon and Hades, as well as his sisters Hera, Demeter, and Hestia bestowing on them rights and privileges in return for their allegiance. Hesiod recognizes Zeus's calculations to consolidate his power. As the intelligent god, not only does he know that he is destined to the same fate as his father and grandfather, who were both overcome by their smarter sons, but devises the way that will allow him to avoid begetting a son who will replace him. As part of the plan, he swallows Metis when she is pregnant and subsequently, his first daughter Athena is born by springing from his head to be the goddess of wisdom and most devoted to her father.

Of course Zeus cares for justice. He is known to regularly punish misdeeds, disrespect or arrogance. His wrath has been targeted at Atlas, Bellerophontes, Phaethon, Prometheus, and Sisyphus among many humans and lesser gods. They are chastised for disobeying gods' wishes, overconfidence or conceit, antagonizing the gods or displaying excessive force and brutality.

Nonetheless, Zeus's justice is not necessarily measured in human dimensions and timelines, and does not always comply with our notions of fairness. To Zeus, justice is important in the sense of humans showing respect towards the gods and not violating certain principles, but there is no one set of divine laws that humans or gods can follow. Those principles are frequently contradicted and do not always fit in a cohesive whole, the way for example Christian, Hindu, or Jewish religions provide a comprehensive and internally consistent set of values. What is considered deplorable at one instance is condoned under some other conditions. Zeus himself frequently behaves uncharacteristically for a god, at least for a god that would meet our Judeo-Christian standards. He habitually allows his urges and desires, his temper and his anger to guide his behaviour towards both gods and humans.

He does not hesitate to pursue women and men for his own pleasure, but few humans survive to claim any privileges that could arise from their encounter. Most unions are accomplished through deception and yield offsprings that singularly glorify their divine father. Conservative accounts have him father gods and mortals with Hera (Hephaistos, Hebe, Ares, Eileuthyia), Demeter (Persephone), Leto (Artemis, Apollo), Maia (Hermes), Metis (Athena), Mnemosyne (the nine Muses), Leda (Helen, Polydeuces), Danae (Perseus), Alchmene (Heracles), Semele (Dionysus), and Europa (Minos, Rhadamanthys, Sarpedon). Yet, Zeus will frequently interfere in the affairs of others to correct wrongs and uphold order, or prevent excesses. On more than one occasion during the brutal battles recorded in the *Iliad*, Zeus will intervene either for the Greeks or the Trojans to balance the outcomes and ensure that neither side has an unfair advantage. In contrast, the other gods, Athena, Hera, and Poseidon, or Aphrodite, Ares and Apollo in particular, are squarely engaged and would not hesitate for one moment to use their divine powers to tilt the result towards their favourite side.

Agamemnon exhibits similarly unique elements of leadership. The king of the most powerful city of his time, Mycenae, and the leader of the Greek army against Troy is set to avenge the insult to his brother's home committed by Paris, the young prince, who has run away with Menelaos' wife, the beautiful Helen. Paris, who was a guest in Menelaos' palace, has violated the fundamental rules of hospitality that have always been very dear to the Greeks. Thus starts a most powerful myth that has captivated the imagination of untold numbers of artists from many countries over the last 30 centuries and speaks of the deeds of men and the powers of gods, of leadership and courage, but also of destiny and fate and of the limitations of human mortality and physical weakness that even gods cannot always change.

Agamemnon and Menelaos are the sons of Atreus, the king whose heinous deeds have brought about the curses of the House of Atreus and have inspired some of the most powerful Greek tragedies ever written. The Atreidai's (sons of Atreus) actions demonstrate a strong sense of purpose and obligation to uphold order, in direct contrast to their father's atrocious acts. Agamemnon eventually becomes king of Mycenae and marries Klytaimnestra, while Menelaos reigns over Sparta with her sister Helen. Parallels between Zeus and

Agamemnon and their fathers are striking, for the sons endure moral battles to assert their leadership against the paternalistic shadows.

Following Helen's and Paris's elopement Agamemnon summons all Greeks to unite on an expedition against Troy. Soon he is presented with a tragic choice when he is asked to sacrifice his own daughter, Iphigeneia to appease the goddess Artemis and bring about favourable winds necessary for the sails of the gathered armada. His sense of responsibility, of upholding the rules and the burden of leadership leave him no choice but to trick his wife and daughter to come and take part in the sacrifice, or as Kershaw (2007) puts it, 'to avenge Paris' transgression, Agamemnon must transgress'. Indeed, mother and daughter arrive in Aulis, where the Greek fleet is waiting, to discover the deceit of the purported marriage between Iphigeneia and Akhilleus. Of course, the sacrifice will spark a series of brutal killings as Klytaimnestra never forgives her husband and in turn, her other children subsequently avenge their father's murderers. Classic Greek tragedy that has been told numerous times by brilliant dramatists since the time of Euripides and Aiskhylos and always demonstrates the limitations of power and the inability even of those in leadership positions to control their destiny.

But Agamemnon is not a simple leader, no more than Zeus might ever be. Agamemnon is also driven by his own personal ambitions and allows his urges and desires, his temper and his anger to guide his behaviour towards both gods and humans. When Apollo is infuriated by Agamemnon for showing no respect to his priest Khryses and his daughter Khryseis, he sends a terrible plague on to the Greek army. Agamemnon does not recede until much harm is caused on the troops and even then, he reluctantly agrees to release Khryseis only after taking in her place Akhilleus' prize, the beautiful Briseis. Of course this will put in motion another tragic series of events as Akhilleus is furious and refuses to fight. His mother, the goddess Thetis intervenes with Zeus to make the Greeks suffer greatly so they would recognize that her son is the mightiest warrior among all of them and most worthy of respect and admiration. The feud with Agamemnon will cause untold hardship and cost the Greeks some of their best warriors, among them Akhilleus' friend Patroklos.

Zeus and Agamemnon represent a rather unique and complex type of leadership. For the most part, they are proud, charismatic, honourable, and do what leaders are best at doing, that is, provide a vision and create the energy that motivates their followers. They build commitment and steer people and resources towards the visionary goal. They are strong and reflect the best attributes of muscular strength and intellectual prowess. They have rightly earned their place at the summit of Mount Olympus or the peak of the citadel. They have a sense of responsibility that comes with their position and see themselves as the bearers of justice and fairness.

Nonetheless, at times, they also exhibit little regard, concern or even respect for others. Zeus frequently does not care what happens to other gods, or to humans. Both Zeus and Agamemnon are capricious and there are instances when they clearly lack integrity. According to some definitions of leadership, those characteristics would probably disqualify them as true leaders; yet, they have been unquestionably bestowed on leadership positions and are revered for their superiority. At the same time, they also have some unique sense of justice and piety, which they frequently want to see being imposed on others. Zeus would interfere to restore justice or to correct wrongs, as much as he could be the cause of wrong behaviour himself. Agamemnon would be ready to sacrifice what is dear to him for the greater good, but then again, he would be petty and short-sighted, as well as vengeful. Both Agamemnon and Zeus frequently react on impulse and their decisions and actions are driven by immediate personal ambitions. They are certainly complex and seemingly inconsistent but always unique and inspirational.

### Herakles (Hercules), Akhilleus

Brave, eminently gifted, and glorious, Herakles and Akhilleus are leaders, as well as heroes. They personify the two complementary facets of great mythological characters more than any other legendary creation of ancient Greece. Both heroes have captivated all kinds of audiences for centuries; they have been celebrated more than any other known mythological creature in every form of art imaginable with paintings, sculptures and plays. From the sculpted metopes over the porches of the temples of Olympia and in the Acropolis of Athens, their stories have been told innumerable times culminating with present day movies from Hollywood and popular Disney characters. They represent the most celebrated of heroes and have inspired countless admirers. Scholars have described them as heroic masters of prodigious feats, tragic figures, who achieve immortality through unparalleled performance (Kershaw, 2007). Yet, their stories also reveal egotistical, brazen, arrogant and self-centred individuals whose lust, violence and brutal force cannot be easily reconciled with our simplistic contemporary notions of magnanimity and integrity that are associated with heroes and leaders.

Herakles is the son of Zeus and Alcmene, a mortal queen from Thebes, who is deceived by the mighty god to believe that she is sleeping with her husband when she becomes pregnant. Herakles is one of Zeus' proudest sons and the nemesis of his main wife, goddess Hera. She will never forget that Zeus has fathered Herakles and repeatedly tries to harm both him and his mother. Interestingly, the name Herakles means 'Hera's glory' and it is indeed the result of Hera's efforts to destroy him that led to the most famous achievements of strength and accomplishment that legendary Herakles has been renowned for through the centuries. For starters, she sends two poisonous snakes to his cradle, but the infant strangles them. She convinces Alcmene's husband to burn her on a pyre for her infidelity but Zeus sends a sudden downpour and puts out the flames. She drives Herakles mad and in his madness he kills his wife and three sons. To repent, the oracles of Delphi tell him to put himself in the service of spiteful king Eurystheus and perform the famous 12 labours that eventually make him immortal. Among them, he kills the Nemean lion, whose hide becomes his distinctive attire; he kills the monstrous Lernea Hydra, captures the Keryneian hind, brings alive the savage boar from Mount Erymanthos, cleans Augeias' stables, and chases away the Stymphalian birds. Then Herakles harnesses the Cretan bull, tames the man-eating mares of Diomedes, steals the belt of the Amazon Queen Hyppolyte, captures the cattle of Geryon, fetches the golden apples of Hesperides, and while he is at it, he kills the eagle that daily devours Prometheus' eternally renewed liver and frees him from his chains. During the same labour, he encounters the titan Atlas, who holds up the heavens on his shoulders. Herakles' last labour is probably the most daring for he brings briefly up to the world Kerberos, the three-headed hound that guards the underworld.

Herakles continues to amass great fame with many achievements beyond the 12 labours that no other mortal could possibly match. Freed from king Eurystheus, he travels the known and unknown world more than any other mythological figure, in search of challenging tasks that would relieve the people of monsters, diseases and curses. He goes on to perform mighty feats and rids the countryside of terrifying animals and the cities of tyrants. In the process, he kills, burns, maims, mutilates, and slays while frequently striking innocent people and avenging parents' deeds by killing their young. In parallel, not unlike his father, he leaves a trail of offspring wherever he ventures. Conservative accounts mention Herakles copulating with at least 62 different women begetting numerous sons and daughters whose acts further celebrate their father's life both in torment and achievement. Other accounts have him inaugurate the Olympic Games and face the famous 'choice of Herakles', when he meets two women at a road junction: Vice is a sexy and alluring woman that promises the easy path of pleasure and quick gratification while Virtue offers a tough road of duty and hard labour. Of course, Herakles chooses Virtue and follows many years of glorious achievements married with hardship and anguish, crowned by a terrible ending from the misguided love and jealousy of his second wife, Deianeira, and ultimately achieves immortality.

Unmistakably, Akhilleus is a leader with all the enviable characteristics. He is handsome, powerful, inspirational, endowed, skilful, and enthusiastic. He leads one of the best armies in the Greek camp during the expedition against Troy and can motivate his Myrmidon soldiers to fight victoriously far superior enemies. His triumphs are legendary and his conquests stretch far and wide across the Eastern Aegean and Asia Minor. His fame causes fear in the minds of great warriors. Yet, none of those attributes compel him to act in any self-less manner or to direct his energies towards anything more inspiring than himself. When he is in battle, he is to achieve more glory and fulfil personal desires. When he retreats, he withdraws from battle only to spite Agamemnon and does not care whether his stance greatly hurts his comrades. At one point he even persuades his mother to use her charm on Zeus to tilt the scales of the war against the Greeks, simply because his tantrums have gone without a response. His *timi* [5] has been gravely wounded and in response it is important, not just that he will be offered a very public apology, but that he will be recognized as the mightiest warrior, who is desperately needed to save the Greeks. He returns again to fight not because of a higher purpose but to avenge the death of his intimate friend, Patroklos. And when he kills Hektor, his friend's slayer, he shows no respect for the brave warrior and drags the body of the Trojan hero, tied behind his chariot, around the walls of Troy for 12 days.

Yet, no one questions his bravery or his prowess. Alexander the Great admired Akhilleus more than any other mythical figure. After all, he is the son of the beautiful nymph Thetis and a student of Chiron, the wisest among the Centaurs. He is blessed with unique gifts and divine weapons, forged by the smith god Hephaistos. Of course, like other heroes of Greek mythology, Akhilleus does fall on account of his heel, to remind us of the fate and vulnerability of all humans.

Both Herakles and Akhilleus are at once phenomenally gifted and powerful, inspirational and driven, as well as self-centred and egotistical, frequently resorting to excessive violence, and their obsession with lust is proverbial. They do not hesitate to act on their emotions with little regard for others or the greater good. Their accomplishments are beyond reproach, while frequently their acts could verge on the immoral. Their arrogance is legendary and guides their actions. They exist to delight themselves not to serve others, whether their actions greatly assist or inhibit others' causes.

## Odysseus (Ulysses)

King of Ithaca, husband of Penelope, is among the Greek leaders taking part in the expedition against Troy. Skilful warrior, brave and daring, he is also known as the most cunning, deceitful, crafty and ingenious among the legendary Greeks of the ancient world. If Machiavelli was writing in classical Greece, he would have found ample inspiration in the ways that Odysseus views the world, how he makes decisions, and how he puts them to action. Ethics is relative for Odysseus and he will not hesitate to kill, sacrifice friendships or put allies in peril in the name of his objectives.

Odysseus is reluctant to join the other Greeks in the war against Troy. He pretends to be crazy, and only after Palamedes tricks him to reveal his acute faculties, does he join the expedition. But he never forgives Palamedes and years later, he sets him up on a fabrication of treachery and has him stoned to death. Odysseus is very competitive, not unlike most heroes of ancient Greece. Such competitiveness is ruthless and frequently misguided leading to much distraction and counterproductive deeds among the supposedly allied men. Only the common enemy in battle unites them, but outside the battlefield, they quickly get back to their acrimonies.

Odysseus can be relied upon to solve difficult challenges that require astute observation, deception, trickery, swift manoeuvres, brilliant improvisations, and an unparalleled cunning. He applies his skills to discover where Akhilleus is hidden by his mother to be protected and not join the expedition to Troy where he is bound to be killed; to trick Klytaimnestra and Iphigenia in Aulis; to ambush Helenos and get the oracles that protect Troy from capture; to fetch the Palladion from within Troy's walls; and is famously the mastermind behind the Wooden Horse that eventually brings an end to the ten-year war and results in the total annihilation of Troy. Odysseus wants the war to end because he really wants to get back to his beautiful Penelope and he does not truly believe that this is his war. Yet, his sense of allegiance not only brings him to the allied camp but makes him one of the most accomplished members of the Greek army.

He is always respectful of the gods, and is especially fond of Athena, who guides him through his ten-year odyssey and the great changes of fortune that see all his comrades perish. He tricks the son of Poseidon, Cyclops Polyphemos and manages to escape with his men, he fights the Laistrygones, survives the winds of Aiolos, succeeds to free his men from the enchantress Kirke, narrowly misses Skylla and Kharybdis, beats the alluring songs of the Sirens, sails on a makeshift raft to flee Kalypso, and manages to entice beautiful princess Nausikaa even though he is shipwrecked and destitute.

Odysseus is shown to be both courageous and sensitive. In true leadership, Odysseus carries a full sense of responsibility to bring his troops back to Ithaca. Of course, the troops constantly quarrel and repeatedly disobey, which eventually leads to every single one of them perishing. In Homer's epic, the suitors that have taken residence in his palace and pilfer and waste everything that is not theirs, are portrayed in offensive deeds and behaviour so their eventual slaughter in the hands of Odysseus, which is so grotesquely described in detail, will be morally justified.

Odysseus has inspired innumerable accounts that capture the dramatic panorama of the human condition. Throughout history, immense artistic expressions such as those of Dante, Goethe, T. S. Eliot, Joyce, and Kazantzakis, as well as Kubrick and Clarke, and of course an internet search engine, 'Ithaki.net' convey our innate need to seek out. Odysseus has also served as inspiration for modern Greek leaders such as Aristotle Onassis – see Commentary box. Arguably, one of the finest inspirations comes from the Greek poet Cavafy and reflects uniquely the culture that has given rise to such a complex illustration of what a man's aspirations in life should be.[6] While leadership is supposed to be about achievement, Cavafy tells us that the journey may be the ultimate reward.

---

## COMMENTARY BOX

### Aristotle Onassis

The life and character of Aristotle Onassis, in many ways, exhibited strong similarities to that of the Greek mythological figure Odysseus ... [he] was fascinated by the story of Odysseus – about his eternal journey in search of chimera and adventures and his ultimate return to his native country to reign in peace over his people. This character always attracted him as he felt the sense of a similar destiny and that he, as did Odysseus, knew how to exist above all will (from Prionas *et al.*, 1996). This is exemplified in the following attributed quotes (from http://www.brainyquote.com/quotes/authors/a/aristotle_onassis.html):

After a certain point, money is meaningless. It ceases to be the goal. The game is what counts. / I have no friends and no enemies – only competitors. / It is during our darkest moments that we must focus to see the light. / The secret of business is to know something that nobody else knows. / To succeed in business it is necessary to make others see things as you see them. / We must free ourselves of the hope that the sea will ever rest. We must learn to sail in high winds.

---

## GLOBAL IMPLICATIONS

Without a doubt, there exist tremendous accounts of leadership in the extensive mythology that adorns ancient Greece. Gods and mortals alike assume leadership positions, inspire, motivate, give purpose, lead and enable others to accomplish unimaginable achievements and in the process, award us with some of the most beautiful and vivid stories ever told. Without a doubt, these bigger-than-life individuals are complex personalities that defy simple characterizations and can be ill-placed in neat categories. Mythology, as well as leadership, is inseparably tied to culture. As such, a study of such rich mythology provides a unique window to its people's culture and can inform us how Greeks tend to view the world and how they relate to the environment around them. They reflect complex and unpredictable personalities that one would not only find in the stories Greeks tell, but on the streets of modern Greece.

Greek leaders exhibit *timi* in abundance. Pride and valour are tremendously important to them. If one wants anything accomplished in modern Greece, one has to speak to people's *filotimo*, their sense of pride and honour. What logic, reasoning, manipulation, incentives, or threats cannot accomplish, a simple call to one's pride can marshal immense energy and get things done. Famously, the Greeks staged an extremely successful 2004 summer Olympic Games, not because they had the resources or the technical expertise but because they felt their *timi* was on the line to be judged by the entire world.

Position, origin, roots, family, genealogy, and city are critical identifiers of each individual, sometimes more so than skill and accomplishment, whether god or mortal. Hofstede (1980; 1991) recognizes those elements and refers to individualism and collectivism as the degree to which individuals in a given cultural orientation are integrated into groups. On the individualist side, ties between individuals are loose. On the collectivist side, people are integrated into strong groups that protect in exchange for unquestioned loyalty. In an individualist culture, people prefer to take care of themselves and their immediate families; they remain emotionally independent from groups, organizations and institutions. Their ties and attachments are rational and emphasize knowledge and information (Bhagat *et al.*, 2002). Greece's individualism places it around the middle, 30th among the 53 countries in Hofstede's (1980) study, but with a score well below the mean. Greeks see themselves as born into families and social systems and identify with those structures more than with the individual and her ability to chart her own course.

Greek mythology emphasizes the central role of the collectivity, yet places that collectivity in small numbers. Greece scores the lowest in performance orientation in the GLOBE (2004) project, reflecting a society that places much more emphasis on family and background than achievement and excellence. Who you know is tremendously more important than what you know in Greece. And when those achievements and rewards are counted, they are directed at the individual rather than the collective. Indeed, Greeks tend to find themselves at the opposite end of institutional collectivism affirming a disdain for social practices and organizational policies that would encourage collective distribution of resources, actions or rewards.

Yet, Greek mythology also shows the complexity and difficulty of such characterizations. Even the family and one's own home are sometimes not a reliable sanctuary; the Greek myths give us many conflicting accounts of the role that the small group may play. At times the family is the all important unit that has to be protected, yet Zeus and Hera, Agamemnon and Klytaimnestra, Orestes and Electra, or Oedipus and Antigoni remind us that those units of collectivism are not always reliable. Family feuds are not uncommon and although rarely an outsider will be allowed to pierce into a Greek family brawl, such notorious battles are legendary in Greece, as long as there are only Greeks around. As soon as an outsider enters the scene, whether in the form of an enemy or a tourist, all that is pushed aside and a façade of calm and harmony is presented.

Greek leaders are tragic characters, in the Greek sense of the word. None of them fully control their destiny. Even the mighty gods are subject to other forces; they have to compromise, have to accept sharing of ultimate control. The good guys don't always win or get rewarded. Justice is not blind and life is just not fair. Although gods do care about justice, they do not necessarily dispense it within time dimensions that would serve the average mortal.

## PRACTICAL APPLICATIONS

While leadership in our textbooks is associated with vision and integrity, Greek mythology seems to have bypassed both of those qualities or at least, not given them the dominance and centrality that one would expect. Honour, integrity and responsibility toward others can be found in all stories, but the opposite is also true, even for the same characters in different settings. It is not that Greek leaders are deceitful and cunning, which at times they are to an extreme, but that neither vision nor integrity seem to be as important as our modern day accounts of leadership portray. Gods and demigods seem to live in comfort and at ease, without a sense of purpose, at least not in the way that humans could understand. There is no higher purpose for betterment, struggle to achieve, evolution, and development that one can detect coming from the gods. Humans in turn simply try to survive, fully aware of the ultimate and cruel ending of all human life.

Gods are elitists and don't care to associate with most humans, with few exceptions among the aristocracy. Even those encounters are brief and typically for the pure enjoyment of the god, with no regard for the human partner who is left traumatized or even dead. Zeus is a notorious womanizer, who abandons his human partners and only cares for his self-indulgence. Lessons of leadership could easily be misconstrued here. A leader's motives are neither consistent nor always noble. Greeks readily accept flaws in their leaders, whether those are mythical gods or contemporary politicians and members of the business elite. In Greek mythology, humans cannot be sure that they have acted properly, or what is truly proper. There is frequently a sense that what might be the right thing in one instance is not necessarily the right thing under different circumstances. Gods in Greek mythology do not provide humans with a moral compass or commandments they should follow. Gods are not human-like and are not to be emulated. It is not that gods don't care about justice. To the contrary, they do. However, their sense of justice is different and rather capricious.

This contrasts sharply with uncertainty avoidance as defined by Hofstede (1980). He refers to it as the tolerance within a given cultural orientation for uncertainty and ambiguity. He explains that it indicates to what extent a culture programmes its members to feel either uncomfortable or comfortable in unstructured situations and whether there is preference toward predictability and stability. The GLOBE project (House *et al.*, 2004) places Greece close to the bottom of the scale reflecting a culture that is opportunistic, relies on only broadly stated rules and strategies, and accepts fluidity and uncertainty/inconsistency. There might be a strong honour code in Greece, but everything else is relative.

There is no doubt that the myths tell stories of great leaders that have been and of their accomplishments, their inspirations and their tribulations. In the process, they reflect a rich culture of a proud people that are human, and guide them how to behave as their mythical leaders. As Kershaw (2007: 467) concludes in his book, 'The Greek myths may go back to time immemorial, but they have a glorious and vibrant future ahead of them.'

## NOTES

1.  Throughout this article, we follow Kershaw's (2007) guidance and employ the original spelling of the various names, as opposed to either Latin or English transliterations, even though most readers may be more familiar with the latter versions than the former. For example Odysseus has become Ulysses, while Klytaimnestra and Priamos are commonly known as Clytemnestra and Priam.
2.  If there is such a thing as an original text; scholars have long questioned whether there was someone called Homer and if there was only one text of that epic story. A cursory survey of our own books, movies, documentaries and other accounts of recent historical events does reveal that today, we are not much further ahead in documenting how things actually happened.
3.  To be precise, we know that restricting the number to an exclusive club of 12 gods is a rather modern invention not supported by the ancient scripts (Kershaw, 2007).
4.  The following account draws from many excellent books and descriptions of Greek mythology that are too numerous to list and would make the reading too tedious if each reference was cited as appropriate. We would like to respectfully acknowledge that our sources consist of a whole range of elementary and high-school textbooks and teachers, story telling, innumerable guided tours of museums and ancient sites, as much as scholarly works. In no way do we want to avoid giving credit to all those excellent students of Greek mythology; as many as possible of them that are known to us and we remember to have read over the last 50 years, are listed among the references at the end of this chapter.
5.  Pronounced (tim-i) and means pride, honour, valour or value. It is particularly central to

Greeks, ancient and contemporary, although very different from the notion of 'saving face' that dominates eastern cultures.
6. Much of the above discussion can be found in many related works, but in this instance, it has been informed by and extracted from the work of S. Kershaw (2007), *A Brief Guide to the Greek Myths*, pp. 421–3.

# REFERENCES

Atwood, M. (1986), *The Handmaid's Tale*, Boston, MA: Houghton Mifflin.
Bhagat, R. S., Kedia, B. L., Harveston, P. D. and Triandis, H. C. (2002), Cultural variations in the cross-border transfer of organizational knowledge: an integrative framework, *Academy of Management Review*, **27** (2), 204–21.
Boardman, J., Griffin, J. and Murray, O. (1986), *The Oxford History of Greece and the Hellenistic World*, Oxford: Oxford University Press.
Bulfinch, T. (1898), *The Age of Fable, or the Beauties of Mythology*, edited by J. Laughran Scott, Philadelphia, PA: David McKay.
Cotterell, A. (2007), *Mythology of Greece and Rome*, London: Southwater.
D'Aulaire, I. and D'Aulaire, E. P. (1962), *D'Aulaires Book of Greek Myths*, New York: Bantam Doubleday Dell.
Dowden, K. (1992), *The Uses of Greek Mythology*, London: Routledge.
Drucker, P. F. (1967), *The Effective Executive*, New York: Harper and Row.
Graves, R. (1957), *The Greek Myths*, New York: George Braziller.
Graves, R. (1959), *New Larousse Encyclopaedia of Mythology*, London: Hamlyn.
Griffin, J. (1980), *Homer on Life and Death*, Oxford: Oxford University Press.
Hamilton, E. (1940), *Mythology*, Boston, MA: Little, Brown.
Hard, R. (2003), *The Routledge Handbook of Greek Mythology*, London: Routledge.
Hofstede, G. (1980), *Culture's Consequences: International Differences in Work Related Values*, New Bury Park, CA: Sage.
Hofstede, G. (1991), *Culture's Consequences: Comparing Values, Behaviors, Institutions, and Organizations Across Nations* (2nd edn), Thousand Oaks, CA: Sage.
House, R.J., Hanges, P. J., Javidan, M., Dorfman, P. W., Gupta, V. and GLOBE Associates (2004), *Leadership, Culture and Organizations: The Globe Study of 62 Societies*, Thousand Oaks, CA: Sage Publications, Inc.
Kakrides, I. T. (1986), *Greek Mythology*, Athens: Ekdotiki Athenon.
Kerenyi, C. (1951), *The Gods of the Greeks*, London: Thames and Hudson.
Kerenyi, C. (1959), *The Heroes of the Greeks*, London: Thames and Hudson.
Kershaw, S. P. (2007), *A Brief Guide to the Greek Myths*, London: Robinson.
Kets de Vries, M. F. R. (2004), Organizations on the couch: a clinical perspective on organizational dynamics, *European Management Journal*, **22** (2), 183–200.
Kets de Vries, M. F. R. and Miller, D. (1985), Narcissism and leadership: an object relations perspective, *Human Relations*, **38** (6), 583–602.
Lefkowitz, M. (2003), *Greek Gods, Human Lives*, New Haven, CT: Yale University Press.
Metaxa, A. and Krontiras, K. (1956), *My Little Dictionary of Mythology*, Athens: Pechlivanidis.
Prionas, E., Kiriazis, C., Elisofon, M., Roberts, A. and Salter, A. (1996), *The Life of Aristotle Onassis: The Man, the Myth, the Legend*, http://www.greece.org/poseidon/work/modern-times/onassis.html
Schwab, G. and Coon, N. A. (1986), *Mythical Heroes of the Greeks*, Athens: Heridanos.

# 7. Cultural mythology and global leadership in Germany[1]

## Sonja A. Sackmann

### INTRODUCTION

Numerous myths, sagas, and legends exist in Germany. These are, on the one hand, an expression of the national and regional culture. On the other hand they have to a certain extent also influenced culture at the national and regional level. Given the specific history of Germany in its European context, it is somewhat difficult to identify specific German mythology and separate it from the mythology of related nations and neighbouring states. Due to ancient tribal movements of Germanic or Teutonic people, of Anglo Saxons as well as changing national borders over time, the mythology found in Germany is to some extent similar to the one that can be found in Scandinavian countries and it has overlaps with British myths. It is therefore more appropriate to talk about Germanic mythology within the borders of the nation-state of Germany. However, other influences such as Romans and Huguenots have shaped German myths as well (Phillipson, 1962).

Before we explore Germanic mythology and its influence on leadership in Germany in more detail, we first want to clarify our understanding and use of the terms in question. In the Oxford English Dictionary, 'mythology' is defined as the body of myths from a particular culture. 'Myths' are defined as 'traditional story, typically involving supernatural beings or forces or creatures, which embodies and provides an explanation or justification for something such as the early history of a society, a religious belief or ritual, or a natural phenomenon'. In modern times, folklorists have differentiated the all-encompassing traditional story and distinguished myths from legends and folktales. In this more differentiated view, myths are seen as sacred stories, concerning the distant past, particularly the creation of the world; legends are considered stories about the more recent past based on some historical events and focusing on human heroes; and folktales are stories whose tellers acknowledge them to be fictitious, lacking any definite historical setting and frequently including animal characters. Based on this more differentiated view, we will predominantly focus on legends and myths while talking about mythology. According to Burkert (1981) myth as a traditional story has the function to structure reality in order to cope with it. In this way, the present time should be bound to the past and at the same time guide future expectations.

Given Germany's history, an examination of German mythology and its myths is not unproblematic. In the more recent past, mythology became relevant for Germanic people during the period of romanticism (1800–50) (Herrmann *et al.*, 1977) when Germany consisted of several independent principalities. In 1806, after the end of the Holy Roman Empire of the German Nation, the nation state of Germany did not yet exist. The idea of Germany as a national state started to develop during those times. Since mythology was used to create patriotism and a sense of national feeling, it was changed or rather adapted for those purposes (Phillipson, 1962). One of the most influential misinterpretations, the so-called 'Nibelungentreue' (loyalty of the Nibelungs), which means unquestioning loyalty unto death toward the emperor, the country, and the superior, influenced Germany's role in the First World War. It also supported the National Socialists in gaining power and eventually the beginning of the Second World War (Heinzl, 2004).

Due to this specific history, the most important influences on Germans' view of their mythology today are the experiences and their critical reflections that resulted from the misuse of that part of Germanic mythology during the Third Reich (1933–45). The National Socialists used Germanic mythology and (mis-)interpreted its myths in line with their ideology. The experience with these events and processes has developed an ideal of leadership that distances itself from a *Führer* (German translation of leader). Instead, it values a team approach, shared leadership and shared power, critical thinking with a focus on the depersonalized aspects of leadership as one way to avoid potential dictatorship in the future. After the Second World War, German society has undergone a thorough democratization process encompassing all spheres of life such as education, military and business life including the structure of organizations.

## OVERVIEW OF GERMANIC MYTHOLOGY

Germany's national culture and leadership behaviour[2] that is considered desirable by people socialized in Germany may be influenced by or is reflected in four aspects of Germanic mythology and history which we will discuss in the following sections. These are the 'Nibelungenlied' (Song of the Nibelungs) a medieval saga; the Prussian virtues; the honour of Hanseatic merchants, and its specific history during the first part of the twentieth century; and the democratization process that followed the Second World War.

## The Nibelungenlied

The 'Nibelungenlied' is probably the most popular and well-known Germanic saga. In the eighteenth and nineteenth centuries, it was often considered the modern Germanic equivalent to Homer and Germany's national epic (Heinzle, 2004). Due to its long tradition, there are different versions and adaptations of the 'Nibelungenlied'. Most popular is the opera 'Der Ring des Nibelungen' (Ring of the Nibelungs) by the German composer Richard Wagner (1813–83). As in many myths of oral tradition, different parts of the story are rooted in different ages. The story has developed from a pure myth to narrative poetry eventually becoming a heroic epic (Heusler, 1921). The oldest – historically-based – parts originate from the invasion of the barbarians in the fifth and sixth centuries and deal with the downfall of the Burgundies. A second version is known from the twelfth century and integrates the – predominantly fictional – story of Siegfried, the dragon slayer (Bischof, 1996; Heinzle, 2004).

The 'Nibelungenlied' tells the story of the Burgundian kings from a narrator's perspective. The first part focuses on the hero Siegfried, his connections to the court of Burgundy and his death. The second part of the epos deals with his wife Kriemhild's revenge. Siegfried, a prince of Xanten (North Rhine-Westphalia), became physically invulnerable after he bathed in the blood of a dragon that he had defeated. During bathing, however, a falling lime tree leaf got stuck on his back leaving one tiny spot of vulnerability. In addition to this physical shield, Siegfried had a cloak of invisibility, a powerful sword, and the legendary treasure of the Nibelungs. Only his wife Kriemhild, sister of the Burgundian king Gunther, knew about this vulnerable spot on his back. Pretending to protect Siegfried, Hagen of Tronje, a Burgundian like her, insisted on getting the exact location of Siegfried's vulnerable spot. In fear for his life, Kriemhild revealed that secret to him. Hagen considered Siegfried, however, an enemy and finally killed him with a lance while Siegfried was drinking water from a well. Wanting to take revenge, Kriemhild married the Hun King Etzel, the historical person Attila. Finally, almost every hero and heroine in the epos and the court of Burgundy dies, including Kriemhild.

Siegfried is a characteristic hero in Germanic mythology. Even though he is very powerful, he also has some weaknesses which make him human. There is no absolute adoration for him, because his actions can not always be approved nor are they always rational. The underlying rationale of the saga implies that power is not an end in itself and needs to be supplemented by wisdom. The 'Nibelungenlied' shows that a 'good' leader uses his power carefully and thoughtfully while respecting the interests of other people. If leaders do not follow this guideline, they may fail or finally die, even if they seem to be invincible.

In the Nibelungen saga, King Etzel is described as centre of attraction for heroes because of his financial and political power, his tolerance and his honour. His court is a popular place for young knights' education. Due to the peaceful coexistence of Christians and heathens in the environment of Etzel's tolerance, this particular court is seen as an ideal court in medieval epics (Springeth, 1996).

The Prussian virtues, the honour of the Hanseatic merchants as well as the recent history are closely linked to the underlying message of the Nibelungenlied. They include virtues and values like honesty, accuracy, reliability and responsibility both for the task and for the people involved. While the former two represented values of certain German regions and the bourgeoisie, the democratization process that followed as an answer to the Third Reich and the Second World War disseminated these values throughout Germany.

**Prussian Virtues**

Originating in Prussia, the Prussian virtues were transferred to the whole of Germany during the German Empire (1871–1918), a time in which the Prussian kings were also German Emperors. Besides Austria, Prussia had been the most powerful and influential Germanic principality from the seventeenth to the nineteenth century. It consisted of the former realm of the Teutonic Order and the electorate Brandenburg. The Prussian virtues originated with the two Prussian kings, Frederick William I (1688–1740) and his son Frederick II known as Frederick the Great (1712–86) who successfully reformed the old feudalistic system. Frederick William I, who was also called 'soldier king', reformed the Prussian administration and created a modern government system based on the military. Major changes and achievements at the time were the development of a standing army, compulsory education, mercantilism and the first chairs in economics at European universities. Frederick the Great supported economic development influenced by the Calvinistic ideals of work (Weber, 1991). These include commitment to fulfil one's duty, shrewdness, conscientiousness and diligence. In 2003, the Prime Minister of Brandenburg Matthias Platzeck characterized Prussia in his speech as 'trying for justice, ready for solidarity and tolerant' (Platzeck, 2003).

During the reign of Frederick the Great, an enlightened absolutist monarch, Prussia became an important place for scientific research, economic development and religious tolerance. Due to economic necessities, tolerance towards other cultures and nations was a major aspect of his policy – ideas that can also be found in the court of King Etzel in the 'Nibelungenlied'. Religious tolerance – a novelty at the time – was one corner-stone of Prussia's history. Until the seventeenth century, Prussia had been a small and poor state. In order to gain wealth and power in Europe, it was necessary to attract talented and wealthy people who wanted to live there. Religious and ethnic minorities were predestined. Frederick the Great also established several other reforms following the ideas of enlightenment, including the abolition of the death penalty. He acted on his maxim: 'Der König ist der erste Diener des Staates' (The king is the first servant of the state).

Frederick the Great was very popular in Germany, especially after his victory in the Seven Years' War against Austria (Heinzle, 2004). One of the most widespread stories about Frederick the Great is the legend of 'The miller of Sanssouci'. The story demonstrates Prussia's tradition as a state that honours the law even when challenged by those in power. Sanssouci was the king's summer palace in Potsdam. In the middle of the park stood a windmill. It is said that the clacking of its blade disturbed the king to such an extent that he instructed the miller to break it down. The miller refused, went to court and won. The story proved historically false. In reality, the king liked the windmill symbolizing country life with clean, fresh air in contrast to the capital Berlin (rbb, 2007).

Despite all these achievements and positive aspects, the Prussian virtues have also negative connotations connected to militarism and obedience. In their extreme portrayal, they have become a source of negative myths about Prussia in connection with experiences of the First and Second World Wars: being overly dedicated to the task, strictly following rules and orders without questioning, cherishing correctness and so on. Prussia's rise to a European state of power in the eighteenth and nineteenth centuries was based on its military power. During the German Empire (1871–1918), the military was ranked higher than civil life. The status of a sergeant outranked the status of a university professor. The Prussian virtues started to develop into fundamentalist beliefs and fostered the beginning of the First World War. In later years, they were further misused and prevented the development of a movement of resistance in the military and in civil life during the Third Reich (rbb, 2007).

**The Honour of Hanseatic Merchants**

The Hanseatic League was a union of Low German merchants from the twelfth to the seventeenth centuries to represent their interests abroad. The seaports of Hamburg, Bremen and Lübeck were connected through this union. Since the nineteenth century, these merchants were famous for their aristocratic behaviour (Wegner, 1999) characterized by dignity, daring in business, reservation and self-mockery (Huret, 1993). Traditionally engaged in sea trade, *Hanseatic* was and still is also associated with cosmopolitanism even though Hanseatics considered their home town the greatest place on earth and the only place to live. In the eighteenth century Von Heβ (1787: 99) described that Hamburg's merchants divided people of the world into 'Hamburger' (people from the city of Hamburg) and 'Butenminschen' (Outsiders). The cities of Hamburg and Bremen received Hanse status and became independent city states.

The honour of the Hanseatic merchants consisted of their pride to be a merchant. This pride distinguished and separated them from all other societal groups in the city and fostered the development of their own identity. The specific Hanseatic identity can still be found in traditional Hanseatic families. According to their honour, business contracts are considered legal by handshake. Oral agreements are kept, even if they imply disadvantages for the merchant (Huret, 1993). During an organizational crisis, it is considered a duty to invest private funds in order to solve the problem and save one's honour. Like the Prussian virtues, the honour of the Hanseatic merchant is connected to the Calvinistic ideals of work (Weber, 1991) implying that trading respectfully and earning money is a way to receive God's blessing. This particular honour was seen to both assist on the way towards reaching heaven and serve as an instrument towards becoming successful in business. To be a reliable business partner, it is necessary to be predictable and honest (Weber, 1991).

Historically, these values were most prevalent in the eighteenth century and included the so-called *virtutes oeconomicae* (economic virtues) – order, diligence and shrewdness (Bizard, 2007). During the period of industrialization and the rise of capitalism in the nineteenth century, the explicit focus on these values and virtues vanished. They have survived, however, as a myth of civic pride and as ideal entrepreneurial behaviour.

## Democratization as Answer to Avoid Pre-Second World War Developments

Germany's democratic tradition is quite young. The first attempt with the Republic of Weimar in 1899 was not successful and was followed by the autocratic, dictatorial system of the National Socialists (1933-1945). After the Second World War, these historical experiences fostered the development of democratic, participative systems first in the area of politics, economics, and the military and later, after the 1968 movement, also in the educational system.

In the sphere of politics unlike its US counterpart, the German Federal President fulfils merely representational tasks that are separated from legislation (parliament) and execution (chancellor and government). A similar separation between supervision, decision making, and execution was introduced into the business world with the two-tiered model of Corporate Governance. The 'Vorstand' (group of top executives) is represented by a speaker. This top executive group is democratically organized and the Speaker of the Vorstand has much less power when compared with an Anglo-Saxon CEO.[3] The

'Aufsichtsrat' (supervisory board) supervises the decisions of the Vorstand. Its chairman can not be the same person as the speaker of the 'Vorstand'.

In addition, co-determination was introduced into German companies to provide employees with an institutionalized voice through the workers' council (Betriebsrat) and provide them with an equal representation in the supervisory board. The German model of social market economy assumes that cooperation and consensus are better ways to achieve economic aims than conflict culminating in strikes or lockouts (Szabo *et al.*, 2002).

Organizational dynamics are influenced by participative ideas on a daily basis and manifest themselves in the German model of industrial relations. Collective bargaining is negotiated between two parties, the specific trade union and the employer respectively the employer's association. The employer, therefore, cannot overrule the resistance of labour, except in deadlock situations (Sackmann, 2007; Szabo *et al.*, 2002).

Another example of this process of democratization and power equalization can be found in the German Federal Armed Forces ('Bundeswehr'). Their leadership guidelines 'Innere Führung' (internal leadership) focus on democratic values and foster critical thinking rather than unreflected obedience towards superiors.

In summary, the beliefs underlying the above described mythology can still be found in today's business and are expected from 'good' leaders. Using power carefully and thoughtfully while respecting the interests of other people (Nibelungenlied), the Prussian virtues of integrity, bound in honour, sense of duty and ambition, diligence and shrewdness (Hanseatic Merchants) are considered important characteristics of a leader in Germany. In addition, the extensive democratization process after the Second World War has strongly influenced today's business life at various levels including the corporate governance structure, co-determination, expectations about participation and younger leaders' behaviour.

## OVERVIEW OF GERMAN LEADERSHIP

Any prototypical view of leadership regardless of country gives a rough idea referring to stereotypes. Stereotypical behaviour usually applies to some people but never to all. In addition, stereotypes render only a superficial and incomplete picture of reality. With this caveat in mind, this section explores leadership behaviour that can be considered prototypical for Germany as well as prototypical expectations towards leaders from a German perspective.

As recent research reveals, this view contradicts, to some extent, other nationals' views of stereotypical German leadership behaviour largely influenced by films of German military leaders in the Third Reich and the Second

World War. It refers to a directive leadership style, asking for loyalty and obedience toward the leader and even more so the cause, following the rules regardless of obstacles, people, and potential negative implications. Tiitula (1995) has collected prevalent stereotypes concerning business life in Germany listed in Table 7.1.

Unfortunately, stereotypes tend to be persistent over time even if change has occurred (Tiitula, 1995). Recent empirical studies of current leadership in Germany somewhat refute this stereotypical view of German leadership. The results show that the Prussian virtues and values may still have an influence in German leadership; however, they are grounded in a democratic understanding and participatory environment.

In this context, the results of the recent GLOBE (Global Leadership and Organizational Behaviour Effectiveness) research project are of particular interest. This study investigated the relationships between societal culture, organizational culture and organizational leadership in a multi-phase, multi-method (quantitative and qualitative methods) project. Leadership was defined as 'the ability of an individual to influence, motivate, and enable others to contribute toward the effectiveness and success of the organizations of which they are members' (House *et al.*, 2002: 5). The GLOBE results position the

*Table 7.1    Stereotypes of German business conduct (Tiitula, 1995: 162f)*

|  | **Germans** |
| --- | --- |
| **Background** | • Exact time schedule, slow speed, correctness |
|  | • Territorial |
|  | • The door as frontier |
|  | • Power is omnipresent |
|  | • Primacy of correctness and discipline |
|  | • Strict categorization |
|  | • Form, politeness, distance |
|  | • Work ethic |
| **Business** | • Authority and control in leadership |
|  | • Participation |
|  | • Written communication, exact and formal |
|  | • Work ethic |
|  | • Stiff |
| **Negotiations** | • Power |
|  | • Fact oriented |
|  | • Exact agreement |
|  | • Well organized |

prototype of German leadership in the Germanic cluster consisting of Austria, Switzerland and the Netherlands. Even though high performance is traditionally valued in German business life, the results show that respondents in all surveyed countries including Germany consider charismatic, transformational leadership, team-orientation and participation as desirable (Brodbeck *et al.*, 2002) and important attributes of 'good' leaders (Szabo *et al.*, 2002). While charisma seemed to be a widely favoured concept (Den Hartog *et al.*, 1999), team-orientation and especially participation were more specific to the Germanic cluster.

The GLOBE researchers developed several leadership concepts for classifying different leadership styles. Two of these concepts are prevalent in Germany. The first one is the transformational/charismatic leader characterized by attributes such as integrity, inspiration, performance orientation and vision. In addition, German transformational leaders showed also administrative competence and team integration values. The second predominant leadership concept in Germany is the so-called humble collaborator. This leader is characterized by a strong collaborative orientation, modesty and humane orientation. The attributes set leaders at an equal base with their followers largely eliminating hierarchical order (Brodbeck *et al.*, 2002). The characteristics of both leadership concepts can be found in the above described mythology and are present in current leaders such as Chancellor Angela Merkel (see below).

Besides the GLOBE studies, there are other studies which have examined German leadership behaviour comparing leadership styles of different countries. These results show that the base of comparison influences significantly the way leadership is experienced rendering different kinds of attributions and characterizations. In a longitudinal study, Vesa Suutari surveyed, for example, Finnish expatriates (Suutari, 1996). Participating expatriates were asked to describe their personal experiences with leadership in certain European countries since differences in leadership behaviour can be expressed particularly well by expatriates who start working in a foreign country, because they are not (yet) culturally bound to the society of their new workplace (Brewster *et al.*, 1993). Ten Finnish expatriates, now working in Germany, reported in their questionnaire that, in comparison with their Finnish peers, German leaders give recognition, reward good performance, criticize little and emphasize production. They also clarify roles and plans, coordinate and set goals more actively. On the other hand, they were characterized to be more passive in the two dimensions decision-participation and autonomy-delegation. The observed differences were, however not that clear and differed between companies due to different organizational cultures (Suutari, 1996).

Using Hofstede's model of culture, Ardchivili and Kuchinke (2002) studied differences between leadership styles found in Germany, the US and four countries of the former Soviet Union. The researchers compared the cultural values and leadership styles of more than 4000 employees in all six countries. Their findings suggest that leadership behaviour in Germany is characterized by high scores on charisma, inspiration, intelligence, consideration and contingency. Styles consisting of attributes such as management-by-exception and laissez-faire were ranked lowest of all attributes and of all researched countries. The authors argue that these do not seem to be important in German leadership concepts (Ardchivili and Kuschinke 2002).

Prior research on culture (for example, Sackmann and Phillips, 2004) suggests that the 'typical' leadership of a firm is not only influenced by national culture but also by the prevalent culture of the respective industry and the specific company. This is supported by the preliminary results of a current study of the author about leadership in a German based international firm. Interviews with top and key executives reveal a generation change in leadership behaviour (older versus younger leaders), industry specifics, and national differences. While both generations of leaders were/are very task- and results-oriented, the benevolent patriarchical leadership style of retired or retiring leaders has been replaced by a stronger focus on dialogue, open discussions, less attention to hierarchy and formality, a team-based approach, and self-leadership. In addition, the 'typical' leadership behaviour of German leaders is described by a Scandinavian as results-oriented/getting things done, hard working (long hours), organized, reliable, very task focused and hierarchically oriented, less open and challenging as compared with Scandinavians who are seen as more direct and open, more people- and team-oriented disregarding hierarchies.

Perhaps the presently most well-known German leader is Chancellor Angela Merkel. Trained as a physicist, the coverage of her activities portrayed in the media can be characterized as modest, down to earth, hard working, performance driven, well prepared, collaboration and humane oriented. In supra-national negotiations, she demonstrated her mediating role (for example EU). She topped 'The World's 100 Most Powerful Women' by *Forbes Magazine* in 2006 and 2007 (MacDonald and Schoenberger, 2007) and was elected most popular politician in Europe and in Germany (Die Welt, 2007). Several incidents indicate that Angela Merkel follows her own ('typical' German) beliefs and values even if this behaviour may lead to diplomatic discord as illustrated in recent diplomatic exchanges with China. She had invited the Dalai Lama into the Chancellery in Autumn 2007. This led to discord in the German-Chinese diplomacy and critical discussions in her government. Despite these problems, Merkel persisted in her view (Stern, 2007). In addition, she addresses openly issues of human rights, product piracy and environmental protection instead of primarily focusing on business issues. Merkel's policy concerning Russia and other countries is based upon the same standards (Bork, 2007; Focus, 2007).

Despite increasing globalization and a move towards an Anglo style business conduct, local specifics can still be observed in Germany as illustrated by Michael Diekmann, CEO of the Allianz Group since 2003. Allianz is a leading global insurance, banking and finance group. Diekmann is not well known in public because – as a 'typical German' – he separates private from business life. Besides business, he studied philosophy and graduated in law in record time. When he finally started at Allianz he was 33. Fifteen years later, he became CEO of the company. His leadership style is described as direct, decisive and sensible (Brost, 2006) as shown in the recent restructuring process of the Allianz transforming the German insurance company into an international player.

## GLOBAL IMPLICATIONS

Myths and legends are critical events and part of the collective memory of a certain group of people (Heinzle, 2004). Like stories (Martin *et al.*, 1983), they help people in their orientation in a particular cultural setting. In addition, they satisfy people's desire to remember their heritage (Graf, 1990) and help them define and maintain their identity. Myths can be seen as a form of narrative story in which heroes fulfil several roles. They may serve as antecessors, role models or even idols (Assmann, 1992). The paradox that Martin *et al.* (1983) found in their research of stories may apply to mythology as well. While members of a certain culture are convinced that their story or mythology is unique, it may, in fact, share several common themes and structures with other cultural settings (Jung, 1968). In addition, stories, sagas and legends are embellished and changed over time and can be interpreted in many and even in opposite ways as we have indicated in regard to the Prussian virtues.

Given the specific Germanic mythology with Siegfried, Hagen and King Etzel of the Nibelungenlied as different kinds of leaders, the Prussian virtues and the honour of Hanseatic merchants, prototypical Germanic leadership can be characterized as patriarchical using position power to get results in a way that tries to respect the interests of other people. It values and promotes a Calvinistic approach to work including commitment, shrewdness, conscientiousness, creating order and expecting loyalty and respect for order in return. However, the results of recent studies on German leadership behaviour suggest that the Germanic mythology relevant to prototypical leadership has been overlaid and changed by a thorough democratization process initiated after the Second World War in all spheres of life. Hence, assumptions of prototypical leadership that are still promoted in other countries may be based on a mythology that has become outlived by processes of modernization and change.

On the basis of this democratization process, leaders who have been social-ized in Germany after the Second World War still tend to be task-focused, results-oriented, loyal, hard working, organized and so on. In addition, younger leaders are less formal, they value and live a stronger team orienta-tion and participative approach than generally recognized. Underlying reasons are a socialization process promoting democratic values. Structural, political and legal arrangements were created such as the Vorstand, the law of co-deter-mination with the Betriebsrat and workers' representation on the board as a framework for democracy in the corporate world.

While all these characteristics can be considered a strength both in a national as well as global context, depending on their mix and mould they may also turn into weaknesses. If the task-focus, factual and performance orienta-tion, diligence and drive are too strong, leaders may be considered stubborn, inflexible, dogmatic, too mechanistic, lacking an orientation towards people, processes, and life balance. In addition, the participative approach takes time in decision making. To be successful as a leader in a global context, the proper mixture is important, combining the 'typical' German attributes with a process and people orientation that meets both the expectations of local people and business needs – see the Commentary box.

---

## COMMENTARY BOX

### CEO (German National) of a German Based International Firm

Leadership is an important topic to us. Our company is still a bunch of firms with their own subculture (due to recent acquisi-tions) … There are clear differences in leadership in these differ-ent firms. In X, leadership is still too focused on the top guy (who is retiring at the end of the year). People need to share leader-ship.

### VP HR (German National) of a Business Unit, German Based International Firm

We have excellent experts. Their know-how is fantastic. Our people in leadership positions are highly qualified, task focused, hard working, and committed to the firm. They get things done even if it is a tight schedule and lots of problems emerge. However, they don't really lead people.

### VP HR (Scandinavian) of an Anglo-Saxon Business Unit, German Based International Firm

In Germany, we have very good managers. Their leadership skills are, however, underdeveloped. They underestimate the value of people leadership. Leadership does not always happen. Their consideration of impact of their own decisions on others could improve. However, they get things done, they move, solve problems. They are much more formal and hierarchically oriented than the Scandinavians but not as direct in their communication.

### Leader (German National with International Work Experience) of an International Business Unit, German Based International Firm

When I worked ten years for the other firm (global Anglo-Saxon based firm), I realized the strong positive side of German leadership: being reliable, valuing high quality, being punctual, getting things done, being knowledgeable about your field, highly committed, taking decisions. In the other firm (Anglo-Saxon), we would sit together, talk for hours but no real decision was taken. When we moved apart, it was not clear what we had agreed on.

Recent research indicates that prototypical leadership may differ not only between nations but also between regions, industries and companies (Sackmann and Phillips, 2004). Given the recent worldwide developments in the spheres of economics, politics and society, individuals may be influenced to a lesser extent by the nationality of their passport. Increasing internalization and globalization of business, enabling telecommunication and transportation, technological as well as political developments have allowed people to travel easily, communicate instantaneously, work in virtual teams around the globe, be exposed to different cultures, and make a choice about their home base (Sackmann and Phillips, 2004). A new breed of cosmopolitical leaders who have lived in different cultures may have developed a mind set that enables them to move around and behave culturally more sensitively and adequately in different parts of the world – regardless of their cultural heritage.

## PRACTICAL APPLICATION

The mythology of a particular country may help to understand a particular heritage and serve as a first orientation in regard to prototypical leadership and expected leadership behaviour in a country like Germany. Such an understanding is, however, rather superficial and based on stereotypes. Stereotypes express general opinions or categories for classifying experiences with a certain group of people. They may apply to some people of that group but not to all and therefore need to be handled carefully. Hence, stereotypical views need to be supplemented by more detailed and context specific understandings in order to be able to do justice to underlying changes and new developments that may be different from the past.

While German style management is often characterized with the 'competence first' principle (Brodbeck *et al.*, 2002: 16) avoiding the German translation of the term leader, leadership behaviour found in a younger generation of leaders and young dynamic industries such as IT related is much more participatory, inclusive, team and dialogue based, less hierarchical and power centred when compared with the older retiring generations of leaders and traditional industries such as banking or insurance. Precision, quality of work, reliability and punctuality, directness in communication, professionalism that strives for perfection searching for the one way or 'the truth' may still be principles that guide the behaviour of a leader socialized in Germany. If these are experienced as helpful or difficult in business interactions depends to a large extent on the beholder. A person socialized in an Anglo-Saxon or Latin-American country may experience some behavioural rigidity while another person may experience the same behaviour as trustworthy and reliable.

We therefore recommend that a person who wants to work or do business in Germany should move beneath the stereotypical view of prototypical German leadership and search for the particularities of individuals and groups, firm, region and industry involved in a specific situation to truly understand the underlying guiding rationale. Dealing successfully with cultural differences of any kind in intercultural, cross-cultural or multicultural encounters requires a general cultural awareness also of one's own cultural biases, openness and tolerance towards differences, an appreciation of these differences as well as the ability to deal with ambiguities and potential conflicts (for example, Phillips and Sackmann, 2002). In a first step, the personal biography of a leader, the specific history of a company, region, industry and country may be a more solid indicator for some of the cultural peculiarities involved.

All in all, 'typical' German leadership behaviour has its value base in Germanic mythology and post-Second World War developments. Valuing traditionally the 'hard' side of leadership such as a task-focus, professional conduct, facts and performance helps getting things done in combination with reliability. The stronger team-based approach of younger leaders is a move to further add and develop the 'soft' side of leadership.

## NOTES

1. I would like to thank Birte Horstmann for her support in researching German mythology.
2. Taking a typical view of leadership behaviour at the national level relates to stereotypes that render a rather rough picture. The reader who is interested in a more differentiated view of culture is referred to Boyacigiller *et al.* (2004), Phillips and Sackmann (2002), and Sackmann and Phillips (2004).
3. Recent changes in some companies such as DaimlerChrysler are influenced by the Anglo-Saxon model.

## REFERENCES

Ardchivili, A. and Kuchinke, K. P. (2002), Leadership styles and cultural values among managers and subordinates: a comparative study of four countries of the former Soviet Union, Germany, and the US, *Human Resource Development International*, **5** (1), 99–117.

Assmann, J. (1992), *Das kulturelle Gedächtnis* [*The cultural memory*], München: Beck.

Bischof, N. (1996), *Das Kraftfeld der Mythen* [*The force field of myths*], München: Piper.

Bizard, P. (2007), '*Welche Seite der Welt soll man jungen Leuten zeigen?*' – *Die literarische Reflexion pädagogischer Konzepte in Prosatexten Johann Karl Wezels* [*'Which side of the world shall be shown to the youth?' – The literary reflexion of pedagogic concepts in the prose of Johann Karl Wezel*] Inaugural dissertation zur Erlangung der Doktorwürde der philologischen Fakultät der Albert-Ludwigs-Universität Freiburg im Br.

Bork, H. (2007), Merkels China Politik. Wenn Peking droht Merkels [China politics. If Beijing threatens], www.sueddeutsche.de/ausland/artikel/783/143463/ [29 November 2007].

Boyacigiller, Nakiye, Kleinberg, M., Phillips, Margaret and Sackmann, Sonja (2004), Conceptualizing culture. Elucidating the streams of research in international cross-cultural management, in Betty Jane Punnett and Oded Shekar (eds), *Handbook for International Management Research*, University of Michigan Press, 99–167.

Brewster, C, Lundmark, A. and Holden, L. (1993), *A Different Tack: An Analysis of British and Swedish Management Styles*, Lund: Studentlitteratur.

Brodbeck, F. C., Frese, M. and Javidan, M. (2002), Leadership made in Germany: Low on compassion, high on performance, *Academy of Management Executive*, **16** (1), 16–29.

Brost, M. (2006), *Hoffentlich gut versichert [Hopefully, you are well insured]*, DIE ZEIT, No. 43/2006, 19 October 2006.

Burkert, Walter (1981), Mythos and Mythologie [Myth and mythology], in Erika Wischer (ed.), *Prophyläen Geschichte der Literatur. Literatur und Gesellschaft der westlichen Welt I: Die Welt der Antike*, Berlin: Propyläen, 11–35.

Den Hartog, D. N., House, R. J., Hanges, P. J., Ruiz-Quintanilla, S. A., Dorfman, P. W.,

Brodbeck, F. C., Reber, G., Szabo, E., Weiber, J. and Wunderer, R. (1999), Culture specific and cross culturally generalizable implicit leadership theories. Are attributes of charismatic/transformational leadership universally endorsed?, *Leadership Quarterly*, **10** (2), 219–56.

Die Welt (2007), Angela Merkel beliebter als der Papst [Angela Merkel more popular than the Pope'], http://www.welt.de/politik/article1343906/Angela_Merkel_ist_beliebter_als_der_Papst.html [6 December 2006].

Focus (2007), Merkel ruft China zur Verantwortung [Merkel holds China liable]', www.focus,.de/politik/ausland/umweltschutz_aid_130629.html [29 November 2007].

Graf, K. (1990), Heroisches Herkommen. Überlegungen zum Begriff der ,historischen Überlieferung' am Beispiel heroischer Traditionen [Heroic origin. Thoughts about the term 'historical tradition' on the example of heroic traditions], in Leander Petzoldt, Siegfried de Rachewiltz, Ingo Schneider and Petra Streng (eds), *Das Bild der Welt in der Volkserzählung*, Frankfurt/M. *et al.*: Lang, pp. 45–64.

Hammer, M. (1987), Behavioral dimensions of intercultural effectiveness: An application and extension, *International Journal of Intercultural Relations*, **11**, 65–88.

Hammer, M., Gudykunst, W. B. and Wiseman, R. L. (1978), Dimensions of intercultural effectiveness: An exploratory study, *International Journal of Intercultural Relations*, **2**, 382–93.

Hawes, F. and Kealey, D. J. (1981), An empirical study of Canadian technical assistance, *International Journal of Intercultural Relations*, **5**, 239–82.

Heinzle, J. (2004), Unsterblicher Heldengesang: Die Nibelungen als nationaler Mythos der Deutschen [Immortal heroic epic: The Nibelungs as the German national myth], in Reinhard Brandt and Steffen Schmidt (eds), *Mythos und Mythologie*, Berlin: Akademie Verlag, 185–202.

Herrmann, H. P., Blitz, H. M. and Moßmann, S. (1977), *Machtphantasie Deutschland [Germany as a imagination of power]*, Frankfurt/M.: Suhrkamp.

Heusler, A. (1921), *Nibelungensage und Nibelungenlied. Die Stoffgeschichte des deutschen Heldenepos Nibelungensaga and Nibelungenlied. [The history of the theme of the German heroic epic]*, Dortmund: Fr. Wilh. Ruhfus.

Hofstede, G. (n.d.), *Values Survey Module 1994 Manual*, University of Limburg: Institute for Research on Intercultural Cooperations.

House, R., Javidan, M., Hanges, P. and Dorfman, P. (2002), Understanding cultures and implicit leadership theories across the globe: an introduction to project GLOBE, *Journal of World Business*, **37** (1), 3–10.

Huret, J. (1997), Hamburg im Jahre 1906 [Hamburg in the year 1906], *Hamburgische Geschichts- und Heimatblätter*, **13** (3), 56–78.

Javidan, M. and House, R. (2002), Leadership and cultures around the world: findings from GLOBE. An introduction to the special issue, *Journal of World Business*, **37** (1), 1–2.

Jung, C. G. (1968), *Man and His Symbols*, New York, NY: Dell.

Knapp, K. (1995), Interkulturelle Kommunikationsfähigkeit als Qualifikationsmerkmal für die Wirtschaft [Intercultural communication skills as a qualification characteristic in economy], in Jürgen Bolten (ed.), *Cross Culture – Interkulturelles Handeln in der Wirtschaft*, Sternenfels and Berlin: Wissenschaft und Praxis, 8–23.

Kroll, F. J. (2002), Executive commentary, *Academy of Management Executive*, **16** (1), 29–30.

MacDonald, E. and Schoenberger, C. R. (2007), The world's 100 most powerful women, *Forbes Magazine*, 9 March 2007, http://www.forbes.com/business/forbes/2007/0903/126.html [6 December 2007].

Martin, J., Feldman, M. S., Hatch, M. J. and Sitkin, S. B. (1983), The uniqueness paradox in organizational stories, *Administrative Science Quarterly*, **28** (3), 438–53.

Phillips, M. E. and Sackmann, S. A. (2002), Managing in an era of multiple cultures, *The Graziadio Business Report*, November 2002.

Phillipsson, E. A. (1962), Phänomenologie, vergleichende Mythologie und germanische Religionsgeschichte [Phenomenology, comparative mythology and Germanic religious history], *PMLA*, **77** (3), 187–93.

Platzeck, M. (2003), Der Umgang mit dem preußischen Erbe in Brandenburg [Exposure to the Prussian heritage in Brandenburg, Speech of the Brandenburgian prime minister], www.preussen.de/de/heute/forum_preussen/ministerpraesident_ matthias_platzeck_ueber_den_umgang_mit_dem_preussischen_erbe.html;jsessionid=A13D9BF528A1C0016ED9F55D895D7371 [5 July 2007].

rbb (2007), Preußen und seine Mythen [Prussia and its myths], in rbb (ed.), Preussen. Chronik eines deutschen Staates, www.preussen-chronik.de/_/thema_jsp/ key=thema_ preu%25dfen-mythos.html [5 July 2007].

Sackmann, S. A. (2007), Unternehmenskultur und Mitbestimmung – Versuch einer integrativen Perspektive [Corporate culture and co-determination – An integrative perspective?], in R. Benthin and U. Brinkmann, *Unternehmenskultur und Mitbestimmung*, Frankfurt: Campus Verlag GmbH.

Sackmann, Sonja and Horstmann, Birte (2008), Unternehmenskultur und Mitbestimmung – Versuch einer integrativen Perspektive [Corporate culture and co-determination – Attempt of an integrative perspective], in Rainer Benthin and Ulrich Brinkmann (eds), *Unternehmenskultur und Mitbestimmung*, Frankfurt and New York, NY: Campus, 97–120.

Sackmann, S. A. and Phillips, M. E. (2004), Contextual influences on culture research: shifting assumptions for new workplace realities, *International Journal of Cross Cultural Management*, **4** (3), 370–90.

Springeth, M. (1996), Der Attila-Mythos in der nordischen und in der deutschen Literatur [The myth of Attila in Nordic and German literature], in Ulrich Müller and Werner Wunderlich (eds), *Herrscher. Helden. Heilige* S. 29-46, St Gallen: UVK.

Stern (2007), Kritik an Merkel's Dalai-Lama-Treffen: 'Entscheide selbst, wen ich treffe' [Animadversion on Merkel's meeting with the Dalai-Lama: 'I decide whom I meet'], www.stern.de/politik/deutschland/603126.html [21 November 2007].

Suutari, V. (1996), Variation in the average leadership behaviour of managers across countries: Finnish expatriates' experiences from Germany, Sweden, France and Great Britain, *The International Journal of Human Resource Management*, **7** (3), 677–707.

Szabo, E., Brodbeck, F. C., Den Hartog, D. N., Reber, G., Weibler, J. and Wunderer, R. (2002), The Germanic Europe cluster: where employees have a voice, *Journal of World Business*, **37** (1), 55–68.

Tiitula, L. (1995), Stereotype in interkulturellen Geschäftskontakten. Zu Fragen der deutsch-finnischen GeschäftskommunikationStereotyps in intercultural business contacts. [Questions about German-Finnish business communication], in Jürgen Bolten (ed.), *Cross Culture – Interkulturelles Handeln in der Wirtschaft*, Sternenfels and Berlin: Wissenschaft und Praxis, S. 162–72.

Triandis, H. C. (1993), The contingency model in cross-cultural perspective, in Martin M. Chemers and Roya Ayman (eds), *Leadership Theory and Research: Perspectives and Directions*, San Diego, CA: Academic Press, 167–88.

Von Heß, J. L. (1787), Hamburg topographisch, politisch und historisch beschrieben [Hamburg described topographically, politically and historically], *Bd. 1, 1. Aufl.*, Hamburg: beim Verfasser.

Weber, M. (1991), *Die protestantische Ethik I. Eine Aufsatzsammlung Ed. von Joachim Winckelmann* [*Protestant ethics I. A collection of essays, ed. by Joachim Winckelmann*], 8, durchges. Aufl., Gütersloh: GTB Siebenstern.

Wegner, M. (1999), *Hanseaten Hanseatics*, Berlin: Siedler.

# 8. Cultural mythology and global leadership in England

## Romie Frederick Littrell

## INTRODUCTION

At least some of the English have had a tradition of viewing themselves as uniquely qualified to be world leaders; Lord Palmerston, in 1858 in Parliament: 'our duty – our vocation – is not to enslave, but to set free; and I may say, without any vain-glorious boast, or without great offence to anyone, we stand at the head of moral, social and political civilization. Our task is to lead the way and direct the march of other nations', and according to Archibald Philip Primrose 5th earl of Rosebery, prime minister 1894–5, the British Empire was 'the greatest secular agency for good that the world has seen'.

England has significant examples of effective leadership in King William I of Normandy, establishing a line of kings who built and adapted a strong, lasting government. King John abused his powers, and was forced by noble English leaders to sign the *Magna Carta,* which limited the powers of the king and established a cornerstone of English Common Law, spread by the Empire around the world. Henry II established laws for all of the people of England. Under the rule of Elizabeth I, England became one of the most powerful nations in the world, growing into the British Empire in the seventeenth to twentieth centuries.

The events of the building of the British Empire actually define the Real First World War, where the pursuit of trade brought British overseas merchants and the military into conflict with other imperial powers, initially with Spain and Portugal and later adding France and Russia. The British Empire outside the islands began in the seventeenth century in North America and eventually achieved global economic hegemony in the late nineteenth century. At its maximum in about 1920, the British Empire was the largest geographically in history, one-quarter of the world's territory and 20 per cent of its population, and for a considerable length of time was the foremost global power. Today the UK and its colonial offshoots comprise six of the 30 major world economies (17 per cent) in the OECD (Organisation for Economic Co-operation and

Development). These numbers are even higher if the Republic of Ireland is included.

## BRITANNIA

This chapter deals with England in the original Britannia sense, and does not include discussion of Ireland, Scotland or Northern Ireland, as they have historic cultural differences. I will also not discuss differences within England between North and South. Generalizing the cultural origins of England, we find an Anglo-Celtic heritage, and a Christian religious background (later heavily influenced by Protestantism).

Britannia was the original name given by the Romans to the province that comprised what is now England and Wales (neighbouring Ireland was known as Hibernia, Scotland was Caledonia, Germany was Germania, Brittany was Armorica and France was Gaul). After the Romans left, the name gradually fell into disuse, but later, in the days of the Empire, it was resurrected, and since 1672 Britannia has been anthropomorphized into a woman wearing a helmet, and carrying a shield and trident. It is a symbol that is intended to blend the concepts of empire, militarism and economics.

Wales is included in Britannia; Morgan and Phillips (2003) report that 'most young people in Wales define themselves primarily as "Welsh"; but there is very little to suggest that they are uncomfortable with a subsidiary identity of "British".' They do not consider themselves 'English'.

During the first millennium of the Christian calendar, England was very much part of Europe, and this link was solidified by the invasion by William, Duke of Normandy, who held a claim to the throne equal to the resident Harold. The victory over Harold, King of England, in 1066 at the Battle of Hastings, established one of the dominant monarchies of Europe, and William's division of his heritage between England and Normandy began the 900-year conflict between England and France.

Many consider the establishment of England as a nation as stemming from the building of the *Domesday Book* to provide national taxation after the conquest of England by William and the Normans.

Though under Norman control, the Anglo-Saxon culture of the common people continued to shape the underlying cultural beliefs of the English (Ashkanasy *et al.*, 2002). The Anglo-Saxon culture of the U.K. derives from the migration of northwestern European communities beginning in the fourth and fifth centuries. Their subsequent conversion to Christianity, exemplified by the legends of Arthur as a Christian king, further defines the national character. The Angeln (Anglians) from Germany and Denmark, the Saxons from Germany, and groups from The Netherlands, Denmark, France, Central

Germany and Rome settled in England, irrevocably influencing the local Briton or Celtic culture (Gupta *et al.*, 2002).

During the mid-sixteenth century England was consumed by internal political and religious unrest. However, its external power was established with the defeat of the Spanish Armada in 1588, marking the global ascension of English naval power. Thereafter began the colonial expansion that underpinned economic success in the centuries to come. For the next 200 years, England embarked on a massive worldwide colonial occupation and social migration. A brief review of the cultural history of England is available in Ashkanasy *et al.* (2002).

Definitions of 'Englishness' have varied over the centuries. An interesting discussion is provided by Richard Hingley (2000) in *Roman Officers and English Gentlemen: The Imperial Origins of Roman Archaeology*. Hingley states that self-identification has ranged from Briton to Celt to Teutonic 'Anglo-Saxon'. Oppenheimer (2006) found that 30 per cent of genes in England derive from Northern Europe, mainly due to ancient cultural links between England and Scandinavia in the Neolithic period or before. The pendulum of socially desirable heritage swung to descendants of Romans, then back to Victorian-Boudican Celts, then to the rise of a theory of a mixed race. We have now returned to 'Anglo-Saxons' or 'Anglos'. Anglo-Saxon was first used in continental European Latin sources to distinguish the Saxons in England from those on the continent, but it soon came to mean simply the 'English'.

The more specific use of Anglo-Saxon to denote the non-Celtic settlers of England prior to the Norman Conquest dates from the sixteenth century. In more modern times it has also been used to denote any of the people (or their descendants) of England, or even the British Isles. This idea gives rise to WASP (White Anglo-Saxon Protestant), and the 'Anglo cluster' in cross-cultural studies, that is, Australia, Canada, New Zealand, the UK, the USA, and White English-speaking South Africa.

## OVERVIEW OF MYTHS IN ENGLAND

The popular archetypical heroic mythical leader is the noble warrior; in English myth this hero is more complex, with the greatest leaders being those who could also govern effectively, such as Beowulf, Arthur, Henry V and Churchill. England does have heroic noble warriors in such as Drake, Nelson, Wellington (who also had a political career), and Montgomery.

Prior to the establishment of the Kingdom of England in the tenth century, several legends influenced the idealization of the national character. 'Scholars continue to find that fictional narratives provide rich insight into the historical development of a modern national consciousness' (Barczewski, 2000). Campbell (1968, and 1993: 9) proposes that comparative cultural studies demonstrate beyond question that similar themes in mythic tales are to be found in every part of the world. The themes that continually show up in multiple cultures are called 'universal myths'. Some of the universals are creation myths, flood myths, dying and rising god myths, punishment myths and hero/heroine myths. This is an important point for students of human social behaviour to understand; human beings have common important concerns; and these can be used as a starting point when comparing cultures. Questions held in common include survival issues, wondering who we are, where we come from, how we fit in our world, and what we are supposed to do with our lives. We will see these kinds of myths in the legends of England.

Leadership myths and stories about the heroes of history, such as King Arthur and the Knights of the Roundtable, are important in understanding cultures. These stories passed on through generations define a culture's mental programming. Leadership myths in a culture give clues about how members see themselves and what constitutes good governance, ethical behaviour and fundamental courage.

England, along with most European nations, remembers a mythical origin, deriving the genealogical descent of their kings from distant roots. Geoffrey of Monmouth's *Historia Regum Britanniae* (Busse, 1994) specified an origin from the Trojan Diaspora.

Most cultures and peoples also have the myth of a 'Golden Age', which involves two perspectives: it looks backward in time towards a lost paradise and forward towards an idealized future. The reign of Arthur fulfils this myth with the ideals of just rule and ancient chivalry and the myth that Caliburn/Excalibur is still held by the Lady of the Lake, and Arthur and Merlin may only be sleeping.

England's oldest folk tales, myths and legends share themes and sources with the Norse, Welsh, Scottish and Irish Celts, and Gauls. Successive waves of invaders and settlers have all influenced the myths and legends of England. Some tales, such as that of The Lambton Wyrm show a distinct Norse influence, while others, particularly some of the events and characters associated with the Arthurian legends show Roman and Norman/Gaulic influence.

The most famous body of English folk tales concerns the legends of King Arthur, although it would be wrong to regard these stories as purely English in origin as they also concern Wales and, to a lesser extent, Ireland and Scotland. They should therefore be considered as part of the folklore of the British Isles as a whole.

Post-1066 stories include the tales of Robin Hood, which exist in many forms, and stories of other folk heroes such as Hereward the Wake and Dunn of Cumbria who, although being based on historical characters, have grown to become legends. Other historical figures have come to have legends associated with them, such as Sir Francis Drake and 'Drake's Drum', which, though in a Naval Museum, can be heard beating when significant events take place involving England. When legends are attached, these figures then move out of the realm of historical fact and into the realm of mythology.

## Beowulf: From Hero to Heroic Leader to Leader

In Beowulf, an early legend combining heroism and leadership, we see the ideals of the Germanic ancestors of the English before they left the Continent to settle on the island. The legend of Beowulf embodies the beliefs of tribes in North Germany on the shores of the North Sea and of the Baltic. The myth depicts a hero who embodies the English ideal, bold to a level of rashness himself, but prudent for his comrades, resourceful, loyal to his king and his kinsmen, generous in war and in peace, self-sacrificing. Beowulf's life is depicted as a struggle against evil forces, and his death comes in a glorious victory over the powers of evil, a victory gained for the sake of others to whom Beowulf feels that he owes protection and devotion.

Beowulf is an Old English poem surviving from a tenth-century manuscript; the text of the poem may have been first written in the eighth century. The story may be the first Western work where the same character plays both hero and then leader and political leader. 'The hero follows a code that exalts indomitable will and valour in the individual, but society requires a king who acts for the common good, not for his own glory' (Boggs, 1990: 94). By the tenth century the roles of heroes and kings were beginning to be differentiated in the minds of the people. A leader's desire for personal glory placed the entire society at risk (p. 98) and, therefore, Beowulf signalled the beginning of the end of the heroic age, tempering his desire for glory with a desire to govern well. 'The greater the hero, the more likely is his tendency to imprudent action as a king' (Leyerle, 1965: 89).

Some believe the end of the heroic age in literature came with the death of another king, Arthur (Boggs, 1990: 98). According to Boggs, Arthur is the first fully developed leader in Western literature (p. 102), destined from the beginning to be king, and as he aged becoming a wise leader, served by greater heroes such as Gawain and Lancelot.

## The Romans

For 350 years, Britain was part of the political union created by the Roman Empire. By AD 43, the time of the main Roman invasion, Britain had already frequently been the target of invasions by forces of the Roman Republic and Roman Empire. Like other regions on the edge of the empire, Britain had long enjoyed trading links with the Romans and their economic and cultural influence was a significant part of the British late pre-Roman Iron Age, especially in the south. Roman towns and cities in England have ruins of the distinctive baths, forums, arches, aqueducts, walls, roads and temples. The Romans also brought literature, legends, and a pantheon of gods and goddesses. They also introduced Christianity and practically annihilated the Druid religion and priests. Many Romano-Celtic deities were based upon old Celtic gods, taking on new Latin names and aspects of Roman divinities, and began to be worshipped alongside the more traditional Jovian pantheon. The cult of Mithras, a god of Persian sources who was particularly popular with Roman soldiers and troops garrisoned on the British frontier, had significant religious/mythological influence on the expected behaviour of leaders and warriors. Mithras had appeal to both the common soldier and officers, and had significant parallels in practices and beliefs with Christianity. The cult remained active in Britain for some time after Christianization, and in his 'Song of the Macrocosm' (*Canu y byd mawr*) the bard Taliesin (sixth century) demonstrated his knowledge of the 'Cult of Mithras' (Matthews, 1991).

### Arthur: The Ideal in War and Peace

Following the departure of the Romans came Arthur, a mix of myth and fragments of history, said to be the son of Uther Pendragon (Ythr Ben Dragwn) of Brittany, and may have been high king from 496–537 (Geoffrey of Monmouth, c. 1136/1977). King Arthur is an influential figure in the mythology of England, where he appears as the ideal of kingship in both war and peace. There is disagreement about whether Arthur, or a model for him, ever actually existed. In the earliest mentions and in Welsh texts, he is never given the title 'King'. An early text refers to him as a *dux bellorum* (Latin: 'war leader'), and medieval Welsh texts often call him *ameraudur* ('emperor'; the word is borrowed from the Latin *imperator*, which could also mean 'war leader').

Arthur was first identified as a fictional high king from Britain's past by a monk of Welsh origin, Geoffrey of Monmouth, who chronicled *The History of the Kings of Britain*, '*Historia Regum Brittaniae*', early in the twelfth century. This chronicle was an important cultural influence on medieval society. Geoffrey gave the world an extraordinary and evocative tale that caught the imagination of rulers, the public and creative minds for generations. Legends of Arthur and his court accumulated in the middle ages, not just in Geoffrey's chronicle, but also in the Welsh *Mabinogion* and in the French romance cycle and the German epics of Parzival and Tristan. Geoffrey's narrative demonstrates clear agendas: national pride, Christianity, and a strong system of justice. Geoffrey exalts the culture and idealistic society of England, as in his account of Arthur's plenary court (pp. 226–37). Although many of the earlier

British kings described by Geoffrey are not Christian, his narrative builds towards the height of the country's power under the Christian King Arthur, and hence, the glorification of the country as a Christian entity.

Arthur was depicted as a popular King, who became known for his outstanding courage and generosity. Confiscated lands were given back to their rightful owners and churches were rebuilt. He married Guinevere, who was of Roman descent, then he conquered Ireland and Iceland. As a result of his wise rule, a golden age followed with peace, stability and dignity in Britain.

King Arthur is perhaps considered 'The Greatest Leader' of England. From the legends his name is synonymous with wisdom and fairness. The names of his wife, magician, and knights are household words. His sword symbolizes righteous power. His capital city is an icon for earthly perfection. The Round Table, first mentioned by Wace in his *Roman de Brut* (Ford, 2000), was not only a physical table but the highest Order of Chivalry at the Court of King Arthur. Its members were supposedly the cream of the British military who followed a strict code of honour and service.

As great warrior, Arthur's victory over the Saxons at Mount Badon is regarded by historians as a real event. Stories relate that during the battle Arthur, calling on the name of the Virgin Mary, rushes into the midst of his enemies and destroys multitudes of them with the formidable Caliburn, and puts the rest to flight.

As a just and generous leader, Arthur established all his knights, and to those who were not rich he gave land, and charged them all never to do outrage nor murder, and always to flee treason; also, by no means to be cruel, but to give mercy unto him that asked mercy, upon pain of forfeiture of his favour and lordship; and always to do ladies, damsels and gentlewomen service, upon pain of death; also that no man take battle in a wrongful quarrel, or a quarrel outside the law, nor for any worldly goods. Arthur required this oath to be sworn by all the Knights of the Round Table, and again at every year at the high feast of Pentecost.

Geoffrey of Monmouth gave the British consciousness a heroic King to rival Charlemagne, King of the Franks. Invading the Roman Empire in Europe with victory after victory, Arthur was planning to cross the Alps and attack Rome itself, but he received the news that Mordred had proclaimed himself as King of Britain and was living in adultery with Guinevere. In later, more popular versions Guinevere committed adultery with Lancelot. Arthur returned home, defeating Mordred's army in Cornwall by the River Camel. During the battle, Mordred was killed and Arthur was fatally wounded. According to the story, Arthur gave the crown to a cousin, while he was taken to the Isle of Avalon for his wounds to be nursed (by, said Geoffrey, Morgan the Enchantress). The Isle of Avalon has always remained a vague, mythical place, and Geoffrey leaves it unclear whether or not Arthur is supposed to have died of his wounds.

King Arthur's new ethos of courtliness, nobility, and selfless bravery became established in common life, and his influence began to extend itself. The Kingdom of Britain had risen above all others, in its riches and in its chivalric codes of conduct. Knights had become famed for their personal bravery and wore armour and colours of their own style. Women vowed only to give their devotion to brave men who had proved themselves three times in battle; the knights became ever more daring and the women ever more virtuous. The rules of Chivalry were codified (Gautier, 1891):

The ten rules of chivalry

- Thou shalt believe all the church teaches and observe all its directions.
- Thou shalt defend the church.
- Thou shalt respect all weaknesses and shalt constitute thyself the defender of them.
- Thou shalt love the country in which thou wast born.
- Thou shalt not recoil before thine enemy.
- Thou shalt make war against the Infidel without cessation and without mercy.
- Thou shalt perform scrupulously the feudal duties, if they be not contrary to the laws of God.
- Thou shalt never lie and remain faithful to thy pledged word.
- Thou shalt be generous and give largesse to everyone.
- Thou shalt be everywhere and always the champion of the Right and Good and the foe of Injustice and Evil.

Giovanni Boccaccio (1363/1962) in *De Casibus Virorum Illustrium* (Examples of Famous Men) says that the 12 basic rules of Arthur's Knights of the Round Table were:

- To never lay down arms.
- To seek after wonders.
- When called upon, to defend the rights of the weak with all one's strength.
- To injure no one.
- Not to attack one another.
- To fight for the safety of one's country.
- To give one's life for one's country.
- To seek nothing before honour.
- Never to break faith for any reason.
- To practise religion most diligently.

- To grant hospitality to anyone, each according to his ability.
- Whether in honour or disgrace, to make a report with the greatest fidelity to truth to those who keep the annals.

This kind of knight evokes images of what the nation should be and appeals across sub-national cultural factions and economic classes.

Gellner (1983) states that nationalism 'imposes homogeneity', in part to organize and structure culture; it therefore must be accompanied by hegemonic tools such as the iconic figure of the knight to symbolize and reinforce the dominant ideology (pp. 125, 140). Thus, out of the need for a specific representation of the desired shared culture the myth of the knight took root and flourished within the national imagination. The stories of the knights were essential to defining England as a nation. Painted as romantic purveyors of right, upholding chivalric ideals, and commencing on exciting, colourful quests, the knights appealed to all – aristocrat, merchant and peasant alike. The timing of the overwhelming popularity of the knights' tales strongly suggests that these tales, and more specifically, the knights depicted in them, provided England with a central icon around which to establish identity as a nation.

The romanticization of the knight continued through such works as the Vulgate Cycle of Arthurian stories written some time between 1215 and 1230, Chaucer's *Canterbury Tales*, the *Alliterative Morte Arthure*, and *Sir Gawain and the Green Knight* in the last half of the fourteenth century, the Stanzaic Morte Arthur at the beginning of the fifteenth century, Malory's Arthurian tales, first written in approximately 1470 and published as *Morte D'Arthur* in 1485 by Caxton, and others. Finally, some time between 1590 and 1596, Sir Edmund Spenser wrote *The Faerie Queene*. The work incorporated Queen Elizabeth I into the chivalric folklore, interesting because of the fact that the queen seems to have been extremely aware of the necessity of cultural homogeneity and encouraged the literary trend of using literature to shape the identity of the nation so long as it fit with her agenda.

Knighthood was eventually glamorized into an elegant ideal called, after the French chevalier (horseman, knight), 'chivalry'. It was soon not enough for the true knight to be merely a capable horseman. He was expected to exemplify courage, piety, generosity, and above all, 'courtesy'. In theory, at least, chivalry was identified with virtue; and later, with increasing emphasis placed upon the protection of the weak, the chivalric ideal became as compelling in peace as in war.

Modern knighthood is a distinction that is granted to commoners, ranking next to baronet, and bestowed by the Crown. Formerly knighthood was a military order, any member of which might create new knights, noble or commoner, establishing an egalitarian opportunity. It was originally the highest rank of chivalry, and in full flower in England and Normandy before the Norman

Conquest. Under the feudal system a knight was generally a vassal holding land as a fief from the lord he served. As noted above, the Christian ideal of knightly behaviour under the rules of chivalry required devotion to the church, loyalty to military and feudal superiors, and preservation of personal honour.

The nature, duties, and responsibilities of the knight expanded over time, and in the twelfth and thirteenth centuries had assumed civil administrative responsibilities (Faulkner, 1996). By the sixteenth century knighthood had become honorific rather than feudal or military. Nowadays one may become a knight by organizing a very successful rock-and-roll band or managing a football league.

The texts that portray knights and knighthood demonstrate their burgeoning role as an archetype whose romanticized depictions served to mask violence, tumult and extreme class stratification. The figure was shaped into a representation of qualities that were already priorities to certain cultural groups, creating a harmonizing hegemony. The narratives served an important function: the focus on chivalry and spirituality as national ideals brought together highly disparate groups, particularly since the knights themselves occupied a nebulous position in a clearly demarcated three estate social structure. In fact, part of what Chaucer addresses in the *Canterbury Tales* is the situation of the members of the 'third estaat' who were actively seeking to carve a niche for themselves, a fourth estate. He does this through an interesting and broadened use of the term and concept 'nobility'. In the *Tales*, often those whom one might expect to have 'nobility' do not. Conversely, those whom, because of social class one might not expect to have the quality, do. Chaucer, himself in a position that did not fit easily into the social strata, seems to have chosen as characters in the *Tales* those in similar, socially mobile positions, such as a merchant, a man of law and a knight.

Taken as a whole, all of the Arthurian narratives drew the members of the oppressed third estate, who participated in the courtly adventures of the knights and identified with the mythologized figures, thereby identifying with and participating in the nationalization movement as well. Thus, the knight and his idealized qualities came to define ideal Englishness and to disseminate nationalist sentiment, which in turn fuelled English nationalism. Moreover, the figure began to open a new social class, a class much different from the landed (or at the opposite end, extremely poor), inherited, limited mobility classes that already existed. Interactions between knights and knights and others comprise much of English myth, with the morals of the stories defining correct values and behaviour.

## The Leader is Owed Duty and Loyalty: The Song of Roland

A legacy of the Normans to English mythology is the rearguard battle of

Roland, nephew of Charlemagne. Says Roland in the *Song* (Ebbutt, 1988: 138): 'Our duty is to hold this pass for our king. A vassal must endure for his lord grief and pain, heat and cold, torment and death; and a knight's duty is to strike mighty blows, that men may sing of him, in time to come, no evil songs. Never shall such be sung of me.'

## Robin Hood: Chivalry and Rebellion

Robin Hood (Robert Hode), was probably an historic person, however his fame and popularity were such that his true identity has been obscured by legend (Phillips and Keatman, 1995). The two heroes Arthur and Robin Hood personify respectively the good Christian knight and the rebel against oppressive injustice. The outlaw of medieval England has always possessed a potent charm for the minds of less overtly rebellious persons. The romance of Robin Hood and his merry band of banished men, robbing the wealthy to generously help the needy and, defying law and authority, gave to the poor an embodiment of the spirit of liberty. Of all the unjust laws which the Norman conquerors laid upon England, perhaps the most bitterly resented were the forest laws,[1] and resistance to them was the most popular representation of independence. In mediaeval English history outlaw heroes were popular, standing in the mind of the populace for justice and true liberty against the oppressive tyranny of the king's subordinate officials, and who are always later taken into favour by the king, the fount of true justice (Ebbett, 1988: 226).

Ebbett (1988: 316) relates a story of Robin Hood in which he states 'The Outlaw's Rules', somewhat similar to the rules of chivalry, 'You are to do no harm to women, nor to any company in which a woman is travelling; this is in honour of our dear Lady. You are to be kind and gentle to husbandmen and toilers of all degrees, to worthy knights and yeomen, to gallant squires, and to all children and helpless people; but sheriffs (especially him of Nottingham), bishops, and prelates of all kinds, and usurers in Church and State, you may regard as your enemies, and may rob, beat, and despoil in any way.'

In nineteenth-century Britain, the legends of King Arthur and Robin Hood played an important role in construction of contemporary national identity. These two legends provide excellent windows through which to view British culture, because they provide very different perspectives. King Arthur and Robin Hood have traditionally been diametrically opposed in terms of their ideological orientation. The former is a king, a man at the pinnacle of the social and political hierarchy, whereas the latter is an outlaw, and is therefore completely outside conventional hierarchical structures. The fact that two such different figures could simultaneously function as British national heroes suggests that British nationalism did not represent a single set of values and ideas, but rather assimilated a variety of competing points of view (Barczewski, 2000).

## Ivanhoe

Another assimilation of a variety of competing points of view, *Ivanhoe* was an immensely popular fiction bestseller first published at the end of 1819. The book inspired literary imitations as well as paintings, dramatizations, and even operas, and recently, movies and TV mini-series. In *Ivanhoe,* the Scottish Sir Walter Scott fashioned a myth of national cultural identity that influenced the popular imagination. Scott drew on the conventions of Gothic fiction, including risky sexual and racial themes, and explored the violent origins and limits of English nationality, with the Saxon Ivanhoe exhibiting all the traits of chivalry, and the Norman knights few, if any.

### Henry V, the Egalitarian Leader

Shakespeare stresses Henry's prowess as an egalitarian leader, for example, the definition of his army as a 'band of brothers', who worked with and for his followers; describing him as 'the Mirror of all Christian Kings'. In a historical treatment of Henry, Allmand (1993) identifies traits of goal-oriented business planner, egalitarian political strategist, tireless academician, merciless warrior and God-fearing Christian.

### Sir Francis Drake

Sir Francis Drake became a national hero for his attacks on the Spanish Armada. After his death, from dysentery or during a failed raid, Drake remained a legendary figure who circumnavigated the globe, destroyed dozens of Spanish warships, and (apocryphally) was the secret lover of Queen Elizabeth I. His depiction as having a jaunty, daring attitude in the face of overwhelming opposition remains a symbol of pride for the English nation. Mant (1977) considered that Francis Drake could be used as a model epitomizing managerial leadership qualities in England.

## OVERVIEW OF ENGLISH LEADERSHIP

The cultural heritage and mythology of England combine to create perceptions about how leaders should behave; and perception is reality.

### Standing Up for What is Right in the Face of Royal Injustice

Early hagiographers claimed that St. George, adopted as the patron saint of England, was a soldier martyred in what is present-day Syria during the reign of Diocletian in the late third or early fourth century AD. One version claims he held the rank of tribune in the Roman army and was beheaded by order of the emperor for protesting against the persecution of Christians. His bravery in the face of royal injustice in defending the poor and defenceless quickly led to veneration. Similarly, Thomas Becket, before his murder was said to have spoken, 'And I am prepared to die for my Lord, so that in my blood the church will attain liberty and peace; but in the name of Almighty God I forbid that you hurt my men, either cleric or layman, in any way' (Grim, 1875–1885).

Robin Hood did not have a problem with authority; he was simply against the misuse of authority, and was against those people whom the king appointed who were unjust. Robin becomes the hero of the people for fighting this injustice. He would have needed the help of the people to survive, so robbing the rich and giving to the poor was a way of bringing the common people on to his side.

**Heroically Defending the Nation**

Sir Francis Drake's exploits as an explorer have become a part of folklore in Europe. Numerous stories and fictional adaptations of his adventures exist. Considered a hero in England, it is said that if England is ever in peril, beating Drake's Drum[2] will cause Drake to return to save the country. (This is a variation of the sleeping hero folk tale; along with that of King Arthur.) Other major heroic defenders include Nelson and Wellington.

**Heroically Defending the Nation in League with the Common People**

A leadership legend expounding upon the inspiration of loyalty and performance from the common solider can be seen in Shakespeare's three plays, *Henry the IV Part 1* and *Part 2*, and *Henry V*. Henry-V-in-Waiting in Parts 1 and 2 spends time carousing with commoners as training to lead as king. This common touch is put into play in this mixing with his infantry and archers the night before Agincourt, and in the inspiring speech Shakespeare gives him immediately before the battle.

Part of Admiral Lord Horatio Nelson's popularity among those under his command and among a wide public was empathy for the common seaman (Cannadine, 2004). As an example, Nelson's first reaction to the news of the Spithead Mutiny in 1797, usually omitted by his biographers, was to sympathize with the mutinous sailors. Much of his self-constructed persona relied upon the open evasion of the orders of his superiors. He was notable for his un-hierarchical consideration of officers and men; this was a key to his successful leadership and to his wider reputation, at a time when a significantly large proportion of the population was in the army or the navy.

## Gender and Leadership in England

Admirable women in leadership roles in English myth are admirable because they emulate the characteristics of men. The Iceni war leader Boudica (Boadicea, or Boudicca) from AD 61 and AD 63 led her people in a glorious, bloody war against the Romans, winning many battles, but losing the war. The military skills of the Roman army finally led to the crushing of the rebellion, perhaps giving us insight into the need for both management and leadership skills, but lack of management skills can be fatal.

Elizabeth I was forceful, resourceful, and shrewd as a leader. She was indeed a role model because she was strong for a woman. Her tutor, Roger Ascham, claimed that, 'her mind [had] no womanly weakness, her perseverance [was] equal to that of a man' (Taylor-Smither, 1984: 47).

Our contemporary, Elizabeth II, a symbol with little real power, sees herself as a Servant Leader (Wenig, 2004). In 1966, Elizabeth II placed a large carved plaque in Westminster Abbey which stated, 'Whoever be chief among you let him be your servant.'

## English Business Leadership

Business leaders are often maligned, especially by those who have never led a business. An example is a quote attributed to Edward, First Baron Thurlow (1731–1806), Lord Chancellor of England, in Coffee (1981), 'Did you ever expect a corporation to have a conscience, when it has no soul to be damned, and no body to be kicked?' However, in the GLOBE study (House et al., 2004), 'Integrity' was no. 3 in the 21 first order desirable leadership characteristics in England.

Hofstede (2001) and Hoppe (1990) find England to be a country with Small or Low Power Distance, Moderate Uncertainty Avoidance, High Individualism (Low Collectivism), and Moderately High Masculinity. (See the following website for more detailed discussion of the dimensions: http://feweb.uvt.nl/center/hofstede/index.htm).

Low Power Distance indicates that there is an expectation that the less powerful members of organizations and institutions find the more powerful to be approachable and that decisions can be questioned, that inequality is not endorsed by either the leaders or followers.

High Individualism indicates societies in which the ties between individuals are loose, everyone is expected to look after him/herself and his/her immediate family, as opposed to being well integrated into strong, cohesive in-groups, often extended families (with uncles, aunts and grandparents) which continue protecting them in exchange for unquestioning loyalty.

The Masculinity cultural dimension, versus its opposite, Femininity, refers to the distribution of roles between the genders, which is another fundamental issue for any society, to which a range of solutions are found. Masculinity is the assertive pole of the dimension, and the modest, caring pole is 'feminine'. The women in feminine countries have the same modest, caring values as the men; in the masculine countries females are somewhat assertive and competitive, but not as much as the men, so that these countries show a gap between men's values and women's values.

Moderate Uncertainty Avoidance indicates a society's moderate tolerance for uncertainty and ambiguity; moderate discomfort in unstructured situations, that is, those that are novel, unknown, surprising, or different from usual. Uncertainty avoiding cultures try to minimize the possibility of such situations by strict laws and rules, safety and security measures, and on the philosophical and religious level by a belief in absolute Truth.

Littrell and Valentin (2005) found English managers indicating that they preferred a leader who:

- uses persuasion and arguments effectively to motivate and lead staff, indicating a low Power Distance society's penchant for consultative leadership;
- clearly defines his or her own role and lets followers know what is expected, tending to avoid Uncertainty;
- performs in the traditional management theory style of directing and guiding, motivating, and leading in an interventionist fashion,
- is able to predict outcomes accurately, accurate forecasting skills being a desirable trait of managerial leaders;
- supports and promotes the organization and its members to higher authority.

These traits indicate a collaborative, team-oriented leader who convinces rather than commands.

House *et al.* (2004), in the GLOBE study, defined six dimensions of leadership. England means were highest for *Inspirational Charismatic Leadership*. Universally endorsed as contributing to a leader's effectiveness, in that Charismatic/Value-based leaders endorse a vision congruent with the values of followers, which are also generally congruent with the values based on national cultural norms.

## Self-protective leadership

This dimension was found universally to impede leadership effectiveness. These behaviours represent a bossy, yet self-interested and evasive leader, who relies on formalities and procedures.

## Team-oriented leadership

Endorsement of this dimension was found to vary between cultures. These behaviours represent a style of leadership focusing on the team and emphasizing the relationships between the members of that team.

## Humane leadership

The endorsement of this dimension was found to vary between cultures. This set of behaviours represents a leader who is generous to subordinates, compassionate, patient, and modest.

## Participative leadership

This is another leadership style where endorsement was found to vary from culture to culture. A participative leader works well with other people and actively participates in the task being undertaken.

## Autonomous leadership

This dimension was based on the single attribute of individualism, and encompasses an independent and autonomous approach. Endorsement of this dimension also varied across cultures.

With a different set of traits we again see a collaborative, team-oriented leader.

*Table 8.1   Detailed characteristics describing leaders in English society*

| Description | Mean | Description | Mean |
| --- | --- | --- | --- |
| Charismatic 2: inspirational | 6.39 | Humane orientation | 4.91 |
| Performance orientation | 6.37 | Calm | 4.90 |
| Integrity | 6.12 | Charismatic 3: self-sacrifice | 4.90 |
| Charismatic 1: visionary | 6.10 | Self-absorbed | 3.91 |
| Decisiveness | 6.00 | Status consciousness | 3.70 |
| Team 2: team integrator | 5.53 | Procedural | 3.55 |
| Administrative competence | 5.40 | Conflict inducer | 3.43 |
| Diplomatic | 5.39 | Autocratic | 2.55 |
| Team 1: collaborative | | Face-saver | 2.53 |
| team orientation | 5.34 | Non-participative | 2.32 |
| | | Isolationist | 2.29 |
| | | Evil/malevolent | 2.13 |

*Note*: Ranking by mean scores (maximum rating = 7.0)

# GLOBAL IMPLICATIONS

The cultural mythologies of England provide a rich array of leadership characteristics that are codified in recent empirical research studies. The character of English leadership equips individuals with a high level of confidence to engage in the global business arena where there are distinct groundings in norms and values associated with honourable and chivalrous practices. English leaders are expected to rule, govern, or lead for the greater good. Endowed with such beliefs as a need to rectify what is not believed to be proper behaviour on the part of others, an English leader may be very effective in situations when there is a need to support processes that are helpful in developing others. Also, valuing leadership characteristics such as courage, wisdom, and generosity equip an English leader to actively engage with the dynamics of globalization. Based upon a range of leadership characteristics that include resourcefulness and servant leadership, English leaders would likely have a relatively higher level of self-confidence to enter into and grapple with the ambiguities and complexities of globalization.

Unfortunately, the alternative perspectives of the English leader's noble ideals may border upon and be perceived by others as being arrogant and imperialistic. These create blind spots that may hinder the development of important business relationships in a global context, even though they may be economically rational. While an English leader may intend to be helpful, some behaviour may be misread as being imperialist and infringing upon the rights and territory of others due to attitudes, behaviours, and beliefs stemming from the success of the British Empire.

In sum, English leadership entails a long history of global engagement that includes being a superpower. This creates a context for leaders from around the world to be comfortable due to familiarity in engaging with English leaders in business relationships. English business leaders might need to be more self-effacing and accommodating in the face of the movement of centres of power around the globe.

# PRACTICAL APPLICATIONS

As we see from the discussion immediately above, there is considerable congruence between English myths of leadership and recent traits identified by academic research.

Taking our analyses of leadership mythology and the recent academic research findings as a model, we can identify a contemporary business leader who exemplifies the traits. Sir Mark Moody-Stuart exemplifies the 'agree' to 'strongly agree' desired traits above. Moody-Stuart was born in 1940 out in the

Commonwealth in Antigua to a wealthy sugar plantation owner. He spent parts of his childhood in the West Indies and his working life in a range of developing countries around the old Empire. In England he was educated at Shrewsbury School and at St John's College, Cambridge. He made his mark on the business world at Royal Dutch Shell, rising to CEO, 1998–2001. At Shell, he was accessible, popular, and had a reputation for listening and thoughtfulness. Moody-Stuart became a Knight Commander of the Order of St Michael and St George in June 2000. Since 2001 he has played a high profile role in promoting sustainable development.

Moody-Stuart stood up for what he believed was right in espousing and practising corporate social responsibility at the risk of compromising profits; strong Christian beliefs; managerial and leadership competence; and an award of a knighthood for his outstanding accomplishments.

Stuart's behaviour also reflects leadership in the burgeoning field of sustainable development. His accomplishments could almost become a cultural icon that lends itself to mythical proportions in the future. The foray into sustainable development would provide an opportunity for other English leaders to support more proactive, self-confident, and persistent participation in dealing with the complexities of the field. Hence, the contemporary Britannia may not necessarily be the colonization of land but of issues and concerns falling within the sustainable development agenda – see Commentary box.

---

## COMMENTARY BOX

### Sir Mark Moody-Stuart – Chairman, Anglo American plc

As a company we are seeking increasingly to play a role in the sustainable development of the communities and countries where we work … we also recognize that we have a role to play, in partnership with others, in contributing to optimizing the governance and human rights impacts associated with our operations at a regional and national level … Whilst it is ultimately for governments to choose whether to participate, we are not reticent about being advocates for EITI in the interests of good and transparent governance. Our commercial interests are served by such an approach since, as long-term investors, it is more likely that we will be able to achieve sustainable outcomes. (from http://www. angloamerican.co.uk/cr/publications/speeches/)

---

# CONCLUSION

There is an expected congruence between the idealized mythical leader in England, and the ideal modern business leader. Taking Arthur as an example, we find inspirational charisma, performance orientation, integrity, vision, decisiveness, team integrator, diplomatic, and collaborative team orientation, all the highly rated traits by modern managers in the GLOBE study, a congruence of the myth and the measures. To quote Cecil Rhodes (n.d., probably 1877), 'I contend that we are the finest race in the world, and the more of it we inhabit, the better it is.'

# NOTES

1.  The 'royal forest' (not necessarily a forest, but any land supporting wild game) concept of land management in England was introduced by William I. A royal forest was an area of land where certain rights were reserved for the monarch or the aristocracy, usually set aside for hunting. At the peak of royal forests in the late twelfth and early thirteenth centuries, some one-third of the area of England was designated royal forests. Forest law prescribed harsh punishment for anyone who committed a range of offences within the forests. When an area was designated a royal forest, any villages, towns, and fields that lay within it were also subject to forest law. This could naturally foster resentment, as the local inhabitants were then unable to use land they had previously relied upon for their livelihoods.
2.  Drake's Drum was taken by Drake when he circumnavigated the world, and was with him when he died of dysentery during a blockade of Porto Belo, Panama, in 1596. The drum, with Drake's coat of arms painted on one side, is currently located in the Drake, Naval and West Country Folk Museum at Buckland Abbey in Devon, owned by the National Trust for Places of Historic Interest or Natural Beauty. It is claimed that the beating of the drum can be heard at times when England is at war or a significant national event takes place. For example, some said they heard the drum when Britain's greatest naval hero, Admiral Lord Nelson was made a freeman of Plymouth. The most recent occasions on which the drum roll was said to have been heard were during the Dunkirk evacuation in 1940 and the Falklands War in 1982.

# REFERENCES

Allmand, C. (1993), *Henry V*, Berkeley, CA, USA: University of California Press.

Ashkanasy, N. M., Trevor-Roberts, E. and Earnshaw, L. (2002), The Anglo Cluster: legacy of the British Empire, *Journal of World Business*, **37**, 28–39.

Barczewski, S. L. (2000), *Myth and National Identity in Nineteenth-Century Britain: The Legends of King Arthur and Robin Hood*, Oxford: Oxford University Press.

Boccaccio, G. (1363), translated by Hall, Louis Brewer, 1962, *De Casibus Virorum Illustrium*, Gainesville, FL: Scholars' Facsimiles & Reprints.

Boggs, D. B. (1990), *Literary Perceptions of Leadership*, Doctoral Dissertation, University of San Diego, CA: ProQuest Theses & Dissertations.

Busse, Wilhelm G. (1994), Brutus in Albion: England's Gründungssage, in P. Wunderli (ed.), *Herkunft und Ursprung, Historische und mythische Formen der Legitimation*, Sigmaringen, Germany: Jan Thorbecke Verlag, pp. 207–23.

Campbell, J. (1968), *The Hero with a Thousand Faces*, Princeton, NJ: Princeton University Press.

Campbell, J. (1993), *Myths to Live By*, New York: Penguin Group.

Cannadine, D. (ed.) (2004), *Admiral Lord Nelson: Context and Legacy*, London, UK: Palgrave.

Coffee, Jr., J. C. (1981), 'No Soul to Damn: No Body to Kick': an unscandalized inquiry into the problem of corporate punishment', *Michigan Law Review*, **79**, 386.

Crook, C. (2005), The good company, *The Economist* (US): 22 January, p. 4.

Ebbett, M. I. (1988), *British Myths and Legends*, London: Crescent.

Faulkner, K. (1996), The transformation of knighthood in early thirteenth-century England, *The English Historical Review*, **111** (440), 1–23.

Ford, D. N. (2000), *Details of the Knights of the Round Table*, http://www.britannia.com/history/arthur/knights.html, accessed 14 April 2007.

Gautier, L. (1891), *Chivalry*, Simsbury, CT: Bracken Books.

Gellner, E. (1983), *Nations and Nationalism*, Ithaca, NY: Cornell University Press.

Geoffrey of Monmouth (c. 1136), Lewis Thorpe, Translator, 1977, *The History of the Kings of Britain*, New York: Penguin Group.

Grim, E. (1875–1885), Vita S. Thomae, Cantuariensis Archepiscopi et Martyris, James Robertson (ed.), *Materials for the Life of Thomas Becket*, Vol. II, London: Rolls Series.

Gupta, V., Hanges, P. J. and Dorfman, P. (2002), Cultural clusters: methodology and findings, *Journal of World Business*, **37** (1), 11–15.

Hingley, R. (2000), *Roman Officers and English Gentlemen: The Imperial Origins of Roman Archaeology*, London: Routledge.

Hofstede, G. (2001), *Culture's Consequences,* Thousand Oaks, CA: Sage.

Hoppe, M. H. (1990), *A Comparative Study of Country Elites: International Differences in Work Related Values and Learning and Their Implications for Management Training and Development*, Ph.D. dissertation, University of North Carolina at Chapel Hill. ProQuest Digital Dissertations.

House, R. J., Hanges, P. J., Javidan, M., Dorfman, P. W. and Gupta, V. (eds) (2004), *Culture, Leadership and Organizations: The GLOBE Study of 62 Societies*, Thousand Oaks, CA: Sage.

Inglehart, R. (2004), *Human Beliefs and Values*, Madrid: Siglo XXI.

Inglehart, R., Basañez, M., and Moreno, A. (1998), *Human Values and Beliefs: A Cross-Cultural Sourcebook*, Ann Arbor, MI: University of Michigan Press.

Leyerle, J. (1965), Beowulf: the hero and king, *Medium Aevum*, **34** (2), 89–102.

Littrell, R. F. and Valentin, L. N. (2005), Preferred leadership behaviours: exploratory results from Romania, Germany, and the UK, *The Journal of Management Development*, **245**, 421–42.

Mant, A. (1977), *The Rise and Fall of the British Manager*, London: Macmillan.

Matthews, J. (1991), *Taliesin: Shamanism and the Bardic Mysteries in Britain and Ireland*, Dartford, Kent: Aquarian Press.

Morgan, A. and Phillips, R. (2003), Wales! Wales? Britain! Britain? Teaching and learning about the history of the British Isles in secondary schools in Wales, *International Journal of Historical Teaching, Learning and Research*, **3**(1), 39–47.

Oppenheimer, S. (2006), *The Origins of the British – A Genetic Detective Story*, London: Constable and Robinson.

Phillips, G. and Keatman, M. (1995), *Robin Hood – The Man Behind The Myth*, London: Michael O'Mara Books Ltd.

Rhodes, C. (n.d., probably 1877), Confession of faith, Appendix in Millin, Sarah Gertrude (1936), *Rhodes*, London: Chatto & Windus.

Smith, P. B. (1997), Leadership in Europe: Euro-management or the footprint of history?, *European Journal of Work and Organizational Psychology*, **6** (4), 385–96.

Smith, P. B., Peterson, M. F. and Schwartz, S. H. (2002), Cultural values, sources of guidance, and their relevance to managerial behavior: a 47-nation study, *Journal of Cross-Cultural Psychology*, **33** (2), 188–208.

Taylor-Smither, L. J. (1984), Elizabeth I: a psychological profile, *Sixteenth Century Journal*, **15** (2), 47–72.

Wenig, R. E. (2004), Leadership knowledge and skill: an enabler for success as a technology education teacher-leader, *The Journal of Technology Studies*, **30** (1), 59–64.

# 9. Cultural mythology and global leadership in Sweden

## Lena Zander and Udo Zander

### INTRODUCTION

The stories we are told as children (and grown-ups) trigger our imagination but also govern it, in still opaque and mysterious ways. What Swedish children consider good and bad or who they conceive as heroes or villains when their parents read them a fairy-tale, or tell them stories about a common past, matters later in life. Stories and myths almost always include authority figures, and they therefore reflect ideas and beliefs regarding leadership.[1]

A question that interests us throughout this chapter is how Swedes have coped with old taboos being discredited, going to pieces, disintegrating, and becoming resorts of vice and disease, while at the same time celebrating ancient stories about leadership. Swedish society, in our view, has coped amazingly well with combining supporting myths of their civilization with the factualized 'truths' of modern science. To answer Campbell's (1972, 1993) fundamental question, we believe that the Swedes over time have managed to find a 'point of wisdom beyond the conflicts of illusion and truth by which lives can be put back together again'.

In this chapter, we will briefly touch upon what we believe are crucial aspects of Swedish (or Norse) mythology and Swedish folk tales. In our discussion of Swedish leadership a picture of leaders embracing concepts like knowledge, common sense, action, collaboration, consensus, conflict avoidance, empowering, independence, control, universalism, fairness and pragmatism emerges. We synthesize by tracing contemporary leadership philosophies and practices back to the myths and folk tales, and by discussing transition and change. Practical applications for interaction with Swedish leaders, including strengths and blind spots of Swedish leadership conclude the chapter.

### OVERVIEW OF SWEDISH MYTHOLOGY

#### Norse Mythology

Norse, Viking, Scandinavian or Swedish mythology comprises the indigenous pre-Christian religion, beliefs and legends of the Swedish people.[2] In the following we will have a brief look at stories of creation, the first humans, prominent gods, and the eschatology in Sweden before Christianity took hold during the eleventh century AD.

## Creation and Human Beings

The Norse creation story[3] begins in the borderland between two cosmic regions, the frozen world of 'Nifelhem'[4] and the hot realm of 'Muspelhem', a setting recalling the ice age and its ending, icy terrain and volcanic activity, but also freezing hostile winters and agreeable, life-bringing summers. Five frost giants including Ymer and Bure, emerging from the interaction of the two regions, ruled the cosmos. Bure's three grandchildren – Oden, Vile, and Ve – eventually killed the cruel Ymer, and his body was transformed by the three cooperating creator gods into the world as we know it.

The Norse creator gods had the power to breathe life into objects and created the first man and woman, Ask (meaning 'ash') and Embla ('elm'), by giving life to a pair of tree trunks. The three creator gods told Ask and Embla that it was their responsibility to look after the plants and creatures, and the couple settled down at Midgård ('the middle farm') to nurture their realm and start their family.[5]

## Gods and Demigods

As in Greek mythology, the Norse deities were easily recognizable to people by their distinctively human traits of emotion, bounded rationality, risk- and loss-aversion, and overconfidence. The familiar struggles for power and prestige among the gods led to continuous fights between deities and between the two divine 'clans'.[6]

The first clan were the 'Asar', the sky gods, who included the three creator gods. The second were the 'Vaner' who were gods and goddesses of fertility, and presided over the sky and the Earth. There was prolonged and very destructive warfare between the clans, which were ended by a truce, where saliva was mixed in a bowl and peace was guaranteed by a hostage arrangement (two gods from each group would spend part of the year with the other group), as well as intermarriage. Although the two clans lived peacefully after the truce, they remained suspicious, thinking that the hostages were spies. A violent act on the part of the Vaner (cutting off the head of the hostage Mimer, who refused to tell them the secrets of wisdom, and sending it back to the Asar) paved the way for the triumph of the Asar, due to them now possessing all the wisdom in the world. Over time, the defeated Vaner gods of fertility, health, wealth and luck were assimilated into the tribe of their rivals, the Asar.

Oden was the wandering and philandering head of the Asa-clan. A complex, pondering character, he was the god of war (helped in battle by his two wolves Gere and Freke), poetry, as well as the dead. Oden decided to first give up one of his eyes for one sip of wisdom and then hang himself on (and later pin himself on to) the trunk of the world tree Yggdrasil for nine days and nights in exchange for knowledge. Having clutched the secret rune letters on his way down, he was now an expert on performing magic spells and could change his shape. In the arts of peace, Oden was helped by mastery of the runes and by the two ravens Hugin (thought) and Munin[7] (memory) who whispered into his ears what was happening in the world. He also picked up expertise in fortune telling from women, and practised it although it was seen as unmanly and led to the other gods teasing him. Frequently, he walked among the humans in Midgård incognito, dressed in a slouch hat and a wide coat, putting him distinctly in touch with common people and their reality.

The most revered god among common Swedes however, was Oden's son, the violent and moody 'Tor'. Interestingly, he was etymologically and functionally more or less identical with the Vedic god Indra. A sworn enemy of the giants, he rode through the sky in a chariot with his mighty hammer 'Mjölner' which had been forged for him by dwarves, and which he used to crush his enemies and bless those he wished well. His chariot was pulled by two goats, and Mjölner produced thunder and lightning when hurled at enemies. Tor's bad temper often complicated his life and led to spells of serious regret and anguish. Psychologically, Tor was a relative simpleton in comparison to his father Oden, but he was often called on by ordinary Swedes to bring order out of chaos.

It seems appropriate in this context to mention the women and their roles in Norse mythology. In general, females in Norse mythology take 'the back-seat', but are instrumental in planning and pulling strings behind the curtain, while other female beings watch over the fate of individuals and clans. The most prominent goddesses are Freja and Frigga. Freja was the symbol of fertility, beauty and seduction, in touch with the powers of the earth and thereby the underworld. Frigga was the stable wife of Oden, a very knowledgeable but secretive mother and governess of the Asgård property. She, in spite of protecting marriage, lived in a separate dwelling. Other very prominent females were the three Nornor which sat at the roots of the tree of life, Yggdrasil, and watered it as well as spun the threads of life, thereby determining the fate of all living beings.

### Folk Tales: Beings of the Dark Woods of Sweden

Over time, some aspects of Norse mythology have passed into Scandinavian folklore and have survived to modern times. We will briefly describe some beings of the dark forests of Sweden and their often complex and vague properties and characteristics, still influencing popular beliefs.

### Potential 'helpers': The Tomte and the Will-o'-the wisp

The Swedish word 'Tomte' roughly corresponds to 'gnome' or 'elf'. The Tomte is small, about the size of a seven-year-old boy, has a long grey or snowy beard and an old and wrinkled face. He wears grey clothes and a pointed red cap, and lives on haylofts, looking after the farm and the animals. He is shy and often not visible but it is of utmost importance to treat the Tomte well. If so, he will help the farmer to bake, carry chopped wood, clean out the stable, and spread the manure on the fields. At Christmas time, people reward him with a big plate of porridge with butter. A Tomte has no sense of humour, so he must never be made fun of, as he may move to the neighbouring farm and take the farmers' luck with him.

A similar helper is the Will-o'-the wisp, a translation from the Swedish name 'Lyktgubbe', which means 'old man with a lamp'. During dark nights a flickering light can be seen at old moss, rivers and lakeshores or where there used to be an old path. Coming too close to the short little 'man' wearing grey or green clothing might lead to illness or disorientation, but he can be nice as well, and help those who are lost in the forest in the middle of the night if asked kindly. If not thanked profusely he will confuse people to not find their own door even if standing right in front of it.

### The allure of beauty and quick fixes: the Water Sprite and the Wood-nymph

'Näcken' or the 'Water Sprite' is mentioned in the old Nordic folktales as early as in the eleventh century. 'Näck' in Swedish means nude. In the most common tales about the Water Sprite, he is a naked man – a very sensuous being – sitting in a stream, playing the most beautiful music on his violin. The Water Sprite is a solitary being and tries to entangle humans with his music close to bridges and water mills. Many fiddlers have told that they have learnt how to play the violin from the Water Sprite, but only by making sacrifices. Others can see the fiddler as a lost soul, and occasionally the fiddler cannot stop playing until someone comes and sets him free. The Water Sprite is especially dangerous to women, whom he tries to seduce or entrap at the bottom of lakes or streams where they are never to be seen again.

Deep in the Swedish woods lives the Wood-nymph, the most beautiful of women. The Swedish name 'Skogsrå' indicates that she is the caretaker of the woods and the wild animals. For a hunter it is very important to treat her well, for example, sacrifice some food, for successful hunting. However, male hunters and charcoal-burners that have fallen in love with the Wood-nymph after following her into the forest lose their soul. She distorts their vision, and

changes shape from the most exquisitely beautiful woman to the most repul-
sive creature. If one takes a closer look, her back is a rotten tree-stump and she
has a tail, of which she is very ashamed. By grabbing the tail, and holding on
to it, one might be able to keep her at a distance and save one's soul.

### The 'neighbours': the Trolls and Giants

Unlike most other forest beings, 'Trolls' like company and live together in
groups. Trolls also like being around human beings, who they unfortunately
abduct if given a chance. They live underground or inside mountains and are
rarely seen as they hate sunlight, which can kill them. They are very greedy
and hoard gold and silver. If running into a Troll, courtesy is law, unless they
are angry in which case only a quick run to the closest church will save a
human.[8]

Giants, or 'Jättar', are a tall family that lived on earth long before
humankind. Most of what we see in nature can be seen as traces of the age of
giants. Round holes in rocks for example are giant cooking pots. Giants are not
always nice, but they sometimes offer their help if properly rewarded. They
are able blacksmiths, and because of their size, work is done quickly and the
quality of their forged tools is excellent. Giants are tall, but not very clever,
and they can be lured into helping humans with construction. If the building
contractor can guess the giant's name before construction is finished, the giant
goes unrewarded.

## OVERVIEW OF SWEDISH LEADERSHIP

'Swedish-style management is profoundly different from what's practised
elsewhere in the world' exclaim Dearlove and Crainer (2002: 21). In the same
breath, they quote Jack Welch as observing that 'pound for pound, Sweden has
probably more good managers than any other country'. The question then
becomes: what characterizes Swedish leadership? We have chosen to approach
this question with broad brush-strokes identifying five essential leadership
themes, detailing nuances and highlighting contradictions within each theme
and illustrating them with Swedish leadership profiles. The Swedish leadership themes are:

1.   knowledge, common sense and action;
2.   collaboration, consensus and conflict avoidance; and
3.   empowering, independence and control;
4.   universalism, fairness and pragmatism;
5.   walking, talking and silence.

## Knowledge, Common Sense and Action

Brought up in a meritocracy, Swedish leaders *par excellence* are not selected on general knowledge but on expertise competence believed as essential for leadership success. Before the latter half of the twentieth century managers were often internally recruited engineers from a very small group of individuals with a similar educational, social and cultural background (Maccoby, 1991). Being a manager is slowly being perceived as an occupation, and this together with a growing market demand has led to increased recruitment from business schools. However, the typical leader profile still features strong technological skills, paired with a large portion of common sense, often unabashedly applied when making and taking decisions. In Swedish media, outstanding Swedish leadership has been associated with 'doers', rather than 'thinkers', who display a strong performance-orientation and an entrepreneurial approach (Holmberg and Åkerblom, 2001). To say that someone is good at getting things done or possesses 'the power of action' (which is one word in Swedish – 'handlingskraftig'), is more than highest praise in a recruitment recommendation.

## Collaboration, Consensus and Conflict Avoidance

One of the important Swedish cultural beliefs is the superior efficiency and results of cooperation and collaboration in comparison to competition and confrontation. Cooperating, or connecting subordinates' interests with superordinates' interests, was expressed as a Swedish value as early as 1809 (Linnell and Löfgren, 1995). Individualistic rather than collectivistic work values were however, identified for Sweden (Hofstede, 1980, 1984), leading Hampden-Turner and Trompenaars (1993) to talk about 'social individualism', that is, individualism rooted in a collectivistic value system. In the Globe study, Sweden was found to be both extremely collectivistic and extremely individualistic, leading Holmberg and Åkerblom (2001) to conclude that Swedes were 'socially concerned individualists'.

Self-managing teams were used to organize work in Swedish firms in the 1970s, for example Volvo's production plant in Kalmar (Gyllenhammar, 1977) and experiments continued into the 1990s, when autonomous teams of skilled workers assembled whole cars without an assembly line in the Uddevalla plant. Twenty years later, Swedish multinational companies' web-based home pages detour readers from technicalities to emphasize how working in teams is a part of their corporate culture. Future leaders are recruited based on their ability to create, manage and be part of teams. According to Kenneth Bengtsson, CEO of the Swedish retailing group ICA Ahold AB, the uniqueness of Swedish business is based on how 'Swedish leadership tends to focus primarily on cooperation and teamwork. Managers put a lot of effort into getting everyone in the team involved' (Bengtsson, 2003). Correspondingly, Swedish employees consider that their managers should encourage cooperation and make the employees feel part of a team, acting similarly to a coach (Zander, 1997). Outstanding Swedish leaders should have 'a great ability in building, integrating, coordinating, and sustaining a team whose members collaborate in a collegial and egalitarian way' (Holmberg and Åkerblom, 2006: 322).

If collaboration and teamwork are the preferred *modus operandi* in Swedish organizations, consensus is the preferred decision-making vehicle. A consensus-based process involves all concerned parties so that when a decision finally is taken it has been well aired, discussed from all parties' perspectives and agreed upon by all involved. This time-consuming process at its best facilitates a smooth, fast and (importantly) conflict-free implementation phase. Conflict avoidance characterizes Swedish culture in general and the importance of agreeing is exceptional. The strong belief in consensus decision-making could be seen as a reflection of this (Daun, 1986; Holmberg and Åkerblom, 2001). A typical Swedish reaction when differing opinions are expressed is that 'there is no use in discussing this as we disagree' (Zander, 1999, 2001), disagreement seen as leading to that dreaded confrontation. Skilled conflict avoiders are sought-after as leaders, as there is a strong belief that conflicts are ineffective and will hamper processes rather than energize and inspire them (Jönsson, 1996).

### Empowering, Independence and Control

Egalitarianism, one of the important Swedish cultural values, has influenced and shaped life in Sweden in general and Swedish management in particular.[9] Equality in the workplace in the form of employee influence and participation in decision making at all levels is legislated in Swedish law. The egalitarian vision has also been pursued in society by abolishing the extensive use of titles and formal way of addressing people in the latter half of the twentieth century. Remaining gaps between groups are difficult to identify as in Swedish culture it is important to be modest and downplay one's achievements. Overt display of status, authority or wealth is abhorred (Lawrence and Spybey, 1997). There is a social requirement not to stand out, not to believe in any way that one is special, as expressed in an old Swedish saying: 'any one person is as good as any other person'.

In parallel to the development of the egalitarian vision in Swedish society, Swedish companies have been transformed from hierarchical organizations to flat decentralized structures, with participatory practices following governmental policies (Gyllenhammar, 1977; Zander, 2002). As predicted in a low power distance society (Hofstede, 1980, 1984), Holmberg and Åkerblom (2006) identified the participative dimension as distinctive to Swedish leadership in the Globe study. From the late 1980s and onwards Swedish Percy Barnevik's (then CEO of ABB) leadership style has inspired many leaders around the globe (Kets de Vries, 1998). Barnevik declared that he was obsessed with decentralization, and he pushed authority, responsibility and accountability down in the organization with a maximum of five people between the shop floor and the CEO (Kets de Vries, 1998). Not only participation in consensus processes, but also actual discretionary authority has been delegated to Swedish employees at lower levels (Lawrence and Spybey, 1997). Swedish employees want their managers to empower them, that is, delegate responsibility to them, give them the opportunity to share decision making, to participate in strategy discussions, and appreciate their initiatives and their advice (Zander, 1997).

---

## COMMENTARY BOX

**Pehr G. Gyllenhammar, Former Group CEO of Volvo (Multinational Producer of Cars, Commercial Vehicles, and Power Systems)**

Participation actually demands better leadership, as well as more self-discipline from everyone involved. Some foreigners talk about Sweden as if management control, in the traditional sense, may be lost in the new industrial environment [that is using work teams instead of assembly lines in Volvo auto factories]. Participation demands more work, not less, from everybody … the manager who is reluctant or just gives lip service to the idea of participation can hold back employee-based changes that are actually in the best interests of both the corporation and its employees. (from *Harvard Business Review* 1977: 112–13)

**Lars Renström, Group CEO of Alfa Laval (Global Provider of Heating, Cooling, Separation and Engineering Solutions). Swedish Leader of the Year 2007**

Good leadership is characterized by being able to make a team move up one level and reach extraordinary results. It is not always the team with the best players that wins. With good leadership, a team of lesser skilled players can win because together they surpass themselves. (from *Affärsvärlden*, 2007-11-06)

---

**Annika Falkengren, President and Group CEO for SEB (North European Financial Group). Ranked in the Top 10 of the Financial Times 2007 List of Powerful Women in Europe**

Leadership is very difficult to explain ... Of course you need a message of where you want to go and why employees should feel that this is a fantastic target and a goal we would like to achieve ... It is very much about communication: to communicate with the employees all the time how you think, what you want, and what they have done well and less well. (IMD CEO video interview 2006-09-05)

'Management by objectives' is praised and favoured by Swedish leaders as well as by subordinates. The importance of independence and self-reliance, that is autonomy, is expressed not only in the desire for empowerment, but also in the limited appreciation of supervision (Zander, 1997; Holmberg and Åkerblom, 2006). In general, supervision is seen as an expression of a manager's distrust in the employees' ability and competence. Far-reaching delegation of authority, questions instead of orders, and vagueness signal egalitarian beliefs and trust, 'See what you can do about it?', is not an uncommon leader expression (Edström and Jönsson, 1998, p. 167 translation in Holmberg and Åkerblom, 2001). Lack of supervision does not however mean lack of control. Formal control is sparse, but informal personalized or culture-based normative control is practised both at organizational and individual levels (Selmer and De Leon, 1996).

**Universalism, Fairness and Pragmatism**

Swedes are occasionally referred to as the Prussians of the North to emphasize their strong organizational skills, a typical Swedish characteristic articulated in the beginning of the twentieth century (Linnell and Löfgren, 1995). Swedish leadership discourse builds on rationality, reason, logic, facts, function and order, as these have been valued in the Swedish context for a long time. Leaders should excel in using ratio-based 'modern' arguments, as emotionally-based arguments signal incompetence as well as the dreaded 'all words but no action' type of leadership. Leaders are expected to embody these fundamental organizing principles produced by a very successful implementation of 'The Modern Project' (see Toulmin, 1990). To Swedes, being 'modern' is essential for future development (Daun, 1992).

In Swedish organizations there are relatively few rules and regulations, as could be expected given the Swedish low uncertainty avoidance score (Hofstede, 1980, 1984), but the few must be followed similarly to policies, procedures and decisions (Smith *et al.*, 2003). Both Swedish society and organizations are governed by universalistic principles (Hampden-Turner and Trompenaars, 1993). People do not expect leaders to make particularistic exceptions to rules and regulations, and 'cries' of unfair treatment will echo if practices and procedures are not applied universally. Non-transparency does not lead to suspicion of shady practice, but to the belief that something unfair is going on. Fairness being vital in Swedish society and organizations, leaders who are not perceived as fair will not be held in esteem for long.

Swedish leaders are expected to apply universalistic principles but there is still ample room for pragmatism (Czarniawska-Joerges, 1993). Pragmatism, one of the central aspects of outstanding Swedish leadership, involves a readiness to listen to others, to compromise if need be, and to realize practical solutions (Holmberg and Åkerblom, 2001). Drawing on, and learning from, experience and knowledge coupled with common sense, pragmatism will always dominate over theory and ideology in leader behaviour. Indeed to be rational, reasonable, pragmatic, and possessing excellent organizational skills were identified as representative for outstanding leadership portrayed in Swedish media (Holmberg and Åkerblom, 2001).

## Walking, Talking and Silence

Non-Swedish managerial colleagues have much to their astonishment found Swedish managers walking around and talking with employees at different levels in the organization, equally comfortable at the shop floor and in the laboratory, personifying the 'management by walking around' concept. 'The 'floors' are our best schools' according to Ingvar Kamprad, founder, owner and executive chairman of IKEA (Hall and Nyman, 2004: 80). For Swedish leaders this is essential for being 'in-the-know', coordination and informal control, as well as for decision making and consensus seeking. Jan Carlzon, famous for his turn-around of Scandinavian Airlines System (SAS) in the 1980s and his published reflections about tearing down the pyramids, explains how effective communication creates a sense of responsibility, eases control and the need for instructions, leading to motivated and empowered employees (Hall and Nyman, 2004). Alvesson (1992) notes how leaders in a Swedish computer consultancy company focus on communication in both formalized meetings and informal settings and encourage the personal dimension in the interaction. Swedish employees correspondingly prefer frequent communication with their managers about both work and personal-oriented matters (Zander, 1997).

Perhaps somewhat paradoxically, silence and shyness are seen as something positive in the Swedish culture. According to an old Swedish saying, 'talking is silver and silence is gold'. Swedes in general are often experienced as 'reserved' or 'stiff' with a limited, if any, capacity for cocktail-party-type socializing and small talk (which in Swedish is translated into 'cold talk'). However, these national cultural values also shape specific leadership skills such as excellence in international negotiations, where the Swedes' silence can make others nervous and give Swedish leaders the upper hand (Laine-Sveiby, 1987).

# SYNTHESIS AND GLOBAL IMPLICATIONS

## Traces from the Past

At the onset the creation myths and the stories of gods and demigods populating Norse mythology seem far removed from contemporary Swedish leadership ideals, but a closer look reveals intriguing similarities with contemporary rhetoric and practice. Examples are the focus on and significance of teamwork, knowledge/expertise, and empowering. Pragmatic solutions to avoid conflicts and 'management by walking around' also shine through in the mythical tales. In addition, the folk tales of beings of the dark woods of Sweden give hints as to what to expect regarding Swedish leaders' work values and attitudes towards their subordinates.

### Norse mythology's influences on contemporary Swedish leadership
In a Swedish context, the world would not have been created without teamwork. By cooperating, Bure's three grandchildren managed to kill the cruel frost giant Ymir and transform his body into the world as we know it. Creation is based on coordinated activity of a group of individuals rather than the bravery, strength or wits of one individual alone. To this day, an obsession with and belief in the virtues of teamwork remains a prominent feature of Swedish leadership. It is seen as the key to organize work and continuously stressed by Swedish leaders. Fostering teamwork attitudes starts early with an emphasis on group activities in the educational system from the very early years all the way to the University level, where in some cases even exams can be written in groups. An interesting question of course becomes: what is the leader's role in this team-oriented approach? Just like in the ancient Norse tales, there is a clear realization that the leader acts as a *primus inter pares* due to special talents, knowledge and a grasp of the art of inspiration. He or she also has a clear mandate to lead and organize work by empowering and distributing roles and responsibilities among team members. In addition, the focus on management teams is prominent in contemporary Sweden. Management teams in Sweden are regularly involved in common problem solving activities, finding

solutions by way of discussion, active participation and dialogue (Edström and Jönsson, 1998; Jönsson, 1996). In such teams leadership is usually vague and imprecise, allowing team members to retain a certain degree of autonomy and 'freedom-under-responsibility'.

The thirst for knowledge among the Norse gods was great. The Vaner-clan broke the treaty of truce due to a failed attempt at obtaining knowledge, and Oden (head of the Asa-clan) gave up one of his eyes and suffered considerably in exchange for knowledge and wisdom. Stories of leaders that make extraordinary efforts to become knowledgeable run through Swedish mythology, and correspondingly contemporary leaders in Sweden should possess expertise and are selected upon being knowledgeable. Both specialist knowledge and common sense (or wisdom) are essential. In fact, Oden's informed and wise leadership seems to be very close to that aspired to by Swedish leaders today. Tor, son of Oden, with his mighty hammer, called upon to bring order in chaos, could be seen as another archetypical leader also prevalent in today's Swedish society. The need to drastically and often dramatically shape up organizations usually involves recruiting a Tor-like leader, a 'hatchet man' for the purpose, who with a figurative hammer or hatchet will implement changes with the speed of lightning, and often the sound of thunder. Turn-around management on a somewhat less dramatic and slower time-table, in the Swedish mind still needs a 'Tor' type rather than an 'Oden' type of leader to be effective.[10] Like in Norse mythology, women are influential, powerful and creative. Unfortunately, like in the myths, they do not yet figure as prominently at the top of Swedish organizations as the high female participation in the workforce would suggest.[11]

Pragmatism as a theme is recurrent in mythology known by Swedes. A typical pragmatic solution to avoid further destructive conflict was the treaty between the two clans of gods, the Vaner and the Asar, which involved yearly exchanges of two gods as hostages and encouragement of intermarriages. The story of the two clans of gods also emphasizes the belief that conflict is inherently destructive and should be avoided at any cost.

After the Norse gods had blown life, senses and intelligence into the two first human beings, they empowered them. The humans were given the responsibility for plants and creatures and the opportunity to settle down and start a family in their own world Midgård. To empower, to give independence and to delegate decision-making throughout the organization are of utmost importance to both Swedish leaders and to Swedes who are led. Similarly to successful contemporary Swedish leaders' 'management by walking around', Oden frequently walked among the humans in Midgård disguised as an ordinary man in order to keep in touch and to stay informed.

### Folk tales: the complexity and vagueness of beings
Swedish folk tales about beings of the dark woods tell a consistent story about

the workings of the world. Unlike other Germanic people, Swedes seem totally at ease with the complexity, vagueness, and opaqueness of the inner nature of humans and other beings. Instead of fully-fledged 'good guys' and 'bad guys', including superheroes and super-villains, Swedish fairy-tales, folk tales and stories are full of people and creatures that can be either good or bad, depending on how one treats them. Interestingly, this view of human nature is very close to Voltaire's view that was promoted during the Age of Enlightenment. The idea that all of us can be both angelic and bestial and should constantly cultivate ourselves is quite different from the Hobbesian idea of 'man as man's wolf' and Rousseau's idea of 'the noble savage'. Rousseau's teachings have been very influential in Sweden during the twentieth century when promoted and applied by Social Democrats in their attempt to reengineer society, but it is quite clear that the ancient (and more nuanced) view of human nature has recently made a comeback.

The implications of this view of the world for leadership are straightforward: treat subordinates with respect and kindness, and reward them in a fair way for their efforts. Just like the Tomte and the Will-o'-the wisp, employees expect to be treated decently, or they will leave for other jobs or even turn on the leader to make his or her life miserable. The loyalty and services of a Swedish subordinate can never be taken for granted, but must be earned by the leader on a recurrent basis. Tales of creatures like the Water Sprite and the Wood Nymph tell a story of the dangers of being enchanted by beauty and what can be seen on the surface of things. Both Swedish leaders and subordinates are suspicious of sweet talking, slick personalities, and are not impressed by quick fixes. Work should be done properly and thoroughly, often at considerable personal cost. Stories of Trolls and Giants, finally, corroborate the observation that not even notoriously wicked creatures are consistently bad. Greedy and stupid people exist and need to be handled, but a skilled leader can outsmart them and make them work by motivating them properly.

**Transition and Change**

The idea that leadership ideals would remain the same for thousands of years despite immense changes in human societies and learning on part of the generations of people involved is clearly absurd. In essence our reasoning around transition and change is that leadership beliefs in Sweden are affected by two major waves of novel ideas: Christianity and the Modern Project. However, Swedish leadership still seems deeply rooted in stories told thousands of years ago, which in turn were based on the human condition in this northern outpost. Ancient stories seem to survive in the background and are brought back into both discourse and practice, in hybridized, reformulated and re-contextualized format.

The first fundamental change in Swedish society is from ancient Norse polytheism to monotheism and Christianity around the year 1000 AD, and the second is the eclipse of the Christian world view caused by the slow but stable progress of the Modern Project, starting approximately at the time of the assassination of the French king Charles IV by the redhead villain Ravaillac in 1610 (Toulmin, 1990), and arguably reaching its peak in Sweden with the Social Democratic government modernization projects of the 1960s and 1970s.

In ancient Swedish society, it seems plausible that people lived at ease with the idea that their gods were more or less just like them, for good and for bad. Society was organized in clans where leaders constantly bought loyalty and appealed to kinship. The arrival of Christianity through the travels of the Vikings constitutes the potentially greatest change to Swedish society of all times. The idea of a single, all-knowing, perfect god and his son was brought back to Swedish shores by Viking tradesmen and warriors who were full of admiration for the wealth and achievements of foreign civilizations. Their leaders rapidly realized the potential of a religion where power was given to them by a single, immaculate god. The change was as revolutionary in the Swedish context as anywhere else in the world and, as any major change, it was initially endorsed by a few and mainly manifested in language, discourse and symbols.[12]

The coming of Christianity, heralding ideas about the possibility of perfection and almightiness, paved the way for a central authority, for example a king, who ruled with powers given by God. Although Sweden's long history of parliamentarism, Swedish kings to this day remain well-known leadership figures and stand statue in most cities.[13] The king usually referred to as the founder of Sweden as a united country, Gustav Vasa (Gustavus I), in the sixteenth century broke with the Catholic Church, declared Sweden a protestant nation and confiscated all property of the wealthy monasteries. For the following 300 years, Swedish kings and queens engaged the country in more or less constant warfare, temporarily turning the Baltic Sea into an all-Swedish 'lake'. Having lost the 'empire' and the belief in autarchy and the gains of warfare, Swedes increasingly turned to more peaceful activities and constitutionally prohibited the monarch from initiating aggressive wars (Moerk, 1998).

The next round of dramatic changes in Swedish society, the coming of modernity and industrialization, added rationality, control through logical and exact science, and machine metaphors to the leadership story.

In Hofstede's (1980, 1984) study, Sweden scores very high on 'femininity', that is endorsing values such as nurturing, caring, focus on personal relationships rather than more materialistic values. Forss *et al.* (1984) comment that no one would characterize Swedish managers of the early twentieth century as 'feminine'. Instead, words like strength and assertiveness fit the history of

Swedish industrialization. It is suggested that 'perhaps the idea of relatively equal, and strong, men united in battle under a commander who is only "primus inter pares" has been wrongly taken as sign of a submissive leadership style' (Forss *et al.*, 1984: 37).

We believe that the historic autarchic leadership style underwent substantial changes under the Social Democrats' long era of reign, starting in 1920, due to major efforts to extend voting rights and democracy. The role of a caring and nurturing leader picked up by Hofstede proved to be compatible with rational ideas of expertise, control and universalism promoted in the modernization of Swedish society, and was curiously emulated on the 'patriarch' of the early raw material extracting industries where the owner (and leader) supplied workers with basic lodging, schooling, health care, and often provided a shop for basic needs where the monthly bill could be deducted from the wages.

As to recently made allegations of Sweden being a country on the cutting edge of cultural change, social innovation and post-modernization (Tengblad, 2006), we agree that Swedish society in general, and its leaders specifically, have handled the often painful sense-making exercise related to major societal and ideological change in a (typical) pragmatic way. Sediments of Christian and Modern Project ideas are important parts of Swedish leadership, but mythology remains a basis for understanding beliefs, language and behaviour of today's Swedish leaders.

## PRACTICAL APPLICATIONS

The complex nature of leaders and other characters in Swedish mythology echoes in contemporary Swedish leadership, leaders have blind spots, weaknesses to external eyes that are paradoxically often viewed as strengths in the Swedish context. Birkinshaw (2002: 11) exemplifies Swedish leadership's main strengths and weaknesses by describing Sven-Göran Eriksson, the famous Swedish coach of the English national soccer team recruited after his success in Italy as follows: 'He comes across as a rather unlikely leader – modest, understated, a man of few words. But at the same time he is evidently very successful'. Associating Eriksson's leadership style with Swedish culture, Birkinshaw (2002) argues that it all boils down to empowerment, teamwork and consensus-based decision-making.

What Birkinshaw (2002) refers to as the 'modest and understated' is in our view a reflection of egalitarian values and the importance of not standing out, tightly related to the relatively flat organizations, the lack of overt displays of hierarchical level, and the leader as being perceived as a team player while in fact being the person in charge. In the Swedish culture, these are among the most appreciated leadership strengths, often expressed as 'she or he is just one of us', while at the same time being acutely aware that this is not completely the case. Internationally, this is often valued when understood but in our experience, this is where most non-Swedes go wrong even if working for many years in Swedish organizations in Sweden. It is undisputedly very difficult to realize that there is an existing, almost invisible, hierarchy based on both level and expertise, and to understand how it plays out in everyday operations. Similarly, role and task boundaries are vague, but Swedes know exactly where these are and how they work. Metaphorically one can speak of infrared lines criss-crossing the organization salient to varying degrees depending on the non-Swedes' cultural lens. Those who come from explicit, almost tangible bureaucratic organizations and societies have problems in detecting those infrared lines. One problem is that bureaucracy in its original Weberian sense assumes a monocratically organized hierarchy. Individuals from a background encompassing this belief often have trouble when trying to locate 'the pyramid' and identify the one leader, as there is seldom one person holding all the power. Instead, discretionary authority is distributed and delegated in the Swedish organization based on expertise as well as position.

The action-oriented Swedish leader spurred by challenges is indeed a person of few words. Verbal acrobats and strong debaters are viewed with the suspicion that the person is superficial, hiding something, or is 'all talk and no action' (Zander, 1999, 2001) whereas a silent person is a good listener, who thinks before speaking and when speaking reflects good judgement and a balanced opinion. This strength in the Swedish context also renders Swedes internationally advantageous diplomatic and negotiating skills. However, there is another side of the coin, a blind spot to many leaders. Non-Swedes often perceive Swedish managers as indirect and unclear in their communication and they are often referred to as 'managing by nods and winks' (Hedlund and Åman, 1984). For example, at international meetings, some non-Swedish subsidiary managers have a problem understanding what, if any, decision was taken, while others do not grasp that a decision actually had been made. This has led some scholars to view Swedes as the Japanese of the North (Daun, 1986). The bottom line is that it is difficult for non-Swedes to capture not just the subtleties but often the main message conveyed. Again, the success in deciphering Swedish communication depends on the non-Swedes' own cultural communication patterns. Those who are used to elaborate (large quantity), as well as direct or confrontational communication styles will have more communication problems than those from other types of cultural background, noting that communication style preferences also vary across the same spoken language (Zander, 2005).

The empowering, the teamwork and the consensus aspects of Swedish leadership are strengths that also may be frustrating but are quite explicit and visible and thus easier to grasp for non-Swedes. For example empowering can be seen as pushed 'too low', or carried out with employees who are 'too young' or 'too inexperienced'. Being expected to be a team player can exasperate those from a culture where competition and individual achievement are rewarded. Teamwork can be experienced as inefficient, seen as generating an outcome of the 'least common denominator' type, rather than 'a sum that is larger than its parts'. Consensus-oriented decision-making is perceived as slow and cumbersome leading non-Swedes to view their Swedish managers as indecisive (Hedlund and Åman, 1984) and lacking both clout and power.

It is the implicit, tacit, invisible, modestly downplayed and understated hierarchies, role and task boundaries that are exceptionally difficult to comprehend and relate to for many non-Swedes. Swedish leaders do not in general perceive these as weaknesses, which make them serious blind spots. Adding communication preferences based on silence, conflict avoidance and action rather than words, is a recipe for unnecessary confusion, complication and communication disorders among many non-Swedes. It may even be the case that non-Swedes in Swedish organizations draw the conclusion that there is no leadership exercised, which is (almost) always wrong.

How then can non-Swedes interact with Swedish leaders in a successful way? The apparent starting point is to know that there are differences and that often these are not visible; neither in the physical environment (for example, department lists of names are usually in alphabetical order without titles), nor in written documents such as policies, rules and regulations as these are scarce. Swedes will seldom point anything out verbally as this is seen as improper and rude. However, Swedish leaders do not mind answering questions and can go to lengths to put a person into the picture.

Taking time for informal talks at the almost compulsory coffee breaks and lunch hours but also when bumping into each other in the corridor is key to understanding the on-goings in Swedish organizations. Given conflict avoidance, this is also a means for non-confrontational exchanges of opinions and partial settling of issues before formal meetings take place. Substantial teamwork is carried out in informal settings and not just in designated formal meetings. Informal conversations also lead to participation in consensus-making processes, staying informed and being able to slowly decipher the flat but existing invisible hierarchies, role and task boundaries. In other words, learning by doing, learning by participating in informal as well as formal settings, and situated learning (Lave and Wenger, 1991) are the most promising paths for non-Swedes to take.

The vague role and task boundaries are also fluid and the importance of volunteering or responding positively to unexpected requests, when troubles arise cannot be overestimated. Reminiscent of historical times, when Sweden's harsh geography and climate led the relatively few people that lived there to help each other out, responding to calls for ad hoc assignments requiring immediate action in today's organizational life is often a fast track to becoming an insider and to learning more about Swedish leadership.

In the informal, invisible, almost incomprehensible realm of Swedish leadership, we in essence recommend non-Swedes to initiate communication, embrace situated learning, and engage in action above and beyond the call of duty as key to successful interaction with Swedish leaders.

## ACKNOWLEDGEMENTS

The authors wish to express their gratitude to the editors Eric H. Kessler and Diana J. Wong-MingJi for inviting us to join this book project, and for insightful, supportive and generous feedback. The authors would also like to thank the faculty at the School of Marketing and International Business at Victoria University of Wellington for providing such an inspiring venue for writing this chapter.

## NOTES

1. In addition, of course stories about where we all come from and daily encounters with the social workings of our family (our first observations of the structure and dynamics of a [semi-] formal organization) define our thoughts and behaviour for longer than we might want.
2. Norse mythology is the best preserved version of the older common Germanic paganism, in turn developed from earlier Indo-European mythology. The mythology was orally transmitted in the form of poetry and had not one set of doctrinal beliefs. Some aspects of Norse mythology have passed into Scandinavian folklore and have survived to modern day times.
3. As creation explains the origin of all things, this mythology reflects deep-seated philosophical, religious, cultural and social beliefs about the nature of reality and the unknown, being and non-being and the relationship between all things. Hence they are in most societies regarded as the most sacred of traditions.
4. In the following, the Swedish forms of names will be used consistently, as the English counterparts only have slightly different spelling.
5. To emphasize the fatalism (but also a messianic message) in Swedish mythology, all the major male gods were mortal and would die fighting at the time of 'Ragnarök', the final great destructive battle. This battle was only survived by a handful of less important gods, the world tree Yggdrasil, and hidden within it, the two human beings who would found a new human race in an idyllic world of goodness and happiness. The new world would be governed by Oden's flawless second-born son Balder, the god of light, innocence, beauty, joy, purity and peace. He would be brought back to life together with his formerly blind brother, the god of winter and darkness, Höder, who would help build the new world.
6. This view of deities is in stark opposition to the later dominant single, all-seeing, all-knowing God introduced to Sweden over a period of 300 years beginning in the ninth century through monotheism in the form of Christianity.
7. 'Munin' is the chosen name for the first Swedish nano-satellite, its scientific objective is to be able to collect data on the auroral activity in both the Northern and Southern hemisphere, the data on magnetospheric activity is to be made available online to be used for space weather predictions.

8.  In the genre of paleofiction, Kurtén has entertained the theory that Trolls are a distant memory of human encounters with Neanderthals by our Cro-Magnon ancestors some 40 000 years ago. A perhaps more plausible explanation for the Troll myth is that they represent the remains of a forefather cult, where a custom was to sit on grave-mounds in order to make contact with the deceased (or mound-dwellers). With the introduction of Christianity, the religious elite sought to demonize the pagan cult and denounced the ancestors as evil trolls.

9.  Understanding Swedish cultural values and attempting to trace their origin historically has peaked the interest of not only academics but also practitioners as witnessed by recent popular management books (see for example, Johansson Robinowitz and Werner Carr, 2001).

10. There seems to be an ongoing specialization of roles among Swedish leaders, where an important minority specialize in and are known and admired for their hard-handedness. Like in other societies, the main reason for these types of leaders to become ousted scapegoats is that they have not been tough enough in their creation of order.

11. There is a striking lack of top Swedish women leaders in our discussion above. Sweden is internationally known for its comparatively large percentage of women in the salaried workforce (about 80 per cent). However, there is a notable gender imbalance across hierarchical levels (Höök, 1995). In Sweden's 70 largest firms, a mere 3 per cent of top management and 4 per cent of the board members are women. Women at the top have not yet reached an iconic status although many, notably Annika Falkengren (President and CEO of the bank SEB), Antonia Ax:son Johnson's (owner and chairperson of the Axel Johnson AB Group) and Christina Stenbeck (chairman of Kinnevik) are soaring to this position as witnessed by their rankings on prominent international lists such as Fortune's Global Power, Forbes list of the 100 most powerful women in the world, and the Financial Times list of powerful women in Europe.

12. Although the Christian cross soon made it on to rune-stones and churches were built, people for hundreds of years to come snuck into their secret hideouts to worship the familiar Norse gods when darkness fell on Swedish farms. Likewise, the ideas of logos and ratio promoted by the modern project over time eroded the hegemony of Christian thought, while religious beliefs were still held by the silent majority.

13. Interestingly, freedom fighters like Engelbrekt in the fifteenth century are also immortalized.

# REFERENCES

Alvesson, M. (1992), Leadership as social integrative action. A study of a computer consultancy company, *Organization Studies*, **13** (2), 185–209.

Bengtsson, K. (2003), Executive commentary, *Academy of Management Executive*, **17** (1), 22–3.

Birkinshaw, J. (2002), The art of Swedish management, *Business Strategy Review*, **13** (2), 11–19.

Campbell, J. (1972, 1993), *Myths to Live By*, New York: Penguin Books Ltd.

Czarniawska-Joerges, B. (1993), Sweden: a modern project, post-modern implementation, in David. J. Hickson (ed.) *Management in Western Europe*, Berlin: Walter de Gruyter.

Daun, Å. (1986), The Japanese of the north – the Swedes of Asia?, *Ethnologia Scandinavica*, **16** (1), 5–15.

Daun, Å. (1992), Modern and modest. Mentality and self-stereotypes among Swedes, in Annick Sjögren and Lena Janson (eds) *Culture and Management: In the Field of Ethnology and Business Administration*, Stockholm: The Swedish Immigration Institute and Museum, and Institute of International Business.

Dearlove, D. and Crainer, S. (2002), Need a CEO? Call Stockholm, *Chief Executive*, **17** (8), 21.

Edström, A. and Jönsson, S. (1998), Svenskt ledarskap, in Barbara Czarniawska, *Organisationsteori på svenska*, Malmö: Liber Ekonomi.

Forss, K., Hawk, D. and Hedlund, G. (1984), Cultural differences: Swedishness in legislation, multinational corporations, and aid administration, Stockholm: Institute of International Business, Research Paper 84/5.

Gyllenhammar, P. G. (1977), How Volvo adapts work to people, *Harvard Business Review*, **July–August**, 102–13.

Hall, A. and Nyman, N. (2004), *Reinforcing Work Motivation: a Perception Study of Ten of Sweden's most Successful and Acknowledged Leaders*, Jönköping: Jönköping International Business School.

Hampden-Turner, C. and Trompenaars, A. (1993), *The Seven Cultures of Capitalism*, London: Currency Doubleday.

Hedlund, G. and Åman, P. (1984), *Managing Relationships with Foreign Subsidiaries – Organization and Control in Swedish MNCs*, Stockholm: Sveriges Mekanförbund.

Hofstede, G. (1980, 1984), *Cultures Consequences: International Differences in Work-Related Values*, Newbury Park, CA: Sage.

Holmberg, I. and Åkerblom, S. (2001), The production of outstanding leadership – an analysis of leadership images in the Swedish media, *Scandinavian Journal of Management*, **17**, 67–85.

Holmberg, I. and Åkerblom, S. (2006), Modelling leadership – implicit leadership theories in Sweden, *Scandinavian Journal of Management*, **22**, 307–29.

Höök, P. (1995), Women at the top – a survey of Swedish industry, in Anna Wahl (ed.) *Men's Perceptions of Women and Management*, Stockholm: Ministry of Health and Social Affairs.

Johansson Robinowitz, C. and Werner Carr, L. (2001), *Modern Day Vikings: A Practical Guide to Interacting With the Swedes*, Boston, MA: Intercultural Press.

Jönsson, S. (ed.) (1996), *Perspectives of Scandinavian Management*, Kungälv: Gothenburg Research Institute and Gothenburg School of Economics and Commercial Law.

Kets de Vries, M. F. R. (1998), Charisma in action: the transformational abilities of Virgin's Richard Branson and ABB's Percy Barnevik, *Organizational Dynamics*, **Winter**, 7–21.

Laine-Sveiby, K. (1987), *Svenskhet som strategi*, Stockholm: Timbro.

Lave, J. and Wenger, E. (1991), *Situated Learning: Legitimate Peripheral Participation*, Cambridge: Cambridge University Press.

Lawrence, P. and Spybey, L. (1997), Sweden: management and society, in David J. Hickson (ed.) *Exploring Management across the World: Selected Readings*, London: Penguin Books.

Linnell, B. and Löfgren, M. (eds) (1995), *Svenska krusbär: En historiebok om Sverige och Svenskarna*, Stockholm: Bonnier Alba.

Maccoby, M. (ed.) (1991), *Sweden at the Edge: Lessons for American and Swedish Managers*, Philadelphia, PA: University of Pennsylvania Press.

Moerk, E. L. (1998), From war-hero to villain: reversal of the symbolic value of war and a warrior king, *Journal of Peace Research*, **35** (4), 453–69.

Selmer, J. and De Leon, C. (1996), Parent cultural control through organizational acculturation: HCN employees learning new work values in foreign business subsidiaries, *Journal of Organizational Behavior*, **17**, 557–72.

Smith, P. B., Andersen, J. A., Ekelund, B., Graversen, G. and Ropo, A. (2003), In search of Nordic management styles, *Scandinavian Journal of Management*, **19**, 491–507.

Tengblad, S. (2006), Is there a 'new managerial work'? A comparison with Henry Mintzberg's classic study 30 years later, *Journal of Management Studies*, **43** (7), 1437–61.

Toulmin, S. (1990), *Cosmopolis: the Hidden Agenda of Modernity*, Chicago, IL: The Chicago University Press.

Zander, L. (1997), *The licence to lead – an 18-country study of the relationship between employees' preferences regarding interpersonal leadership and national culture*, Published Ph D dissertation, Stockholm: Institute of International Business.

Zander, L. (1999, 2001), Management in Sweden, in Malcolm Warner (ed.) *International Encyclopedia of Business and Management*, Vol. 4., London: International Thomson Business Press, pp. 345–53.

Zander, L. (2002), Empowering Europe: a study of empowering, national culture and cultural congruence, in Pat Joynt and Malcolm Warner (eds) *Managing Across Cultures: Issues and Perspectives*, London: International Thomson Business Press, pp. 103–23.

Zander, L. (2005), 'Communication and country clusters: a study of language and leadership preferences', *International Studies of Management and Organization*, **35** (1), 84–104.

# 10. Cultural mythology and global leadership in Poland

## Christopher Ziemnowicz and John Spillan

## INTRODUCTION

The roots of myths and legends in Poland can be traced to its geography that made it an easy target for invaders as well as its tumultuous history. The nation has had many neighbors, which generally means problems, but also centuries-long cohabitation, annexation of its territories, and collapses as an independent nation. Not only has Poland shared its territory with other people, but also others have claimed its heroes. Examples include the poet, Adam Mickiewicz, who called himself 'Lithuanian' – even though he was born in Belarus. The hero of the Polish uprising as well as the American War of Independence, Tadeusz Kosciuszko, is also claimed by both nations. The famous woman scientist and two-time Nobel Prize recipient, Maria Skłodowska who worked with her husband, Pierre Curie, is likewise claimed by both Poland and France. The heroic exploits of its people are legendary, as is their nationalism in spite of overwhelming odds as repeatedly illustrated through the willingness to put everything on the line to protect their country.

Cultural mythology in Poland goes back to the country's early history. A seminal event took place in 966 when Prince Mieszko adopted Christianity as the main religion for all of the Polish land. This also established Poland as a state within which Roman Catholicism became the primary religion of the Polish people. It became, and continues to be, a primary influence and integral component of Polish life and behavior. As Poland became the first Christian country in Europe, Polish patriots supported and defended their chosen faith from many intruders. For example, when the Tatars (Mongols) invaded Poland and Central Europe, they were held in check due in part to the deep-rooted Polish faith answering the call to protect the church. The vows taken by Poland to the Virgin Mary are taken very seriously. Even under the most desperate of conditions throughout history, the Poles have remained loyal to their country and their faith.

# OVERVIEW OF POLISH MYTHOLOGY

Events during its early history became some of Poland's most enduring mythological stories that impart on critical beliefs and values. The origin of the Hejnał Mariacki (hymn to Mary) has several versions. A popular myth describes birth of the tune from one of the Tatar attacks on Kraków. A guard sounded an alarm so the city gates could be closed as warriors approached. The bugler was on the tower of St Mary's church (Kościół Mariacki) and was shot with an arrow before completing the tune. This five-note Hejnał became a legend and is used as a national symbol. For example, during World War II, Polish soldiers in the Battle of Monte Cassino played the Hejnał Mariacki to proclaim victory.

Another ubiquitous Polish folk myth dating back to the eleventh century is Krakus, a legendary prince. He is the mythical founder of Kraków and is also credited with building Wawel Castle. The legend begins before the establishment of the city when an evil dragon lived in a dark cave inside Wawel hill. No one would dare to get near the cave entrance out of fear to awaken the creature. The greenish dragon, named 'Smok', would occasionally emerge hungry from its sleep to grab a hapless animal or even a child for its meal. The locals tried to slay the dragon, but even their combined efforts and weapons were ineffective against the fire breathing Smok. However, one of the wise men in the small settlement was named Krakus and he prepared magical herbs that healed the sick. Krakus made a paste that was placed on a sacrificial sheep. The tainted sheep was then thrown into the cave. After some time, the dragon came out from the cave and went to the nearby Vistula River. The secret paste on the sheep had caused the dragon a great burning in its gut. It drank massive amounts of water until it swelled and eventually burst. The locals rejoiced the riddance of the dragon's curse. Because of his knowledge and innovation, Krakus was asked to rule over them. Krakus built the fortified city that was named in his honor.

An enduring symbol remains from King Boleslaw and his Knights. The legend can be thought of as a Polish version of King Arthur. The Polish king unified the territories and his leadership made it a great nation. His exploits as a warrior together with his Knights were legendary and he earned the title of Boleslaw the Brave. When he died, he went into a mountain called Giewont. From certain angles, the mountain looks like the head of a sleeping Knight. Legend has it that King Boleslaw and his Knights are ensconced within a cavern, still mounted on their horses and ready to come to the aid of Poland when awakened.

Another enduring legend was the outlaw, Jerzy Janosik. He is also known in neighboring cultures sharing similar roots. Janosik was the Slovak version of Robin Hood and the myth inspires modern opposition movements.

According to the folk myth, Janosik robbed the rich merchants and nobles in a most chivalrous way and often shared the spoils with the poor. However, this legend of a hero taking from the rich and giving to the poor had transformed over time into a highwayman character among the mountaineers in Poland, as well as a symbol of resistance to oppression in Slovak and Czech literature.

Poland achieved several major milestones during the sixteenth century. The country became politically stable as a truly democratic country as well as affluent and powerful in the region. It benefited from exports of raw materials including timber and grains. Poland's prosperity was manifested in numerous educational and cultural advancements. Education, business and culture became significant aspects reaching Polish society involved in skilled trades and the guilds. Business activities transformed the way of life and increased the standard of living for those taking on new ventures during this period of time. This 'golden' period is also thought to have provided Poland with the cultural identity to help the country survive through the dark ages.

The eighteenth century brought on a major change. War and internal conflict created serious stability problems. It was during this century that Poland was divided up by Austria, Prussia and Russia. This geographical arrangement lasted for almost 100 years. Uprisings and revolts dominated this period of time and thus shaped many aspects of Poland's propensity to be almost ungovernable and the people's disobedience to authority. It was not until after World War I that Poland again became a stable entity and again was considered one whole independent state. Shortly thereafter with the invasion of Poland by the German Nazis, Poland was once again no longer an independent state. The domination by the Germans and the Russians lasted until 1989 (Thompson, 2002).

The complex structure of Polish culture, interrelationships among levels in Polish society, and the nation's historical trials and tribulations continue to contribute to mythology, as well as the conflicts between some of the myths and the practical reality of Poland's environment. Among the most enduring recurring events shaping beliefs and dominating Polish values are the partitioning of the nation by outside forces and the severe brutality against the people by the nation's captors. Two representatives of historical memory now deeply rooted in Polish cultural heritage and that continue to manifest themselves in decision-making are the Nation's Anthem and the Warsaw Uprising of 1944.

The first is a song that became popular after Poland lost its independence after it was partitioned by Austria, Russia and Prussia. It was written after the final effort to save Poland, the Kosciusko Insurrection in 1794, was suppressed by the Russians. Polish soldiers were scattered from their homeland and General Jan Henryk Dąbrowski wanted to create an army that could eventually liberate Poland. It was written to inspire Polish legionnaires serving under

Dąbrowski. While they were fighting in Napoleon's wars, the song's purpose was to rally the soldiers to return to Poland and reunite the nation. The song's exhortation that 'Poland is not dead as long as we live' became a symbol of Poland's indestructibility, as well as generating hope and enthusiasm for the nation that did not exist and for the Polish diaspora. The song was banned over the centuries by various totalitarian governments that occupied Poland or its historic territories. It became, and continues to be, a rallying call for all Poles at times of difficulty.

The second example recalls just one of the many atrocities that befell Poles during one of the nation's many struggles for independence. The 1944 Warsaw Uprising was a heroic and tragic 63-day attempt to liberate Warsaw from the German occupation. The casualties suffered by Poles during this brief resistance are the equivalent of the 11 September 2001 attack on the World Trade Center repeated each and every day for two months. About one quarter of the buildings in Warsaw were destroyed during urban combat that engulfed every man, woman and child. Taken together with earlier damage and the systematic German destruction of the city block by block following the surrender Home Army (Armia Krajowa, AK), almost 90 percent of the city was leveled. This was not a planned collapse of only two high-rise towers because by January 1945, when the Soviet 'liberators' finally entered, Warsaw had practically ceased to exist as a city.

During the domination of Poland by Russia, the Poles did not share the vision of the Soviet imposed state controlled socialist worker's utopia. Even ordinary citizens could see through the myth of a worker's paradise that held as the goal of the Soviet system. They observed the discrepancy between the myth of a utopian worker's society and the actual day-to-day reality. The Soviet propaganda actually was counterproductive because rather than being the beneficiaries of their hard work, they were actually the victims. This produced completely opposite behavior since socialism cannot exist under a system of state ownership, if the workers do not have control of the state.

Workers and managers learned to exploit and manipulate the system not only for individual gain, but also to spite the authorities, regulations, or the Soviet domination. This became a cultural phenomenon best described in saying 'Czy sie stoi, czy sie lezy, dwa tysiace sie nalezy' (Whether you stand up, or whether you lie down, 2000 Polish zlotys are your due). The Polish mythology became so pervasive that the Polish worker's productivity itself became a myth. British historian, Norman Davies, stated, 'Poles, above all, are patriots. It has been proved time and again that they will readily die for their country; but few will work for it' (Davies, 1982). In the 1970s, the Communists initiated the 'Czyn Partyjny' (Party Actions) or spectacular deeds done usually on Sundays to promote the bond of party members with the nation. This was yet another myth that people should voluntarily work rather than enjoy a holiday and participate in a religious tradition. There was no doubt hardly any real work was accomplished.

The dominant cultural values in Poland have been ingrained in the collective memory of its people not only from famous and defining symbols or from the events that have transcribed the nation and its citizens in the past several decades, but over the previous centuries. These myths and legends affect leadership, management, and worker behavior. These are typically problems that were the result of occupation, disobedience of the law, destruction of traditional links within society and religion. For example, cheating was a necessary ingredient for people's survival under the occupation of various empires. Forced migration and wars moved people to new areas with no local roots, traditions or business enterprises. As a Catholic nation for over 1000 years, people in Poland have been told that what is going to happen has already been destined for them and accumulation of wealth is a sin. The communist system added another attitude and belief system that the passivity helplessness is rewarded as more than enterprise and innovativeness. Such a morality is deeply ingrained and inherited from one generation to another. A recent example of this historical memory in policy-making was when the Polish Prime Minister Donald Tusk refused to attend the opening of the 2008 Olympic Games in China in support of the demonstrators in Tibet. Hoping to influence other world leaders, Tusk reminded them 'human rights are unusually important for Polish society after years in which they were violated in our country' (Miler and Andrusz, 2008).

Another characteristic of shared memory among Poles that persists relates to the 'before' situation. This is the place that the nation, its people, its traditions, or even a particular situation were at the so-called before. The concept of the Polish 'before' is at the root of many cultural myths. It is where Poland and its people had come from. Not even in the past 50 years, but from over the last five centuries. This is more deeply rooted than the occasional longing for the 'romanticized era' before any of the barbaric and totalitarian occupations. This is particularly evident in the sense of before the Nazi and Communist occupations in Poland because it continually endures and drives people's behavior. In that sense, the 'before' is not a myth, but a deep historical memory.

There exists an ingrained nationalistic opposition to any imposed regime in Poland. This attitude was most pronounced in recent history during the Soviet domination. Starting with the bourgeoisie and middle-class intellectuals, but also incorporating almost all segments of society, opposition was based on Polish nationalism against Soviet imperialism. The 'Russian brothers' and 'Country of Advice' espoused a socialist 'freedom' for Poland by removing the capitalist exploitation of workers by the bourgeoisie and imposing a centrally planned economy whose focus was to be on the production of goods and services needed by people, as well as the Polish government becoming a puppet following the policies established in Moscow. However, Soviet-style socialism was incompatible with Polish nationalism. Polish people wanted a freedom that enabled them to be 'free' to decide their own fate and to be able to manage their own economy and carry out their own relations in the international arena. Since the Soviet domination of Poland seemed so comprehensive and sandwiched geopolitically as to have no room to maneuver, the Polish perspective was turned back to its periods of freedom in history.

An example of the effect of this was shown in an ethnographic study by Kostera (2006) that attempted to learn about ideas of the future as seen by Polish managers. The interviewees were to discuss their visions. Instead, the managers talked of the past, some even going back to the 1950s. They did not want to speak about future visions, even though a few talked about the present.

The Communist occupation of Poland had a particularly insidious influence on its people. This was a major conflict between an imposed myth and the daily life and business of Polish citizens. For example, employee participation in enterprise management began in 1918. Indigenous patriotic movement as well as the October Revolution in Russia spurred Restoration of Polish independence after World War I. The two major parties, the Polish Socialist Party (Polska Partia Socjalistyczna, PPS) and the Communist Workers' Party of Poland (Komunistyczna Partia Robotnicza Polski, KPRP) viewed the worker's voice differently. The socialist view was that of employee participation organizations supporting the development of a new government. On the other hand, the communists' view was that they could use the employee participation to initiate a revolution to establish a so-called dictatorship of the proletariat. The role of the councils of workers and union movement was tempered by the reconstruction of Poland's democratic system, as well as by establishment of pro-active social legislation, which was complementary to the demands of the workers. During this period Poland faced political and economic difficulties, but it fostered an enlightened, courageous and patriotic society. This challenging time for fledgling democratic Poland became a legendary and romanticized era in spite of the numerous social and economic problems.

After World War II, Poland entered a new era of state ownership and the employee participation in enterprises became a tool where workers were viewed as a manifestation of socialist democracy. The workers' councils were supposed to be the voice of the enterprise. In reality, their function was to supervise working conditions and make sure that discipline and productivity were continued. The assumed communist ideology meant that worker-management relations had no conflict because both sides had the same interests to improve output and thus the standard of living. Moreover, there was no need for worker or management participation, as central planning became the only force of administrative direction. Both managers and workers revolted due to the lack of confidence in workers' councils and public authorities. Following the October 1956 Workers' Riots, authentic and spontaneous employee participation in enterprise management was established under communist rule.

This was another disparity and conflict between the management myths and practical reality. Production for profit exists under capitalism as well as under socialism. In economic terms, surplus wage labor production accrues as profit to an individual entrepreneur or capitalist. On the other hand, when enterprises are under state ownership, it is the central authorities that appropriate the workers' surplus labor. This means that the state itself is capitalist.

Workers had no say in the control and affairs of the state. Regardless of the Soviet imposed propaganda machine statements, Polish worker interests were not satisfied. There was a disconnect between the ideals of the communist system and the day-to-day reality of the working class. Neither the workers, nor their councils, had any real impact on the decision-making within state enterprises. The communists introduced a new law in 1958 that established an obligatory 'Worker's Self-Management Conference' that ostensibly empowered the staff and trade union workers under the rule of the Communist Party. However, the national bureaucracy constrained self-management with increasingly centralized economic planning and management. Moreover, there was little support for developing the socialist working class in Poland and the ideals of communism. Because the open market system for prices and labor was ended by the Soviets, the traditional relationships of risk and return no longer applied and any entrepreneurial innovation was squelched due to limits on private ownership.

The ideological foundation of communism was focused on ordinary workers and farmers rather than the so-called intelligentsia that was regarded with suspicion. It was also easier to indoctrinate people without education, particularly if the system would provide for a better life. A system was built to provide special privileges to peasants and blue-collar workers – particularly in the heavy industry sectors of steel and mining. This changed the structure of Polish society by empowering a new working class who would be devoted to the new system while the old intelligentsia was considered the source of ideas opposed to the new system. This radically changed the whole system of values. A career thus depended on the ideological attitude rather than on experience and education. This had a further negative affect on the work ethic and productivity at all levels.

A significant contributor to the culture of cheating could be observed from the standard of living statistics. Workers were not much better off under the communist system than since the devastation of Poland in World War II. Survival competencies included the need to cheat the system and not just nationalistic needs for freedom. Because they were subjected to exploitation by the state, workers were motivated to act because of material reasons. Since many Poles lived below the official 'minimum standard of living' and the salaries of workers would not buy much, corruption became endemic. During this time it was not work but rather sabotage that was of value. Acting against the communist government was considered an act of courage.

The influence of imposed communism on Poland continues to influence decision-making and leaders. A special morality developed that is summarized in the 'it is not mine, thus I don't care' approach. The attitude pervaded the economy that often lacked a rational and a commonsense basis. Values sometimes had no meaning. A culture of cheating evolved because it was more profitable than solid work. Moreover, the communist economy divorced rewards from merit. Corruption was often the principal means to secure a life and provide housing as well as a telephone and even meat to make meals.

Success was often attributed to effective propaganda and the creative use of key cultural symbols and myths to inspire the citizens. For example, Wincenty Pstrowski became a new hero of the working class, where workers worked above their quota and the centrally planned increase in output was reached ahead of schedule. Nevertheless, under the thin veneer of development, most of the Poles calculated that about 20 percent was real progress and 80 percent did nothing. The socialist ideal encouraged the belief that the state is responsible for the welfare of all citizens. The 'I don't need to care' attitude hindered growth and development. Furthermore, the communist system encouraged deception. Unvarnished truth that went against official propaganda could not be told. People learned to read between the lines, as censorship was pervasive.

A bad attitude was thus inherited from generation to generation. Passivity and helplessness became deeply ingrained. Internationalization was discouraged. Poland was thus a fallen nation under the guidance of the Soviet Union. Not only was entrepreneurial spirit suppressed, but also the ability to cooperate was reduced. The Soviet culture imposed a sclerosis on the nation. This was evident in political and economic policies. The consequence was a refusal or an inability to modify policies in response to changing conditions.

Perhaps the most damaging element of the 'it is not mine, so I do not care' philosophy was the prevalence of corrupt practices in business and social life. There are many reasons why corruption became so popular in Polish society. First is the partitioning and occupation of Poland by the Russian, Prussian and Austrian empires that lasted over 150 years. Another related factor was the resettlement and migration of people to new areas. This tore traditional links in the social and economic areas. Having been deprived of their roots they had no sense of homeland. Some traditions did not match the local areas.

The 'I don't care' approach was even prevalent in the education system. The famous '4Zs' best describes the minimalism of some Polish students. The 4Zs stand for the first letter in four Polish words:

Zakuc = to cram the subject
Zdac = to pass the examination
Zapic = to drink in excess because of the success
Zapomniec = to forget the subject

The centralized decision-making of Poland's command economy could not continue without radical change. The nation's economy was heavily regulated and the state impeded private enterprises. Compounding inefficiencies included the overly large government and state run industries, continuing economic malaise associated with maintaining a welfare economy, as well as the insistence of maintaining a fortress-type trade policy closed to international markets. However, the Soviets bowed to pressure and thus prevented more serious unrest in Poland by making concessions in economic policies that included allowing more private ownership, dismantling of collective farms, and better trade terms. This allowed for improvements in the living standards.

Nevertheless, workers in Poland continued to struggle under austere conditions. The economic system was broken beyond repair and a full crisis ensued. Moscow was forced to bail out the Polish economy even though this meant spreading Poland's economic and political problems into other Warsaw Pact countries. The basic demand for change in material circumstances gave rise to the development of Solidarity and its eventual role as a model for international revolution. The state was not providing the promises made to the working class in Poland. The lie of communism was now exposed as workers struggled to establish 'free trade unions' and 'workers' self-management of production'. Solidarity was a turning point in the culture of management as new champions and role models emerged for positive achievements and a can-do attitude, as well as in the development of new myths. The historical changes that occurred in Poland since World War II therefore offer a unique opportunity to investigate the role played by mythology among Polish managers and its impact on decision-making. For example, in place of the previous oxymoron was to assume that people work.

The recent revolutionary changes in the nation's governance as well as its economic structures and environment help highlight the effect of established work rituals and standards that were pervasive. The environment has been radically changed to an open, market-based system within which new entrepreneurial and innovation based myths emerged while the old stereotypes are no longer applicable. For example, studies have shown that Polish workers now have high competencies and qualifications. This is particularly the case among the responses voiced by foreign investors. Managers of new business ventures that have established operations in Poland do not agree that 'the labor force is inefficient' and that 'it is hard to get anything done without a kick-back'.

Studies show that Poland is also a source of management best practices. For example, creating team building within a marketing department, an unneeded function in the centrally planned system. Another example is Mr Stanislaw Zon, president and CEO of Geofizyka Torun, who has demonstrated innovative management practices by acquiring Input/Output's VectorSeis technology. This new acquisition has already contributed to successfully finding recoverable reserves on the northeast border of the Wolsztyn ridge in Poland. VectorSeis imaging of PS waves from lower Zechstein limestone reefs brings new, important information, that helped the company achieve its objectives. This sale strengthens the company's strategy to expand international sales and increase its worldwide presence in emerging markets (Geofizyka Torun). These two examples illustrate the movement toward positive and progressive management practices much different from the old hard line command oriented focus that was the historical benchmark for managers.

Business leaders have grown out of the old mythological environments of Polish history and become vibrant, progressive leaders. On 15 February 2006, Prochem SA-Poland awarded its president Marek Garliński the Prochem Business leader recognition. The Business Centre Club has a Gold Statuette of the Polish Business Leader 2005 in the large company category. Selection of the winners was based on economic indicators, quality and modernity of products, investments – particularly pro-export and job creation, in addition to commitment to charitable activity and a focus on maintaining a sustainable natural environment (Warsaw Voice, 2006). Another case of indigenous advancement led by Polish workers was when they established a self-imposed system of critical steps at which the team measured their actual service performance by evaluating whether they were adding, or subtracting, customer value (McClenahen, 1997). These are examples of the radical transformation among companies and workers that has led to the existence of a clash of cultures. This is where the old values and myths are confronting entirely new ideas about how business should be run. Cross-cultural management issues have provided a challenge for organizational development in Poland's new market economy.

## PRACTICAL APPLICATIONS

Cultures exist not only in countries, but also in business organizations. Because they are so important to our existence, many scientists in a variety of settings study them. Business organizations are a diverse sector of every society. Employees in these organizations represent the primary area in corporate operations where a clash of cultures can most frequently occur. Organizations consist of a collection of people with different points of view working together to achieve a common goal. Because there are at least two points of view, corporate culture disparities can erupt and alter the compatibility or success of groups of workers. Workers are the foundation of corporate cultures. Workers themselves determine whether the corporate culture will help, or hinder, the achievement of goal attainment. Examples of endeavors that encounter culture clash include wholly owned subsidiaries operating in multi-cultural environments.

For example, the American and Polish management groups represent two culturally different work forces possessing different beliefs, values, and patterns of thinking. When Americans brought in their new high productivity goals that were very efficiency oriented, Polish employees became angry because there was such a marked departure from the old management rules and myths of the past. The old ideas of 'it is not mine, so I do not care' philosophy cannot exist in a market oriented economy. However, productivity and increased sales are critical to the workers' success and survival.

How people work together in international ventures is important to analyze. In many organizations culture is a low priority and managers tend to regard it as an imprecise variable that will adjust automatically with the application of proper business tools. Culturally different work forces possess different beliefs, values, and patterns of thinking. Different work forces create structures, factors and strategies that influence the achievement of organizational goals. Many conceptual and methodology issues are yet unresolved and, hence, the discipline does not have solid answers to many questions. The lack of findings and the methodological complexity of cross-cultural research are major disadvantages of the field (Zaleska, 1992: 1).

In a paper entitled 'Cross-cultural interaction between Polish and American managers', Zaleska begins a major attempt to examine a variety of issues that affect the ability to transact business in an international environment. Zaleska's work provides insights into the interaction between American and Polish managers. Her work substantiates the thesis of a clash of corporate cultures when two different nationalities of management interact. Zaleska further states that: 'no major methodologies have been established that focus on analyzing the impact of corporate culture clash on the final outcomes of business activities.' The essence of her work is that corporate culture clashes exist; that these clashes affect a company's economic performance, and those other methods for studying these phenomena must be developed. Zaleska describes some of the problems of culture clash when American and Polish workers come together.

This problem is worsened by the lack of inter-cultural communication skills, as well as by the management practices established by international management teams. Betty Ann Korzenny (1979), in a work entitled 'Cross-cultural issues in the process of sending US employees of multinational corporations for overseas service,' found that large American multinational corporations, who are otherwise sophisticated in organizing their business tasks, have not systematically organized their inter-cultural management functions. The relationships between firms from different cultures create challenging problems for international managers. As Terpstra states: 'issues of cultural miss-communication arise from the fact that individuals in any business firm are triply socialized – into arise culture, into their business, and into their corporate culture' (Terpstra and David, 1991: 8).

A review of the literature clearly states that corporate culture is a major factor in the management of a business. All businesses have cultures whether they label them as a culture or not. However, describing the particular culture is not an easy task. For example, some companies may have an entrepreneurial culture, others may be bureaucratic, while still others may exhibit a customer-oriented culture. All of these labels, on the surface, may mean different things to different people. Almost all aspects of work, culture and management that have been integral and critical to the delivery of management practices in the Polish economy have taken on new dimensions. They have become, in some cases, substitutes for the old myths that were pervasive in the old Polish management environment.

As Poland has moved through its transition it has encountered a very steep learning curve. The basic foundation myths and principles that were embedded in the society had to be discarded or reshaped. One of the first areas to change was the work environment itself. This factor is an important element that influences the ability of company staff and management to generate ideas. Without an environment that supports staff participation in decision-making and idea development, the firm will move towards decay and decline. Managers believe that a staff with a participative work environment is critical to innovation. Another new approach is the learning organization where continuing employee development and training is emphasized. A learning organization keeps its human resources competent, skillful, and current with state-of-the-art capabilities. For any company this requirement cannot be waived, eliminated, or devalued. It must be supported with continuous resources.

Because the American style of free market system is pervasive in many markets, there is often a clash between American and Polish management principles and beliefs. As Zaleska's research demonstrated, there is a clear difference in the way Polish managers view a variety of management practices. This is significant because of the possible potential conflicts that can have an impact on productivity. Additionally, different perspectives influence the composition of the firm's corporate culture that is directly related to strategy development. Since strategy development is at the nucleus of goal attainment, it would seem important that there should exist a balance between the joint management philosophies of each group.

The bureaucratic structure has been a huge burden and obstacle to the transformation from a command oriented society to a market system. Management structures would be expected to shift away from bureaucracy and towards flexibility and entrepreneurship. Teamwork is also an important aspect of idea development and innovation process within the new Polish environment. While independent thinking is important and individual participation is required, most successful firms achieve their goals because they are committed to teamwork.

Another shift has been in risk-taking, which was previously an unknown in the old Polish management structures. Workers did what they were told and carried out the centrally determined five-year plans, whatever they may be. As Poland moved towards the market-system and new competitors come to Poland the need to wager various resources is a necessity to make short- or long-term gains. Few enterprises can escape the need to introduce products, processes, or markets that are not guaranteed to provide the desired return. This is important because without taking risks, survival is impossible.

Management leadership is now at the center of any successful venture. Poland previously had linear leadership that was often focused on unproductive methods that retarded rather than promoted its economic development. The old myths about producing products to meet plans that had no market are no longer acceptable. The leadership factor is critically important in any country and corporate culture. Without its existence all other factors flounder and companies become aimless in their pursuits. Without proper leadership, corporate culture is doomed, management strategy is worthless, and goal attainment is almost impossible.

A new hierarchy of values relating individual ownership and entrepreneurship in Poland have encountered old values and beliefs promoted by the previously centrally planned economy. While they are rapidly fading away, these myths and values can still be a barrier to this transition in ideology. In other words, these old methods may need to be eradicated before they create a major clash of corporate cultures and adversely affect the economic reforms.

However, opinions have been confirmed about Poland's ubiquitous bureaucracy, inefficient judiciary, poor infrastructure, and its complicated tax system. Similar to many other nations, the bureaucracy myth continues with its vested interest in maintaining the status quo.

## OVERVIEW OF POLISH LEADERSHIP

The true definition of myth indicates a set of stories, traditions or beliefs associated with a set of particular groups or the history of an event arising naturally or deliberately fostered, that is the Fascist mythology of the interwar years (Dictionary.com Unabridged (v1.1) based on Random House unabridged dictionary, Random House, Inc. 2006). The myths of the old Polish management functions related to how the society was socialized after its domination by the Soviets. The events and beliefs that were inculcated into the culture and the mass society determined the way the people thought, worked and lived their lives. These beliefs determined the way organizations were managed and how the managers conducted business. While management education teaches students skills and competencies to manage processes and decision making, in the Polish society the education not only provided the manager with skills to do his/her job but also a status in the society and the enterprise (Kostera *et al.*, 1995). The competencies provided the roles and conditions for the managers to perform and present an image to his/her peers and the community.

In communist Poland, the task related skills and the professional standards of the manager were context specific requiring different attributes that were not seen in western managers. The manager in the Polish context was an administrator with their task focused on performing and not on creativity. The manager was greatly restricted by regulations and directives he received with a very limited degree of freedom. The manager's role was determined by the 'production plan' prescribed by the centrally planned bureaucracy. The manager was required to enforce labor discipline by making the labor force obey the rules and regulations promulgated by bureaucracy (Sarapata, 1992). The managerial role was associated with conventionality rather than imagination. Management was not a superstar career. They were not to be too noisy or visible. They should not be overzealous (Kostera *et al.*, 1995). In order to survive, the managers played various games with authorities, the party and the secret police that had considerable power over the enterprises. The games were political negotiations including formation of coalitions aimed at maximizing power, as well as countering the symbols created and transmitted by the political authorities (Kostera and Wicha, 1995). Playing these games successfully without making him/herself vulnerable nor his/her company and employees was considered the most important quality of the former professional role of the manager, and also kind of a virtue (Kostera *et al.*, 1995). The games were part of the managerial role but were also a necessity – the managers had to play for more power if they wanted their companies to survive and perhaps also to grow (Kostera and Wicha, 1994).

The social responsibility of the communist manager was then very broadly defined as related to the society as a whole. Individuality was banned, initiative and stressing of one's own position were not popular. Managers were not to provide 'individualistic gains' but were to subject themselves to the needs of the society (Kostera and Wicha, 1995). The professional role contained a high degree of hypocrisy: declaring loyalty to the communist party and commitment to the system without really thinking so was an important element of the manager's career. Knowing the right people was tremendously important in the Polish manager's life and role as a manager of an enterprise. These insincere declarations and personal networks were tools for accomplishing the most important informal aim of Polish managers: assuring that the central plans for their companies were minimal so that it would be easy to accomplish and not exceed them. This was needed to gain extra financial and material means for social programs, bonuses for employees and foreign travel. The managers who could achieve this were considered good managers (Kostera and Wicha, 1995).

The transition of Poland during the late 1980s and through the 1990s until the present day witnessed unprecedented change in the role of the manager. The roles of the new manager are becoming increasingly more like that of Western managers focused on a market economy (Kozminski and Obloj, 1990). The new Polish managers are involved in organization and motivation of teams. They are now working with and managing autonomous organizations, which no longer are under several layers of bureaucratic control. The managers believe that their new role is that of organizing tasks, and strategy formulation (Kostera and Wicha, 1995).

Kwiatkowski and Kozminski (1992) indicate that there is currently a large group of well-educated management professors in Poland and quite a few institutions offering high quality education. Today managers emphasize competence and professionalism and a code of ethics. According to Kostera *et al.* (1995) the key point to emphasize is that managerial roles develop in two parallel tracks that seem to be independent of each other. The first is the mythical one, and it corresponds to the use of the right slogans. The mythical role has changed considerably in Poland. It is entirely different from the communist era, even if the myth it is now based on is in the distant past. The second track is the substantial or enacted role and it can best be described by words: wait and see.

## GLOBAL IMPLICATIONS

Since we live and work in a dynamic global world, it is imperative for managers and business operators to understand that other cultures have different perspective on issues. We can see with many Polish examples. For a long time the Poles were required to reject the Western world's point of view and sustain their allegiance to the Soviet Union's linear central command point of view. All that has changed in the twenty-first century. Yet, culture and ideas about other people that are not understood continue to be obstacles to our interactions with other business cultures. The study of Polish management mythology provides another view; another lens for us to see how cultures can change and cultures can make adaptations to different patterns of living. For many years those in the West considered the Poles 'backward', unable to compete with the fast growing Western ways. It is interesting that since the incredible transformation of Poland which started in 1989, Poland has made historic changes that allowed Poland to be part of the European Union and an equal partner in global business activities. Clearly, Poland has gained enormous strength by transforming its economy and its society. It is now a nation in transition diligently moving forward with continuous improvement. All of this progress emerged because Poland had courageous leaders who were always looking for ways to make the quality of life better for its citizens, for example Lech Walesa's leadership in the streets of Poland when he led Solidarity toward freedom. His perseverance demonstrated to the world that Poland may be old and may be constrained by the central command of the Soviet Union but it will not be enslaved any more – see Commentary box. Those courageous days led to the fall of communism and the historic change in Central and Eastern Europe. Leadership was also demonstrated with Dr Leszek Balcerowicz's implementation of the 'shock therapy' economic program that established the foundation for the economic success that exists today among the Polish enterprises. Both of these leaders broke away from the old mythology of defeat and 'can't do' to a positive, progressive proactive approach. Their methods were difficult for the Polish people to understand and accept but in the end they brought about a new society that is growing and continually improving. These leaders wanted a better quality of life for their citizens and worked to make that goal come true. The successes of the transformation and the old mythologies that were so embedded in the uneducated observer and reader are now long part of history.

---

## COMMENTARY BOX

### Lech Walesa

When it comes to struggle, almost everybody is nervous and afraid, in every struggle all over the world ... We had the Soviet troops stationed in Poland for 50 years ... There were not so many people who would claim to be very courageous. Then again, you have people of different characters. Some are really put off by the hardships, by the difficulties, whereas the others actually strengthen. I was among the latter, who became stronger due to the hardships, and I got involved in my struggle with much more determination. (from Academy of Achievement, 2000: http://www.achievement.org/autodoc/page/wal1int-3)

Viewing the firm's corporate culture suggests that each enterprise establishes a corporate culture conducive to accommodating the values and myths held by managers in Poland, as well as meeting the goal attainment as established by the organization. The major factors of culture that invigorate, promote and sustain decision-making, as well as developing new approaches such as innovations are available within each enterprise. There has to be a positive attitude about idea development and a traditional bureaucratic approach to management will lead to suboptimal results. Studies of successful and sustainable new enterprises in Poland highlight their structure as embracing the modern entrepreneurial culture. They are willing to take risks that have the probability of generating gains either in the short- or long-run.

The most important critical factor in building and sustaining a successful and effective corporate culture is leadership. There is no question that leadership is the key variable or the nucleus of any corporate culture. Without strong leadership that sets the direction, vision, and culture for goal attainment, no firm can be successful in the long run. In his work, *Organizational Culture and Leadership*, Edgar Schein (1992) examined companies with a vision to establish a corporate culture that emphasized goal attainment and success and found in all instances that successful firms have strong attitudes or beliefs towards leadership.

One of the greatest assets that a businessperson, or even a tourist, possesses is the ability to respect and appreciate the history of the country they are visiting. Some countries have had more difficult struggles than others. Poland is a country that has had to meet many challenges both internally and externally. The preceding discussions have outlined in detail the people, factors and events that have made Poland what it is today. Presently, Poland is positioned to be a significant economic power in the world. It has the geography and the demographics that are very helpful in its pursuit of becoming a prominent nation with a high quality of life for its citizens. The insights that have been presented in this chapter can provide some major suggestions toward effectively engaging with the managers and leaders from Poland. Some of these suggestions are as follows:

(a)  respect the history of Poland;
(b)  appreciate the tenacity, brilliance and perseverance of the Polish people;
(c)  understand that Poland is eager and anxious to continue to make improvements by discarding the old myths and acquiring new and innovative ways of doing business;
(d)  appreciate the Polish culture as it is; and
(e)  continue to work to understand and interact with the Poles no matter where they come from.

In conclusion, Poland is a very old country with a broad and deeply rich culture developed from actual experiences, tale, folklore and myths. The traditions and conventions that have grown out of these myths and cultural norms have had a major impact on the management behavior and style of Polish Administrators. The experiences that Poles have witnessed over the life of the country have been embedded into their pattern of thinking and living. In many instances the myths and legends have been the glue that has held the management together. With the many cultural and political changes that have occurred in Poland, the myths and legends have provided an alignment mechanism that has filtrated through the years to the present day society. It is obvious that the pace of change during the ninth and tenth centuries was much slower, but nonetheless it had a major impact on the content and direction of the society. The values and traditions that have followed the Poles through the years have a major impact on the way businesses are managed today in Poland.

## REFERENCES

Academy of Achievement (2000), Changing the face of the world, www.achievement.org/autodoc/page/wal1int-3

Business Wire (2003), Geofizyka Torun and input/output announce sale of VectorSeis System Four, *Business Wire*, 2 June 2003  www.findarticles.com/p/articles/mi_m0EIN/is_2003_June_2/ai_102672462

Davies, N. (1982), *God's Playground*, Columbia University Press.

Deresky, H. (1994), *International Management: Managing Across Borders and Cultures*, London: HarperCollins.

Hall, E. T. and Hall, M. R. (1987), *Hidden Differences – Doing Business with the Japanese*, Garden City, NY: Anchor/Doubleday.

Korzenny, B. A. (1979), Cross-cultural issues in the process of sending US employees of multinational corporations for overseas service, Paper presented at the 65th Annual Meeting of the Speech Communications Association, San Antonio, TX, November, 10–13.

Kostera, M. (1995), Differing managerial responses to change in Poland, *Organizational Studies*, **16** (4), 673–97.

Kostera, M. (2006), The narrative collage as research method, *Storytelling, Self, Society*, **22** (Spring), 5–27.

Kostera, M. and Wicha, M. (1994), Ponad blokami: Organizacja i otoczenie [Beyond blocks: Organization and environment], *Przeglad Organizacji*, **2**, 7-1.

Kostera, M. and Wicha, M. (1995), The symbolism of the communist manager roles: A study of scenarios, *Scandinavian Journal of Management*, **11** (2), 139–58.

Kotter, J. P. and Heskett, J. L. (1992), *Corporate Culture and Performance*, New York: The Free Press.

Kozminski, A. K. and Obloj, K. (1990), From innovative to systematic change: the transformation of Communist systems, *Communist Economics*, 2/3, 335–45.

Kwiatkowski, S. and Kozminski, A. (1992), Paradoxical country – management education in Poland, *Journal of Management Development*, **11** (5), 28–33.

McClenahen, J. S. (1997), Europe's best practices, *Industry Week*, 17 March, 17.

Miler, M. and Andrusz, K. (2008), 'Polish Premier skips Olympic opening to protest Tibet Update2, *Bloomberg News*, March, 27, http://www.bloomberg.com/apps/news?pid=20601085&sid=aHhXLAzSqu0c&refer=europe

Sarapata, A. (1992), Society and bureaucracy, in Ploszajski, P. and Connor, W. D. (eds), *Escape from Socialism: the Polish Route*, IFIS, Warszawa, pp. 98–114.

Schein, E. H. (1992), *Organizational Culture and Leadership* (2nd edn), San Francisco, CA: Jossey-Bass.

Schermerhorn Jr., J. R. (1993), *Management for Productivity* (4th edn), New York: John Wiley and Sons.

Terpstra, V. and David, K. (1991), *The Cultural Environment of International Business* (3rd edn), Mason, OH: South Western.

Thompson, B. (2002), Polish folk tales, legends and myths, SLIS 5440, December.

Warsaw Voice (2006), Prochem SA – Polish business leader, *The Warsaw Voice*, 15 February, http://www.warsawvoice.pl/view/10558/- accessed 4/1/08.

Zaleska, K. J. (1992), Cross-cultural interaction between Polish and American managers: a case study of an American firm in Poland, Central European University, Prague, Master's Thesis.

# PART III

# Africa and the Middle East

# 11. Cultural mythology and global leadership in South Africa

## David N. Abdulai

### INTRODUCTION

The commonly held notion of a myth is that it is a traditional story mostly emanating from primitive societies that deal with the supernatural, ancestors or heroes that serve as primordial types. It could also be a collection of stories that appeals to the character, emotions and consciousness of a people. But such definitions of myths or mythologies of a people in the view of this author are static and stale. The definition of a myth that has not been explored is how lies and half-truths have gained currency as truths in our society today. This is because fictitious stories were written and peddled by people with a certain agenda, ideology or worldview which have succeeded in turning their half-truths into truths and facts. The consequence of such half-truths or fiction is that they are now used to make decisions that affect the lives of people. Some of these half-truths have also created negative perceptions that can have a devastating impact on a people. The definition per this elaboration therefore is any issue that is a fallacy, a fiction, half-truth which in most cases evolved out of a certain ideology or worldview. This definition of a myth by this author is different from the mainstream definition offered at the beginning of this chapter. This latter definition is what this author will use in the course of this chapter.

This chapter will explore how ancestral veneration by Africans[1] has now come to be widely believed abroad and by even some Africans as 'ancestral worship' – a myth. Thus, because ancestral veneration plays an important role in the worldview of the African, this myth definitely has implications for them, their leaders and culture. Equally, it has global implications in how the outside world sees Africa, its culture and belief systems. But equally important is the fact that because cultural mythology deals with the character, emotions and consciousness of a people, the importance of ancestral veneration as such cannot be emphasized enough. The role of the ancestors in the mythology of the African forms part of their being, culture and worldview. Hence the veneration of such ancestors can thus be regarded as important in any discussion of cultural mythology that deals with the belief systems and culture of the African. The chapter will start by explaining the role ancestors play in the life and worldview of the African and how such has been misconstrued as 'ancestor worship'. An in depth analysis will be offered to help readers understand the important role of ancestors in the life of the African. It will then touch on ancestor veneration and the role local leadership plays in this process among the Zulus of South Africa. The chapter will also point out why ancestral veneration is not 'ancestral worship'. It will argue that it is a myth perpetuated by anthropologists, ethnographers and missionaries who either do not truly understand why Africans venerate their ancestors or have an alternative agenda. The possible reasons why such a myth has been perpetuated will be explored and the global implications delineated. Finally, the chapter will suggest how this knowledge can be used to do business or deal with leaders in Africa in general and the Zulus in particular.

## ANCESTORS IN THE AFRICAN COSMOLOGY AND THE MYTH OF THEIR WORSHIP

The role of ancestors in the worldview and cosmology of the African cannot be emphasized enough. The ancestors in the cosmology of the African serve as an intermediary between them (the living) and God (the creator). This creator is known by the Ashantis as *Nyame*, by the Zulus as *Inkosi Yezulu*, or *Mklunlunkulu* and by the Xhosa as *Quamata*. The ancestors who are referred to as *nananom* by the Akans, *togbuiwo* by the Ewes and *amalozi* by the Zulus in Africa guide and protect their people or clans from evil, diseases, famine and disasters (Dzobo, 1985). In most African societies, the ancestors are the custodians of the culture and way of life of the people, hence they serve as a source of reminder or symbols of the moral and value systems that a particular society or group of people stand for. But who are these ancestors and what must one do to qualify as an ancestor? The ancestors in the African tradition are the 'living dead' (Mbiti, 1969). To qualify as an ancestor in the African tradition, a person must die. There are no living ancestors in the African tradition and it does not mean that everyone who dies in the African tradition automatically becomes an ancestor. Certain conditions apply.

The first condition therefore of becoming an ancestor in the African tradition is that one must be an adult. In most African cultures adulthood has nothing to do with age. In most cases it is determined by a person's marital status. For example, a 50-year-old man who dies a bachelor in some African cultures is not regarded as an adult whereas a teenager who is married is considered an adult. The reason why bachelorship disqualifies one from becoming an ancestor seems to be the conviction that a bachelor, because he refused to help increase the number of his relatives, is a useless person whose name should be blotted out of memory (Sarpong, 1974).

Another important condition for one to become an ancestor is that one must not die a tragic or uncertain death. It is also the case for people who die of unclean diseases such as leprosy, epilepsy and madness to mention a few. Tragic deaths are believed to be brought about due to a person's dubious crimes. The only difference is the case of those who die in a war which is regarded as bravery. Those who die of unclean diseases are thought to have been punished for their sins. In the case of a suicide, the person is considered to have committed a crime that was going to be revealed in the long-run, hence they are evil. Thus, to be considered as an ancestor in most African cultures, one must die a natural death (Sarpong, 1974; Pobee, 1976).

A final condition is that one must not be a bad or wicked person during one's days on earth. To be honored as an ancestor, one must have lived an exemplary life by the standards of the particular ethnic group or clan. A person who was a thief in their life time cannot be an ancestor because he or she was a public nuisance and hence his or her spirit is unreliable. The same applies to all evil persons but also lazy people as well. It is also the belief of most African societies that a person cannot be a good ghost if during his or her life time they were evil. The rationale is that, it is usually a good ghost that blesses the people; hence evil people cannot be ancestors (Sarpong, 1974). The importance of these conditionalities points to why ancestors play an important role in the lives and worldview of Africans and why it is not just anyone who dies that becomes an ancestor. The elaborate rites and rituals, almost religious in nature and the reverence accorded ancestors in many traditional African societies have led many Africans, particularly those who subscribe to the Christian faith as well as foreigners to believe that Africans worship their ancestors. The misunderstanding of this worldview of the African has led to the erroneous conclusion by some Western scholars and some Western oriented African scholars that Africans indeed worship their ancestors (Fortes, 1965; Callaway, 1970; Mbiti, 1969). This is far from the truth.

Sadly, this is the root of the myth of 'ancestral worship' by Africans. This myth of 'ancestral worship' by Africans has since been perpetuated over the years by numerous scholars (Goody, 1962; Fortes, 1949, 1959; Callaway, 1970) who misunderstood the African worldview and cosmology and tended to interpret such worldview using Western lenses (Jahn, 1961). But this myth has also been bought into by numerous Western oriented African scholars and some Christianized Africans who have made no effort to debunk the myth or to truly understand the practice of the veneration of the ancestors which has nothing to do with 'ancestral worship'. If one can use the case of the Catholic Church as an example, their veneration of saints does not mean that Catholics worship them. Then why is it that as it pertains to Africans the veneration of their ancestors is regarded as worship? To understand the important cultural value of ancestor veneration, hitherto, the myths of 'ancestral worship' in African societies, an understanding of the role of the ancestors in the cosmology and worldview of the African is paramount.

## Role of Ancestors in the Worldview of the African

The dead in Africa go to inhabit the spirit world and become ancestors. Those Africans who die and do not get admitted into the spirit world for one reason or another become ghosts and go around frightening people until they are reborn into this earth again and given the opportunity to fulfill the conditions necessary for them to enter the spirit world when they die. But it is also the belief of the African, particularly Ghanaians, that some ancestors who consider their work on earth not completed before their death may decide to come back to complete it (Sarpong, 1974). The relationship therefore between Africans and their ancestors is a unique one. They believe the ancestors are more powerful than the living and they get this power from the creator (God) which they can use independently of the creator and it is through such powers that they are able to supply the needs of their subjects. Mitchell (1977) for example, states that ancestral spirits have the potential power to affect the living positively if they respect and venerate them or are adversely punished if they don't. Thus, the ancestors can help or punish their subjects by virtue of the power bestowed on them by the creator. This power of the ancestors is below that of the creator but higher than that of humans.

Africans also believe that the ancestors keep close watch and contact with the living members of their lineage or group. It is believed that they can only be seen by those members of the living among their people that have special powers. Because these ancestors partake albeit invisibly in the life of the group members, they must be respected and the living are rather careful to keep cordial relations with their dead ancestors for fear of their wrath. For example when calamities befall a people or a village in some African societies, it is believed that it is because the ancestors are angry or are showing disapproval of certain misdeeds of their people. The ancestors can also show their contempt or indignation of certain acts of some members of the clan or lineage by punishing them with some misfortunes. According to Nyamiti (1984), although ancestors are feared by the living, they equally expect from them care and protection from sickness, death or calamities. For example they are believed to help their relatives either by showing some of their people through dreams the remedy for certain diseases that have been inflicted on their community, bless their daughters with fecundity (a rather important issue in the African culture) or bless their people with material wealth and abundant harvest. The ancestors are also consulted by the diviners (see p. 215) in the community on behalf of the living in times of sickness, crises, droughts, harvests and when individuals or people in the group are about to undertake a rather difficult or dangerous journey. From the foregoing, it is thus safe to say that in the worldview of the African, the ancestors are continuously involved in the affairs of the living and form the basis and rationale for their veneration. This is manifested in how they exert their power and interest in the daily life of the African, which is the driving force for the veneration of their ancestors.

## Ancestor Veneration and the Role of Local Leadership

Now that the reader is familiarized with some of the reasons why the African venerates, honors and respects his or her ancestors, let us now see the different ways such veneration is expressed. The honor, respect and reverence for the ancestors in traditional African societies can be expressed in three different ways, physically, materially or through propagation. Material reverence is done through offerings of food, drinks, pouring of libation, animal sacrifices and generally through gifts of love. Physical reverence is expressed through bowing before ancestors in their shrines or sacred grounds, working for the ancestors or putting up physical structures to remember them. Finally, propagation reverence is where names of ancestors are given to children and where living family members are expected to continue with the customs and rites of the lineage. The differential attitude of the African towards his or her ancestors occupies a big part of their lives. When the African is in need or in difficulty they call upon their ancestors to come to their aid. They sometimes invoke them to bear witness that what they are saying is true. They also often commend themselves and those who are dear to them as well as their activities or work to the care of their ancestors (Sarpong, 1974).

A very important way of venerating their ancestors is by naming their children after the dead ancestors (propagation reverence) as an honor or to celebrate the good work they did when they were alive. Their names are mentioned during funerals and they are remembered when setting out on long journeys. This is another way of keeping the dead living among their people for a long time for their name never dies and will be in the memory of their people. In most African cultures, a fetish priest is one who is in charge of catering for the needs of the ancestors. In the absence of such a fetish priest in the culture, such a responsibility is left to the heads of villages and towns, chiefs and paramount chiefs. The cadre of local leadership allowed to carry out ancestral veneration on behalf of the people is important for it is not just anyone that is allowed to do that. It requires special training or calling and the occupation of a certain leadership position amongst the people. In most African cultures, there are special days in the year that are set aside for the veneration of ancestors. On those days, the people and their chiefs and priest must exercise their sacred duty in the performance of special rites to the ancestors lest they incur the wrath of the ancestors. These special days are also a time for the chiefs to show their leadership responsibilities by making sure that all the taboos and laws as put in place by the ancestors are observed. If any of these taboos and laws has been infringed, it will infuriate the ancestors and the leaders must make the requisite sacrifices to pacify them. In fact some leaders in traditional African societies are believed to have ascended their positions because of the divination and will of the gods and ancestors. Hence, it is their sacred duty to see to it that all necessary rites and rituals to venerate the ancestors are timely and performed correctly. Ancestral veneration is mostly a lineage affair, assuming national or tribal proportions in the case of the cult of the ancestors of the ruling lineage. On the tribal level, it is the deities who are in the forefront. In this case God's power surpasses all, then the ancestors, then the lesser gods or deities, then the traditional leaders or the fetish priests (Sarpong, 1974).

## Ancestral Veneration amongst the Zulus

The Zulus of South Africa are a Bantu speaking people who are believed to have migrated from central Africa and settled in what is today known as Kwazulu Natal in the Republic of South Africa. Traditionally, the Zulus live in Kraals, or small villages. The Kraals of the Zulus are the primary locus of their rituals. This is the crucial space where religious performances occur periodically. These Kraals consist of circular arrangements of thatch huts. These circles of huts surround a circular cattle enclosure at the center of the village. One important thing to note is that the huts in the circular arrangement are significant for it indicates the social and ritual relationships of the occupants. The hut usually located at the west side of the circular arrangement is that of the headman also the priest of the Kraal. To each side of the hut of the headman are the huts of his wives. Lower down are huts for the children and that of visitors and guest (Lawson, 1985; Kuper, 1993; Monteiro-Ferreira, 2005).

So how does this reflect the realities of an urban contemporary working place in Africa today? Despite the dynamic changes in the contemporary working environment in Africa due to globalization, much of traditional businesses in Africa and indeed South Africa reflect some aspects of the Kraal. The head of some traditional African businesses[2] are appointments due to old age and in most cases it is a member of the family. This is because according to African tradition, an older person is believed to have the wisdom, vision and the ability to maintain harmonious working relations in the workplace, despite the fact that they might not have the requisite expertise. In addition most of the hiring especially to important positions in the organization may be based on kinship ties (Mangaliso, 2001). In the West, such action would be frowned on as it would be associated with nepotism. But in traditional African organizations, kinship elicits trust, a source of psychological and emotional support and above all fosters teamwork.

In each hut there would be found the *umsamo*. This is a place set aside for special objects of ritual significance used to communicate with the ancestors. It is a place where all offerings to the ancestors are made and it is the place where all the important guardian spirits of the Kraal reside. For example the ritual spear of the Zulus (*isipuku*) is also kept there. The headman of each Kraal leads the rituals (*amasiko*) for the ancestors and represents them before the ancestral lineage of the people. The Zulus as well as many Africans believe that the ancestors have great power and can act for good or ill toward the people. As mentioned earlier, Africans and in this case the Zulus believe that the ancestors are an intermediary between them and the 'God of the sky'. The ancestors thus require reverence and veneration and the headman is responsible for these rites (*amasiko*), either birth, marriage or death rites. The ancestral spirits are known as *amalozi, amakhosi* or *amathonga*. These ancestral spirits are the departed souls of deceased relatives. These spirits are believed to have relationships with those who still live in the Kraal. They are able to communicate with them through dreams and through other manifestations. Consequently, dreams play an important role in the Zulu culture. As mentioned earlier in this chapter, certain conditions apply in the African culture before one becomes an ancestral spirit. The same applies with the Zulus. This is because these spirits are believed to have positive or constructive presence amongst the living (*abaphilayo*) and can also mete out punishment when they have been wronged or ignored.

Furthermore, failure to show proper respect and veneration of them invites misfortune, but on the other hand, a proper veneration of the ancestors ensures benefits. When an ancestor brings misfortune to a Kraal, it is viewed as a legitimate expression of their anger due to the failure of one of the members of the Kraal to perform their requisite veneration duties (*amasiko*). In cases of misfortune that do not have an easy solution, the Zulu will consult a diviner or *Sangoma* or *isangoma*. To become a *Sangoma* or diviner, one must receive a calling from the ancestors. The calling could be to a male or female member of the group and this is in most cases through a dream. Once they accept the calling, they have to go through tutorship under an experienced diviner for a considerable period of time. The *Sangoma* may be able to tell them specifically whether the misfortune is due to the ancestors or an envious acquaintance (Krige, 1950; Fernandez, 1967). Some of these diviners also practice traditional medicine.

The ancestors of the Zulus are regarded as living in or under the earth (*abaphansi*). They have two important places in the Kraal which they are associated with, the *umsamo* and the cattle Kraal which are regarded as sacred grounds. It is from there that they are always watching over the activities of their descendants. Because the Zulu society is patrilineal, important ancestors for a Kraal are male ancestors such as a headman/priest and also the great chiefs of the Zulu people. Lately, some educated women of the Zulu ethnic group have complained that this practice is discrimination against female ancestors of this ethnic group (Malange, 1992). Sadly, the response is to label these women as feminist and people who do not respect their culture. This is akin to the current debate in the modern work environment as it pertains to minimal representation of women in top management positions. Such is often referred to as 'the glass ceiling'. Hence this is not only an African phenomenon but a global one. The head of the Kraal who leads the rituals for the veneration of the ancestors which is usually a male is also responsible for the decisions that affect the everyday lives of the inhabitants of the Kraal.

The headman of each Kraal not only performs the ancestral ceremonies but is also the chief official of the village. He does play a political, social and religious role in the Zulu culture and is referred to as the *umnumzane*. Amongst the Zulus to become an ancestor, the deceased is buried with his 'short shadow', while his 'long shadow' or soul (*isithunzi*) leaves the corpse and becomes a spirit. This spirit does not immediately go to the spiritual world until the ceremony of 'bringing home' the spirit to the spirit world is performed (Du Toit, 1960). This is called *ukubuyisa idlozi* in Zulu. On this special day, an ox is sacrificed and special portions are placed on the *umsamo*. Some of the portions are burnt in rituals. The rest of the ox remains in the hut of the deceased headman/priest. The next day, the rest of the ox is eaten and parts given as gifts with food to members of other Kraals. The ancestors then are guided from the new graveside by the new headman/priest, who is also the chief son of the former headman/priest by making marks with twigs. At the *umsamo*, the *idlozi* is called upon to return to his rightful place (Lawson, 1985).

So far the important fact established by this chapter as to why Africans and in this case the Zulus venerate their ancestors is because they regard them as intermediaries between them and the supreme God or 'God of the Sky' as the Zulus will call him. But another important fact that needs to be mentioned is that ancestral veneration forms part of the African extended family and kinship ties system. This communal nature of the extended family kinship system is characterized by interdependence. As argued by Mbiti (1969), Africans locate their individual identity within the group. Hence, the belief by Africans that, 'I am because we are; and since we are, therefore I am'. This is beautifully expressed in Zulu as '*Umuntu Umuntu ngabantu*' literally interpreted as 'human being becomes a person through others; only through you do I become an I, I am because we are'. This is popularized amongst South Africans as '*Ubuntu*' (Edwards *et al.*, 2006; Choon, 2004) – see Commentary box.

---

## COMMENTARY BOX

**Ketan Lakhani, former director of the National Productivity Institute of South Africa and commissioner of South Africa's Conciliation Service**

Ubuntu – it's fundamentally a human- or people-based leadership. I think in many traditions leadership is goal-oriented or objective-oriented 'end justifies the means' kind of conversation. Traditional African philosophy of humanism, which is 'caring for people first' shows that leading requires humanity. That there's very little that demands that you lose your humanity in whatever goal you choose. (from Hamson and Lakhani, 2001)

**Desmond Tutu**

Ubuntu ... comes from the root [of a Zulu-Xhosa word], which means a 'person'. So it is the essence of being a person. And in our experience, in our understanding, a person is a person through other persons. You can't be a solitary human being. It's all linked. We have this communal sense, and because of this deep sense of community, the harmony of the group is a prime attribute. (from Jaffrey, 1998)

---

Mangaliso (2001), in his article, 'Building competitive advantage from ubuntu: Management lessons from South Africa,' points to how the concept can offer competitive advantage to businesses through the enhancing of relationships with others, communication, decision making, understanding the African attitude towards time, enhancing productivity and efficiency as well as age and seniority in leadership which comprise the core of *Ubuntu*. For the purpose of this chapter, *Ubuntu* and its application, particularly in modern African workplaces, calls for a rather compassionate leadership as opposed to contractual/transactional types that pertain in the West. The compassionate leadership example of Nelson Mandela is expressed in his lack of bitterness toward his fellow white South Africans when he became the first black president of his country despite the suffering endured by him and black South Africans under Apartheid.

Thus if ancestors are part of the African extended family system, then their veneration is a form of communicating and communion with them and the fact that they are dead should not diminish the family and kinship ties. Looked at critically, ancestral veneration among Africans and Zulus in particular is more of an extension of the African extended family system which includes the ancestors. They believe that the ancestors have left them in flesh but live amongst them in spirit and will intercede between them and the 'God of the Sky'. In sum, there is a symbiotic relationship between the living and the dead because they are part of the African extended family system – '*Ubuntu*'.

## GLOBAL IMPLICATIONS

So far, the effort in the preceding sections of this chapter was to share with readers the unique relationship that exists between Africans and their ancestors. A specific case of the Zulu of South Africa has also been looked at in this regard in an effort to shed more light on why ancestral veneration is an important part of this unique relationship between the African and his ancestors. Veneration and honoring of their ancestors are important because they believe that these ancestors serve as intermediaries between them and the supreme being, God and in the case of the Zulu, 'God of the Sky' (*inkosoyezulu*) in their times of difficulty and need. The Zulu for example believe that the gap between God and the living is the ancestral spirits. The ancestors are seen as part of reality for African people, and thus they occupy center stage in their worldview. They thus venerate these ancestors because they believe that they sustain and nurture the interest of their descendants and serve as a bridge between the physical and spiritual worlds. When they pray to God, they do so via the ancestors (Ngubane, 2004). According to Fortes (1940), 'the ancestor cult, the supreme sanction of kinship ties is a great stabilizing force counteracting the centrifugal tendencies inherent in the lineage system. However widely the lineage may be dispersed, its members can never escape the mystical jurisdiction of their founding ancestors.'

It is this unique relationship that has been misunderstood or misinterpreted by many as ancestral worship (Fortes, 1965; Callaway, 1970). There is nowhere in the belief system or worldview of the African in general and the Zulu in particular that states that they 'worship' their ancestors. In the African cosmology, God is the Supreme Being. God is the origin and sustenance of all things. Traditional African societies believe that a person has to go through intermediaries such as the ancestors or the 'living dead' to get to God. Acts like the pouring of libation, giving food to the 'living dead' or ancestors are some of the symbols of communion and fellowship and sometimes such acts are performed to seek help from the intermediaries to plead on their behalf in difficult times. Mention should be made in passing that the act of pouring libation or giving food to the living dead has nothing to do with what some may regard or misconceive in the West as 'ancestor worship' (Abdulai, 2000). Mbiti

(1978) puts it best when he says that, 'the phenomenon that Westerners call "ancestor worship" is not really worship at all. Giving food and drink to ancestral spirits is a symbol of communion, fellowship and remembrance.' When the priests of a Catholic church during Mass venerate saints, they are honoring the dead. During such process, the priests bow, make the sign of the cross before an icon or relic or statue of the saint. In some cases, they may even kiss the statue. This veneration of the saints is called *dulia* by the Catholics. It must be added that it is not only the Catholic Church that practices such veneration. Others include the Eastern Orthodox Church and some members of the Anglican Church.

Sarpong (1974) adds his voice to this chorus. Writing on the same issue with examples drawn from Ghana in West Africa, he insists that, 'the Ghanaian does not worship his ancestors as Christians worship God or Muslims worship Allah. He venerates them, honors them and respects them and this deferential attitude occupies a big part of his religious life.' Sarpong should know better because at the time of writing, he was the Catholic Bishop of Kumasi in Ghana. A final observation to drive this point home is that made by Edwin Zulu. He argues that, 'I am fully informed of the assertion by Western oriented scholars, including Africans who make a generalization by suggesting that ancestors are worshipped in Africa. However, to worship a human being in the real sense of the word is foreign to this part of Africa (South Africa). Ancestors are human beings and Africans here worship God alone' (Zulu, 2002). As it pertains to the Zulus, Berglund (1976) adds, the 'Zulu are explicit that there is no worship of the shades (ancestors) in the sense that there is a veneration of them. If there is worship, then it is the veneration of the "Lord of the Sky" ' (*inkosoyezulu*).

What are therefore the implications of this myth or misperception of ancestral veneration as 'ancestral worship' for Africans and globally? Definitely, it has implications for Africans. These implications can be analyzed at two levels. At the first level, it casts the African culture and belief system in negative light as primitive and backward. This has played into the hands of racists and those who subscribe to such racist ideologies and theories that the African and his beliefs are backward and primitive; ergo he is less intelligent than whites[3] (Conrad, 1969; Herrnstein and Murray, 1994). It could also be argued that it has given racist currency to denigrate Africans and their leaders as well as their culture and worldview in any opportunity they get. The impact on the growth and development efforts of Africa and its people cannot be emphasized enough.

A flip side to this is a strong urge to African leadership not to cower from the negative stereotypes of their unique culture or any aspects of their culture that underpin their Africanness. They should stoically hold on to their culture and belief systems in the fast-changing synthetic world of today. For such will truly be their bulwark against the fast erosion of their values and strength as leaders in this sea of constant change.

On the second level, it has wittingly or unwittingly encouraged the forced imposition on Africans of foreign or Western cultures. If the African can be made to feel and believe that their worldview or culture is primitive and backward or that they are engaged in devil worship, then it paves the way for their introduction to Western culture, belief systems and way of life. This is another form of colonization that African leadership has to deal with. Currently, there is a huge debate among Christian churches in Africa and among some African Christians whether to Christianize ancestral veneration or continue to see it as 'devil worship' (Afeke and Verster, 2004; Mulago, 1965; Kuckertz, 1981). The outcome of this debate, if ever there will be one, will have a huge impact on the practice of Western Christianity in its current form in Africa. A study was conducted amongst Zulu Christians in 1978 by one Father Jean-Louis Richard as to whether these African Christians will reject their ancestors; the majority of them responded that it was unthinkable. Many see it as an abominable act to reject one's parents and origins (Richard, 1978).

At another level, it is refreshing to note that despite the devastating impact of colonialism and neocolonialism on Africans and their way of life, in the case of the Zulus despite the numerous wars they fought with settlers, they have been able to preserve their culture, especially ancestral veneration. Even with increased urbanization in Africa with more and more Africans moving from rural to urban areas in search of better livelihoods, there is still an increase in appreciation of African culture and traditions. More and more modern and urbanized Africans are naming their children after their ancestors and great kings or chiefs of their ethnic origins. There is even a resurgence of this phenomenon amongst even Africans in the Diaspora. The naming of urban African children with names of great African chiefs, kings and queens offers them identity, shows a respect for the dignity of their past and its leaders as well as a sense of pride in such great leaders of a great continent; otherwise denigrated by the Western press and media. As future leaders, these urban African children will grow to be proud of their past and ancestry and it would have a positive psychological effect on them to embrace who they are in the often racially diverse societies in which they may be living and working. Furthermore, this also points to the macro issue that the cultural dimension of development, often relegated to the backburner in development policy, should be emphasized by African and international leaders if any development programs targeting Africa are to be sustained. The case of ancestral veneration by Africans is just one example of how culture plays an important role in the life and worldview of the African. Those who ignore this important observation do so at their peril if they have to deal with Africans or design programs and projects targeting Africans.

The case of how a Western aid agency that decided to alleviate the suffering of women in an African village who trudge numerous miles to fetch water from a stream is an excellent example worth mentioning here. The aid agency decided to build a bore-hole in the middle of the village. The women ignored the bore-hole and still trudged to the stream to fetch their drinking water. What the aid agency did not understand was that it was part of their socialization and bonding process not just an act of going to 'fetch water'. Consequently, their good intentions failed to bring about the perceived outcomes because of a misunderstanding of the culture.

On a positive note, the recognition of how certain myths about Africans and their culture and the negative perceptions that these myths have created in the West about Africans is galvanizing African leaders, intellectuals and theologians to speak up and write to correct these myths and perceptions. The myth that Africans worship their ancestors is a case in point and the response to such a myth by this author is an example to this effect. The hope is that if some of these myths about African traditional culture are shattered, it would go a long way to neutralize the negative perceptions and reporting about Africa and Africans by Western media. Hopefully, that will help influence positively policy decisions of the West that affect Africans.

Most importantly, a better understanding of the cultural traditions of Africans by the West and indeed the global community will go a long way to reducing conflict. For the global village that we are becoming due to advances in technological innovation, it will go a long way to fostering cross-cultural communication and dialogue between Africans, Westerners and the rest of the world. Such an understanding will go a long way to avert a further 'clash of civilizations' as postulated by Samuel Huntington's thesis. According to him, the 'clash of civilizations' will be a great threat to world peace because the critical distinctions between people today are mostly cultural (Huntington, 1996). If this is so, the fostering of a better understanding of global cultures would be a right step in averting global conflicts. Fostering cross-cultural communications among global leaders is another way to enhance global understanding and cooperation. One of the ways of doing that is through cultural immersion by Westerners who are truly interested in understanding African culture. Programs like the US Peace Corps, and other volunteer programs by Western countries that allow their university graduates to live and work in developing countries, particularly Africa, is one of the best ways of fostering cross-cultural understanding, education and communication.

So how does one use this knowledge (ancestral veneration) in dealing with Africans or to do business with them? First, this knowledge that Africans venerate their ancestors not worship them will help allay the fears and anxiety of Western business people as well as multinational companies and multilateral organizations who undertake projects in Africa or are building infrastructure in certain communities on the continent. They would not be surprised if the elders insist on pouring libation to the ancestors or to seek permission from them before work can proceed. The ability of Western organizations and individuals doing business in Africa to understand and appreciate these cultural norms will go a long way to gaining respect and appreciation in the communities in which they work. This will pave the way for the smooth operation and delivery of their projects on time. Because it will also show that they respect the customs and traditions of the people, this will elicit a buy-in of their projects from the people in the communities in which they are operating.

Finally, because the belief in ancestral spirits is so strong among Africans, if such a relationship is genuinely acknowledged by Western business people through the show of concern and respect in their dealings with their African counterparts, it could serve as a strong foundation to ensure that these counterparts are honest and deliver on the strength and belief in their ancestral spirits. Most of them will do well to deliver; after all, they do not want to incur the wrath of the ancestors. This in a way could serve as a strong insurance policy because indirectly the ancestral spirits become part of the business relationship.

## CONCLUSION

There is an African proverb that says that, 'a stranger's eyes might be big but they cannot see all the happenings in the town' (Abdulai, 2000). The same can be said of Western anthropologists, ethnographers, theologians and researchers who write about Africa's social-political, cultural and economic issues. Their 'eyes might be big' but they definitely cannot see all the happenings in the Africa they propose to intimately know and write about arrogantly. The lack of hubris on their part has created and continues to create a lot of misperceptions, half-truths and myths about Africa, its people, culture and way of life. The impact on the growth and development prospects of the continent cannot be emphasized enough. Ancestor veneration is a case in point. As clearly pointed out in this chapter, Africans do not 'worship' their ancestors. They venerate them. My goal in this chapter has been to look at what a myth consists of in a different way. 'Ancestral worship' by Africans was given as an example of a myth perpetuated by Western anthropologists, ethnographers and theologians. Ancestral veneration was given and explained as the true way Africans treat their ancestors. The Zulus of South Africa were used as an example to illustrate this. The implication and application of this new knowledge were offered. Hence, if this chapter has contributed in a small way to rectifying this perception in the minds of some of the readers and future readers of this chapter, then the effort has not been in vain. Above all, the chapter has shown that ancestral veneration is an important aspect of the culture of traditional Africa and leaders in these traditional societies cannot afford to ignore it. They will do so at their own peril. It has also shown how leaders in traditional African societies employ ancestral veneration in leading and serving their people.

## NOTES

1. Africans as used throughout this chapter refers to the people of Sub-Sahara Africa unless otherwise noted.
2. These are businesses that are not Western owned or multinational companies operating in Africa.
3. For example Nobel Prize-winning scientist James Watson in October 2007 said that Whites are more intelligent than Blacks. American academic, Arthur Jenson in 1969 delivered a paper that claimed that Whites were innately more intelligent than Blacks.

## REFERENCES

Abdulai, D. N. (2000), *African Proverbs: Wisdom of the Ages*, Denver, CO: Dawn of a New Day Publications.

Afeke, B. and Verster, P. (2004), Christianization of ancestor veneration within African tradition religions: an evaluation, *In die skriflig*, **381**, 47–61.

Berglund, A. (1976), *Zulu Thought-Patterns and Symbolism*, London: C. Hurst and Company.

Callaway, H. (1970), *The Religious System of the Amazulu*, Cape Town: C. Struik Ltd.

Choon, S. B. (2004), Ancestor worship in Korea and Africa: Social function or religious phenomenon, *Verbum et Ecclesia*, **25** (2), 389–56.

Conrad, J. (1969), *Heart of Darkness*, Original published in 1902, 1st edn. New York: Bantam Books.

Du Toit, B. M. (1960), Some aspects of the soul-concept among the Bantu-speaking Nguni tribes of South Africa, *Anthropological Quarterly*, **33** (3), 134–42.

Dzobo, N. K. (1985), African ancestor cult: a theological appraisal, *Reformed World*, **38**, 333–40.

Edwards, S., Makunga, N., Thwala, J. and Nzima, D. (2006), African breathing and spiritual healing, *Indilinga-African Journal of Indigenous Knowledge Systems*, **5** (2), 135–44.

Fernandez, J. (1950), Divinations, confessions, testimonies: Zulu confrontation with the social superstructure, Occasional Paper No. 4, Institute of Social Research, Durban: University of Natal.

Fernandez, James W. (1967), *Divinations, Confessions, Testimonies: Zulu Confrontations with the Social Superstructure*, Durban: University of Natal, Institute for Social Research.

Fortes, M. (1940), The political system of the Tallensi of the Northern Territories of Ghana, in M. Fortes and E. E. Evans-Pritchard (eds) *African Political Systems* Republished,1987. London: Kegan Paul International.

Fortes, M. (1949), *The Web of Kinship among the Tallensi*, London: Oxford University Press.

Fortes, M. (1959), *Oedipus and Job in West African Religion*, Cambridge: Cambridge University Press.

Fortes, M. (1965), Some reflections on ancestor worship, in M. Fortes and G. Dieterlen (eds), *African Systems of Thought*, London: Oxford University Press.

Goody, J. (1962), *Death Property and the Ancestors*, London: Tavistock.

Hamson, N. and Lakhani, K. (2001), Ned Hamson interview with Ketan Lakhani, *Journal for Quality and Participation*, **243**, 14–15.

Herrnstein, R. and Murray, C. (1994), *The Bell Curve: Intelligence and Class Structure in American Life*, New York: Free Press.

Huntington, S. P. (1996), *The Clash of Civilizations and the Remaking of World Order,* New York: Simon and Schuster.

Jaffrey, Z. (1998), February. 'Desmond Tutu', *Progressive*, **622**, 18.

Jahn, J. (1961), *African Culture and the Western World*, Revised, 1990. New York: Grove Weidenfeld.

Krige, E. J. (1950), *The Social System of the Zulus*, Pietermaritzburg: Shuter and Shooter.

Kuckertz, H. (ed.) (1981), *Ancestor Religion in Southern Africa*, Transkei: Lumko Institute.

Kuper, A. (1993), The 'House' and Zulu political structure in the nineteenth century, *The Journal of African History*, **34** (3), 469–87.

Lawson, E. T. (1985), *Religions of Africa*, New York: HarperCollins.

Malange, N. (1992), Discriminated ancestors, *Agenda, No. 13, Culture and Tradition*, 20–1.

Mangaliso, M. P. (2001), Building competitive advantage from ubuntu: management lessons from South Africa, *The Academy of Management Executive*, **15** (3), 23–33.

Mbiti, J. S. (1969), *African Religions and Philosophy*, London: Heinemann.

Mbiti, J. S. (1978), *The Prayers of African Religion*, Southampton: Camelot.

Mitchell, R. C. (1977), *African Primal Religions*, Niles, IL: Argus.

Monteiro-Ferrera, A. M. (2005), Reevaluating Zulu religion: an Afrocentric analysis, *Journal of Black Studies*, **35** (3), 347–63.

Mulago, V. (1969), *Un visage africain du christianisme- L'union vital Bantu face á l'unité vitale ecclésiale*, Paris: Présence Africaine.

Ngubane, S. (2004), Traditional practices on burial systems with special references to the Zulu People of South Africa, *African Journal of Indigenous Knowledge Systems*, **3** (2), 171–7.

Nyamiti, C. (1984), *Christ as Our Ancestor*, Harare: Mambo.

Odhiambo, E. S. Atieno (2000), Mugo's Prophesy, in B. A. Oget and W. R. Ochieng (eds), *Kenya: The Making of a Nation, 1895–1995*, Maseno, Kenya: IRPS Publications.

Pobee, J. (1976), Aspects of African traditional religion, *Sociological Analysis* **37** (1), 1–18.

Richard, Jean Louis (1877), *L'epérience de la conversion chez les Basotho*, Roma: Universita gregoriana.

Sarpong, P. (1974), *Ghana in Retrospect: Some Aspects of Ghanaian Culture*, Accra-Tema: Ghana Publishing Corporation.

Zulu, E. (2002), Reverence for ancestors in Africa: interpretation of the 5th Commandment from an African perspective, *Scriptura*, **81**, 476–82.

# 12. Cultural mythology and global leadership in Kenya

## Fred O. Walumbwa and George O. Ndege

## INTRODUCTION

Africa is the world's richest continent in terms of natural resources. It has 50 per cent of the world's gold, most of the world's diamonds and chromium, 90 per cent of the cobalt, 40 per cent of the world's potential hydroelectric power, millions of acres of untilled farmland, as well as other natural resources. Since the 1960s, more than $400 billion in Western aid and credits have been pumped into Africa and yet many of its problems seem to be as pervasive as in the past. Despite its natural wealth and massive Western aid and credit, Africa is still home to the world's most impoverished people. A variety of reasons have been given for this state of affairs in Africa, including the legacy of colonialism, neo-colonialism, cultural differences, bio-geographic diversity and many others. Yes, there is no question that colonialism, for example, had a big impact on some of the nagging problems confronting Africa. Yet, in the post-colonial era most of Africa has infrastructures such as roads, railways, bridges, schools, universities, hospitals, and even the civil service machinery that are in worse shape today than they were over 40 years ago.

While all of the above factors significantly contribute to Africa's problems, many have argued that there has been a pervasive failure of leadership that keeps the African continent from advancing beyond its current state. For decades, African leaders have focused on blaming external factors like colonial legacies, lingering effects of the slave trade, unjust international economic systems, and predatory practices of multi-national corporations, among others, to explain the miserable economic performance of the continent. To be fair, a lot of studies have already been done about the external factors and it is no secret to say that these factors have had their impact on the African continent's plight. Yet, a big obstacle to economic growth in Africa is the tendency to place blame, failures and shortcomings on outside forces.

Many now believe that to address the current challenges facing the African continent, Africa must improve the quality and capacity of leadership in all sectors and at all levels. Already, African nations are banding together in such organizations as the New Partnership for Africa's Development (NEPAD) to take control of their own economic destiny and sovereignty. Some African leaders are calling for African countries to unite under a single government – the United States of Africa or USA so it could compete in a globalized world and to deal effectively with the critical problems on the continent, from the Darfur crisis to dictatorship, human rights, corruption, and poverty that the African leaders prefer not to confront. Africans are also pulling their own military forces together to come into countries in chaos to provide peace keepers and peace makers. Economic activity in countries such as Botswana, South Africa and Nigeria is beginning to show signs of positive growth and change.

In this chapter, the focus is on Kenya. Specifically, since leadership is inexorably intertwined with culture, knowledge of this dynamic is essential for developing and succeeding as a leader in the global business context. Below, we begin first by providing a brief overview of the history of Kenya. Next, we provide a brief description of culture and leadership in traditional society. We then introduce two leadership theories that we believe are applicable to the Kenyan context and the myriad of challenges facing the country. Our hope is that these two leadership approaches may also apply to the rest of the African continent given the similarities of the challenges, such as leadership and economic management issues, governance, systemic corruption, and capital flight. We conclude with some general suggestions on how these two leadership theories could be used to enhance human motivation, behavior, and performance that drive exemplary, sustainable organizational outcomes. In doing so, we also offer some specific suggestions on how such leadership behaviors can be developed and sustained.

## KENYA: A BRIEF HISTORY

Kenya as a country is a colonial construct whose genesis dates back to 1895 when it became a British protectorate. The British brought together disparate ethnic groups who had their histories, rituals, myths and symbolisms all of which defined the way authority and power were exercised before the onset of the colonial period. Kenyan communities were forced to submit to British colonial power, which for many of them was after protracted wars of pacification.

Britain exercised power and control over the new colony of Kenya through an appointed special commissioner, later Governor, who was the chief executive authority in the country. He was accountable to Britain on all matters of governance within the country. The citizens were considered as mere subjects whose loyalty to the colonial government was supposed to be absolute. The colonial government embarked on the development of a colonial economy, institutions of governance, and physical infrastructure in the country. In institutionalizing colonial governance, a number of legislations were passed by the legislative council to regulate the movement of people, demarcate internal boundaries, and to provide legal basis for the taxation of Africans as well as forced labor (Berman, 1990).

The British government initially envisioned Kenya as a European settler colony (Sorrenson, 1967). The rhetoric, however, was that the colonial government would guarantee African interests until such time that the country would be ready for African leadership. Yet the colonial government was anything but an impartial arbiter in mediating competing European and African interests. The arbitrary alienation of African land and subsequent confining of Africans to various designated areas, reserves, exemplify the partiality and unequal power relations that defined British colonialism in Kenya.

African participation in national politics was curtailed. They were not allowed to form nation-wide political parties. Instead, the colonial government allowed limited political participation at the local level through the Local Native Councils. The councils were tightly controlled by the colonial administration. The purpose of this localization was to ensure that grievances were domesticated and dealt with at the local level. Problems and challenges came to be viewed through the prism of ethnicity (Ndege, 1992). This development suited the state's divide and rule strategy. However, the strategy failed to forestall the development of African nationalism because Africans interacted in towns, schools, churches and professions. The denominator of frustration united Africans against colonial governance.

The emergent African elite began to challenge the colonial system more aggressively than ever before in the period after World War II. Trade Union leaders, Kenyan World War II veterans, and nationalists began to demand the dismantling of the colonial system. They mobilized the masses in their endeavor to present a unified front against the colonial government. Africans were no longer preoccupied with the reform of colonialism as their agenda was firmly the dismantling of colonialism. This demand reached its explosive high point in the central part of the country in the early 1950s following the outbreak of the Mau Mau uprising (Kaggia, 1975; Kanogo, 1987; Elkins, 2005). Anti-colonial violence rocked the country leading to bloodshed in many parts of the Central and Rift Valley regions.

The colonial government's counter-insurgency measures proved too formidable for the Mau Mau forces, which were crushed by the end of 1956. However, the government came to the conclusion that the future of colonial rule in Kenya was dim. Forced by the emergent circumstances of resentment against colonial rule and the violent Mau Mau uprising, the government proceeded to heal the nation and to accelerate the process of decolonization by working with the Kenyan elite. In central Kenya, the government embarked on registration of land and issuance of title deeds, both of which were aimed at rewarding the collaborators and marginalizing the freedom fighters. Most Mau Mau fighters were denied the opportunity to own land for which they were fighting (Sorrenson, 1967; Kitching, 1980). The development left bitterness among the fighters and their descendants who have argued that collaborators worked with the colonial government to disinherit them. The politics of land has continued to be one of the thorny issues in postcolonial Kenya.

Following protracted negotiations in London with the African leadership, representing various political parties, Kenya attained independence in 1963 with Jomo Kenyatta as the Prime Minister. Kenya African National Union (KANU) emerged as the dominant majority party having defeated the Kenya African Democratic Union (KADU). Britain bequeathed Kenya the Western style of multiparty democracy. The independence constitution was a compromise document aimed at allaying the fears of the KADU party, which opposed a strong centralized government. It divided the country into eight provinces, including Nairobi the capital city. Kenya became a Republic in 1964 under the presidency of Jomo Kenyatta.

The attainment of independence marked the beginning of experiment in nation building, which included safeguarding the constitutional framework for a multi-ethnic and multi-racial society. Also of enormous significance was how to guarantee economic growth with a view to eliminating poverty, boosting literacy, and providing health care to the citizenry. These were weighty issues viewed against the backdrop of the ideological battles of the 1960s as well as the competing interests of the ruling elite. With the common enemy of colonialism dismantled, the struggle for the control of the state's resources assumed an ethnic dimension.

Kenyatta wanted a strong and imperial presidency. Thus, within two years of assuming power, he presided over the abolition of the devolved government. Kenyatta instituted an administrative hegemonic regime in which ethnicity and patron-client relationships emerged as key determinants in the control and distribution of resources. His Kikuyu ethnic group came to disproportionately monopolize key positions in government and businesses. Kenyatta made Kenya a de facto one party state. His successor, Daniel Arap Moi, did little to reform the structure of governance. Domestic as well as international pressure forced the Moi government in 1992 to embrace reforms, which included the return to multiparty politics, end of detention without trial, and a fixed two five-year term for the president.

Moi retired in 2002 and the KANU party that had ruled Kenya since independence was defeated. Mwai Kibaki who succeeded Moi as the third president was more of a status quo leader. He has failed miserably on devolving power from the center, eradicating political ethnicity, containing corruption and guaranteeing security. In fact, Kibaki unapologetically returned the country to the dark days of 15 years ago as he elected to be another African despot.

It is against this backdrop that the country faced a catastrophic conflict following the flawed and outright election rigging of the 2007 Presidential elections. Instructively, it is the current Prime Minister, Raila Amolo Odinga, who was in and out of detention during the 1980s fighting for an open, transparent and accountable political system that is leading what has been dubbed the final liberation of the Kenyan people.

## OVERVIEW OF KENYAN MYTHOLOGY

Kenya's population of slightly over 30 million is made up of 43 ethnic groups, each with a different language and culture. The ethnic groups are normally determined by language and common culture and customs. The Kikuyu, Embu and Meru communities inhabit Central Kenya, while the Luyia, Luo, Gusii and Kuria are in Western Kenya. The expansive Rift Valley is the home of the Maasai, the Kalenjin, Turkana and the Kikuyu migrants from the central province. The coastal communities include the Mijikenda, Swahili and the Taveta among others. The Somali, Oromo and Borana people are in the northern part of Kenya. Each of these ethnic groups has myths that narrate their origin, religious beliefs, and interactions with their neighbors.

The Kikuyu claim descent from a common ancestor Gikuyu. He was called by the Divider of the universe, *Mogai*, and given his share of land (Kenyatta, 1962). *Mogai* took Gikuyu to his abode atop Mount Kenya and showed him the beauty of the country he had given him. Gikuyu was given a wife named *Moombi*. The marriage was blessed with nine daughters and no sons. Gikuyu sought *Mogai*'s indulgence in getting men that would marry the daughters with a view to ensuring the continued existence of his community. It is instructive that the Kikuyu still recognize the nine daughters as the basis of their clans. The Kikuyu had by the twentieth century evolved into a patriarchal society. They performed ceremonies and rituals at various times and developmental stages in the life of the individual. One of the most important rites was circumcision, which marked the transition from childhood to adulthood. It was the gateway to marriage, guaranteed access to the community's secrets, as well as leadership status.

The Maasai who now occupy Rift Valley province are a predominantly pastoral society that believe their supreme being *Enkai* is the creator of the earth (Kipury, 1983). Enkai is the guardian over rain and fertility. He also gave the Maasai all cattle on earth. This myth of *Enkai*'s providence explains the centrality of cattle in Maasai cultural, economic and political life. The amount of cattle and children one had determined one's status in society. Cattle were and still remain the main source of wealth and income among most of the Maasai. Institutionalized leadership among the Maasai was vested in the

*Laibon*, who was a religious cum political leader. He was invested with vast powers ranging from shamanistic healing and divination to prophecy and insuring success in war.

The Luos are found around Lake Victoria, which is the largest fresh water lake in the world. The Luo claim common ancestry from *Ramogi*. Belief in a common God, *Nyasaye*, as well as culture that tended to be communalistic identified them as a single homogeneous community. Leadership among the Luo was chosen based on ability and clear contributions to the community (Odinga, 1967).

The narrative of common heritage or ancestor from whom all members of an ethnic group, as presently constituted, came forth is a myth. There is no pure ethnic group. Kenyan communities have been intermingling and inter-marrying for centuries. What is of critical importance in the history of various Kenyan communities is not how homogeneous they are, but rather how they came to assume a given kinship or ethnic identity. Myths therefore give meaning and cement this perceived identity through various rituals that members of the community share. Thus myths not only define social relations, but also are useful during times of political uncertainty and transition. Nowhere is this more evident in Kenya than during the dawn of the British conquest.

Among the Kikuyu, the legendary prophet and seer Mugo wa Kibiru fore-told the coming of 'strangers who would carry magical sticks which would produce fire ... very much worse in killing than poisoned arrows ... they would later bring an iron snake with as many legs as a centipede, that this iron snake would spit fires and would stretch from the big water in the east to another big water in the west of the Gikuyu country' (Kenyatta, 1962: 42–3). Similarly, both Mbatian among the Maasai and Kimnyole among the Kipsigis foretold the arrival of the White man and 'his iron train that would belch smoke and traverse the lands from east to west' (Odhiambo, 2000: 5). The Gusii prophet Sakawa echoed similar prophecy (Ochieng, 1974). These narra-tives represent anxiety and tension during colonial invasion, as well as how traditional leaders exhibited uncanny ability to make predictions and optimal decisions during such times.

The magical sticks refer to the rifles, which were weapons of choice widely used by the British during conquest. The iron snake and/or iron train symbol-ized the locomotive train, which was evidenced by the construction of the Uganda Railway from the coastal port of Mombasa in the east to Kisumu in the west. There were no words in the languages of the communities for rifles or locomotives. The rifles and locomotives were instrumental in not only subduing the indigenous populations, but also opening up areas that were hith-erto inaccessible to Europeans. The narratives are thus instructive of the dawn of a world of vulnerability and unequal power relationships that defined the colonial order.

In traditional society, especially chiefly societies, like the Maasai or Nandi, the central authority of the chief was reinforced by several factors that included control of the warriors, his powers of appointment and removal, and the mystical qualities associated with his office. Besides, there were several other officials, his council of elders, diviners, seers, who had a decisive voice in the chief's investiture. The arrogation of royal power and authoritarianism was abhorred. Dissatisfaction with an authoritarian leader would lead to sanctions as prescribed by the society, or in some cases, migration by sections of the community to other areas thereby reducing the number of the governed under the chief's jurisdiction.

Leadership whether at the kinship, clan, or community level had inbuilt mechanisms of ensuring accountability to the governed. Decisions were reached through participation of the community members present and by consensus. Leaders were chosen on the basis of their ability to provide good and moral leadership. Leadership outside of the family at the clan and community level invariably went to those who had proved themselves as reliable, confident, brave and impartial. Effective leaders were creative and imaginative people. They knew that leadership is a responsibility and service.

Traditional leaders were invariably wealthy. They were generous with their wealth because of the communalistic nature of most traditional societies. They assisted the less privileged members of society. It was a way of showing compassion for one's kinsmen, clan and subjects. This endeared people to their leadership because they desired the most good for the greatest number. Trust and truth were cherished. Leaders were bound to keep their word. Power stemmed from people who gave it royal sanction through their rituals, symbolisms, and most important of all respect for the office.

The British undermined traditional leadership by unilaterally appointing chiefs, who were accountable to them, without reference to the preexisting context and situation. Emphasis was put on loyalty to the British Crown rather than the governed. The newly appointed colonial chiefs were from the communities, but governed with authority from outside the community. They had enormous powers bestowed on them to control the people they governed. The office of chieftaincy was elevated to an authoritarian institution. It represented colonial despotism at the local level. The result was the split between colonial leadership and their subjects. The colonial discourse on governance was framed in terms of 'them versus us'. Africans distrusted not only the chiefs, but the appointing authority as well. In essence, the destruction of consultative leadership and the subsequent introduction and enhancement of imposed leadership eroded people's confidence in the new local leadership styled to suit the purpose and mission of colonial government.

# OVERVIEW OF CONTEMPORARY KENYAN LEADERSHIP

There is no single theoretical or comprehensive definition of culture that is widely accepted. Alternative perspectives exist for diverse academic disciplines that have used the concept of culture. For example, anthropologists use the concept of culture to refer to customs and rituals that societies develop over time. Organizational researchers focus on the practices that organizations develop to handle their employees and the relationships between such practices and organizational outcomes. Ambiguity aside, culture has been linked increasingly with the study of leadership. Schein (1992) points out that culture and leadership are two sides of the same coin and neither can be understood in isolation. He observes that while cultural differences may hinder or aid leadership effectiveness, it is also through leadership that cultures are changed and formed.

Although there may be many cultural influences on a person's life, our focus here is primarily on the subcultures or what we call 'microcultures' within one given country – Kenya. This is because past research dealing with the impact of national culture on leadership and various work-related attitudes and behaviors often assumes national culture is fixed and invariant within a given country. Yet there might be multiple 'microcultures' within a given country. For example, according to culture-fit theory (e.g., Kanungo *et al.,* 1999), the socio-cultural environment such as societal subcultures can influence individual behavior to the extent that internal individual values are shaped by the larger subcultures or societal values in which individuals are embedded, which in turn would affect individual perceptions, attitudes and behaviors. Indeed, Walumbwa *et al.* (2007) found that the extent to which leadership style affects follower work-related attitudes varies as a function of individual cultural orientations, defined in their study as either 'allocentrism' (that is, viewing oneself in terms of the in-groups to which one belongs) or 'idiocentrism' (that is, viewing oneself as the basic social unit where individual goals have primacy over in-group goals).

A word of caution is necessary before we proceed. Although we focus here on national subcultures and leadership, it is also important to recognize that there are also other factors other than leadership that might influence both sub- and national cultures. Hofstede (1998) found that economic development is strongly associated with cultural changes. That is, as people become more affluent, they are able to act more independently and do not require the support of an extended family or some sort of patron to whom they must be loyal and deferential.

## Transformational Leadership

Transformational leadership theory has received more conceptual and empirical scrutiny than all other leadership theories over the last two decades (Lowe and Gardner, 2000). Over the last two decades, transformational leadership has been found positively associated with a number of important organizational outcomes in many different types of organizations and situations, across different levels of analysis, and across cultures (Avolio, *et al.*, 2004a).

Transformational leaders appear to be effective because they motivate followers to identify with the importance of their work, encourage followers to think critically and take independent action, seek new ways to approach their jobs, enable them to take on greater challenges, and stress the importance and values associated with desired outcomes in ways that are more easily understood by followers, while simultaneously setting higher performance standards (Bass and Avolio, 1994; Walumbwa *et al.*, 2008a). By getting followers to think through more deeply the obstacles confronting their success, they enable them to develop a better understanding of what needs to be done to be successful and therefore are considered more empowering (Bass and Avolio, 1994).

**Authentic Leadership**

Although the concept of authenticity (that is, owning one's personal experiences, be they thoughts, emotions, needs, preferences or beliefs, processes captured by the injunction to know oneself) has its roots in ancient Greek philosophy, 'to thine own self be true', a theory of authentic leadership has just emerged in the last five years from the intersection of the leadership, ethics, and positive organizational behavior and scholarship literatures (Avolio *et al.*, 2004b; Cameron *et al.*, 2003; Cooper and Nelson, 2006; Gardner *et al.*, 2005; Ilies *et al.*, 2005; Luthans and Avolio, 2003).

Walumbwa *et al.* (2008b) defined authentic leadership as a pattern of leader behavior that draws upon and promotes both positive psychological capacities and a positive ethical climate, to foster greater self-awareness, an internalized moral perspective, balanced processing of information, and relational transparency on the part of leaders working with followers, fostering positive self-development. Although a relatively new construct, it has been suggested that authentic leadership may positively affect employee attitudes and behaviors (Avolio *et al.*, 2004b; Gardner *et al.*, 2005; George, 2003; Ilies *et al.*, 2005). Avolio and colleagues (for example, Avolio *et al.*, 2004b; Gardner *et al.*, 2005) argued that more authentic leaders promote employee engagement and well-being by more often recognizing and valuing individual differences and talents, thus helping followers convert their talents into job-related strengths.

## Application of Authentic and Transformational Leadership Theories to Kenya

We need to discuss explicitly the transferability of authentic and transformational leadership theories into the Kenyan culture (Walumbwa, 1999). On the surface, it might seem that the notion of authentic and transformational leadership may not be compatible with Kenyan culture. For example, in Kenya, individual achievements frequently are much less valued than are interpersonal relations (although this is changing). Moreover, because hierarchical societies like Kenya tend to generate very top-down leadership practices, it is possible that such cultures may not be compatible with authentic and transformational leadership styles, which stress inclusiveness and empowerment of followers to make independent decisions.

Several other African leadership and management scholars also have argued that the Western theories of leadership may not apply to the African context. Taken together, proponents of this school of thought argue that Western leadership theories are inadequate because leadership challenges in Africa are embedded in very different cultural, economic, historical, political, and social contexts (Jackson, 2004). For example, Blunt and Jones (1997) argued that it is unrealistic to think that the Western paradigms of leadership apply to Africa, which has a totally different cultural and economic context. Nyambegera *et al.* (2000) argued that most managers in Africa (and Kenya is a good example) still practice leadership styles that are largely authoritarian, which they argued, are responsible for lowering employees' social status, engagement, and motivation while demanding unquestioning personal allegiance to the manager. Others (for example, Mbigi, 2005), in reacting to the domination of Western-oriented leadership theories have argued for a rejection or a limitation of Western leadership theories. Indeed, such reactions would be expected given that in an extensive review of the leadership literature, House and Aditya (1997) revealed that about 98 per cent of leadership theory emanates from the United States.

However, to argue for a rejection or a limitation of the so called 'Western leadership' theories, in our view, misses the point and as a matter of fact, is to deny reality. Yes, we need African management approaches (such as Ubuntu), but at the same time we must accept evidence of the influence of globalization and the fact that Africa is a multicultural and multi-ethnic continent. Considered carefully, we believe there are certain leadership theories that are very compatible with Kenya's culture and Africa in general. Of course, this is not to deny there are no differences; such differences are bound to exist even in Western or Asian cultures. Below, we advance several reasons to explain why we believe authentic leadership and transformational leadership could have similar positive effects in this part of the world.

First, in Kenya like many African countries, there are multiple, and some-times, conflicting forces at work shaping Kenyan management systems: bureaucracy rooted in the legacy of British colonial rule, Kenyan traditional values rooted in subcultures, communism or the extended family, and a hybrid conventional Western business values (promoted by Western multinationals and Kenyan managers born in Kenya and educated in the West). Moreover, the distance between leaders and subordinates is very deferential to superiors; but the superior's authority is rooted not just in position, but moral integrity. Africans like any other group of people also expect their leaders to be aware of their strengths and weaknesses as well as to have high ethical standards. Thus, the overall belief of the working men and women in Kenya is that lead-ers should provide care and affection to subordinates, as well as provide balance, challenge, guidance and inspiration. These are the core elements of both authentic and transformational leadership theories (Bass and Avolio, 1994; Avolio *et al.*, 2004b; Gardner *et al.*, 2005; Walumbwa *et al.*, 2008b). For example, Avolio and Walumbwa (2006) argued that authentic leaders posi-tively impact followers' performance by helping them understand how aware-ness of their own and others' beliefs and values facilitates the development of skills, attitudes, and behaviors required to optimize performance. The influ-ence of transformational leadership is also based on such leaders' success in connecting followers' self-concept to the mission of their organization so they become self-expressive or what has been referred to as, 'an absolute emotional and cognitive identification' (Bass, 1988: 50). Such leaders influence follow-ers by activating an identity-based organizing construct in their working self-concept that serves to shift followers' conceptions of their identity in line with the goals, mission and vision of their organization.

Second, the nature of paternalistic leadership is complex and multifaceted. Linquist and Adolph (1996) argued that African societies tend to be egalitar-ian within age groups, but hierarchical between age groups. The implication here is that although top-down leadership is commonplace, the culture also incorporates leadership techniques that are rooted in benevolence, team work, and moral example, which are aspects of authentic and transformational lead-ership theories. Moral, ethical, and challenging leaders such as more authen-tic and transformational motivate subordinates through exemplary and virtuous behavior, while benevolent leadership involves care and considera-tion for the welfare of subordinates. Those exercising moral and benevolent leadership techniques would seem to be employing authentic and transforma-tional leadership perspectives (that is, providing inspiration, intellectually stimulating, individualized consideration, balanced processing, internalized moral perspective, ethical leadership, self-awareness).

There is some evidence to support the above arguments. Walumbwa *et al.* (2005), using data collected from several bank institutions in Kenya reported that transformational leadership has a strong and positive effect on followers' organizational commitment and job satisfaction. Similarly, Walumbwa *et al.* (2008b), using data drawn from 11 diverse companies in Kenya found that authentic leadership was positively related to supervisor rated performance. Thus, it appears that the theories of authentic and transformational leadership, although originally conceived and developed in the United States tend to result in positive employee attitudes and behaviors in Kenya. Note, however, that our point of discussion here is not to claim that authentic and transformational leadership is necessarily commonplace in Kenyan organizations; clearly it is not. Rather, there are aspects of idealized notions of leadership in Kenya that are indeed quite compatible with authentic and transformational leadership behaviors and thus are more likely to make workers presumably receptive to such leadership perspectives.

## GLOBAL IMPLICATIONS

We believe that authentic and transformational leadership has several implications for businesses in Kenya. Kenyan leaders are still faced with daunting challenges, including how to deal with adverse labor relations and ethnicity in the workplace. Breaking down these misconceptions and mistrust among the several ethnic groups and replacing them with positive expectations may not only raise the expectations that leaders have of their followers, it may also change the way they behave with each other. Such changes may not only enhance work engagement, commitment and performance, it may also help prepare Kenyans to take on increased leadership responsibilities. Therefore, managers must be able to come up with new ways of thinking about how to engage and transform the multi-ethnic Kenya's work force to enable employee empowerment and to develop more effective leadership at all levels of organizations – see Commentary box.

---

### COMMENTARY BOX

**Dr Bani Orwa, Business Consultant, Nairobi, Kenya**

Kenyan leadership style has changed over time. It is no longer the question of which style of leadership and management is best for you. A key to success is to empower employees and utilize every available talent to meet the expectations of both internal and external customers. Given the diversity, the style of leader-

> ship best suited for a particular leader in Kenya depends upon the particular group a leader is trying to influence. I think managers should use the style of leadership that works best for the organization's objectives taking into account the uniqueness of Kenyan cultures. Managers should also strive to build a good relationship with their employees to create a healthy working environment.

We suggest that authentic and transformational leadership styles may play critical roles in motivating diverse work groups and the multi-ethnic Kenyan society. In particular, transformational leadership style has been described as having greater relevance in situations where significant change is needed (Bass and Avolio, 1994). For instance, being aware of the subcultural differences may help managers to identify individual and organizational contexts where authentic or transformational leadership is more (or less) likely to enhance organizational commitment, satisfaction and job performance. Helping leaders to be more aware of their impact on individuals with different orientations and backgrounds, would help them to best adjust their leadership style to the individual values of their followers, organizations and societies in which they are leading.

Finally, given sweeping concerns regarding corruption, ethnicity, ethics and management issues in organizations in Kenya, we suggest that authentic leadership (Walumbwa *et al.*, 2008b) and transformational leadership (Bass and Avolio, 2004) measures can serve as practical means through which organizations seeking to provide authentic and transformational leadership development training can begin to design programs and interventions. That is, the scales offer organizational human resource professionals reliable and valid instruments for examining the level of authentic and transformational leadership exhibited by its managers and their subordinates. In addition, the conceptual models of both theories offer the content that training should focus on in order to 'create' authentic and transformational leadership. More importantly, given that both authentic and transformational leadership have been found to be positively related to a variety of follower outcomes, including job satisfaction, organizational commitment and performance, suggests that training leaders to be more authentic and transformational may provide substantial returns on the investment and thus spur socioeconomic and political developments. This is especially critical as Kenyans seek ways to improve their productivity and competitiveness in the global economic arena. However, we must emphasize that for such training programs to be effective and successful, they must be appropriately designed to reflect the multi-ethnic and racial complexity of the Kenyan culture, and where appropriate use a balanced combination of authentic/transformational and traditional local leadership styles to avoid potential possible conflict and resistance.

## PRACTICAL APPLICATIONS

Based on considerable research on authentic and transformational leadership theories, we suggest a number of practical guidelines that can be used to develop authentic and transformational leaders in Kenya. First, the development of authentic and transformational leaders can start with human resource development (HRD) interventions aimed at individuals (direct reports, leaders, and so on) or teams (that is, collective leadership) as well as organization development processes. We recommend that leaders and their direct reports be allowed to set stretch goals that are specific and challenging, and yet achievable and realistic. Such goals could be broken down into manageable sub-steps that will mark progress and enable at least small wins and success. However, for such training interventions to be effective in enhancing authentic or transformational leadership, we recommend that they must be appropriately designed to reflect the complexity and uniqueness of the Kenyan culture and history. By integrating local cultural context into the leadership development processes, there is greater opportunity for authentic and transformational leadership behaviors to be sustained, while also potentially altering the work context itself to make it more favorable to the further development of authentic and transformational leaders and followers. In addition, management from top to bottom must provide strong support for such developmental efforts. That is, they must act as role models and take the first step in 'walking the talk' of an authentic and transformational leadership.

Second, leaders and their direct reports can be exposed to discussion and considerable self-reflection. In particular, leaders and their associates can be sensitized to the extensive nature of the consequences of authentic and transformational thoughts. Moreover, leaders' and associates' perspective-taking abilities can be enhanced through exposure to and discussions of authentic or transformational situations with role models they respect and relate to. In addition, training in different models of authentic and transformational thoughts can also expand organizational leaders' capacities to think about issues in alternative ways.

Third, authentic and transformational leadership behaviors can be further developed by coaching and mentoring high ethical standards and challenging strategies. This can be done through participation in leadership development programs designed to incorporate high ethical standards. In particular, the Authentic Leadership Questionnaire (ALQ) (Walumbwa *et al.*, 2008b) and the Multifactor Leadership Questionnaire (MLQ) (Bass and Avolio, 2004) measures can be used to help assess the most appropriate tactics needed to enhance overall authentic or transformational leadership.

Finally, the authentic or transformational leadership development can use rehearsals and experiential exercises. Such standard training and development techniques can be used to build skills of when and how to take authentic actions or how to deal with challenging situations. That is, the leader and/or the individual empowered employee must know, for example, when persistence toward a goal is no longer feasible.

# REFERENCES

Atieno-Odhiambo, E. S. (2000), Mugo's prophesy, in B. A. Ogot and W. R. Ochieng (eds), *Kenya: The Making of A Nation, 1895–1995*, Maseno, Kenya: IRPS Publication.

Avolio, B. J. (1999), *Full Leadership Development: Building the Vital Forces in Organizations*, Newbury Park, CA: Sage.

Avolio, B. J. and Walumbwa, F. O. (2006), Authentic leadership: Moving HR leaders to a higher level, in J. J. Martocchio (ed.), *Research in Personnel and Human Resources Management*, **25**, 273–304. Oxford: Elsevier/JAI Press.

Avolio, B. J., Bass, B., Walumbwa, F. and Zhu, W. (2004a), *MLQ Multifactor Leadership Questionnaire: Technical Report, Leader Form, Rater Form, and Scoring Key for MLQ Form 5x-Short* (3rd edn), Redwood City, CA: Mind Garden.

Avolio, B. J., Gardner, W. L., Walumbwa, F. O., Luthans, F. and May, D. R. (2004b), Unlocking the mask: A look at the process by which authentic leaders impact follower attitudes and behaviors, *Leadership Quarterly*, **15** (6), 801–23.

Bass, B. M. (1988), Evolving perspectives on charismatic leadership, in J. A. Conger and R. N. Kanungo (eds), *Charismatic Leadership*, San Francisco, CA: Jossey-Bass, pp. 41–77.

Bass, B. M. and Avolio, B. J. (1994), *Transformational Leadership: Improving Organizational Effectiveness*, Thousand Oaks, CA: Sage.

Bass, B. M. and Avolio, B. J. (2004), *Multifactor Leadership Questionnaire: Manual Leader Form, Rater, and Scoring key for MLQ, Form 5x-short*, Redwood City, CA: Mind Garden.

Berman, B. (1990), *Control and Crisis in Colonial Kenya: The Dialectic of Domination*, London: James Currey.

Blunt, P. and Jones, M. L. (1997), Exploring the limits of western leadership theory in East Asia and Africa, *Personnel Review*, **26**, 6–23.

Cameron, K. S., Dutton, J. and Quinn, R. (eds) (2003), *Positive Organizational Scholarship*, San Francisco, CA: Berrett Koehler.

Cooper, C. and Nelson, D. (eds) (2006), *Positive Organizational Behavior*, Thousand Oaks, CA: Sage.

Elkins, C. (2005), *Imperial Reckoning: The Untold Story of Britain's Gulag in Kenya*, New York: Henry Holt and Company.

Gardner, W. L., Avolio, B. J., Luthans, F., May, D. R. and Walumbwa, F. O. (2005), 'Can you see the real me?' A self-based model of authentic leader and follower development, *Leadership Quarterly*, **16**, 343–72.

George, W. (2003), *Authentic Leadership: Rediscovering the Secrets to Creating Lasting Value*, San Francisco: Benett-Koehler.

Hofstede, G. (1998), *Masculinity and Femininity: The Taboo Dimension of National Cultures*, Thousand Oaks, CA: Sage.

House, R. J. and Aditya, R. (1997), The social scientific study of leadership: Quo vadis?, *Journal of Management*, **23**, 409–74.

House, R. J., Hanges, P. J., Javidan, M., Dorfman, P. W. and Gupta, V. (2004), *Culture, Leadership, and Organizations: The GLOBE Study of 62 Cultures*, Thousand Oaks, CA: Sage.

Ilies, R., Morgeson, F. P. and Nahrgang, J. D. (2005), Authentic leadership and eudaemonic well-being: Understanding leader-follower outcomes, *Leadership Quarterly*, **16**, 373–94.

Jackson, T. (2004), *Management and Change in Africa: A Cross-Culture Perspective*, London: Routledge.

Kaggia, B. (1975), *Roots of Freedom, 1921–1963: The Autobiography of Bildad Kaggia*, Nairobi, Kenya: East African Publishing House.

Kanogo, T. (1987), *Squatters and the Roots of Mau Mau*, London: James Currey.

Kanungo, R. N., Aycan, Z. and Sinha, J. B. P. (1999), Organizational culture and human resource management practices: The model of culture fit, *Journal of Cross-cultural Psychology*, **30**, 501–26.

Kenyatta, J. (1962), *Facing Mount Kenya: The Tribal Life of the Kikuyu*, New York: Vintage Books.

Kipury, N. (1983), *Oral Literature of the Maasai*, Nairobi, Kenya: East African Publishing House.

Kitching, G. (1980), *Class and Economic Change in Kenya: The Making of an African Petite Bourgeoisie*, New Haven, CT: Yale University Press.

Linquist, B. J. and Adolph, D. (1996), The drum speaks – are we listening? Experiences in development with a traditional Gabra institution – the yaa Galbo', in P. Blunt and D. M. Warren (eds), *Indigenous Organizations and Development*, London: Intermediate Technology Publications, pp. 1–6.

Lowe, K. B. and Gardner, W. L. (2000), Ten years of the Leadership Quarterly: Contributions and challenges for the future, *Leadership Quarterly*, **11**, 459–514.

Mbigi, L. (2005), *The Spirit of African Leadership*, Johannesburg: Knowledge Resources.

Ndege, G. O. (1992), Ethnicity, nationalism and the shaky foundation of political multipartyism in Kenya: The colonial origins, in B. A. Ogot (ed.), *Ethnicity, Nationalism and Democracy in Africa,* Maseno, Kenya: IRPS Publication.

Nyambegera, S. M., Sparrow, P. and Daniels, K. (2000), The impact of cultural value orientation on individual HRM preferences in developing countries: Lessons from Kenyan organizations', *International Journal of Human Resource Management*, **11**, 639–63.

Ochieng, W. R. (1974), *A Pre-Colonial History of the Gusii of Western Kenya, 1500–1914*, Nairobi, Kenya: East African Literature Bureau.

Odinga, O. (1967), *Not Yet Uhuru*, London: Heinemann.

Schein, E. H. (1992), *Organizational Culture and Leadership* (2nd edn), San Francisco, CA: Jossey-Bass.

Sorrenson, M. P. K. (1967), *Land Reform in the Kikuyu Country: A Study in Government Policy*, London: Oxford University Press.

Walumbwa, F. O. (1999), Rethinking the issues of international technology transfer, *Journal of Technology Studies*, **25**, 51–4.

Walumbwa, F. O., Orwa, B., Wang, P. and Lawler, J. J. (2005), Transformational leadership, organizational commitment, and job satisfaction: A comparative study of Kenyan and the United States financial firms, *Human Resource Development Quarterly*, **6**, 235–56.

Walumbwa, F. O., Lawler, J. J. and Avolio, B. J. (2007), Leadership, individual differ-ences and work attitudes: a cross-culture investigation, *Applied Psychology: An International Review*, **56**, 212–30.

Walumbwa, F. O., Avolio, B. J. and Zhu, W. (2008a), How transformational leadership weaves its influence on individual job performance: The role of identification and efficacy beliefs, *Personnel Psychology*, **61**, 793–825.

Walumbwa, F. O., Avolio, B. J., Gardner, W. L., Wernsing, T. S. and Peterson, S. J. (2008b), Authentic leadership: Development and validation of a theory-based measure, *Journal of Management*, **34**, 89–126.

# 13. Cultural mythology and global leadership in Iran

## Afsaneh Nahavandi

### INTRODUCTION

Until 1979 Iran, or Persia as it used to be known in the West, had been a monarchy for over 3000 years. The monarchic identity, presence of a central powerful government symbolized by a king and the cultural elements that accompany such traditions are an indelible part of Iranian culture and ideals of leadership. During its long history, the country has been subject to numerous invasions including those of Alexander the Great in 300 BC, and the Arab invasion of the seventh century AD, which brought Islam to Iran. As a result, Iran experienced cultural battles between its imperial and Indo-European roots and the cultures of the invaders. What some would consider the 'true' Iranian identity has survived through many conflicts, sometimes going underground, with adjustments and adaptations.

Iranian mythology reflected in fairy tales, folklore and literature has survived for thousands of years and continues to be taught in schools and used in popular story telling and art. The courageous, caring, humble and daring leader-hero who rises to save the nation against various supernatural, foreign or domestic evils, while showing unwavering loyalty to country, king and father, kindness to the weak and his enemies, and caring for his followers is an ever present character.

This chapter will consider the dominant cultural themes that run through Iranian mythology, shape ideals of leadership in Iran and help understand current leadership.

### OVERVIEW OF LOCAL CULTURE AND MYTHOLOGY

Although Iran is at the heart of the Middle East and shares the Islamic religion with some of its neighbors, its culture is distinct. Iranians' ethnic roots are Indo-European, part of the tribes that populated Asia and Europe in prehistoric times. Traces of evolved human civilization are found in some parts of

Iran dating back to 5000 BC, with the first Persian Empire, dating back to 500 BC, one of the largest and first world powers that stretched from modern day Libya and Egypt to parts of India and China, Turkey and central Asian countries.

Existing cross-cultural studies such as Hofstede's (1980, 1992) and GLOBE (Global Leadership and Organizational Behavior Effectiveness, House, *et al.*, 2004) support the cultural distinctness of Iran. For example, the GLOBE studies classify Iran in the South Asian along with India and Malaysia, rather than the Middle-Eastern cluster, which includes several Arab countries (House *et al.*, 2004). The countries in the South Asian cluster rank higher than Middle-Eastern ones on humane orientation (fairness, altruism, generosity and caring for others), a factor that is, as we will discuss later, essential to leadership in Iranian mythology. Iran further ranks higher than Arab countries on performance orientation and power distance. Like Middle-Eastern countries, the South Asian cluster countries lean towards in-group and institutional collectivism and, on the other dimensions of future-oriented action (investing in future), assertiveness, and gender egalitarianism, South Asian countries fall in the moderate category (House *et al.*, 2004). This tendency towards moderation, rather than extremes, appears to be in and of itself a valued cultural trait in Iran.

The leadership dimensions of GLOBE further indicate that Iran ranks high on visionary leadership, and that compared to the Middle-East cluster, South Asian countries are higher on charismatic, team-orientated, participative, humane, autonomous and self-protective leadership (House *et al.*, 2004). Research about leadership style in modern Iran points out that, while Western concepts may have some applicability (for example, Javidan and Carl, 2004), Iranian ideal leadership is characterized by benevolent paternalism whereby the leader is a kind, warm, powerful, accessible and a stern father figure (Ayman and Chemers, 1983; Chemers, 1969). In comparison, studies of Arab leadership style point to a tendency toward egalitarian decision-making influenced strongly by the Bedouin and Islamic traditions (for example, Sarayrah, 2004; Yousef, 1998).

Iranian mythology is defined by one dominant repository of stories in verse, the Shahnameh (the Book of Kings) written by Abol-Qassem Ferdowsi[1] in the tenth to eleventh centuries.[2] This chapter will therefore focus on the mythology as presented in the Shahnameh and touch upon religious folklore that further shapes the Iranian psyche. While the Shahnameh is about kings, as its name indicates, it is not a simple glorification of kings. In many cases, the kings are weak and even incompetent. The Shahnameh is, however, a glorification of Iran and its leader-heroes as guardians of the nation and saviors of its people. In that regard, the Shahnameh is a complex work about leadership addressing issues concerning ideal leader characteristics, factors that lead them to succeed or fail, and their relationships with followers (Davis, 2006). Whereas the epic has been subject to considerable analysis and study, there is strong agreement on its common themes.

## OVERVIEW OF IRANIAN MYTHOLOGY

Ferdowsi was commissioned to write the epic at the end of the tenth century by the last king of the Samanid dynasty which was the first Persian-centric dynasty following the Arab invasion of Iran. The Shahnameh tells the history of Iran from the beginning of time through the Arab invasion of the seventh century through a series of poems of various lengths, the large majority of which are titled after individual heroes. The themes that run through the Shahnameh have their roots in prehistoric times and in Zoroastrian teachings dating back to approximately 1500 to 1000 BC that emphasize purity and goodness of thoughts, words, and behaviors (Brélian-Djahanshahi, 2001). However, in spite of their age, the Shahnameh's themes continue to represent and define the culture and expectations of ideal leadership, as is evident by the literature that follows several hundred years later.

In its original language, the Shahnameh consists of 60 000 verses, which given their length, are equivalent to 100 000 verses by Western standards (Davis, in Introduction to the translation of the Shahnameh, Ferdowsi, 2004). Whereas similar to other Western epics such as the Iliad and Odyssey by its theme of heroism, conflict, and human weakness, it is approximately seven times longer. It is considered to be an unparalleled masterpiece by the Persian-Iranian (the language is called Farsi) speaking world, which includes, not only Iran, but Afghanistan, Tajikistan, and several parts of Central Asia, India and Pakistan (for example, Levinson and Christensen, 2002; Davis, 2006).

Ferdowsi's work is somewhat unique among historical epics in that it is highly patriotic and focused on the country of Iran from its earliest emergence, rather than on a king, an individual hero, or a religious figure. While the poem was written during a time when Islam was highly dominant, references to religion are almost non-existent. A higher power is often acknowledged; Islam is not. The glory of Iran, its struggles, and survival are overriding themes. The heroes of the Shahnameh only exist in relation to their country and their ability to serve it.

The Shahnameh has significance on three separate but related dimensions. First, as a literary masterpiece, it is a symbol of the Persian language and a vehicle for its continued survival, a topic that is not the focus of this chapter, but is essential to understanding the work and its impact. As Dante played a role in shaping the Italian language, so did Ferdowsi have a formative impact on determining the Persian language. Second, it presents the mythology of the country. Finally, it defines its key cultural themes, particularly as they relate to leadership. The influence of the Shahnameh on the Iranian culture and psyche cannot be overstated. The book connects Iranians to the early part of their long history (Forouqi, 1320)[3]. While the actual existence of many of the heroes, particularly those in the first two parts of the Shahnameh, is probably more myth than historical fact, their omnipresence in education, folklore, literature, and social life makes them as significant as real role models. Children and adults, many of whom are named after the heroes of the book, regularly refer to the epic stories, symbols and themes. A required reading in schools, the book is also the basis for popular street theatre and the subject of common story-tellers (called naqqals). Additionally, many Iranian rulers, to symbolically reinforce their unbreakable connection to the past, commissioned new editions of the epic, outdoing one another in the quality and artistry of the publication (Nahavandi and Bomati, 1998).

## Key Leadership Themes and Characteristics

The focus of the Shahnameh is the leader-hero as guardian and savior of the nation. In many cases, these heroes have noble origins; in a few cases, they are ordinary people who outshine their kings by their integrity and courage. While the kings' authority is always accepted and loyalty to them is undisputed, the epic notes their weakness, without detracting from royal status or power (Davis, 2006). The numerous leader-heroes of the Shahnameh are the catalyst for all actions, and the source of all successes, failures, happiness and misery. According to several well-known scholars of Iranian literature, the Shanameh's key themes include the importance of leadership, integrity, humility, loyalty, fairness, kindness, moderation, courage, forgiveness, seeking knowledge and advice, and patriotism (Forouqi, 1320; Khaleqi-Motlaq, 1993). Furthermore, the Shahnameh is a reminder for people not to accept failure, no matter how dire the circumstances may appear (Forouqi, 1320).

### Importance of and need for leadership

The Shahnameh's stories unambiguously and repeatedly emphasize the essential role leaders play. Without leadership, all falls into chaos. One of the most revealing stories is that of King Bahram Gur, who because some villagers do not show him proper respect, asks his priest to punish them (Ferdowsi, 2004: 626–9). The punishment the priest devises is equality among all people, which quickly leads to the disintegration of the social fabric of the village, scarcity and bloodshed. When the priest returns and picks a wise old man to lead the village, order and prosperity are restored. Similarly, the story of Mazdak who preaches and practices equality among people (many concepts are akin to principles of communism) and who gains considerable popularity but is eventually killed by order of the king, illustrates the importance of hierarchy in maintaining social order (Ferdowsi, 2004: 677–83). Followers in the Shahnameh state repeatedly that they, the country or the army cannot function without a leader.

### Integrity and honesty (*dorosti*; *rasti*)

The most essential characteristics of a leader are integrity and honesty. He (not surprisingly they are almost all male), must remain true to his word and must at all times keep faith with his followers. Without fail, the leader-heroes of the Shahnameh demonstrate integrity. Rostam, perhaps the best-known hero of the epic and in Iran, unfailingly stays true to his word and repeatedly advises his king to keep his promises even when breaking them may be beneficial (Ferdowsi, 2004: 162). The importance of integrity is further reinforced through the bad luck and misery that befall those who lack integrity. Salm and Tur who are jealous of their younger brother Iraj and who deceive and kill him, are themselves killed by their nephew (Ferdowsi, 2004: 37–62). Integrity can therefore be considered the *sine qua non* of the ideal Iranian leader.

### Humility (*ferootani*)

Leaders must not become arrogant and distant from their followers; they must remain accessible and remember that they are subject to greater powers. Arrogance and hubris inevitably lead to the fall of heroes and kings. One of the early kings in the Shahnameh, the superhuman Jamshid, is credited with establishing social classes, inventing iron tools and brick making, and instituting the festival of No-Ruz, which to this day is celebrated as the Iranian new year around the world. In spite of his accomplishments, however, he loses God's glory (*farr*) when he becomes arrogant and imperious (Ferdowsi, 2004: 7-8).

### Loyalty (*vafadari*)

Being loyal to elders, family – particularly fathers, and ruler – is essential. Even when the king is less than competent, the leader-hero is duty-bound to remain loyal to legitimate authority. The leader-hero remains in service of the nation and the king. No matter how justified, acts of disloyalty are always punished to preserve social order. Followers must obey their king to the point of knowingly taking poison when ordered to do so, as is the case in the story of Izad-Goshasp (Ferdowsi, 2004: 719–20), or entering into a battle they know is lost when asked to do so by their king (Rostam) (Ferdowsi, 2004: 151).

### Fairness and pursuit of justice (*edalat; dad khahi*)

The leader-hero is responsible for righting wrongs; for pursuing justice for all and demonstrating fairness and impartiality in his decisions. The letter of

Nushin-Ravan, one of the most celebrated Sassanid kings emphasizes the need for justice that will ensure the king's security, world prosperity, and the king's and his followers' happiness (Ferdowsi, 2004: 715). One of the book's early heroes, Kaveh, the ironsmith, who although is not of noble descent, is known for his courage as the liberator of Iran from an unjust king, and his willingness to stand for those who are weak. (Ferdowsi, 2004: 18–21). He uses his simple leather apron (derafsh-e Kaviani; the flag of Kaveh) as the symbol of his pursuit of justice. The flag is still used as a metaphor for Iranian identity and the importance of taking a courageous stand.

### Kindness to all, particularly the poor and weak (*mehrabani*)

The ideal leader is kind to all and champions the cause of those who are weak, and taking advantage of the powerless is frowned upon particularly for those who hold power. Every military victory ends with celebrations that distribute wealth to the poor (for example, Kavus' return from Mazandaran, Ferdowsi, 2004: 172–3) and kings add to their glory by opening their treasury to take care of their subjects.

### Moderation (*miyaneh ravi*) and patience

The leader-hero must follow the path of moderation rather than extremes. While considered a model king on all dimensions, Bahram Gur is chided for his excess (Ferdowsi, 2004: 635). In the story of Kebrui (Ferdowsi, 2004: 623–4), the head of a village is blinded by ravens while he is unconscious from drinking wine to excess, leading the king to outlaw wine. Rostam, the archetypal leader-hero, is prone to excess and pride, characteristics that cause him to put himself, his family, and his country at risk, and unknowingly kill his own son. The theme of moderation and patience is further present in king Nushin-Ravan's letter where he exhorts his son to be patient and not to rush into decisions.

### Courage and chivalry (*javanmardi*)

Courage and chivalry are central to epics of all cultures. In the Shahnameh, many of the leader-heroes are compared to lions for their courage and hunt the animal to demonstrate their bravery and skill (for example, Bahram Gur; Ferdowsi, 2004: 616–21). One of the most well-known set of stories involves the seven trials of Rostam (Ferdowsi, 2004: 152–73), where the hero's bravery and loyalty are tested by the challenge to overcome seven impossible obstacles (*Haft khan-e Rostam* – the seven tests of Rostam), a reference to which is still commonly used in Iran to represent impossible odds and courage.

### Forgiveness (*bakhshesh*)

Another leadership theme in the Shahnameh is the need for leaders to forgive those who stray or make mistakes while the leader-hero himself is held to higher standards and cannot be forgiven for missteps. The leader-hero must show clemency whenever warranted. While there are many instances of decimating enemy armies in battle and beheading of their leaders, leader-heroes who are unkind to their fallen and repentant enemy are considered unjust.

### Seeking knowledge and wisdom (*danesh amoozi; kheradmandi*)

The leader-heroes are expected to make decisions and take charge. However, they must consult wise and knowledgeable counsel before doing so. Nushin-Ravan tells his son that a king who seeks guidance from experts assures his good reputation (Ferdowsi, 2004: 715). Leaders who act on their own find themselves in dire straits. For example, Hormozd, one of the most evil kings in the epic, starts his reign by killing his father's wise confidants (Ferdowsi, 2004: 717) and rules through deceit and without the benefit of good counsel. His tragic end, blinded by two noblemen who rise against his injustice and incompetence, points out the potential fate of those who do not take advantage of others' wisdom.

### Patriotism (*mihan doosti*)

As integrity is the *sine qua non* of Iranian mythical leaders, patriotism is their reason for being. The Iranian leader-hero is first and foremost the symbol and defender of the nation. His patriotism is unquestioned and the primary driver of his actions. Like Kaveh and Rostam, many other heroes are first and foremost patriotic, inherently tied to their native land, and emotionally connected to its culture and people. The story of Bahram Choubineh provides a telling illustration. While possessing most of the leader-hero qualities and leading men and armies to victory in the service of his king, Choubineh's failure is that his patriotism is not absolute (Ferdowsi, 2004: 790–1).

The characteristics presented above shape the ideal of the Iranian leader who is all-powerful and decisive, while remaining humble, accessible, and caring. It is significant to note that the only female leader-hero, Gordyeh, while she does not reach the stature of the epic's others, possesses the same qualities that define other leaders and champions (Ferdowsi, 2004: 774–91). The themes of Persian mythology, as presented in the Shahnameh, date back to prehistoric times, but they are manifest in writings that predate the epic and in literature that follows it. One of the earliest treatise of governance and advice to rulers was written by Ardeshir Babakan, the first king of the Sassanid dynasty.[4] The principles of the short treatise are akin to the themes represented by the heroes of the Shahnameh with a focus on rulers being honest, fair, kind, forgiving and relying on experts (Mashkoor, 1367). These themes are further reprised in later literary works indicating their prominence in Iranian leadership. Most notably, several books that provide advice to kings and rulers, such as the 'Siasat Namet' (Book of Politics) written by a prominent minister Khajeh Nezamolmolk e Toosi in the eleventh century, and M. M. Saadi's 'Nasihat ol Molook' (Advice for Kings, 1977) written in the thirteenth century reiterate the leadership themes found in the Shahnameh.[5] For example, Saadi (1977) provides specific advice to rulers in much the same manner Machiavelli does in *The Prince*. However, the leadership themes are starkly different focusing on generosity, fairness, humility and kindness.

## OVERVIEW OF IRANIAN LEADERSHIP AND PRACTICAL APPLICATIONS

An indication of the importance and significance of the Shahnameh is the struggle of the current Islamic government with it. Because denying and downplaying the 3000 year old monarchic past has been a focus of the current government that has changed names of streets, cities, towns and even historical sites to erase references to kings and to create an Islamic rather than Iranian identity (Nahavandi, 1984), versions of the Shahnameh that were printed early during the revolution were renamed 'Collection of Ferdowsi's Poems' instead of its actual name, the Book of Kings. However, the new title did not prove popular and the name of the epic has been restored. The Shahnameh is still the primary source of Iranian mythology even in the Islamic Republic, even though religion is not a central focus of the epic.

Mythology and modern research (Ayman and Chemers, 1983; Chemers, 1969) both indicate that the ideals of a fair, powerful, decisive, but caring and accessible father figure are key to Iranian leadership. An examination of the recent and current political arenas further reveals that Iranians have searched for honest and patriotic leaders consistently before and since the 1979 Iranian revolution. The last dynasty (Pahlavi; 1925–79) was brought to power by a highly patriotic, domineering father figure. Correspondingly, corruption is cited as one of the major causes of the disillusionment of the Iranian population with the same dynasty, and a cause of the revolution. While Iranians are comfortable and often appreciate even ostentatious demonstrations of wealth and glory, maybe still seen in the cultural unconscious as indicators of divine *farr*, they also expect their leaders to be humble and to care for those who are powerless and weak. Many expressed disappointment and resentment at losing access to their ruler (shah; the Iranian term for king), when the last king of the Pahlavi dynasty, citing security reasons, started traveling by helicopter rather than by car where he could be seen among his people and during which time they had access to him for petitions and requests. The humility and accessibility to followers are coupled with their expectations for the leader's strength and decisiveness. The end of the Pahlavi dynasty offers yet another example.

Iranians who were demonstrating all over the country in 1978 and 1979 against the government, considered the last shah's speech admitting that mistakes had occurred during his reign to be a sign of weakness, an admission that helped further destabilize his government and hasten his overthrow.

The current president of Iran, Mahmood Ahmadi-Nejad was elected, to a great extent, because of his reputation of integrity and honesty, and his connection to the common people, much in contrast to his powerful political rival Ali Akbar Rafsanjani. Ahmadi-Nejad was perceived as a defender of the weak, a champion of the unfortunate and an accessible leader, all qualities of an ideal Iranian leader. Although the current leadership is far from representing all the ideals of the Shahnameh on many dimensions, it is interesting to note that Ahmadi-Nejad and other current Iranian leaders' popularity increases when they emphasize links to the imperial past, rather than association with Islamic principles. While early in the revolution, imperial history was ignored, references to the 'glorious' past return when leaders feel the need to unite the country.

The Shahnameh and its themes are well-established ideals of leadership in Iran. However, there is a divergence between the Islamic ideals projected by the current government and those of the Shahnameh. The Shahnameh is unequivocal about the importance of Iran, not religion. Leader-heroes must champion Iran first. The previous government of Iran, and many other past dynasties such as the Safavids, were similarly focused on patriotism and the pre-eminence of Iran. In contrast, the Islamic ideal, often presented by the current political leadership, is that of a global religion that unifies all Muslims regardless of nationality (Omat-ol-Islam; people of Islam). Khomeini, the father of the Islamic revolution, advanced analogous principles and considered nationalism a creation of the West and a crime (Nahavandi, 1984). Such views are in stark contrast with the nationalistic, and occasionally ethnocentric, message of the Shahnameh. The relationship of religion and state in Iran has posed an on-going challenge for leadership. For example, during the Safavid dynasty when Shiism was established as the national religion, partly to combat the influence of the Sunni, Ottoman Empire, rulers such as Shah Abbas, kept religious leaders at arm's length preventing them from getting involved in political events (Nahavandi and Bomatti, 1998). Such separation has not been the case in other Muslim countries, most notably in Saudi Arabia, where religion and affairs of state are closely integrated and intertwined. The separation of 'mosque and state' was continued under the last Iranian dynasty, and some suggest, carried too far and another one of the causes of the 1979 revolution. Therefore, while Islam has been since the seventh century the primary religion of Iran, because of historical and ethnic differences, it has not brought Iran into the pan-Islamic fold made up of Arab nations.

The Muslim ideals and legends, however, do play a role in Iranian culture and views of leadership. In addition to the Shahnameh, one of the most cited legends in Iran is that of the third Shiite Imam, Hussein, who was killed (martyred, according to Shiite belief) by the caliph Yazid when he was hopelessly outnumbered by Yazid's army. Hussein's battle was over establishing the succession after the death of prophet Mohammad, which he, as the prophet and his son-in-law's relative, claimed must go to him.[6] The Shiites' claim to succession and Hussein's legend offer another window in the strong nationalistic sentiments in Iran. By some accounts, Shiism, and the legend of Imam Hussein along with it, were a vehicle for Iranians to establish their separation from the Arab invaders and distinguish themselves from other Muslims with a distinctive identity, based on the monarchic, therefore Iranian, rather than the caliphate, therefore Arab, right of succession to the prophet. This separation from other Muslim-Arab nations continues to dominate Iranian culture and leadership.[7]

The current theocracy in Iran is an exception to this rule with a focus on Islam rather than Iran as the center of government, although hero worship similar to the one evidenced in the Shahnameh is ever present in the glorification of the 'martyrs' of the war against Iraq and others who have been killed since the revolution (Economist, 2007). Nevertheless, the religious hero, for example Imam Hussein, shares in the Shahnameh's ideals of integrity, courage, rising against injustice, and representing the weak. Since the Islamic revolution, Islam appears dominant and religious themes govern speech in Iran; such locus has two potential explanations. First, it may indicate an actual shift from a secular, Iranian-patriotic-based identity to a global, Islamic identity. Second, it may be an age-old Iranian coping behavior when faced with assaults on the culture where people change behaviors as needed while maintaining their original identity. Such practice has been evident throughout Iranian history from the time of Alexander the Great, through the Arab, Mongol and other invasions. Recent research indicates that despite the superficial changes and a dominance of Islam, the deeper cultural identity remains present and unchanged (Javidan and Dastmalchian, 2003).

## IRANIAN LEADERSHIP THEMES

Ideals of leadership in Iran have much in common with other cultures. The greater than life hero is not unique. However, Iranian leadership ideals present several distinct themes. First, the Iranian leader-heroes are the source of all powers. According to the mythology, they created the world and brought civilization to mankind. Without the leader, there is only chaos.[8] Either for organizational or political purposes, the centrality of the leader in Iran must not be overlooked. Stating that the leaders, not the followers, are the drivers may not be an exaggeration based on Iranian ideals. While consultation is required and participation appreciated, the leader still legitimately holds power. Iranian followers expect their leader to be decisive and strong-minded. Group discussions and public exchange of ideas are not necessary when the leader fulfills his/her role as a caring father figure. If the leader demonstrates the ideals of leadership including strength, kindness and humility, then followers are cared for and do not need to participate for the sake of participation.

The Iranian ideal leader is responsible for transformation, which is typical, but his/her responsibility goes beyond change to the renewal of the culture. Without the leader-hero, the nation and culture may disappear. The leader-heroes are responsible for the rebirth of Iran. They rise, like the Phoenix[9] and fade away when crisis subsides. Another unique theme in Iranian mythology and leadership is that the change agent is often not directly tied to the existing power structure. The leader-hero has loyalty to the king, but he comes from the fringes. Kaveh is a simple blacksmith, unassociated with power. Rostam is not part of the ruling dynasty, but part of the family that serves the king. The leader-heroes are external enough to have perspective but are still insiders and have unwavering dedication to the ultimate goal, which is to safeguard and assure the survival of the nation. Being of Iranian origin is only one determinant of a leader's insider status; however, while many of the leader-heroes have non-Iranian blood, a complete outsider cannot be the savior, no matter how brave. This theme of change coming from the fringes, but still the inside, is another key concept to consider when working with Iranians. Outsiders, or those supported by outsiders, have never been and cannot be the leader-heroes. They must come from the inside, have ties to the culture and its values – whether national or organizational – and have complete loyalty to the culture.

Along with high status and power, the ideal Iranian leader carries a heavy responsibility for justice, fairness, humility, and caring for followers. Abuse of power, even when the ends are justified, is unacceptable. The leader, like a father, is benevolent, accessible, kindhearted and compassionate. Caring for followers is a source of power rather than a sign of weakness. According to ancient Persian traditions, the leader is duty-bound to hear his subjects' requests and petitions and honor them when possible. From an organizational point of view, the role of father puts managers in a caretaker role that is not typical in many Western organizations. Business is not simply business; it is about people and relationships. Similar cultural values are present in other countries, such as the Philippines and Mexico, and have required changes in Western management and human resource practices that make caring for the individual a central priority. As evidenced by the second example in the commentary, the powerful caretaker role is integral to leadership in Iran, not an optional peripheral behavior – see Commentary box .

# COMMENTARY BOX

## Iranian Business Owner-manager with Business Interests in Iran and Europe

In Iran, we have very high expectations of our leaders. I some-times wonder if anyone can really live up to them. We want them to be kind and take care of their subordinates like a father would. If they don't, we think they are cruel. We want them to make deci-sions wisely and know what the right answers are every time. If they don't, we think they are weak. If they don't consult with others, we think they are too autocratic; but when they consult too much, we think they are incompetent. Iranian leaders must be able to do all that at the same time.

## Iranian Political Leader

Change in Iran is only accepted if it comes from the inside. The leader who brings change must prove his or her 'Iranian-ness', as a pre-requisite. Iranians are a very hospitable people, open to outsiders, and tolerant of those who are different, but they are also very proud of their heritage. Their leaders, especially those who want to bring change, have to come from within. The person who makes the change has to be perceived as one of them, not an outsider. The leader is the insider who has the courage to stand up, raise the Kaviani flag, and claim the mantle of leader-ship.

## British-educated Iranian Executive-Business Owner

I have a business to run and must make money. My family depends on that and so do my employees and their families. But, I can only do that if I take care of my employees. They rely on me for much more than their paycheck. The same managers and many of the same employees have worked for me for over ten years, ever since I started my business. We have very little turnover. I have helped my employees buy homes and find suit-able spouses for their sons and daughters, gone to their cousins' funerals and to their children's weddings, given them days off when their grandfather was sick, and made sure that I know what

> is going on with their life. That is part of being a leader. In exchange, I know they will do anything for me. It is more like a family than a business, but there is no doubt who is in charge. There is a clear line between us that they will not cross.

As in any cross-cultural situation, knowing and understanding the other culture is indispensable. When working with Iranians, whether they are still in Iran or part of the diaspora who migrated abroad after the 1979 revolution, recognizing their culture and rich history is essential to building effective relationships. Iranians' patriotism and love of their country and of its culture are deep-rooted values that must be acknowledged and appreciated to establish successful connections with them. Likewise, familiarity with the ethnic and cultural differences between Iran and its neighbors is another step in successful interaction. Primarily focusing on the task and results alone, a well-accepted and common practice in Western business, is not a wise option. The Iranian leader's focus on followers is an entrenched obligation and leaders from any other culture who lead Iranians must understand that responsibility.

## CONCLUDING THOUGHTS

The strength and survival of the leadership themes present in Iranian mythology are startling. The themes can be traced to Zoroastrian teachings, glorified in the Shahnameh, the source of Persian mythology, reiterated in Iranian-Islamic traditions, and recounted by many other writers up to the modern day. The image of the ideal Iranian leader as a charismatic change agent fits, to some extent, ideals of leadership in the West and those that are currently proposed by much of leadership theory. Leaders are charismatic change agents, spiritual and authentic. Their power is unquestioned. However, the power also carries the considerable and unwavering responsibility to care for followers and champion their cause, to listen to their concerns, and to put their well-being ahead of the leader's.

Understanding Iranian mythology can provide considerable insight into modern Iranian leadership. Findings of research about the culture and leadership of Iran are evident in the leadership themes found in the Shahnameh. Because of the ingrained and ancient nature of these themes and their existence in cultural values, understanding of modern Iran is much informed by consideration of its mythology. The goals of the country and its leadership have remained the same for at least 3000 years: Glory of the nation, a recognized place in history, and cultural and national independence. Persia-Iran dominated the world in antiquity. Throughout their history, Iranians have attempted to regain that place of prominence they believe is rightfully theirs. Respect for the national identity, recognition of the role of the leader as the change agent who must be from the inside, and as the person who is responsible not only for accomplishing the goals – business-related, economic, social, or political, but also for being the defender of the weak are all essential to understand Iranian leadership.

## ACKNOWLEDGMENTS

The author wishes to thank Professor Houchang Nahavandi, former chancellor of Tehran and Shiraz Universities, Honorary Professor at Paris University, and Associate Member of the French Académie des Sciences Morales et Politiques for his help in preparation of this manuscript; and Professors Ali Malekzadeh of Xavier University and Mirna Lattouf of Arizona State University for their comments on earlier drafts.

## NOTES

1. Phonetic spellings of Iranian names are used; in most cases, many alternative spellings have been used.
2. Several excellent translations of the book both in prose and verse are available in English, including one by Dick Davis used in this chapter.
3. When Iranian publications are cited, the original dates are used. They are based on the modern Iranian solar calendar which started at the Islamic era; equivalent Western dates are provided in the reference section.
4. The dynasty ruled Iran from 224 AD to the Arab invasion of the seventh century.
5. Saadi is best known for his works the *Golestan* (*The Rose Garden*) and the *Boostan* (*The Orchard*). One of his poems about the common nature of all humans graces the entrance of the Hall of the Nations at the United Nations.
6. The disagreement over succession after the prophet is one of the fundamental differences between Shiites and Sunnis.
7. For example, the assassination of the caliph, Omar of the Umayyad dynasty by an Iranian slave is still celebrated in remote Iranian villages 1400 years after it occurred (djashn-e Omar koshi; the celebration of the killing of Omar). During the previous dynasty, protests by Arab nations over celebration of this assassination led to its ban in major cities.
8. A much-cited story of an anonymous general of the army of Nadir Shah, the Iranian conqueror of India in the eighteenth century, recounts that he pointed out that the Iranians failed many times in their attempts to invade India. The general responded to Nadir Shah's inquiry regarding the reasons for failure by stating that they were all there, but that the King was not.
9. The Phoenix is called the *simorq* in Iran. The last 'poet laureate' (malek ol shoara; king of poets) of Iran, M. T. Bahar has labeled Iran the country of the Simorq for its ability to repeatedly rise from ashes.

# REFERENCES

Ayman, R. and Chemers, M. M. (1983), Relationship of supervisory behavior ratings to work group effectiveness and subordinate satisfaction among Iranian managers, *Journal of Applied Psychology*, **68**, 338–41.

Brélian-Djahanshahi, F. (2001), *Histoires légendaires des rois de Perse* [*Legendary History of the Persian Kings*], Paris, France: Edition Imago.

Chemers, M. M. (1969), Cross-cultural training as means of improving situational favorableness, *Human Relations*, **22**, 531–46.

Davis, D. (2006), *Epic and Sedition: The Case of Ferdowsi's Shahnameh*, Washington, DC: Mage Publishers.

Economist (2007), Heroes of the revolution, *Economist.com/Global Agenda*, 5 July: 1.

Ferdowsi, A. (2004), *Shahnameh: The Persian Book of Kings*, New translation by Dick Davis, New York: Penguin Books.

Forouqi, M. (1320/1941–2), *Introduction to the Shahnameh*, Tehran: Ministry of Education Publications.

Hofstede, G. (1980), Motivation, leadership, and organization: Do American theories apply abroad?, *Organizational Dynamics*, **9** (1), 42–61.

Hofstede, G. (1992), *Culture and Organizations*, London: McGraw-Hill.

House, R. J., Hanges, P. J., Javidan, M., Dorfman, P. W. and Gupta, V. (2004), *Culture, Leadership and Organizations: The GLOBE Study of 62 Societies*, Thousand Oaks, CA: Sage Publications.

Javidan, M. and Carl, D. E. (2004), East meets West: A cross-cultural comparison of charismatic leadership among Canadian and Iranian executives, *Journal of Management Studies*, **41**, 665–91.

Javidan, M. and Dastmalchian, A. (2003), Culture and leadership in Iran: The land of individual achievers, strong family ties, and powerful elite, *The Academy of Management Executive*, **17** (4), 127–42.

Khaleqi-Mutlaq, J. (1993), Iran Garai dar Shahnameh [*Seeking Iran in the Shahnameh*], *Hasti Magazine*, **4**, Tehran: Bahman Publishers.

Levinson, D. V. and Christensen, K. (2002), *Encyclopedia of Modern Asia*, Farmington Hills, MI: Charles Scribner's Sons, p. 48.

Mashkoor, M. J. (1367: 1987–8), *Tarikh e siyasi e Sassanian* (2nd edn), [*The Political History of the Sassanid*], Tehran: Doniyay e Ketab.

Nahavandi, H. (1984), *Le grand mensonge: Dossier noir de l'integrisme Islamique* [*The Big Deception: The Black File of Islamic Fundamentalism*], Paris: Nouvelles Editions Debresse.

Nahavandi, H. and Bomati, Y. (1998), *Shah Abbas: Empereur de Perse 1587–1629* [*Shah Abbas: Emperor of Persia 1587–1629*], Paris: Perrin.

Nasr, S. T. (1350/1971–2), *Perenité de l'Iran Adabiyat e Iran*, Tehran: Kayhan.

Saadi, M. (2536/1977), *Complete Works of Saadi* (2nd edn), M. A. Forouqi (ed.), Tehran: Amir Kabir.

Sarayah, Y. K. (2004), Servant leadership in the Bedouin-Arab culture, *Global Virtue Ethics Review*, **53**, 58–80.

Yousef, D. A. (1998), Predictors of decision-making styles in a non-Western country, *Organization Development Journal*, **19** (7), 366–73.

Zarrin-Koob, A. (1367/1988–9), *Tarikh e mardom e Iran* [*History of the Iranian People*], Vol. 1. Tehran: Amirkabir.

# 14. Cultural mythology and global leadership in Egypt

## Mohamed M. Mostafa and Diana J. Wong-MingJi

## INTRODUCTION

The Egyptian pantheon of cultural mythologies goes back to one of humankind's most ancient beginnings and the myths themselves are 'reconstituted from prolific but fragmentary allusions in funerary formulas' (Kirk, 1975: 207). Ancient Egypt extends back to 3000 BC with the beginning of the pharaohs that was followed by the Hellenistic period with the rule of Alexander the Great starting in 332 BC, the Muslim conquest in 639 AD, the Ottoman Turks in 1517, the Napoleonic invasion in 1798, the onset of being a British protectorate in the late 1800s until 1922, a ruler who started to modernize the country, and with the ending of the monarchy in 1953, Egypt became a republic. Cultural mythologies evolved through the different ages and any original versions are mired in a distant murky past.

Nietzsche once stated that 'without myth every culture loses the healthy natural power of its creativity: only a horizon defined by the myth completes and unifies a whole cultural movement'. The myths of Egypt are found in ancient monuments like pyramids and incredible artifacts that serve as tangible symbols of lives before. The monuments and remains of pharaohs indicate that their role was one of divine mediation between the gods and humanity. While some myths prevail in the national mindset, there are many variations along with different names at the local level. The selection of myths for this project provides a very select view from the wealth and variations of Egyptian cultural mythologies available.

## OVERVIEW OF EGYPTIAN MYTHOLOGY

The Ennead, also known as the Nine Gods of Heliopolis, make up a significant family of Egyptian gods. The first was Ra-Atum who rose from the primeval mound. He was the most powerful God with the ability to change forms. The power of Ra was in his secret name that was kept hidden and as he spoke other names, the things came into being. After speaking mankind humans came into being; Ra took the form of a man and became the first pharaoh ruling Egypt for thousands of years.

Ra also created other deities. He sneezed out the first division of male and female – Shu, the god of air and Tefenet, the goddess of moisture. The union of the two brought forth Geb, the earth god and Nut, the sky goddess. From Nut, two pairs of twins were born – Osiris and Isis, and Set and Nephthys. A drama love, hate, murder and vengeance are woven into the myth among family of deities. Different localities in Egypt worshipped one or more of the deities with variations in the telling of the myths related to the four deities.

The four most important figures in Egyptian mythology needed for under-standing the influence of cultural mythology on leadership style are Set, Isis, Osiris and Horus. In earliest times, Set was the patron deity of Lower (Northern) Egypt, and represented the fierce storms of the desert, who the Lower Egyptians sought to appease. However, when Upper Egypt conquered Lower Egypt and ushered in the First Dynasty, Set became known as the evil enemy of Horus (Upper Egypt's dynastic god). In Egyptian religion Set or Seth came to stand for the forces of chaos and destruction and of misplaced energy. His most famous act was in murdering his brother and gaining a throne. He was the enemy of light and the champion of darkness. Set was the principle of all which burns and consumes.

In later periods, Set was identified with the Greek genie Typhon who had a serpent's body. The snake is a symbol long associated with Set which undoubt-edly influenced the use of the snake as the evil influence in the story of Adam and Eve. In the dynastic periods, when Osiris, Horus and Isis were worshipped, followers of Set were persecuted and his priesthood was finally destroyed in the XXV dynasty. When the Hebrews emigrated from Egypt during the XIX dynasty, it is clear that they took with them the character of Set which was later used along with Angra Mainyu as the model for Satan. Even the word Satan was probably derived from the Egyptian hieroglyphic Set-hen, one of Set's formal titles.

The next major Egyptian character who had a large influence on the early Egyptian mythology was Isis. Perhaps the most important goddess of all Egyptian mythology, Isis assumed, during the course of Egyptian history, the attributes and functions of virtually every other important goddess in the land. Her most important functions, however, were those of motherhood, marital devotion, healing the sick, wisdom, and the working of magical spells and charms. With her intelligence and wisdom, Isis tricked Ra into giving up his hidden secret name to her. She used the secret name and the knowledge of pronouncing the name to bring her husband, Osiris, back to life.

Isis was the sister and wife of Osiris, sister of Set, and the mother of Horus the Child (Harpocrates). Isis was responsible for protecting Horus from Set during his infancy; for helping Osiris to return to life; and for assisting her husband to rule in the land of the Dead. The cult of Isis was widespread in Egypt and spread from there to Phoenicia, Syria and Palestine; to Asia Minor; to Cyprus, Rhodes, Crete, Samos and other islands in the Aegean; to many parts of mainland Greece – Corinth, Argos and Thessaly amongst them; to Malta and Sicily; and, finally, to Rome. In the first century BC, Isis was perhaps the most popular goddess in Rome, from which her cult spread to the furthest limits of the Roman Empire, including Britain: her only rival was Mithras.

Osiris was the god of the dead, and the god of the resurrection into eternal life; ruler, protector and judge of the deceased. Osiris was the brother of Set and Isis, who was also his wife by whom he fathered Horus. Osiris ruled the world of men in the beginning, after Ra had abandoned the world to rule the skies, but he was murdered by his brother Set. Isis is known for devotion in mourning and looking for Osiris's body. When she found him, she used her magic to give life back to him. By Dynasty XVIII, Osiris was probably the most widely worshipped god in Egypt. Reliefs of Roman emperors, conquerors of Egypt, dressed in the traditional garb of the Pharaohs, making offerings to him in the temples exist to this day. His death was avenged by his son Horus, who defeated Set, castrated him, and cast him out into the Sahara. Horus then became the divine prototype of the Pharaoh. As Heru-Ur, 'Horus the Elder', he was the patron deity of Upper (Southern) Egypt. Initially he was viewed as the twin brother of Set (the patron of Lower Egypt), but he became the conqueror of Set around 3100 BC when Upper Egypt conquered Lower Egypt and formed the unified kingdom of Egypt.

Ra primarily represents the role of the all-powerful creator but not one who ruled humans eternally. Osiris was considered to be the bringer of enlighten-ment. He forced no man to carry out his will. He induced them to practice what he preached by means of gentle persuasion. His lessons were often imparted to his listeners through hymns or songs. After Isis, the family relationships and drama of the gods were also reflected in some of Egypt's ruling pharaoh fami-lies where siblings murdered one another to gain power. But more often, family relations were often a powerful unit for building empires that spanned multiple generations.

Each of the four core mythical deities represents key interrelated cultural dynamics. Ra certainly represents the role of the creator and the patriarchal figure for the family of deities. But one needs to be ready for the opportunities with major changes. Set personifies chaos, destruction, and darkness which are commonly associated with major cultural shifts, with political conflicts and wars. Horus stands for the conqueror or pharaoh, and unifier. Following destructions of war, there is often a period of peace with rebirth and growth in prosperity. Osiris symbolizes resurrection, judge or protector, enlightenment, and fertility in agriculture. He is considered to be the rightful ruler who inherited the monarchy from Ra until Set murdered him. Isis signifies motherhood, devotion, healing, wisdom, and magical powers. Her search for Osiris illustrates devotion to a beloved family member. Hence, the following section highlights Egyptian leadership with some reflections of the cultural characteristics that unfold through different major periods of major transformations.

## OVERVIEW OF EGYPTIAN LEADERSHIP

As one of the most ancient civilizations, the study of Egyptian leadership is deeply ingrained to its cultural mythology where actual leaders from the distant past ascend to mythological proportions over time with the telling and retelling of their stories. The selection of leaders for this section is for the purpose of highlighting some key Egyptian leadership qualities while recognizing that space limitations somewhat restrict a more comprehensive roster. Both the leader's actions and followers' responses inevitably reflect the forms of behavior which are regarded as legitimate and appropriate within Egyptian society.

Pharaohs of ancient Egypt revealed by archeological digs leave only sparse remnants as evidence of their leadership. Women actually defined much of the royal lineage of the ancient pharaoh dynasties and men from outside the lineage had to marry a queen in order to become king. Two of the most famous were Hatshepsut who reigned from 1479 BC to 1458 BC and Cleopatra VII from 51 BC to 30 BC. Both women's fathers directly named them as direct heirs and both women married their brothers as was the custom to have heirs from the lineage. Interestingly, the female pharaohs donned fake beards to symbolize a continuity of the male identity. Hatshepsut is known for both reigning peacefully as well as engaging successfully in military campaigns. She was one of the most prolific builders in ancient Egypt who established extensive trade networks and brought forth a prosperous time. King Tutankhamun was identified as one of her descendants. One myth debated by scholars questions whether Hatshepsut was the princess who found Baby Moses floating among the reeds of the Nile.

Cleopatra VII Thea Philopator is likely the most famous of Egyptian leaders through Shakespeare's play, Bernard Shaw's film, and the propagation of Hollywood movies, in particular with one starring Elizabeth Taylor in the role. Cleopatra was actually a Hellenistic ruler with Greek as her primary language who directly descended from Alexander the Great. Cleopatra was likely the first to adopt Egyptian beliefs and deities where Isis was her patron goddess and propagated the idea that she was a reincarnation of the deity. Becoming a joint monarch at the age of 17 with her 12 year old brother was the start of Cleopatra's dramatic life. Her story was woven with wars and murders in the family, love and politics with Julius Caesar and Mark Anthony, and a dramatic suicide that not only ended her life but also the end of all Egyptian pharaohs with the expansion of the Roman Empire.

The Muslim conquest of Egypt brought forth other notable leaders with the most famous being Salah al-Din Yusuf ibn Ayyub, often referred to as Saladin who ruled from 1174 AD to 1193. He restored Sunnism in Egypt, rejuvenated its economy, reorganized the military, and most importantly, successfully resisted the Crusaders from Europe with expansions beyond Egypt to Syria, Iraq, Yemen and Hejaz. To this day, reference to his leadership inspires the notion of a chivalrous knight and Arab unity. Even in defeat and differences in religion, European Christians, including King Richard, had great respect for Saladin. *Salah ad-Din* means 'Righteousness of Faith'. His reputation continues to inspire Muslims through the ages and respected to this day beyond Egyptian culture to Turkish, Arabic, Kurdish and Muslim ones.

More recently, prominent Egyptian leaders continued to play significant roles in international affairs with resulting major transitions in their country. A global orientation is an inherent quality in the nature of Egypt's leadership that continues from the earliest ages through to the country's modernization. Often referred to as the Father of modern Egypt, Mohammad Ali Pasha, an Ottoman officer, was of Turkish origins from Kavala, a Macedonian seaport of the Aegean. He and his descendants ruled Egypt for 147 years until 1952 when King Ahmed Fouad II abdicated his throne. In 1805, Mohammed Ali Pasha rose to power as the Ottoman Viceroy of Egypt based on his political skills developed from a context with constant conflict in the Balkans, military lessons learnt from observing Napoleon's disciplined military forces, and the gall to switch sides multiple times in the battles between the Ottomans and Mamluks, the feudal landowners. Through various battles with the British, Ottomans, and Mamluks, Egyptians saw Mohammed Ali as being capable of standing up to the oppressors. As a result, he received public support to fulfill the pasha position. He had a reputation for being very clever in military affairs. To support military reform, he rebuilt Egypt's economy with cotton as a cash crop industry. His reputation and his family's name continue to be very prominent in Alexandria.

Following World War II, the Egyptian Revolution of 1952 led to the demise of King Farouk I which ended the monarchy and the country became a republic. Although Mohamad Naguib was Egypt's first president, he was arrested less than a year into the position by Nasser. Gamal Abdel Nasser became President of Egypt for 15 years and rose to international importance for his leadership in advancing a pan-Arab agenda, industrial reforms, modernizing the educational system and developing progressive economic and social transformations. On the international stage, Nasser was a prominent leader of the Non-Aligned Movement and helped found the Palestine Liberation Organization. To this day, the Arab world reveres Nasser as a leader who stood up to western imperialism and restored the respect of Arabs through numerous conflicts with Israel and western countries. Prior to the Six Days War, Nasser (1967) stated, 'We can achieve much by Arab Action, which is a main part of our battle. We must develop and build our countries to face the challenge of our enemies.' Following Nasser's death of a heart attack in 1970, attendance at his funeral was estimated at 5 million people with a 6 mile procession.

Muhammad Anwar El Sadat was a confidante of Nasser and succeeded him as President. Sadat made significant departures from Nasser's pan-Arab agenda which resulted in Egypt being ousted from the Arab League. Under Sadat's leadership, Egypt regained the Sinai in the famous 1973 October War and subsequently signed the Israel-Egypt Peace Treaty. Sadat, often referred to as the 'Hero of War and Peace' (Meital, 2003), was the first Arab leader to officially visit Israel in a meeting with Prime Minister Begin with the agenda of achieving peace in the Arab-Israeli conflict. The signing of the Camp David Peace Agreement led to the Nobel Peace Prize awarded to Sadat and Begin. At the same time, Sadat faced criticism within Egypt about the nation's role in history and geography (al-Shazly, 1980; Heikal, 1983). Egypt's dramatic shift toward a nationalist focus had broad support in the country but angered many in the international Arab and Muslim community. Within Egypt, conflicts between those loyal to Nasser's vision of Egypt and Sadat's shift to alliances with the west continue to this day. Subsequently, Sadat was assassinated in 1981 with a fatwa from Omar Abdel-Rahman.

Following Sadat's death, Muhammad Hosni Mubarak became President and has ruled Egypt under a state of emergency since 1981. He has become the longest serving ruler since Muhammed Ali. While Mubarak extends the line of notable Egyptian leaders, a few prominent leaders in the business community bear mentioning.

Osman Ahmed Osman is the famous founder of the Arab Contractors that led the building of the Aswan Dam. He also became a Minister of Housing and Development. Osman is known for a strong work ethic, intelligence and talented organizational skills. His belief in building positive relationships with employees and providing them with security and comfort led to helping employees solve problems which led to the nickname, 'the Teacher'. Osman's management practices such as employee pension funds and medical insurance started within his firm but also later expanded to cover all public employees. He started a contracting firm during Nasser's administration when all such firms in the Middle East were European. Later, Nasser nationalized the business but Osman remained in control. He was also a close friend and ally to Sadat. Today, the company is one of the largest construction firms in Egypt and remains privately held by family members. Within his political and business leadership roles, Osman advocated for a nationalistic and pan-Arab agenda where business and economic development were national priorities above political issues.

Egypt has many other prominent business leaders such as Talaat Pasha Harb who established the first Egyptian Bank, Banque Misr (Bank of Egypt) with additional holdings in textiles, shipping, insurance, publishing, airline, and movie making; Ahmed Ezz who is the Chairman and Managing Director of Al Ezz with businesses in steel manufacturing and ceramics; Talaat Moustafa, former Chairman and founder of The Talaat Moustafa Group with interests in construction, agriculture, and real estate; and Onsi Sawiris has a Forbes estimated worth of about $5.2 billion and is founder of Orascom Telecom Holding SAE which is one of Egypt's largest and most diversified private businesses with interests in telecommunication, construction and tourism. Several of the prominent business leaders also had political leadership roles in the national government and integrated family members into multiple parts of the business operations. Thus, Egyptian business leaders integrate the personal, public and private sectors much more fluidly than in many other countries where the different spheres are often more segregated.

## GLOBAL IMPLICATIONS

The particular cast of deities in Egyptian mythology represents interesting interrelated dynamics in the different phases of change, in particular cultural transformations through the different historical periods of Egypt's development. Ra creates the initial stage and context that is cultivated for growth and maintained in a second phase by Osiris. But then disruption caused by Set creates a shift that requires reconciling through Isis's healing to restore a stable course. The phases of organization development are outlined in Greiner's (1972) description where stages of incremental growth with evolutionary changes (Osiris) are disrupted by a crisis or revolutionary changes (Set) that need to be resolved for subsequent growth (Isis). In addition to the phases of change, the mythological figures are also reflected in different Egyptian leaders.

While it is difficult to precisely trace the values and beliefs of today's Egyptian leaders back to the ancient myths and times of pharaohs, the cultural mythologies of Egypt are kept very much alive with broad diffusion through formal studies in broad educational curriculums around the world and various processes of cultural institutionalization. For example, Mubarak named the machinery for Cairo's major metro construction project Hatshepsut. An Egyptian cultural identity spawns not just one of the earliest civilizations but also evolves through a multi-layered process of broader global dynamics with Islam from the eleventh century onwards, modernization with industrial developments, and western power stakeholders in the Arab-Israeli conflict over the last several decades.

The Egyptian pantheon of gods and goddesses in cultural mythologies serves to illustrate both the conditions in different periods of cultural evolution and the characteristics of Egyptian leadership. The different conflicts and wars that Egypt engaged in are certainly captured by the mythological figure of Set. Chaos and destruction are attributed to him. Leaders such as Saladin, Muhammed Ali Pasha and Nasser can be linked to the leadership qualities of Osiris who was considered as the rightful ruler, the god of agriculture who brought humanity enlightenment and civilization. All three rulers were broadly supported by the masses albeit for different reasons. The story of Horus in defeating Set and unifying Egypt under the rule of pharaoh can be found in Sadat's storyline when he launched the 1973 October War which provided the country with a victory over Israel and led to peacemaking treaties.

The explicit role of leadership in the cultural evolutions of Egypt unfolded with international influence from as early as Cleopatra's reign to Saladin's rule and throughout to the period of Muhammed Ali Pasha's modernization spanning the nineteenth and twentieth centuries. Interestingly, all three rulers engaged in foreign conflicts and brought significant foreign influences into the country with resulting cultural transformations. For a long time, cultural transmissions in Egypt occurred on two levels: On one level was the urban ruling class of 'high culture' among the governing elites that was composed of religious scholars (*ulama*), men of letters (*udaba*), and scribal officials in government. Many of these cultural traditions originated from Arab, Persian, and Turco-Ottoman societies. On another level was the 'subject classes' that derived cultural origins from both Sufi Islam and local Egyptian traditions from the Nile Valley region. Egyptian nationalism provided the forum for socio-cultural evolution and erosion of the dualistic culture with educational reforms and diffusion from the high to subject cultural norms (Dekmejian, 1975; Gershoni, 1992). Thus, Egyptian leaders carrying forth the modernization agenda from Muhammed Ali Pasha onwards brought forth a much greater diffusion of international and western influences.

The integration of an international dimension, family life, and political engagement is a common pattern also found in Egyptian business leadership. 'Social relations, the traditional extended family structure and nepotism have a strong influence on business behavior' (Rice, 1999: 353). Just as importantly, Egyptian identity and leadership styles encompass characteristics attributed to Egyptian, Arab and Muslim cultures albeit not necessarily in equal proportions (Rice, 1999). Osman exemplifies the multiple roles of an Egyptian business leader who also served in prominent political roles in government with porous influence between the two spheres which included human resource policies from the business being influential in broader public policies. In addition, his multinational business is run much like a family business with different family members in significant leadership roles.

Egyptian leadership cultural values of service, surrendering self, truth, charity, humility, forgiveness, compassion, thankfulness, love, courage, faith, kindness, patience and hope are popular in not just the Qu'ran but also Islamic literature including Sufism (Fry, 2003; Giacalone and Jurkiewicz, 2003; Kriger and Hanson, 1999). Within the Islamic faith, researchers identified the importance of socialized power with the servant-caretaker model where the leader and the led have a reciprocal relationship (Kriger and Seng, 2005). The struggle of Egyptian leaders such as Saladin and Nasser for social justice against imperial forces certainly attracts respect from the masses and much of the Arab world. As a comparison, Sadat's leadership was not perceived in a similar servant-caretaker model and the reciprocal cycle of support broke down.

As part of the Arabic cluster based on the GLOBE studies, additional descriptions of Egyptian leadership included being high in group orientation, hierarchical, masculine, and low future orientation (Kabasakal and Bodur, 2002). Sadat's charismatic leadership style illustrated the group orientation in his extensive relationship building and maintaining key people to deal with both domestic and foreign policies (Hermann, *et al.*, 2001). His leadership is not without controversy in spite of the relationship building. Mubarak also emphasized the collective contributions of both Nasser and Sadat within public commemorations.

Many of the values identified were also found in a research study by Shahin and Wright (2004) who examined the impact of culture on Egyptian leadership styles. The research results indicated that Egyptian leaders exhibited inspirational motivation, intellectual stimulation, individualized consideration, passive management-by-exception and laissez-faire, positive leadership, social integration, and autocratic leadership. The researchers analyzed the cultural need to cooperate due to the agricultural society along the geography of the Nile and socially integrate due to Islam. The transition from the authoritarian rule of the pharaoh to the Wali in Islam was not a dramatic shift and today separating the lineage is difficult with over 13 centuries of Islamic influence in the country. At the same time, some Muslim leaders in Egypt may elicit the term 'pharaoh' to criticize a leader as a heathen ruler like the one who denounced Moses. Thus, the linkage between the images of Egyptian leadership in the past to those in the present is a complex one that is multi-dimensional, fragmented and contradictory all at the same time – see Commentary box.

## COMMENTARY BOX

### Anwar Sadat (attributed)

There can be hope only for a society which acts as one big family, not as many separate ones. There is no happiness for people at the expense of other people.

### Gamal Nasser (attributed)

I have been a conspirator for so long that I mistrust all around me. / People do not want words – they want the sound of battle – the battle of destiny.

### Hosni Mubarak (attributed)

The people gave me the responsibility of building the future of this nation. And I did it with honor.

### Mohamed Al-Fayed: Harrods Department Store Owner (attributed)

I am just a person who is human, down to earth enjoying life. Whatever god blesses you with. Enjoying life for me is just normal.

(From http://www.brainyquote.com/quotes/nationality/egyptian_ quotations. html)

## PRACTICAL APPLICATIONS

The influence of Egypt's cultural mythology on leadership has important implications for leadership practices. The coercive style of management is a common phenomenon in Egypt (Bakhtari, 1995). The coercive or authoritative manner is a style involving clear instruction to subordinates without listening to or permitting much subordinate input. Immediate compliance and obedience are expected and tight control is maintained. Egyptian firms tend to be extremely formalized and bureaucratic. In organizations characterized by coercive management, according to the western management perspective, a high level of negative energy grows. People use their creativity to work against autocratic leaders or in spite of them; they refuse to contribute positively to the organization (Wheatley, 1999). As the consultative environment is deeply engrained in the Arab Muslim mind and the Qur'an indicates that rewards will be for 'those whose affairs are a matter of counsel between them' (Naqvi, 1981), senior management should promote a consultative environment. Such an environment can nurture the creativity and originality so vital for business success today.

Rice (1999) discussed the bifurcated nature of today's Egyptian culture that creates interesting challenges for outsiders. The prevalence of Islam entails unity, trusteeship, and justice as ethical business principles but social and economic challenges lead to struggles for survival which may directly conflict with ethics. As a result, Egyptian behaviors may also include indecision, procrastination, and indifference to deal with hardships in life.

With respect to providing an enabling environment, the characteristics of the Arab culture relating to power distance and hierarchy imply that senior managers must be deeply committed to improving the environment for creativity. They must recognize the true implications of consultation and must implement a more consultative style of management. If typically risk-averse Arab employees are not provided active encouragement and do not see that their input is valued and acted upon, they will be reluctant to provide it. The transition to a free market society also raised the issue of risk taking behavior regarding entrepreneurship and how Egyptian Islamic culture shapes attitudes toward money for entrepreneurial pursuits (Farid, 2007).

In contrast to western individualistic culture, the Egyptians are an extremely collectivistic people (Hofstede, 1980) and there is ease in social interactions and formation of groups. This collectivism can result in strong group loyalty and cohesiveness (Ali, 1993) and is a potential source of beneficial 'social capital' – the resources derived from the network of relationship in a workgroup or organization (Napahiet and Ghoshal, 1998). Egyptians value the person and the relationship more than the task. The challenge for an Egyptian work team, then, is maintaining a focus on powerful influence on group performance. While this can be positive, it can simultaneously limit the group's openness to alternative ways of doing things. This would imply that employee teams should be allowed to decide how to achieve their goal; permitting such freedom and autonomy makes intrinsic motivations soar. Based on research studies of Arab managers and workplace environments, however, it is not at all clear whether this effect would occur in the high power distance of Arab culture. Another implication here is that rather than focusing on outcomes, managers should focus on how people approach work and the strategies being used, provide coaching to overcome problems and clarify approach. Zuckerman (1978) found that successful scientists typically had mentors – more senior scientists – who not only imparted knowledge but also strategies and methods for approaching problems.

Egyptian leadership will likely continue to play a significant role within an increasingly interdependent world. The cultural mythologies from the ancient past will always remain significant as people around the world seek to understand our collective human origins. For Egyptian leaders, their cultural mythologies provide not only a rich heritage to anchor valued leadership characteristics in chaotic cultural transformations but also help to inform and bridge cross-cultural understandings with outsiders in a shrinking global society.

## REFERENCES

al-Shazly, Sa'ad al-Din (1980), *The Crossing of the Suez: The October War 1973*. London: Third World Center for Research and Publications.

Ali, A. J. (1993), Decision-making style, individualism, and attitudes toward risk of Arab executives, *International Studies of Management and Organization*, **23** (3), 53–73.

Baha al-Din Ibn Shaddad (2002), *The Rare and Excellent History of Saladin* (trans. D. S. Richards), Aldershot: Ashgate.

Bakhtari, H. (1995), Cultural effects on management style: A comparative study of American and Middle Eastern management styles, *International Studies of Management and Organization*, **25** (3), 97–118.

Dekmejian, H. (1975), *Patterns of Political Leadership: Egypt, Israel, Lebanon*, Albany, NY: State University of New York Press.

Fahmy, K. (1998), The era of Muhammad Ali Pasha, 1805–1848, in M. W. Daley (ed.), *The Cambridge History of Egypt: Modern Egypt, from 1517 to the End of the Twentieth Century*, Vol. 2, Cambridge: Cambridge University Press, pp. 139–79.

Farid, M. (2007), Entrepreneurship in Egypt and the US compared: Directions for further research suggested, *Journal of Management Development*, **26** (5), 428–40.

Fry, L. W. (2003), Toward a theory of spiritual leadership, *The Leadership Quarterly*, **14**, 693–727.

Gershoni, I. (1992), The evolution of national culture in modern Egypt: intellectual formation and social diffusion, 1892–1945, *Poetics Today*, **13** (2), 325–47.

Giacalone, R. A. and Jurkiewicz, C. L. (1991), Toward a science of workplace spirituality, in R. A. Giacalone and C. L. Jurkiewicz (eds), *Handbook of Workplace Spirituality and Organizational Performance*, New York: M. E. Sharpe, Inc., 3–28.

Greiner, L. (1972), Evolution and revolution as organizations grow, *Harvard Business Review*, **50** (4), 37–49.

Heikal, M. H. (1973), *The Cairo Documents: The Inside Story of Nasser and His Relationship with World Leaders, Rebels, and Statesmen*, New York: Doubleday.

Heikal, M. H. (1983), *Autumn of Fury: The Assassination of Sadat*, London: Random House.

Hermann, M. G., Preston, T., Korany, B. and Shaw, T. M. (2001), Who leads matters: the effectives of powerful individuals, *International Studies Review*, **32**, 83–131.

Hofstede, G. (1980), *Culture's Consequences: International Differences in Work-related Values*, Beverly Hills, CA: Sage Publications, Inc.

Kabasakal, H. and Bodur, M. (2002), Arabic cluster: a bridge between east and west, *Journal of World Business*, **37** (1), 40–54.

Kirk, G. S. (1975), *Myth: Its Meaning and Functions in Ancient and Other Cultures*, Berkley, CA: University of California Press.

Kriger, M. P. and Hanson, B. J. (1999), A value-based paradigm for creating truly healthy organizations, *Journal of Organizational Change Management*, **12** (4), 302–17.

Kriger, M. and Seng, Y. (2005), Leadership with inner meaning: A contingency theory of leadership based on the worldviews of five religions, *The Leadership Quarterly*, **16**, 771–806.

Lyons, M. C. and Jackson, D. E. P. (1982), *Saladin: The Politics of the Holy War*, Cambridge: Cambridge University Press.

Meital, Y. (2003), Who is Egypt's 'Hero of war and peace'? The Contest of Representation, *History and Memory*, **15** (1), 150–83.

Napahiet, J. and Ghoshal, S. (1998), Social capital, intellectual capital and the organizational advantage, *Academy of Management Review*, **23**, 242–66.

Naqvi, S. N. H. (1981), *Ethics and Economics: An Islamic Synthesis*, Leicester: Islamic Foundation.

Nasser, G. A. (1967), Statement by President Nasser to Arab Trade Unionists, Source: http://www.mideastweb.org/nasser26may67.htm; Downloaded: 1 March 2008.

Rice, G. (1999), Islamic ethics and the implications for business, *Journal for Business Ethics*, **18** (4), 345–58.

Shahin, A. I. and Wright, P. L. (2004), Leadership in the context of culture: an Egyptian perspective, *The Leadership and Organization Development Journal*, **25** (6), 499–511.

Shaw, I. (2000), *The Oxford History of Ancient Egypt*, Oxford: Oxford University Press.

Tyldesley, J. (1998), *Hatshepsut: The Female Pharaoh*, Oxford: Penguin Books.

Vatikiotis, P. J. (1991), *The History of Modern Egypt: From Muhammad Ali to Mubarak*, Baltimore, MD: Johns Hopkins University Press.

Wheatley, M. J. (1999), *Leadership and the New Science: Discovering Order in a Chaotic World*, San Francisco, CA: Berrett-Koehler Publishers, Inc.

Zuckerman, H. (1978), Theory choice and problem choice in science, *Sociological Inquiry*, **48**, 65–95.

# 15. Cultural mythology and global leadership in Israel

## Shay S. Tzafrir, Aviv Barhom-Kidron and Yehuda Baruch

## INTRODUCTION

Israel is a country characterized as unique in many aspects, and while geographically located in the Middle East, its political, social and economical systems as well as the Jewish religion of the majority, and particularly its culture, differ substantially from its neighboring countries. These features and the scarcity of natural resources are reflected in the Israeli leadership style. The dominant national and managerial culture of Israel is close to that of Western societies (that is, the educational, political and legal systems, the welfare state, and the ethical values). With scarce natural resources, Israel looks for economic benefits from the human factor, and thus leadership plays a major role in Israeli society (Tzafrir *et al.*, 2007).

Israel has a legacy of a nation surrounded by enemies, which requires fighting against all its opponents in order to survive. One myth that helps in such endeavor and prevails from the Biblical times, throughout the life in the Diaspora, up to the establishment of the state of Israel and up to date, is being the few standing up against the many. A complementary theme, typically coupled with 'the few against the many' is that of being 'the chosen people'. Again, deeply rooted in the Bible, this theme is concerned with determination and pride, serving as self-fulfilling prophecy in many struggles along the Jewish and Israeli history.

The aim of this chapter is to present research and literature on both historical and empirical findings about leadership style and myth in Israel. Myths refer to people's sacred stories about origins, deities, ancestors and heroes. Within a culture, myths serve as the divine charter, and myth and ritual are inextricably bounded (Schwartz, 2004: xliv). Myth does not need to be empirical history but a story that makes something psyche in our souls (Gabriel, 1991). Myths compel respect, not necessarily because they are true, but because they are needed. A myth that has survived has met legitimate needs in time and place. It reflects the way a particular individual or group of individuals attempts to establish a distinct identity, and often is vital in laying the basis for a societal self-perception (Schmidt, 2004). The unique integration of historical and empirical facts illuminates the origin of Jewish/Israeli leadership style, and its present and future directions in Israel. In our analysis, we first highlight the relationship between myth and Judaism. We than present famous myths and discuss how these myths build and develop a comprehensive pattern of Israeli leadership across history. We further explicate how dominant cultural values are extrapolated from them. Next, we discuss how leaders have led in the past in order to understand the leadership myth while trying to explore what is going to happen next in the Israeli leadership arena. Finally, we examine how we can utilize these insights in working relationships with leaders from Israel. Our analysis is at both national and individual level, and is based on circumstantial evidence and logical argument.

## OVERVIEW OF MYTH AND JUDAISM

Myth is not a simple, clear-cut concept, but a complex phenomenon that can be explained differently from various perspectives. Myths are meant to create attitudes, stir emotions, and help construct particular social realities conductive to the purposes of those transmitting the myth (Ben-Yehuda, 1995). Myths constitute very central motivating forces in a variety of domains such as politics, economy, religion and education (Hegy, 1991). Heyne and Herder became interested in local customs and legends, and found myths to be an expression of the intuitive and traditional knowledge of national and local particularities – in short, of the people's soul (see Weik, 2001, 13). Thus, understanding the perceived myth from any country should not ignore its background, in this case, the fact that Israel is a society populated by a majority group, namely Hebrew-speaking Jews (76 per cent of the population). *Encyclopedia Judaica* (Berenbaum and Kolnik, 2007) helps us to connect myth and Judaism by providing a specific definition for myth: A myth is "a story about the universe that is considered sacred. Such a story deals with the great moments of a person's life: birth, initiation, and death, referring them to events that took place in mythical times in 'mythical times' ". They added that myths are often recited during a dramatic representation of the event they narrate, and conclude that 'Through the ritual, man becomes contemporary with the mythical event and participates in the God's creative actions' (p. 710). Let us explore the roots and development of the local mythology in Israel, and how it builds on the past.

The most profound 'mythology' underpinning Israeli culture is the Bible (the Old Testament). The Bible not only serves as the basis to the monotheistic religions (Judaism, Christianity and Islam), but also as the basic way of education, values and culture for most Israelis. The Bible encompasses a wide range of stories, relating to both general human values and the unique case of creation of a national, religion-based identity, under the strong leadership of several key figures. Further, Israel develops by using its relative advantage in a range of areas such as military to high-tech by shifting the knowledge from one to another. Thus, we focus in this section on myths that shape the local mythology in social, political, military and economical issues.

Just when the Biblical stories move from the general story of the creation to the roots of Judaism, one of the first strong narratives is that of Abraham and his argument with the Lord. This case represents the vital principles of distributive and procedural justice. Realizing that God almighty might be making an unfair decision (destroying Sodom and Gomorrah), Abraham starts arguing with God, requesting justice (under the principle of not destroying good people together with the evil ones), and haggling with God, until gaining a promise that God will alter his plan if there are ten righteous people living in Sodom and Gomorrah. Here we witness the value of justice, so strong that it allows a mortal human being to challenge God to give them a hearing before deciding. A bit of *Chutzpa* (and it is quite revealing that the word Chutzpa does not exist as an English word) and determination, coupled with strong negotiation skills.

While the Abraham story is about individual values, Moses represents the archetypical leader. He sets a vision, provides individual example, takes risks, represents his people against Pharaoh, the Egyptian ruler, and leads his people into a dangerous journey to the Promised Land. Moses knows how to delegate (for example fighting is done under the guidance of professional fighters while he provides the moral and supports the morale), ready to learn from consultants (for example when Jethro advises him how to create a hierarchical managerial structure), and prepare the next generation of leadership to follow him. Moving ahead, King David represents a different leadership style, more political, interwoven with internal struggles and battles against external enemies. Also, King David is the combination of a warrior, poet, ruler, unifying the nation and making it a significant regional power. Yet, his personal values manifest mixed morality. Moreover, King David's son, Solomon, is well established in the narratives of wisdom and Jewish genius. The story about King Solomon's trial (the dispute over the baby, which he suggests to cut in two, and this way reveals the true mother) offers deep understanding of human psychology and manifests both wisdom and justice. To end the biblical mythology, one needs to note the lack of gender balance. Very few women heroines appear, as was typical in those days. Debora the prophet is an exception to the rule, where she is the leader figure admired by the people, and only with her blessing is the military leadership ready to charge for the battle (which is won, by the help of another female, Yael). The absence of female leadership is manifested in many other areas; even though Israel was one of the first nations to elect a female political leader (Golda Meir), she was not a female-type person (Ben Gurion is alleged to have said that 'she is the only *man* in the cabinet').

Justice, wisdom, and other humans' knowledge, ability and benevolence are one part of the equation. The other part is the belief in God. Thus, the internal and external trust served as a unique source of power for Judaism. This can be learned, for example, in the ten plagues afflicted by God himself as well as many other interventions by God and his messengers. Nevertheless, there is no reference in the Bible of faith such as the Christian or Islamic sense of the term. That is not to say that faith does not exist – but rather implicitly as a confidence in God. In Judaism the primary emphasis is not on profession of faith but on conduct. According to Yehudah Halevi, a medieval Jewish philosopher, belief applies only to things known by means of authority, and God possesses all knowledge and understanding. Accordingly, belief is an acceptance of the doctrines of Scripture based on authority. Maimonides, on the other hand, maintains that belief applies only to things known by way of demonstration. Belief is more than verbal acceptance; it requires understanding and a rational basis. While in medieval philosophy the description of faith formed an integral part of the theory of knowledge, the rise of modern science and the concomitant decline of belief in the divine revelation of Scriptures have made faith a matter of trust in God rather than of the affirmation of certain propositions. Martin Buber and Abraham Heschel see faith as a relationship of trust between man and God, which arises from, and manifests itself, in personal encounters between man and God, and man and man, which Buber calls the I-Thou relationships. Another tendency among modern philosophers, which reflects the influence of psychology, is to view belief as a psychological state which is valuable insofar as it motivates man to act in an ethical manner (Berenbaum and Kolnik, 2007). Thus, trust and confidence could help us to understand many other narratives in Jewish history.

The Masada mythical narratives for legacy of freedom as well as stand of a few against the many, ready to pay the ultimate cost to avoid betrayal of their religion and slavery, have served as very important functions for the Zionists as well as for military purposes. Along the same line are the freedom fights of the Maccabees (Hebrew *Makabim*), a national liberation movement in the second century BC that fought for and won independence from the Hellenistic Antiochus IV Epiphanes, and later, the military uprising of Bar-Cochva, against the Roman army, that have led to the exile to the Diaspora. A different manifestation of bravery coupled with trust in God is in the story of Daniel and the lions' den.

The symbol of Jewish heroism was constructed, delivered, and believed as an authentic emphasized proud Jews fighting for their liberty and land and helped to create and maintain a 2000-year-old link alive. This narrative carried the legacy through the Warsaw Ghetto rebellion against the Nazis, into the underground movements during the Turkish, and then the British rule in Palestine of the first half of the twentieth century, the Israeli army, and later on, into Israeli schools and youth movements. Individuals drew their strength to stand up to some real and utterly horrendous historical challenges from this myth. However, during the late 1970s much of the myth was already dissipating (Ben-Yehuda, 1995). The possible reasons for this vary, but one major reason is the 'wake-up call' of the Yom Kippur war, where initially the Israeli army was caught by surprise and suffered significant casualties. This was coupled with a significant disillusionment with the political system (leading later to political upheaval in 1977).

Yosef Trumpeldor is known as the Tel-Hay hero and a symbol of self-sacrifice for the country. He established the He-Halutz movement in Russia, whose aim was to organize and prepare young Jews for settlement in Eretz Israel. Trumpeldor was asked to organize the defense of the settlements, and reached Tel-Hay. Soon after (early in 1920), the settlement was attacked by a large number of armed Arabs. During negotiations with their leaders, an exchange of fire took place in which Trumpeldor received a fatal stomach wound (Berenbaum and Kolnik, 2007). Toward evening, Trumpeldor was evacuated, but died on the way. His last words were, '*Ein davar, tov lamut be'ad arzenu*' ('Never mind; it is good to die for our country'). The life and death of Trumpeldor became a symbol to pioneer youths and military service as a leader ready to fulfill himself what he was asking from others (Laskov, 1982).

Ghetto revolts and other armed Jewish resistance during the Holocaust are among the formative elements of Israeli Holocaust collective memory and Israeli national identity. The armed Jewish resistances play a central role in making the resistance an important element of Israeli identity. Their fighting in the spirit of Massada has been integrated into the narrative of national heroics (Cohen, 2003). This special case of fighting during the Holocaust strengthens the myth of the stand of a few against the many when life hangs by a thread in order to cope with massively pressuring circumstances.

Another legacy building on medieval myth is the Jewish as learners, wise and bright. While many nations built their wealth on agriculture and heroic legends on fighting (for example the knights stories), the Jewish were typically forbidden from owning land, thus wealth creation was typically in finance and banking, whereas the heroes were the Torah rabbinical students. The myth of the 'Jewish genius' as a problem solver shapes the high-tech industry by building, developing and investing major effort in entrepreneurship of start-ups in pharmaceutical, bio-tech, electronics and so on in the high-tech sector. These start-up products have attracted new global investors such as IBM, Intel, HP and Motorola, which have made significant investments in the Israeli economy (Tzafrir and Eitam-Meilik, 2005). Over the last three decades, Israel's home-grown high-tech market has expanded dramatically (Yeheskel *et al.*, 2001; Zilber, 2007). These leaders represent the culture of initiation, entrepreneur-ship, high ambition, great talent and improvisation ability, characteristics of Israeli management (Baruch, 2001). We elaborate on these elements later in the economical and industrial leadership section.

## OVERVIEW OF ISRAELI LEADERSHIP

Archetypical Leader may emerge from many different arenas. Clearly one cannot cover the full range of such arenas and their unique consequences in a single chapter; however, the strength of our division to political, economical, and military limited to the independence period will well reflect on Israel building and development over recent decades. In Israel, which gained inde-pendence in 1948, history and mythological leaders played a significant role in the struggles for independence, and in the fight of existence ever since. In later years, the feelings of independence and strength as well as the moving towards individualistic values (versus collectivist ones) led to that self-reflection often associated with abandonment of several myths. Much of this followed 'wake-up calls' succeeding major events, mostly wars (like the euphoria after the Six Days war, or the crisis following the Yom Kippur war, and the mourning of Rabin's assassination).

### Political Leadership

The establishment of the State of Israel in 1948 strengthened the dominance of political elites in the elite structure. The dominance of political power arose from five main sociopolitical factors: the political elites' control of state resources (political, material, and symbolic); the importance of the Arab-Israeli conflict; immigration absorption; the internal solidarity of the political elite, especially among the leaders of the leading party, Mapai; and, finally, the weakness of the other elites (Horowitz and Lissak, 1989). However, the estab-lishment of the state, in addition, led to increasing differentiation of the vari-ous elites from the political elite, such as the new state-administrative elite (Maman, 1997).

Our mythical journey starts with one of the most representative of the generation of Israel's founding fathers, David Ben-Gurion. Early biographies, written shortly after the establishment of the state, clearly identified Ben-Gurion with a myth (Keren, 2000). Ben-Gurion employed authoritarian lead-ership combined with certain democratic norms and values. For example, in the 1950s, serving as its first Prime Minister and Minister of Defense, Ben-Gurion led Israel's state-building efforts, absorbing Jewish immigrants from the wide Diaspora, establishing a working democracy, and constructing a modern army as well as various enterprises. Ben-Gurion is also remembered for his attempts to establish a new mission, rejuvenating the desert. In 1953, as part of his call for young Jews to settle in the Negev desert, he moved his residence to 'Sde-Boker', a Kibbutz in the Negev (Keren, 2000).

Golda Meir was the first Israeli woman to take over the Prime Minister role and as such she served as an image of a strong equal opportunity myth (Lieblich and Friedman, 1985). Even though she was clear about the fact that she was neither a feminist nor sympathetic to the feminist movement, in biography after biography she is portrayed as an ideal woman, not only as 'the uncrowned queen of Israel' but also as 'Israel's intrepid grandmother', a successful politician who also possessed the essence of motherly 'warmth and wisdom'. Meir was a shining example for other women not only in exemplifying how to fulfill their potential but also of their ambivalent feelings. Accordingly, Meir did not fit into the feminist myth, but to a myth of motherly/grandmotherly figure. Despite her major contributions to the founding and building of the state of Israel, after the Yom Kippur War in 1973 she was afraid that she would be remembered for this one thing only (Schmidt, 2004) and as criticism directed at Minister of Defense Dayan and her continued, Meir decided to resign (Diermeier and Roozendaal, 1998).

Menachem Begin had a heroic view of leadership. He was a gallant, authoritarian, and at the same time kind, honorable and decent gentleman (Hurwitz, 1994). Begin's character as a leader was shaped, above all, in the relationship developed with the masses. Throughout his long political career, he displayed a brilliant ability to control his followers. Begin's most conspicuous leadership quality was his orator's skill. He brought the use of rhetoric for political ends to a great height (Sofer, 1988). It was not only his oratorical skills that made the impression, but the content of his speeches, his statements and the logic of his argumentation (Hurwitz, 1994). Begin accepted the notion that Judaic religion and nationality are inseparable (Sofer, 1988), in line with the Israeli declaration of independence. He viewed the modern state as the continuation of the long saga of an ancient people and stressed this fact in his speeches and articles (Hurwitz, 1994). He was closed to the view that the establishment of the state and the liberation of the homeland, after the Holocaust, marked the beginning of Messianic redemption. From that point of view, Begin objected Ben-Gurion's dictum that Israel is merely a state of law (Sofer, 1988).

Yitzhak Rabin's case manifests the Israeli political and military in terms of myth and leadership. Following a long army career, starting in the Palmach, the pre-state commando forces, he served Israel as the Chief of Staff during the Six Days war and was elected twice as the prime minister. The tragedy of Rabin's assassination is of unique importance to the Israeli collective memory. In shaping collective identity, collective memory builds on dramatic events to serve as symbolic milestones in the collective history. The Rabin myth that developed following the assassination is highly significant in that it forms part of the nation-constitutive myth. The media promoted the political ritual surrounding Rabin, building the myth of the man who became a symbol in his death. The media used elements of Rabin's biography to shape a collective memory in order to construct a collective identity for Israeli society. 'He was us,' wrote Yonatan Geffen (*Ma'ariv,* 6 November, 1995).

Although the assassination took place nearly 50 years after the establishment of the state in 1948, it is related to the 'battle for peace'. The fact that in November 1995 Israelis were still dealing with the story of the 1948 War of Independence was expressed in the description of Rabin's death. His death was portrayed not as a passive act of weakness, but as an act of heroic sacrifice and supreme courage – the fall of a soldier on the battlefield. The death of Rabin turned him into a 'peacemaker', the symbol of Israeli society's longing for peace (Peri, 1999). This myth serves as a basis for the invented tradition (Hobsbaum and Ranger, 1983) on which the imagined political community is built (Anderson, 1987; Bhabha, 1990). This myth is fostered by various 'state cults' and provides them with legitimacy (Azaryahu, 1995: 8–10). The battle that Rabin was fighting was widely described as 'the battle for peace' that would bring the War of Independence to an end. Rabin called himself 'a soldier of peace' (Peri, 1996), and that was how King Hussein eulogized him at the funeral: 'Yitzhak Rabin lived as a soldier and died as a soldier for peace' ('The Speech of King Hussein,' Ha'aretz, 1995: A4). This image continued to follow him in the collective memory. Peri (1999) described that the most dramatic expression of the attempt to make Rabin a mythical, larger-than-life hero was the reference to him as someone still living in the world above, appealing to him directly to act from there. Signs of deification were evident in sentences such as, 'Guard me from above, because I'm afraid now', which appeared on stickers, graffiti and posters, and in songs, such as one that said, 'Be strong up there', and in a poster relating to him in words taken from a prayer addressed to God, 'He who makes peace in the heights'.

## Economical and Industrial Leadership

The separate formation of the economic elite from the political elite originated with changes in the political and economical structure. It was not surprising then that socialism was the leading socio-economic ideology during the first decades of Israel's existence. This helped to generate a strong sense of cohesion in the country and enabled it to cope with enormous difficulties such as security and the heterogeneity of its population. Tzafrir *et al.* (2007) summarized that global and political changes (the loss of the hegemony of the ruling Labour Party in 1977) were the driving forces behind shifting ideology from the social model to the capitalist one. Since the early 1990s Israel's core economy has been composed largely of high-tech companies (including pharmaceutical), alongside more traditional markets like textiles and agriculture with extensive investment in high technology. Reflecting on the above, we will draw one organizational example and discuss several individual leaders.

The Israeli hostile environment raising defensive needs and the Jewish genius create an outstanding defense industry. The creativity and new products development (high-tech in nature) resulting in a huge success in the battle fields gave the defense industry a special status in Israel. Rafael is a fine example of a legendary organization, nationally owned, with roots set up before the establishment of the state. Rafael with its expertise gained extensive experience in design, development, and production of weapon systems in several arenas such as Satellite Propulsion Systems and Air-to-Air Missiles. Rafael's core employees comprising scientists, engineers, and experienced employees have managed to be at the cutting edge of high-tech and develop most progressed systems under professional leadership at all levels in the organization.

The defense industry symbolizes one part of this phenomenon while military leadership represents the other part. The military elite represents one of the most powerful elites in Israel and established its power from several sources. First, the significant meaning of the Arab-Israeli and Israel-Palestine conflicts. Second, the military elite's relative autonomy, the extension of IDF and defense system functions to many civil areas, the IDF's organizational growth following the 1973 Yom Kippur war and, above all, the centrality of security issues in the Israeli experience (Grinberg, 1991; Kimmerling, 1993). Last but not least is the significant proportions of high-ranking officers' contacts with people in other elite groups who were once themselves part of the military elite (Maman, 1997). There are many examples for the diffusion from the military arena to national politics (Dayan, Rabin, Sharon, to mention a few), local (Mitzna, Holadai, and others) as well as to the business one (for example, Peri, Ben-Noon). The shift from military leadership to civilian and the importance of these leaders to daily life in Israel is an example per se for how strong and relevant is the role of military leadership in Israel.

## Business Leadership

Examples of specific individual leadership in the industry will be manifested by the cases of Horvitz, Wertheimer, Lautman and Shwed: Eli Horvitz is an example of a leader with a great business vision. He led Teva, a pharmaceutical company, from a modest organization to a significant MNC in the global market. Constant entrepreneur, he expanded the company through mergers and acquisitions, keeping public activities (including chairing the Israeli Confederation of Business and Industry) alongside his industrial leadership (Sasover, 2001; www.education.gov.il/pras-israel). Like Horowitz, Stef Wertheimer started his career in the military – in the pre-Israel commando, and moved to the industry. Following his vision, he established Iscar, which has now become one of the two leading global firms in production of metal cutting tools and techniques for machining. Its innovative products, home-designed, have made Iscar a world leader in manufacturing industries such as automotive, aerospace and die and mold production (www.education.gov.il/pras-israel). Similarly, Lautman moved to the business world after a successful short military career, and became a global entrepreneur in the textile business. Later he became involved in public services in roles such as chair of the Israeli Confederation of Business and Industry and an ambassador for peace and progress of Israel's industry. People like Stef Wertheimer and Dov Lautman not only declare a business vision but integrate their vision into the Zionist vision to contribute to the economical flourishing of Israel.

Gil Shwed represents the younger generation of entrepreneurs starting-up and leading high-tech, IT companies. He is the founder, Chairman of the Board and Chief Executive Officer of Check Point Software Technologies Ltd, the leader in internet security. In 1993, Shwed invented and patented Stateful Inspection, now a de facto standard technology. Together with two co-founders, he wrote the first version of FireWall-1, the company's flagship software solution that became the world's first commercially available firewall product in 1994. During the following years, he led Check Point to be a leader in both firewall and VPN (virtual private networks) markets. Check Point redefined the internet security landscape, a multi-billion dollar industry, under Shwed's leadership. The company has operations around the world, and its intelligent security solutions secure hundreds of thousands of customers, including 100 percent of Fortune 100 (Asis, www.nrg.co.il, 2000; www.checkpoint.com/corporate/gilshwed). Shwed and Check Point are not an isolated example. Mirabilis, another Israeli firm, that invented the internet ICQ search engine, was bought by AOL for over $400M in the late 1990s.

## COMMENTARY BOX

### Commander of the Israeli Air Force

When asked about leadership, Major General Eliezer Shkedy said that it is essential to say what you think, no matter what your rank is. This is a sign for openness to critical thinking, and organizational democracy. Young pilots will operate as leaders to those senior to them on certain activities and will learn to be the future leaders.

### CEO of NICE Systems

The leader as a source of inspiration came also from the business sector. Mr Haim Shani indicated that their challenge is to identify uprising leaders that can take others with them with their initiative and passion.

### Chairman of Macabi Tel Aviv Basketball Team

This sentiment fits well with recent writing on leadership, whereas other accepted leadership qualities are appreciated. For example, the Chairman of Macabi Tel Aviv basketball team, former Europe champion, talked about the leader as one who is ready to take risks and responsibility, using the example of who will take the critical shot in the last seconds of a basketball game.

### CEO of Fisher Pharmaceutics

Dr Fisher praised the ability of Israelis to be entrepreneurs, but at the same time to collaborate with down-to-earth managers in order to take the great ideas and enable them to materialize.

### Expert Consultant for Political Leadership

Moving to the political arena, Prof Yechezkel Dror is more skeptical about the effectiveness of the governance in the Israeli political system. He argued that it is much harder to develop and establish political leadership in the complex political environment of post-1967 Israel. Yet Israel benefited from leaders who had the bravery, self assurance, and zeal, as manifested in former Prime Ministers on both sides of the political map – for example, Rabin and Sharon.

# GLOBAL IMPLICATIONS

Stepping into the twenty-first century, Israel has to cope with globalization, a volatile and dynamic high technology-dominated environment, diffusion of a new generation, and a hostile environment. These require an advanced leadership to keep the cohesion of the people in order to deal with new emerging problems. Harel and Tzafrir (1999) mentioned that Israel provides a convenient laboratory for researchers and practitioners in as much as it is a 'Maduradam' (microcosm) for leadership in small countries that based their market position on their human capital. Therefore, many small countries who wish to gain economic development could learn and benefit from the analysis of the case of Israel as a departure point for their growth.

Since the beginning of Jewish history and Abraham, as the first Jewish leader, the Jewish and Israeli leadership have shared several characteristics in common: (a) the myth of 'a few against many' helps to unify the group into achieving common goals and missions; (b) using human capital as a source for competitive advantage is strengthened via the myth of the 'Jewish genius'; (c) the myth of the 'pioneer' leading the way to entrepreneurship with great vision in various domains; and (d) 'justice' as a guiding principle helps to create a collectivist environment and to cope with constraints. These principles, coupled with incredible trust in God, moral and legal rights, and competence, have guided many Israeli leaders since the beginning of its history.

Each of the above four myths is manifested by and drives Israeli leaders to behave in creating a unique national culture. These myths help leaders to lead and transform the ideas of a democratic Jewish state into a reality. For example, the myth of 'a few against many' has encouraged both political and military leaders to unite the nation in the face of attacks and possible collapse. Such were David Ben-Gurion's decisions on the establishment of the State of Israel in 1948 despite the overwhelming presence of enemies, and Yitzhak Rabin, as Israeli military Chief of Staff, in the Six Days war leading an exceptional winning campaign against many countries served as the basis for the wide international agreement for Israeli borders. Second, the high-tech industry is an exceptional example manifesting the myth of 'Jewish genius' as a reality. Israel is one of the global leaders in the high-tech industry because of both internal and external phenomena. The external phenomena via an increasing investment of multinational firms in building and maintaining research and development laboratories. The internal one synthesizes national firms that have reached a significant export success with different products (such as the defense industry) as well as national firms which become a multinational organization – Teva for example (Yeheskel *et al.*, 2001). The integration of the myths of the 'Jewish genius' with the myth of the 'pioneer', plays a major role for business leaders' success. The examples presented of Horvitz, Wertheimer,

Lautman and Shwed paved the way for business pioneers and many translated their dreams into reality, trusting the Israeli's human capital in establishment and development of their companies. Finally, the state of Israel, according to the myth of 'justice' states, offers equal rights for all its citizens. This terminology of justice is also serving the Israeli Supreme Court to protect equal rights for minorities.

## PRACTICAL APPLICATION

What can people from different nations learn in order to better understand how the Israeli mythology works, and engage effectively with Israeli leaders? The answer varies across issues. Political leaders are caught in between the needs to be strong, in particular military-wise because of the continuous threats that have accompanied Israel and its people for over a century, and do not seem to fade away. While in any country, economy, culture, external and internal issues are very important, in Israel, life depends at the outset on security issues. The very existence of Israel as a nation requires constant struggle, and thus, security is crucial for day-to-day living. A person who deals with Israeli leaders must understand this and take it into account when negotiating, because political leaders are well aware that this is existential and as a result, serves as a crucial measure for their evaluation in the future.

There is a clear need to prompt and progress creativity and innovation with great confidence in abilities, knowledge, and competence in facilitating new ideas into reality. Israeli businessmen are happy to be entrepreneurs, take risks, and exploit inventions and their human capital (Avrahami and Lerner, 2003). Their leaders capitalize on these qualities, as can be seen from how the MBA flourished in Israel, in line with western norms and practice (Baruch and Peiperl, 2000). Nevertheless, one must acknowledge the fact that a shift from collectivist to individualist society has recently emerged. There is a clear change, where Americanization has taken over, and money speaks, so doing a business requires more than just a dream. Finally, global companies which recruit and/or work with Israeli employees have to understand and utilize the direct attitude of their local employees and managers.

Trying to aggregate Israeli leadership style is easier said than done. Taking the entire context of this chapter, one could ask how the past and the present history will shape leadership behavior for the future. In this chapter we discussed several characteristics for driving Israeli leadership that exemplify the attitudes and actions in a political and business context. There are, of course, many other possible causes of behavioral outcomes in addition to these, personality traits for example, but they are beyond the scope of this chapter. Turning back to our point of departure helps us to summarize the possible weaknesses as well as strengths of Israeli leadership style. The combination of some myths, such as 'pioneer' and 'Jewish genius' with trust and confidence in their knowledge, skills, and abilities, convinced the Israeli leadership to initiate and to encourage entrepreneurship. Specifically, many Israelis establishing start-up companies that are building on inspiring ideas and dreams have based their progress on informal relationships. This is in line with Hofstede's study (1980), where Israeli culture has a very low power distance. Thus, on the one hand investors in Israeli high-tech firms need to check the balance between organizational life stage and the human resource management formal system. This recommendation is one step ahead from Krau (1993) who believed that the need for achievement explains the lack of planning among Israeli managers: they do not plan – they improvise. On the other hand, firms need to pay attention to the difference between the stage of creating knowledge and the stage of knowledge utilization.

Concerning the above, investors as well as other people doing business with Israeli business people should realize that they will not get into a dead-end road. The fighting spirit based on the combination of 'a few against many' and the Jewish genius helps to encourage creative ideas until the last minute. Nevertheless, this attitude and behavior could bias rational decision making, reinforcing the illusion that we can always win and survive even under awful circumstances, for example, neglecting the economic idea of sunk cost. Last but not least, Tzafrir *et al.* (2007) argued that in the earlier days of Israel it had a clear collectivist culture, but the shift towards individualistic society is stronger now than ever, and is reflected also in business behavior. Thus, managers look for individual success and use the organization as a vehicle to achieve it which could impact the level of team work. However, team work still exists, representing one of the major strengths of Israeli industry. Thus, this change is performing in accordance with the myth of justice, proving that myths do survive in day-by-day reality.

# REFERENCES

Aharoni, Y. (1991), *The Israeli Economy: Dreams and Realities*, London and New York: Routledge.

Anderson, B. (1987), *Imagined Communities*, London: Verso.

Asis, Y. (2000), Gil Shwed – Check point CEO: A rare mix of manager and entrepreneur in Hebrew, www.nrg.co.il

Avrahami, Y. and Lerner, M. (2003), The effect of combat service and military rank on entrepreneurial careers: The case of Israeli MBA graduates, *Journal of Political and Military Sociology*, **31** (1), 97–118.

Azaryahu, M. (1995), *State Cults*, Sede Boker: Ben Gurion University Press, in Hebrew.

Baruch, Y. (2001), Management in Israel. An entry, in M. Warner (ed.) *IEMB Management in Europe,* Tampa, FL: Thompson International, pp. 267–73.

Baruch, Y. and Peiperl, M. A. (2000), Career management practices: An experimental survey and theoretical complications, *Human Resource Management*, **39** (4), 347–66.

Ben Yehuda, N. (1995), *The Masada Myth: Collective Memory and Myth Making in Israel*, Madison, WI: University of Wisconsin Press.

Berenbaum, M. and Kolnik, F. (eds) (2007), *Encyclopedia Judaica* (2nd edn), Detroit, MI: Macmillan.

Bhabha, H. K. (1990), *Dissemination: Time, Narrative and the Margins of theModem Nation,* in Homi K. Bhabha (ed.), *Nation and Narration*, London: Routledge, pp. 290–322.

Bichler, S. (1991), *The political economy of military spending in Israel*, Unpublished Doctoral Dissertation, Hebrew University of Jerusalem, in Hebrew.

Cassirer, E. (1923 / 1994), *Philosophie der symbolischen Formen [Philosophy of symbolic forms]*, Darmstadt, Germany: Wissenschaftliche Buchgesellschaft.

Cohen, B. (2003), Holocaust heroics: Ghetto fighters and partisans in Israeli society and historiography, *Journal of Political and Military Sociology*, **31** (2), 197–213.

Diermeier, D. and van Roozendaal, P. (1998), The duration of cabinet formation processes in western multi-party democracies, *British Journal of Political Science,* **28** (4), 609–26.

Eisenstadt, S. N. (1985), *The Transformation of Israeli Society: An Essay in Interpretation*, London: Weidenfeld and Nicolson.

Eliade, M. (1963), *Myth and Reality*, New York: Harper and Row.

Gabriel, Y. (1991), On organizational stories and myths: Why it is easier to slay a dragon than to kill a myth, *International Sociology*, **6** (4), 427–42.

Gil Shwed: www.checkpoint.com/corporate/gilshwed

Grinberg, L. L. (1991), *Split Corporatism in Israel*, New York, NY: State University of New York Press.

Groleman, D., Boyatzis, R. E. and McKee, A. (2008), *Primal Leadership: Realizing the Power of Emotional Intelligence*, Cambridge, MA: Harvard Business School Press.

Harel, G. and Tzafrir, S. S. (1999), The effect of human resource management practices on the perceptions of organizational and market performance of the firm, *Human Resource Management*, **38** (3), 185–99.

Hegy, P. (1991), *Myth as Foundation for Society and Values: A Sociological Analysis,* Lewiston, NY: Edwin Melen Press.

Hobsbaum, E. and Ranger, T. (eds) (1983), *The Invention of Tradition*, Cambridge: Cambridge University Press.

Hofstede, G. (1980) *Culture's Consequences. International Differences in Work-Related Values*, London: Sage.

Horowitz, D. and Lissak, M. (1989), *Trouble in Utopia: The Overburdened Polity of Israel*, New York: State University of New York Press.

Hubner, K. (1985), *Die Wahrheit des Mythos [The Truth of Myth]*, Munich: C. H. Beck.

Hurwitz, H. Z. (1994), *Begin: A Portrait*, Washington: B'nai-B'rith.

Kant, I. (1781 / 1986), *Kritik der reinen Vernunft [Critique of Pure Reason]*, Frankfurt: Suhrkamp.

Keren, M. (2000), Biography and historiography: The case of David Ben-Gurion, *Biography*, **23** (2), 332–51.

Kimmerling, B. (1993), Patterns of militarism in Israel, *European Journal of Sociology*, **2**, 1–28.

Krau Edgar (1993), Values of managers of Israeli organizations, in A. Shenhar and A. Yarkoni (eds) *Israeli Management Culture*, Tel Aviv: Cherikover, pp. 147–68.

Lang, R. (1996), Wandel von Untemehmenskulturen in Ostdeutschland and Osteuropa [Change of corporate cultures in East Germany and East Europe], in R. Lang (ed.) *Wandel von Unternehmenskulturen in Ostdeutschland and Osteuropa*, Munich: Hampp, pp. 7–21.

Laskov, S. (1982), *Trumpeldor: His Life Story*, Jerusalem: Keter (In Hebrew).

Lieblich, A. and Friedman, G. (1985), Attitudes toward male and female homosexuality and sex-role stereotypes in Israeli and American students, *Sex Roles*, 12 (5/6), 561–70.

Lissak, M. (1981), *The Elites of the Jewish Community in Palestine*, Tel Aviv: Am Oved Publishers (in Hebrew).

Maman, D. (1997), The elite structure in Israel: A socio-historical analysis, *Journal of Political and Military Sociology*, 25 (1) 25–46.

Peri, Y. (1996), Afterword-Rabin: from 'Mr. Security' to Nobel Prize winner, in Y. Rabin (ed.) *The Rabin Memoirs*, Berkeley, CA: University of California Press, pp. 339–79.

Peri, Y. (1999), The media and collective memory of Yitzhak Rabin's remembrance, *Journal of Communication*, 49 (3), 106–24.

Pras Israel: www.education.gov.il/pras-israel

Rafael: http://www.rafael.co.il/marketing/homepage.aspx?FolderID=203

Reissig, R. (1994), *Transformation: theoretisch-konzeptionelle Ansatze, Erklarungen and Interpretationen [Transformation: Theoretical-conceptual Approaches, Explanations, and Interpretations]*, Riga, Latvia: BISS Public.

Rosenfeld, H. and Carmi, S. (1976), The privatization of public means, state-made middle class, and the realization of family value in Israel, in J. P. Peristinay (ed.) *Kinship and Modernization in Mediterranean Society*, Rome: Center for Mediterranean Studies.

Sasover, D. (2001), The balance of Eli Horvitz at the head of the flagship (in Hebrew), www.nrg.co.il

Schmidt, S. (2004), Hagiography in the Diaspora: Golda Meir and her biographers, *American Jewish History*, 92 (2), 157–88.

Schwartz, H. (2004), *Tree of Souls: The Mythology of Judaism*, Oxford: Oxford University Press.

Shalev, M. (1992), *Labour and the Political Economy in Israel*, Oxford: Oxford University Press.

Smith, A. D. (1991), *National Identity*, Reno, NV: University of Nevada Press.

Sofer, S. (1988), *Begin: An Anatomy of Leadership*, Oxford: Basil Blackwell.

Speech of King Hussein of Jordan, The (1995), Haaretz, 7 November, p. A4.

Tzafrir, S. S. and Eitam-Meilik, M. (2005), The impact of downsizing on trust and employee practices: A longitudinal analysis in high tech firms, *The Journal of High Tech Management Research*, 16, 193–207.

Tzafrir, S. S., Baruch, Y. and Meshoulam, I. (2007), HRM in Israel – New challenges, *International Journal of Human Resource Management*, 181, 114–31.

Weik, E. (2001), Myths in transformation processes, *International Studies of Management and Organization*, 31 (2), 9–27.

Yeheskel, O., Senkar, O., Fiegenbaun, A., Cohen, E. and Geffen, I. (2001), Cooperative wealth creation: strategic alliances in Israeli medical technology ventures, *The Academy of Management Executive*, 15 (1), 16–25.

Zilber, T. B. (2007), Stories and the discursive dynamics of institutional entrepreneurship: The case of Israeli high-tech after the bubble', *Organization Studies*, **28** (7), 1035–54.

PART IV

Asia and the Pacific Rim

# 16. Cultural mythology and global leadership in China

## Diana J. Wong-MingJi

### INTRODUCTION

This chapter explores *shen-hua; shen* means 'god', 'divine', 'holy' and *hua* means 'speech', 'oral narrative' or myths to explore Chinese leadership. The *shen-huas* provide insights into Chinese leadership and the culture as well as for Chinese managers to reflect upon their own heritage. The following discussion outlines major historical shifts in Chinese culture with broad brush strokes before outlining a sampling of *shen-huas* and their impact on leadership in a rapidly changing global context.

China is one of the most ancient civilizations dating back over 5000 years. The national origin of China dates back to the Qin dynasty in 221 BC to 206 BC but numerous dynasties can be traced further back to a legendary period of about 3000 BC (Yang and An, 2005). China has had four different political systems – feudal before 221 BC, imperial 221 BC to 1912, republican 1912–49, and communist 1949 to present. During the Cultural Revolution (1966–76), the Po Si Jiu Campaign (Destroy the Four Old Things – old thoughts, old culture, old customs and old habits) called for the destruction of obstacles to communism (Yang and An, 2005). Cultural artifacts, statues, and temples of mythical beings were destroyed. Storytelling of myths became taboo and worshipping deities went underground until the last decade.

Within a relatively large isolated geographical area hemmed in by deserts, mountains, and seas, 56 nationalities make up China. The Han is the dominant group at about 92 percent of 1.3 billion Chinese people. Hence, Chinese myths evolved as scattered and fragmented pieces that are derived from sources including bones, shells, pottery, paintings, bronze vessels, written records and oral traditions (Birrell, 1993). In 1984, the national government initiated the San Tao Jicheng Project to create a comprehensive collection of myths, stories, songs, rhymes, proverbs and poetry.

Chinese cosmology centers on an 'organismic process, meaning that all parts of the entire cosmos belong to one organic whole and that they all interact as participants in one spontaneously self-generating life process' (Mote,

1989: 15). Changes in one part of the system impact its other parts. When everything in existence is part of the cosmos, the binary separation of good and evil is illogical. Thus, humans call upon mythical deities to bring forth good fortune while at the same time ward off bad luck and evil.

The cosmos encompasses the situational context, leaders and their relationships, and flow of activities or events. Choosing dates for important activities helps with optimizing good fortune. Feng shui (wind and water) practices channel flows of chi (energy) in the environment. The circumstances and timing of a child's birth may portend a significant role in his/her future. Socializing into the community starts with naming by placing the family name first, often a middle one shared among siblings and then the child's name. This is the reverse of western naming traditions. Hence, this chapter retains the Chinese convention of family name followed by the individual name.

## OVERVIEW OF ANCIENT CHINESE MYTHOLOGIES

The evolution of Chinese mythologies is intertwined with imaginations and reinterpretations over time. There are about 154 Chinese deities but a mythical figure may have four to six names (Saunders, 2007). The aliases capture qualities associated with the leader and significant events. The myths below are samples that are integral in Chinese culture – the Yellow Emperor, the First Emperor, Queen Mother of the West, the Eight Immortals, the Monkey King and the Goddess of Mercy.

### Huang Di, The Yellow Emperor

Myths of the Yellow Emperor's reign date back to 2697–2597 BC or 2674–2575 BC in the Huang He River basin region in northern China. He was the first of the five legendary sage kings with the others being Zhuanxu, Di Ku, Tang Yao and Yu Shun. Writings from the Warring States period (403–221 BC) documented a part-real, part-legendary leader of an earlier tribal federation in the Yangshao Neolithic age. After a 24 month pregnancy, his mother Fubao gave birth as loud thunders and lights flashed in the heavens which some refer to as the aurora borealis shining around the Big Dipper. Huang Di was famous for many battles but the pivotal one was defeating Chi You with the invention of a south pointing compass (Rice and Egge, 2006). He unified over 40 warring tribes in a region that spanned from the west of today's Gansu province to the sea in the east and north in today's Shanxi and Hebei provinces to the south by the Changjiang (Yangtze) River. Later, he transformed from a warrior to a ruler.

He became the Yellow Emperor in relation to the yellow earth, the Yellow River, his yellow imperial clothing, and the yellow skin of his people, the Han.

His other titles included the 'Ancestor of the Chinese' and 'Originator of the Chinese Culture' because his rule coincided with a golden age of many key Chinese inventions. They included the art of war, the rule of government, invention of the wheel and cart, agriculture and animal husbandry, acupuncture and traditional Chinese medicine, a writing system based on ideograms, a number and mathematical system, astronomy, a calendar with daily time structure, manufacturing of boats, a 12 tone musical scale and musical instruments, clothes, the building of various structures such as homes and palaces, and even ideas on love with the 'Handbooks of Sex' dating back to 2697–2598 BC. The text, *Huang Di Nei Jing* (*The Yellow Emperor's Canon of Medicine*), formed the foundation of traditional Chinese medicine for over 24 centuries. He was also a patron of Taoism and known for a reign that was humane and wise. His queen, Lei Tzu, is credited with discovering the cultivation of silkworms that led to the industry of silk clothing.

Huang Di is also referred to as the 'Son of Heaven' which is a title for subsequent emperors of China. The title evolved from how he ascended to the sun on a dragon with great thunder after 100 years of rule and became immortal. His tomb is located on Mount Qiaoshan in Shanxi Province. Today, the Chinese pay their respect to the Yellow Emperor on 4 April, Chinese Memorial Day.

## Qin Shi, the First Emperor of China

The First Emperor of China was Qin Shi Huang Di (260–210 BC) who established the Qin Dynasty. His reign began at the age of 12 in 247 BC. He united most of China by 221 BC with a network of roads, canals and the Great Wall. Qin Shi developed the basic structure for imperial China with dynasties to follow until the demise of the Qing dynasty in 1912. He conscripted able bodied males for one year of army service and they helped to push the boundaries of the empire by unifying the warring factions from the prior period. As a leader, he standardized currency, the writing system, legal codes, bureaucracy and even cart sizes for the road system.

Qin Shi's burial site includes an army for his after life, famously known today as the terracotta warriors of Xian. In addition, 300 concubines who had not borne him children were also buried alive with him. The secret of the burial site was sealed by executing the workforce who knew the location until farmers in 1974 discovered it as they dug for a well. Hence, Qin Shi became a mythical leader by establishing China as a nation.

## Xiwang Mu, Queen Mother of the West

Myths of the Queen Mother of the West date back to 985 BC. She is the highest ranking Chinese goddess. Earlier myths depict her as a beastly goddess of destruction and calamity with subsequent transformation into a beautiful woman, guardian of the western paradise, matriarch of the Taoist tradition, and Goddess of Longevity and Immortality. Her fame revolves around the peaches of immortality that take 3000 years to form and another 3000 years to ripen. They are served at the end of her birthday banquet that includes dishes of delicacies made from bears' paws, monkeys' lips, dragons' liver and phoenix marrow. She lives in a palace constructed from pure gold by the Lake of Jewels and travels on a white crane with bluebirds as messengers. The myths of the Queen Mother of the West take place in the K'un Lun Mountains and Isles of P'eng-lai. She had nine sons and 24 daughters with her consort, the Jade Emperor who is the highest ranking god.

## The Eight Immortals

The Eight Immortals were humans transformed by the peaches of immortality from the Queen Mother of the West for their good works. They represent eight factors of daily life, eight stages of life, eight body parts in martial arts, eight directions, and eight precious items of Confucianism. Eight forms the numeric basis of Taoism with the eight trigrams of the I Ching. As an auspicious number in the Chinese culture, eight also represents prosperity. The Eight Immortals are:

1. Zhongli Quan (Explosive Revelations), the Fat Man is considered Chief of the Immortals who carries a fan and sometimes a peach. He is a deity for the military.
2. Li Tie Guai (Body Snatcher or Iron Crutch) carries a gourd and/or a crutch to represent the sick.
3. Lan Cai He (Drunk and Disoriented) is a woman or a young boy who carries flowers as a deity for florists.
4. Zhang Guo Lao (Stubborn Old Mule) rides a mule and carries a bamboo tube drum to represent old men.
5. He Xian Gu (Self-Raising Flower) is an immortal female who carries a lotus flower and sometimes a shang reed organ.
6. Lu Dong Bin (Tactical Withdrawal) is a scholar with a magic sword and acts as a deity for barbers.
7. Han Xiang Zi (The Flying Philosopher) plays a flute from which music can soothe wild animals and acts as a deity for musicians.
8. Cao Guo Jiu (Royal Outcast) is the most finely dressed with court clothing and plays a pair of castanets or hold a jade tablet. He is a deity for actors.

In sum, the Eight Immortals represent people from different walks of life – young, old, men, women, civil, military, poor, rich, sick, cultured and nobility.

The belief is that the Eight Immortals can use their tools to bring a good life and combat evil.

## The Monkey King

The myth of *Monkey: A Journey to the West* was one of the four classic novels from the Ming dynasty (1500–82) which inspired numerous movies, operas and shows. The story revolved around a pseudo-historical account of a seventh century monk who traveled to India to bring back the holy sutras of Buddha to China. But Monkey was a central character in the quest. Born of a rock, Monkey gained immortality by stealing and eating the peaches of immortality from the Queen Mother Wang of the West (Walters, 1992). Monkey's desire was to be ruler of the universe over all the gods including the Jade Emperor. All of Monkey's antics earned him the wrath of the heavenly forces and Buddha intervened with a wager. If Monkey could escape Buddha's grasp, Monkey could get his wish. Monkey was capable of covering 108 000 li (33 534 miles) in a single somersault, 72 transformations of different animals and objects, strength to lift 13 500 pounds, and equipped with high intelligence.

But Monkey failed in the wager with Buddha and acquiesced to protect Tripitaka, the monk on a journey to retrieve the holy sutras. They were accompanied by two other figures, Pigsy and Sandy and a white horse. Their journey lasted 14 years over 108 000 miles with 81 trials and tribulations that wove together humor, suffering, hardship, compassion, friendship and victory. The story can be read on many different levels including as a critique of religious, social and political institutions. Monkey symbolizes the mind, intellect and wit that must be brought under control. Pig represents physical pleasures. Sandy stands for patience and strength. Tripitaka, the monk, characterizes human frailties of self-centeredness, fear, survival and naivete. Buddha, Lao Tzu and Confucius are woven into the story, not as competing faiths, but as three coexisting divine beings responsible to higher universal forces.

## Kuan Yin, Goddess of Mercy and Compassion

Kuan Yin, also known as Avalokitesvara in India, is a Buddha whose popularity extends well beyond China to many parts of Asia. As a Buddha, she has many forms but is often depicted as a female in China versus the male god in India. There are many different versions of her origins. In the Chinese version, Kuan Yin was first known as Miao Shan, Wonderful Goodness, who was the third daughter of a king. She was most unusual as a baby with a body that glowed brightly to light up the whole palace.

Upon reaching the age of marriage, she violated her filial duty by refusing to wed a suitor chosen by her parents. Her compromise was to marry someone who would alleviate the misfortunes of sickness, old age and death. The exasperated king condemned Miao Shan to a monastery and then sentenced her to execution. But a tiger rescued her. Later the king became ill and the medicine for recovery was an elixir made from a purely unselfish person's eyes and arms. A hermit offered to make such a sacrifice and the king was healed. Upon paying respect to the person, the king found that the hermit was his third daughter. He begged her forgiveness and ordered a statue to commemorate Miao Shan's purity in compassion and healing power. Hence, she was transformed into Kuan Yin, a goddess to relieve pain and suffering for all.

In a different version, Kuan Yin was a widow that turned to prostitution to survive. Her father-in-law became furious with the shame and had her executed. When she entered hell and found many souls suffering, she began reading the holy books to ease their pain. The god of hell became furious that souls were not suffering and sent the widow back to earth upon which she was transformed into a Buddha, an immortal to care for anyone who called upon her for help.

One story tells of how Buddha gave her 11 heads to respond to all the cries for help. But when she tried to help so many, her arms shattered. The Buddha Amitabha enabled her once again by giving her a thousand arms. Thus, figures of Kuan Yin are commonly depicted by different versions. Myths of Kuan Yin illustrate a bridge between Confucianism and Buddhism. She sought to fulfill filial responsibility, a primary directive of the Confucian tradition while remaining true to Buddhist beliefs and practices by offering sacrifices of the body with ascetic living to attain knowledge and peace.

## OVERVIEW OF CHINESE LEADERSHIP

Western researchers of Chinese mythology tend to seek myths or cultural understandings that are equivalent to ones in their own culture (Yang and An, 2005; Mote, 1989). This approach decontextualizes Chinese myths and creates a fractured telescopic lens for viewing them. Although some leadership characteristics are related to western notions, insights about leadership from ancient Chinese myths need to be understood within China's multiple historical shifts. The myths above illustrate Chinese leadership characteristics that include a holistic orientation, ingenuity for problem solving, hierarchical power, compassion for others, balancing conflicts with sustainable peace, and events of phantasmagorical proportions.

The leadership capabilities from Chinese myths are related to some key contemporary leadership ideas such as self-management (Manz and Sims, 1980), collectivism and power distance (Hofstede, 1997), transformational change (Ackerman, 1996), creativity in innovations, and empathy in emotional intelligence (Goleman, *et al.*, 2002). However, their meanings in a Chinese context differ from western ones. For example, the western meaning of self-management refers to motivating and committing one's self to goals that support organizational performance and minimize supervisory leadership oversight (Manz and Sims, 1980). In the Chinese context, self-management is a virtue and a moral obligation based upon pragmatic Confucian principles because one is part of the large cosmological system. Chinese mythologies emphasize moral responsibilities that require both self-examination and self-correction as a practical norm for a better life. This theme can be identified in the co-existence of the three major philosophical traditions of Taoism, Confucianism and Buddhism.

The cosmos as an organic whole offers a particular perspective to Hofstede's idea of China as a collectivist culture. Morality in Chinese culture means that 'the human domain be at one with the cosmos' (Sivin, 1995: 27). The title, 'Son of Heaven' signifies the unique role of Chinese emperors where they are considered as supreme regulators of everything under heaven; their character, power, and virtue are reflected in natural processes (Smith, 1957). When the emperor is depraved and lacking moral character, the dynamic balance is impaired. Calamities happen because the transformative power is distorted. Leaders need to practice earthly rituals to correspond with heaven and behave in a moral manner to sustain prosperity. Powerful leaders such as the Yellow Emperor and the Qin Shih Emperor succeeded over warring factions because their humane rule brought forth civility, peace and prosperity.

The immense power and unquestioned authority of leaders exemplify Hofstede's (1997) classification of China as high in power distance. Chinese leaders demonstrate different types of power – legitimacy, coercive and reward (French and Raven, 1960). Leaders like the Yellow Emperor may also hold expert power; Kuan Yin has referent power; and the Queen Mother Wang of the West reward power. Furthermore, legitimate power arises from the position and relative status of a person's age, family position, community role, and personal affinities. Power based on age and family positions are significant factors in Chinese family owned businesses.

Chinese cosmology also has important implications for managing time and space. In contrast to atomistic and sequential linear logic, the Chinese cosmos has a cyclical orientation without a definitive beginning or end and a network-like interwoven structure of events with generative logical relationships. Deities, numbers, symbols, and construction of environmental context are employed to improve good fortune for auspicious events. Chinese business leaders do not necessarily abandon economic rational decision making and depend on luck, but rather augment decisions by deploying symbols of good fortune to optimize their potential for success.

## Contemporary Chinese Leaders

Legendary leaders in Chinese mythology are often evoked in reference to contemporary ones who manifest key characteristics and qualities. Although the Cultural Revolution eradicated many cultural traditions, especially the worshipping of deities, the Communist Party evoked the idea of the Eight Immortals in reference to a powerful group of octogenarian leaders. They held substantial political power in the 1980s and 1990s. They are also referred to as the Eight Elders – Deng Xiaoping (1904–97), Peng Zhen (1902–97), Chen Yun (1905–95), Yang Shangkun (1907–98), Li Xiannian (1909–92), Bo Yibo (1908–2007), Wang Zhen (1908–93) and Song Renqiong (1909–2005). Mao Zedong is sometimes added into the mix. These leaders played an important role in shaping the political and economic context.

Of course no contemporary Chinese business leader exemplifies all the qualities of any particular ancient mythical deity. But certain leaders reflect attributes of particular mythical figures. Three contemporary Chinese business leaders are selected as case studies to trace the manifestation of leadership characteristics from Chinese mythologies in growing and managing international businesses.

### Zhang Ruimin of the Haier Corporation

Zhang Ruimin is the Chair and CEO who was appointed as director of the Qingdao Refrigerator Factory in Shandong Province, a small poor performing factory in 1984. Over a 20 year period, he transformed the business into the Haier Group, a leading global appliance manufacturer. In 2005, the operation had a 50 000 member workforce in over 240 subsidiaries, sales in over 100 countries, and revenue of RMB 103.5 billion. In 2004, a joint global survey by the Financial Times and PricewaterhouseCoopers ranked Haier as one of the World's Most Respected Companies.

Zhang's leadership is highly respected in the international business community. In 2005, he was the only Chinese entrepreneur ranked as one of the 50 most respected business leaders by the Financial Times and one of the top 25 most powerful business leaders in China. His leadership philosophy integrates Chinese wisdom and international management principles with a dual focus on innovation and excellence. Zhang literally hammered home the message when he ordered 76 defective refrigerators destroyed. He used a sledgehammer to destroy one himself to make the point. Today, the refrigerator can be found in Haier's museum symbolizing that poor quality goods are not acceptable.

Zhang's leadership resembles the general myth motif of the Yellow Emperor. The leader successfully battles conflicts or warring factions from a prior period and then prospers with multiple innovations that become broadly diffused. Zhang demonstrated the moral responsibility expected of virtuous Chinese leaders, the unity principle in Chinese cosmology, integration of opposites such as destruction for creation, and the absorption of knowledge for innovation to solve problems. Like the Yellow Emperor, Zhang also created an organizational culture that emphasized dynamic regeneration by integrating talented people and giving back to society. Zhang used the metaphor of the sea to emphasize the input of tributaries flowing into it where every drop functions under the sea's command to generate resources. In return, the sea offers its bounty to all and sustains its existence by providing for all.

## Sir Li Ka-Shing, Hutchison Whampoa Limited and Cheung Kong Holdings

Sir Li Ka-Shing has a rags-to-riches story. He is the Chairman of Hutchison Whampoa Limited (HWL) and Cheung Kong Holdings in Hong Kong. In 1928, Li was born in Chaozhou, Guangdong Province as a teacher's son and later as a refugee fleeing to Hong Kong. Due to the death of his father, he left school before the age of 15 to support his family. Today, Li ranks on Forbes' 2007 list as the world's ninth richest man with an estimated wealth of US$23 billion.

Li is often referred to as 'Superman' due to his business acumen (primary data from Gurtler and Nohria, 2005; Vines, 2006). Descriptions of Li's leadership characteristics include the strength of his internal moral compass, prudence, integrity, hard work ethic, modesty and visionary. Li is also dedicated to self-directed learning. Recently, Li also developed a strong reputable track record for his philanthropy. HWL has a workforce of 220 000 with five core operations – shipping port operations, property, retail, energy and infrastructure, and telecommunications – in 56 countries.

Li's success in building a global empire with infrastructures echoes Qin Shi's nation building of China. Building the Great Wall is symbolic of ancient infrastructure for protection of territory as well as maintaining tight control over the populace. Furthermore, Li also exemplifies Confucian primary values concerning family responsibilities in giving up an education to support his family and later, incorporating his two sons, Victor and Richard, into the business.

Li's binding word leads to his honorable reputation as a leader who generates a high level of trust from others. He has foresight with numerous business deals in timing his buying and selling. The combination of his integrity and business acumen generates a following of supporters and investors. Li's first business was in making high quality plastic flowers for export. Then a major opportunity arose with the drop in real estate prices due to China's political turmoil in 1967. While others fled, he looked upon the situation as an opportunity to buy property at low prices which paid off significantly after the political difficulties dissipated. Li repeated this approach of being able to identify and exploit opportunities multiple times when few would consider them.

### Cheung Yan, Nine Dragons Paper (Holdings) Limited

Cheung Yan (also written as Zhang Yin) leads a born-global entrepreneurial venture. Cheung, also known as the Queen of Trash or Paper Queen, is the founder and Chair of Nine Dragons Paper (Holdings) Limited, a global paper recycling company. In 2006, she became the richest self-made woman in the world and China's richest woman at US$3.4 billion. In a period of about 12 years, Nine Dragons Paper is poised to become the largest single paper producer by 2008.

Cheung was born in 1956 in Heilongjiang Province as the first of eight children to a military officer family. Cheung's early life was very difficult with the jailing of her father as a 'counterrevolutionary' during the Cultural Revolution. As the oldest child, she went to work in a textile factory to support her mother and seven siblings with a wage of 40 yuan per month, about US$6 (The Economist, 2007). After the Cultural Revolution and the release of her father, Cheung worked in a foreign Chinese joint venture paper trading company in southern China and learnt about the business.

By 1985, Cheung moved to Hong Kong to start her own paper company with US$3800. Her ambitions led her to Los Angeles. She married for the second time to a Taiwanese dentist and the two started a paper brokerage firm called America Chung Nam. Nine Dragons Paper was established in 1995 with a giant paper making machine that had a capacity of 200 000 tons in Dongguan near Hong Kong. The rapid economic expansion in China entailed growth in demand for corrugated cardboard packaging. Hence, Cheung added ten more machines with three additional sites for capacity totaling 5.4 million tons by the end of 2007. Today, Cheung employs 5300 people and has annual revenue of about $1 billion. She took her company public on the Hong Kong stock exchange in March, 2006 and raised US$500 million. The share prices multiplied a few times over for a market value of $6.5 billion by mid-2007. The Cheung's family stake is about 70 percent.

Cheung is a very private person. She has a reputation for being a visionary, a tenaciously hard worker and rapid learner, an intelligent negotiator, and an intense energetic personality. Cheung does not hesitate to hold employees accountable or to reward them accordingly. In this manner, she is known to be fair. Relating Cheung's leadership to Chinese mythologies requires relating her life to the dynamic social and economic global changes as well as Confucian influences from Chinese cosmology (Hutton, 2006).

The early part of Cheung's life during the Cultural Revolution provided critical lessons. Her earlier experiences allowed her to navigate and develop positive relationships with government officials as well as build bridges across international boundaries. Even though the Communist reign created chaos, Mao's championing of women's equal rights and Deng Xiaoping's subsequent pro-market reform created a supportive environment for Cheung to prosper. Furthermore, the Central Chinese government does not consider recycling scrap paper to be a strategic resource which is helpful to minimize government attention in her growing business.

The primary Confucian principle of filial piety and family values surfaces in Cheung's leadership. Supporting her family continued from difficult times to prosperous ones. She considers the global corporation to be a family business with her husband, younger brother, and son holding significant leadership and equity positions.

When Cheung's leadership is examined from the perspective of a dynamic cosmological whole, the difficulties fold back upon themselves to create a strategic launching platform for prosperity. By having to support her family at an early age, she acquired a deep level of industry knowledge about international trading to support her own entrepreneurial business. Then, leaving China for the US during the tense period after Tiananmen Square enabled her to identify global opportunities when she returned to China to build her business. Her determination perpetuates a positive feedback cycle of transformational growth that requires further development before the Nine Dragons Paper story is finished.

## GLOBAL IMPLICATIONS

The three cases of contemporary Chinese business leaders reflect some of the characteristics of mythical Chinese leaders. While the mythical figures are not necessarily direct role models, they form part of the cultural fabric in socializing current Chinese leaders. Many also reflect the elements of the Monkey King's Journey to the West with global ventures in different directions but returning home to prosper. Chinese myths socialize leadership characteristics by transmitting ideals over more than 4600 years.

Some common themes among the four Chinese business leaders, Zhang, Li and Cheung, include rising above their humble beginnings, integrating working and learning, adapting to environmental changes, and engaging in positive feedback cycles of regenerative transformations. Integrated philosophical beliefs and ideals from Taoism, Confucianism, and Buddhism sometimes overlapped in their daily practices. The Chinese leaders often demonstrated Confucian values of filial piety, hierarchical social relationships from within family to community to the government, duty to humanity, and responsibility for scholarly understanding.

Family is a dominant constituent in the two cases of Li and Cheung, the two examples of rising from rags to riches. Both have a very high level of family control over their publicly traded global corporations and integrate the next generation into key leadership positions. The Confucian ordering of filial relationships means that the younger generation is responsible for learning and making good decisions consistent with their parents' values. Victor Li says that his business thinking is aligned closely with his father where they often independently arrive at the same conclusion (Schuman, 2004). Cheung's response to questions of nepotism in Nine Dragons Paper was that as a family business, her 25 year old son knows the business and may be the successor in the future if he qualifies (Rao, 2007).

The hierarchical order of social relationships extends out to the workplace. Employees have a duty to respect and obey their leader to maintain harmony while at the same time the leader must behave in a morally virtuous fashion in managing their workforce. Reflective of mythical leaders, current Chinese business leaders also have extensive power. In addition to legitimate, coercive, reward, expert and referent powers (French and Raven, 1960), their age, family position, and social network position create additional sources of power. The ability to wield power enables subordinates to follow rapidly once a leader makes a decision and gives the order, as described by a manager of an engineering company – see Commentary box.

A number of writers explain how complex exchanges between family, friends, colleagues, and work relations construct a social network referred to as guanxi (for example Chen, 2003; Su, *et al.*, 2007; Zhang and Zhang, 2006). Central to guanxi are trust and face. Trust mitigates opportunistic behaviors and allows for rapid adaptation. At the same time, outsiders to the guanxi in the social network are often excluded.

Both business success and a virtuous character are important for Chinese leaders to have face. Li is known to have 'big face'. Li's business success, philanthropic generosity, and moral character generate significant goodwill in the Chinese community where others would invest where he invests. For non-Chinese, the connection between a morally virtuous leader and guanxi with a long term perspective can be mystifying at best or unethical at worst. While business transactions are much quicker and smoother with guanxi, outsiders often have different interpretations because forging a business deal based on relationships or family connection seems unfair. Also, foregoing a beneficial exchange with future long term reciprocation to build guanxi may not be reciprocated between Chinese and western leaders because western business practices tend to focus on one transaction at a time versus building a business relationship for the long term.

The primacy of the family unit and significance of filial responsibility in organizing hierarchical relationships often run counter to ideals of meritocracy

---

## COMMENTARY BOX

### Branch Office Manager, Rail Signalling Systems Engineering Company

In the Chinese culture, leadership is very hierarchical and authoritarian. Directives are dutifully followed by subordinates who
rarely challenge or question what is being asked of them, even if
the instructions do not make any business sense or add any
value to the company. This is very different from Western companies which are more cost conscious with an eye on the bottom
line ... One of the most impressive qualities of Chinese leadership is the ability to get things done very quickly. Unlike Western
companies which tend to have more checks and balances,
Chinese leaders seem to have the ability to cut through the layers
of bureaucracy, bypass roadblocks, and do whatever it takes to
get the job completed.

### Chief Technical Officer, High Tech Company

The strength of Chinese managers is their analytical skills.
Many managers take a trial and error approach to problem solving. The down side is wasted efforts and the creation of unin-
tended consequences but it shows quick and immediate action
that upper management likes to see. Chinese managers tend to
take more time analyzing the data and devising a more complete
action plan. It is the turtle versus the rabbit kind of thing. The
turtle may win at the end but it is the rabbit that gets noticed. My
advice to Chinese managers is to go ahead and devise a detailed
plan but come up quickly with an immediate action item and get
going.

---

in western management. Placing family members in leadership roles is often
seen by westerners as nepotism with negative repercussions. The difference
can be a source of tension in managing a global organization.

In international business, cultural differences can lead to different interpretations and implications of leadership practices. Clarity in vision, integrity,
virtuous morality, hard work, intelligence, and a long term view are important
qualities for Chinese leadership. An example of differing interpretation is what
'long term' means. Western managers think 5–10 years as being long term

while Chinese leaders tend to think of long term as multiple future generations. The difference impacts decisions and development of business relations
in situations such as strategic planning for the future. In the second entry into
Commentary box, a Chinese manager invokes the analogies of the turtle and
the rabbit in comparing Chinese leaders with western ones.

Another Chinese leadership characteristic that is often misinterpreted
relates to integrity and honesty. The difference lies in high versus low context
orientation between cultures. The Chinese high context stems from its cosmology of dynamic organic wholeness which requires understanding a simple
word like 'yes' within the context of a situation. An overt 'no' would be
avoided because it would cause a loss of face and be too confrontational. A
Chinese leader would maintain his/her integrity and honesty with 'yes' to
maintain the harmony and protect the face of the other. A non-Chinese person
may misunderstand the 'yes' to mean agreement when no agreement has been
reached. Due to the cultural differences in meaning, the Chinese leader may be
considered misleading and untrustworthy in conducting international business
dealings. As a result, conscious effort needs to be made by all stakeholders to
bridge cultural differences.

## PRACTICAL APPLICATIONS

The ancient myths of the Yellow Emperor, the First Emperor, Queen Mother
Wang of the West, the Monkey King, the Eight Immortals, and Kuan Yin
provide a rich venue for gaining access into the cultural attributes of contemporary Chinese business leaders such as Zhang, Li, Cheung and many others.
Ancient myths provide a window into the Chinese culture that goes beyond
homogenizing western concepts. A mythological perspective paints a more
complex existence that can further our understanding of constructs supported
by empirical research studies with statistical measures. For Chinese leaders,
myths are venues for historical self-awareness and articulation of taken-for-
granted realities.

A few salient implications of Chinese mythologies for global leadership
include the importance of developing contextual literacy for cross-cultural
communication to develop guanxi relationships; engaging in self-directed
learning to compete with a virtuous character; and building competencies and
knowledge during difficult struggles to take advantage of future opportunities.
These leadership practices help build relationships across cultural boundaries
into Chinese organizations.

An important caveat to remember is that myths have a dynamic co-evolu-
tionary process in Chinese culture. During different political regimes, revised
interpretations of ancient myths also serve to advance political agendas. An

example is the shift in meanings and claims about the Yellow Emperor. In establishing the republic during the early nineteenth century, Sun Yat-sen argued that authentic Chinese were descendants of the Yellow Emperor while excluding other minorities (Leibold, 2006). In 1949, the political shift to Communism created a contradiction between using myths of rebellion where Mao often referenced the Monkey King and banning the practice of telling myths to worship deities. Myths were seen as superstitious and contradictory to socialist ideals. In 1978, the opening of China included a revival of myths as cultural artifacts. The resurrection of the Yellow Emperor myth included a shift in meaning where he was more inclusive as the ancestor of all Chinese nationalities everywhere, including Taiwan (Sautman, 1997; Yang and An, 2005). The political use of the Yellow Emperor myth argues for the return of Taiwan to China, a return to the 'family'.

The development of China's market economy entailed a revival of folk and cultural artifacts as resources to support the tourism industry. Chinese myths help to market local attractions, sell souvenirs and export Chinese designs. Hence, myths form a bridge across time and geographical space within Chinese society. Held up as mythical ideals, global leaders can gain insights from the interaction between context and myth to develop cross-cultural relationships with Chinese leaders. At the same time, myths provide Chinese leaders with a means to gain a level of self-awareness to build guanxi in the broader international business context.

Chinese myths provide a vehicle to access the 'inscrutability' factor into the complex layers and dimensions of Chinese culture and its leaders. Seeking to understand the dynamic connection between ancient and contemporary Chinese leaders and their contexts provides fuller insight into important leadership characteristics. As myths form a bridge for Chinese leaders from different geographical locations to cross-cultural boundaries, their crossing will likely perpetuate future cultural evolutions in China. The future use of ancient Chinese myths will likely develop new myths of Chinese leaders.

## ACKNOWLEDGMENTS

I wish to express my gratitude to Desmond Ng and Anthony Tai for their helpful review and feedback on earlier versions of this chapter.

## REFERENCES

Ackerman, L. S. (1996), Development, transition or transformation: bringing change leadership into the 21st century, *OD Practitioner*, **28** (4), 5–16.

Barboza, D. (2007), China's 'Queen of Trash' finds riches in waste paper, *International Herald Tribune*, 15 January, Retrieved from http://www.iht.com/articles/ 2007/01/15/business/trash.php

Birrell, A. (1993), *Chinese Mythology: An Introduction*, Baltimore, MD: Johns Hopkins University Press.

Birrell, A. (2000), *The Legendary Past: Chinese Myths*, Austin, TX: University of Texas Press and London: British Museum Press.

Chen, M. J. (2003), *Inside Chinese Business: A Guide for Managers Worldwide*, Cambridge, MA: Harvard Business School Press.

Coleman, D., Boyatzis, R. E. and McKee, A. (2002), *Primal Leadership: Realizing the Power of Emotional Intelligence*, Cambridge, MA: Harvard Business School Press.

Dunning, J. H. and Kim, C. (2007), The cultural roots of guanxi: An exploratory study, *The World Economy*, **30** (2), 329–41.

The Economist (2007), Paper queen, face value, *The Economist*, 9 June (3838532): 80.

French, J. P. R. Jr. and Raven, B. (1960), The bases of social power, in Cartwright, D. and Zander, A. (eds), *Group Dynamics*, New York: Harper and Row, pp. 607–23.

Gurtler, B. and Nohria, N. (2005), *Li Ka Shing*, Revised case. Harvard Business School Cases, Boston, MA: Harvard Business School.

Hofstede, G. (1997), *Cultures and Organizations: Software of the Mind*, New York: McGraw-Hill.

Hutton, W. (2006), Thanks to Mao, Zhang Yin's a billionaire, *Observer*, 15 October, retrieved from http://observer.guardian.co.uk/comment/story/0,,1922797,00.html

Kherdian, D. (retold) (1992), *Monkey: A Journey to the West*, Boston, MA and London: Shambhala Publications Inc.

Liebold, J. (2006), Competing narratives of racial unity in Republican China: From the Yellow Emperor to Peking Man, *Modern China*, **32** (2), 181–220.

Manz, C. C. and Sims, H. P. (1980), Self-management as a substitute for leadership: A social learning theory perspective, *Academy of Management Review*, **5**, 361–7.

Mote, F. W. (1989), *Intellectual Foundations of China* (2nd edn), Columbus, OH: McGraw-Hill.

Rao, A. (2007), Cheung Yan, interview on Talk Asia. CNN.com, 3 June, retrieved from http://www.cnn.com/2007/WORLD/asiapcf/06/03/talkasia.cheungyan/index. html?iref=newssearch

Rice, R. and Egge, R. (2006), Huang di, http://www.stirlingsouth.com/southptr/ needham/legend.htm

Saunders, C. (2007), Chinese mythology: The gods of the Middle Kingdom, retrieved from http://www.godchecker.com/pantheon/chinese-mythology.php

Sautman, B. (1997), Racial nationalism and China's external behavior, *World Affairs*, **160**, 78–95.

Schuman, M. (2004), Families under fire: The Li family. *TimeAsia*, 16 February, retrieved from http://www.time.com/time/asia/covers/501040223/li.html

Sivin, N. (1995), State, cosmos and body in the last three centuries BC, *Harvard Journal of Asiatic Studies*, **551**: 5–37.

Slater, J. (1999), Consuming passions, *Far Eastern Economic Review*, **16211**: 46–9.

Smith, D. H. (1957), Divine kingship in Ancient China, *Numen*, **43**: 171–203.

Stonehill, P. (n.d.), *Mysteries of the Yellow Emperor*, retrieved from http://www. mystae.com/streams/ufos/emperor.html

Su, C., Mitchel, R. K. and Sirgy, M. J. (2007), Enabling guanxi management in China: a hierarchical stakeholder model of effective guanxi, *Journal of Business Ethics*, **71**: 301–19.

Vines, S. (2006), Li Ka Shing: the richest man in Asia built a global empire out of an ailing British conglomerate, *Time Asia*, retrieved from http://www.time.com/time/asia/2006/heroes/bl_li.html

Walters, D. (1992), *An Encyclopedia of Myth and Legend: Chinese Mythology*, Hammersmith: Diamond Books.

Yang, L. and An, D. (2005), *Handbook of Chinese Mythology*, Santa Barbara, CA: ABC-CLIO Inc.

Zhang, Y. and Zhang, Z. (2006), Guanxi and organizational dynamics in China: A link between individual and organizational levels, *Journal of Business Ethics*, **67**: 375–92.

# 17. Cultural mythology and global leadership in India

## Shanthi Gopalakrishnan and Rajender Kaur

### INTRODUCTION

India is a kaleidoscope of diverse cultures and religions all of which have contributed to its numerous myths and legends. These in conjunction with its long history of colonial rule by the British for over 300 years, and the consequent introduction of Western systems of thought and education, have all gone into molding the unique sensibility of its people, and especially its elite classes, to which most corporate leaders in India belong. Increased multinational operations means increased multiculturalism within the organization and increased interaction between employees and managers of different cultures (Adler, 1983). Therefore, it is useful for foreign companies dealing with India to understand the customs, beliefs, and specific socio-cultural factors that drive the leadership, management techniques and decision making styles of their Indian partners.

It is a commonplace truism in academic discourse in social and cultural anthropology that myths and religions are closely related. In 'Redefining myth and religion: introduction to a conversation' Loyal de Rue (1994) defines myth as 'story' and religion as 'ties that bind'. He argues that 'myth and religion are closely associated because a shared myth is the most efficient and effective means for achieving social coherence' (315). This understanding of the relationship between myth and religion becomes useful in illuminating the extraordinary cultural currency that Rama and Krishna, two of the most popular cultural icons in India, enjoy, not just as beloved religious deities, but also as role models in conducting oneself in everyday life, as well as offering specific lessons in leadership and conflict resolution to Indians across the country.

Further, as culture constantly evolves in response to changing socio-economic conditions, so too the perception and deployment of myths in light of changed circumstances in everyday life. Not only do changing customs influence the understanding of age-old myths but often these myths are manipulated in the service of specific political and cultural agendas, both progressive and obscurantist. For instance, Gandhi was able to mobilize the masses in an anti-colonial freedom struggle against the British precisely because he understood the tremendous power of myths and cultural symbols in the daily life of the people. He motivated the peasantry by casting the independence struggle as a fight to achieve a new 'Ram-Rajya', a utopian moral and political ideal of post-independence India modeled on the legendary reign of Lord Rama, as a golden age. Gandhi himself, with his high-thinking ascetic lifestyle and inspirational leadership, was perceived as a modern day Rama by much of the peasantry (see Rao, 1938). More recently, the Bhartiya Janta Party, one of the key political parties in India, has sought to mobilize the masses by invoking the holy name of Lord Rama.

T. S. Eliot (1948), too, in his *Notes Toward a Definition of Culture* argues that one of the bases of cultural myths is religious beliefs. Besides religion, the culture and a history of the nation also influence prevailing myths and beliefs, and its subsequent emergent leadership styles. In comparative management studies, culture is considered to be a background factor that sets the context in the development and reinforcement of beliefs (Smircich, 1982; Cummings and Schmidt, 1972). In this chapter we view culture as a system of shared cognitions or a system of knowledge and beliefs (Rossi and O'Higgins, 1980). Culture is seen as a unique system for perceiving and organizing material phenomena, things, events and behavior.

This chapter is structured in three parts. First we present the factors – religion, culture and past history, that influence and shape the mythology that prevails in a country. Second, we look at the profiles of four very influential Indian leaders, Narayana Murthy, Ratan Tata, Verghese Kurian and Vikram Sarabhai, relative to the culture, mythology and historical background of India. Finally we showcase aspects of Indian leadership that are unique and different from the West and how they can help us to understand Indian leaders in their context.

## OVERVIEW OF INDIAN MYTHOLOGY

The religion of the majority in India, Hinduism, the unique cultural context, and the historical past of India, have all been the drivers that have influenced the development and gradual evolution of Indian myths. These three drivers and the subsequent myths that have evolved give India its own ethos, which is then expressed in the belief systems, activities and language through which its people sustain themselves (Smircich, 1983a, b). Here, we examine each of the three drivers and their influence on Indian mythology and leadership.

### Religion and its Impact on Mythology and Leadership

The predominant religion in India, Hinduism, is also one of the oldest religions in the world and dates back over 3500 years. Many Indian myths have their origins in religious stories and embody key values that have been handed down through the central characters in these legends. The Hindu Trinity of gods consists of Brahma the creator, Vishnu the preserver and Shiva the destroyer. According to myth, Vishnu the preserver, over the centuries, has taken on many incarnations and come to earth to uphold righteousness, rid the world of evil, and maintain the universal spiritual and moral order of things. Two of his incarnations, 'Rama' and 'Krishna' have been immortalized in the great Hindu epics, the *Ramayana* and the *Mahabharata*.

These epics, some of the oldest narrative poems in the world, are the source of many of the myths and legends in India. Dating back to a long enduring oral tradition, the *Mahabharata* and the *Ramayana* have continued to be revised and retold, each version 'making a particular argument appropriate to its own time and place [and] have contributed to shaping the spheres of religion, politics, everyday morality to a degree unmatched by any other work in Indian history' (Damrosch *et al.*, 2008). The version of the *Ramayana* to which many retellings explicitly or implicitly respond is one in Sanskrit ascribed to Valmiki dating to 200 BC, while the *Mahabharata* is dated to 300 BC.

In contrast to the dystopian world of the *Mahabharata* where brothers and kinsmen are ranged in battle against each other, casting the principal actors, Arjuna of the Pandavas, and the Kaurava elders, in a paralyzing moral dilemma, the *Ramayana* transforms the enemy into the monstrous other, the demon Ravana. This narrative strategy effectively distances the forces of evil from self and kin and simplifies the moral action of the epic. Consequently, the *Ramayana* 'offers positive paradigms for life, and no other work remotely approximates it for the didactic force it has exercised throughout India's history' (Damrosch *et al.,* 2008: 612).

Rama, the eponymous hero of the *Ramayana,* and Krishna, Arjuna's charioteer, and the orator of the *Bhagvada Gita*, exhorting a grief paralyzed Arjuna on the battlegrounds of Kurukshetra to do his duty, personify different qualities and consequently provide different role models for leadership. Rama and Krishna are both incarnations of Vishnu, and are considered visionary, semi-divine personages who affirm the value of righteous actions undertaken in the cause of duty. But while Rama embodies a selfless and humane idealism in which the warrior's duty or *dharma* is deemed subservient to the higher law of hierarchical obedience – of son to father, and younger brother to elder brother, Krishna articulates a pragmatic idealism that is undergirded by the larger irony of cosmic justice that transcends the bonds of familial kinship.

Rama was compassionate and sensitive to people's needs. He cared for every one of his citizens individually (Sekhar, 2001). Recent empirical work shows that this style is still prevalent in India, even though its extent is not firmly established. Sinha (1980) labels this as a 'nurturant task' leadership style. In contrast to Rama, Krishna personifies more a pragmatic leadership style, one which is achieving in adverse conditions (Sekhar, 2001). This style of leadership is more relevant to the turbulent times that India is going through as some of the leadership qualities associated with Krishna have a practical, goal oriented overtone.

Rama was an efficient leader because he was courageous and upheld values of tradition, righteousness, and self-sacrifice while Krishna was an effective leader because he knew how to be diplomatic which helped him deal with different kinds of people. The leadership qualities associated with Rama include righteousness, humility, and being a kingmaker. Righteousness implies doing what you believe is morally right, even though there may be no immediate perceivable benefits to yourself. When asked by his father to spend 14 years in exile, he humbly accepted his fate, despite being the rightful heir to the throne. Finally, Rama had an amazing ability to create and nurture leaders. He did not seek to usurp power but share it with the deserving. Rama's ability to nurture leaders and create collaborators is seen in his crowning of Sugriva, after he vanquished Valli his wicked brother. Sugriva then aids Rama in rescuing Sita from the powerful Ravana, the demon king who had abducted her. Similarly, he welcomed Vibhishana, Ravana's brother, even though he belonged to the enemy camp, and eventually crowned him King of Lanka, after the defeat of Ravana. In both these instances, Rama's actions were motivated by righteousness and compassion, but these also proved to be long-sighted strategic choices since they eventually help his cause against Ravana. Krishna's effectiveness, on the other hand, lay in that his ideas were farsighted and clever, somewhat cunning and pragmatic. Armed with such a 'skill set' Krishna offered key advice on leadership to his friend and devotee Arjuna, which has been passed down to us as the *Bhagvada Gita* which preaches the disinterested execution of one's *dharma* or duty. In *Dominance and Hegemony: History and Power in Colonial India,* Ranajit Guha (1997: 35) defines *dharma* as 'the quintessence of virtue or moral duty, [which] implies a social duty conforming to one's place in the caste hierarchy as well as the local power structure.' He further argues that this is an ideal that has been consecrated by myth, as in the ideal of King Prthu in the *Bhagvada Gita*, the primordial provider and protector, but also that *dharma* implies 'not only the prerogatives of coercion (*danda*)' but also an obligation to protect, foster, support, and promote the subordinate.

The *Bhagvada Gita* also articulates the Indian ideology of *bhakti*. *Bhakti* is key to our discussion of leadership because it is a philosophy and way of life that is deeply imbued in the consciousness of the people in India. Guha calls *bhakti* 'an ideology of subordination *par excellence*. Inferiority in any relationship of power structured as dominance and subordination within the Indian tradition can be derived from it' (50). Within the Vaishnavite tradition (to which worshipers of Rama and Krishna belong) the Krishna/devotee or leader-subordinate relationship can be classified in three essential dyads of the *Palalka/Palya, Prabhu/Dasa,* and *Lalaka/Lalya.* Broadly understood, the three dyads can be translated as protector/servant, master/subject, and superior relative/inferior relative (50). In analyzing the close ties of loyalty and benevolent paternalism that characterize relations between workers and leaders in Indian corporations, an understanding of the deeply held cultural idioms of *bhakti* that define the world view of most Indians is of critical importance.

Another key concept of leadership in the *Gita* is being aware of the importance of followers and their needs. To be successful as a leader, the leader needs to recognize the unique needs of every follower and address them accordingly. The recognition of the distinctiveness of the followers is more likely to motivate people being led to believing in the leader and being influenced by him or her.

Choudhary (2006) argues that the leadership styles mentioned and used in the *Gita* varied based on the maturity level of the followers. When followers display lack of capability, one needs leadership by direction, the more mature followers need to be given incentives (dand), so one leads by attraction or charm (daam), if their level of maturity is higher, then leadership by association (saam) where the followers are involved in the decision making. Finally, the most mature followers should be left alone and trusted completely, which is leadership by delegation (bhed). Many of these concepts of leadership have gained universal acceptance today. These differences in leadership styles are today expressed as authoritative, participative and delegating leadership styles. While leadership and decision making include morality as a central principle, the myths also allow for pragmatism, the inclusion of the led, as well as a sense of the context in decision making.

## Culture and its Impact on Leadership

The cultural values in India, while unique in many ways, are also a study in contradictions. There are many cultural traits that are unique to the Indian context and some of these have been emphasized by Hofstede's (1980) comparison of cultures. Hofstede (1980) uses five dimensions to compare cultures across the world. They include power distance, individualism/ collectivism, masculinity/femininity, uncertainty avoidance, and long term orientation. The three dimensions on which India was significantly different from Western cultures (US and UK) were power distance, individualism/collectivism, and long term orientation (Figure 17.1).

India has power distance as the highest Hofstede dimension with a ranking of 77 compared to a world average of 56.5. Compared to Western nations like the United States and UK, India accepts a high degree of power inequality. In

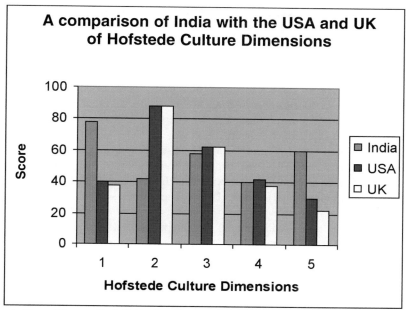

1= Power Distance; 2= Individualism/Collectivism; 3= Masculinity/Femininity;
4= Uncertainty Avoidance; 5= Long Term Orientation

*Figure 17.1    Cultural dimensions of India*

India, the less powerful accept relations that are more autocratic and paternal-istic (Hofstede, 1980). A sense of hierarchy and a respect for authority are deep rooted and have their origins in the caste system, among other factors already discussed in this paper. The caste system has created many vertical and hori-zontal divisions in Indian society and has influenced social practices. This system has accorded opportunities and privileges to some groups and denied the same opportunities to other groups (Srinivas, 1957). Members belonging to higher castes that had the experience of being leaders have learnt to use their power and authority while members of other groups or lower castes have developed a deep, unquestioning respect for authority. This has created a non-egalitarian value system which remains institutionalized in the Indian social system, but is being increasingly called into question. The high power distance lends itself to a leadership style that can be characterized as benevolent pater-nalism where the leader is autocratic but has the best interests of the led at heart. Indian leaders are used to respect from their subordinates. The position of authority they hold affords them legitimate authority to carry out their wishes.

In the context of corporate governance, the high power distance has in some instances resulted in consolidation of top management power, particularly in large family owned firms, and this has resulted in marginalizing the power of the boards of directors and minority share holders (Verma, 1997). The concentration of power in the hands of some groups has inhibited the development of systems of checks and balances. Consequently, in some instances, fewer options may be evaluated in the decision making process, and sometimes innovative solutions may be swept aside or not considered if they do not benefit the parties or people in power.

India scored very low on the individualism dimension compared to countries like the US and UK. This implies that Indians were well integrated into strong cohesive in-groups, often extended families, which protect them for unquestioning loyalty (Hofstede 1980). The strong sense of 'collectivism' influences their priorities in managing and leading groups. Until recently, the average Indian displayed loyalty to the companies that he or she worked with and tended to stay with one organization for a considerable length of time. The leaders considered their organization and its followers as their 'kutumb' or family in managing them (Sinha, 2004). Many leaders displayed nurturing qualities towards their subordinates and many companies display a sense of responsibility to the communities in which they operate. This trait in the Indian culture dates back to the myth of Rama and his nurturing qualities and this core cultural value has endured over generations. For example, Tata Steel led by Ratan Tata, Chairman of Tata Sons, and Muthuraman, CEO of Tata Steel in 2006 and 2007 spent millions of dollars on education, health, and agricultural development projects, in 800 villages near Jamshedpur the headquarters of Tata Steel. The company had a paternalistic attitude and for many years did not lay off employees even though their profitability was seriously threatened. Like the employees, the company culture valued the notion of the 'employee family' (Engardio and McGregor, 2006).

Masculinity versus Femininity refers to the values placed on traditional male versus female values. Masculine cultures value competitiveness, assertiveness, ambition and accumulation of wealth and material possessions, whereas feminine cultures place more value on relationships and quality of life (Hofstede, 1980). India, the US and UK seem to be similar and tend to value competitiveness, assertiveness and ambition more. This common affirmation of masculine values in the three countries speaks also of the cross-cultural prevalence of patriarchal values. In Indian culture, the ideal of the Ardhnarieshawara, that blends masculinity and femininity in equal measure, is true only in its absence in everyday life. Relationships or collectivism being valorized more is not really a contradiction of this index. Perhaps it is this valuing of competitiveness, assertion and ambition, that accounts for the similarity in uncertainty avoidance discussed below.

The scores of India on uncertainty avoidance are somewhat similar to the US and UK and the scores on uncertainty avoidance are the lowest compared to other dimensions. This can be interpreted that as a people, Indians are more open to risk and uncertainty. A tolerance for ambiguity that has added to the richness and variety of Indian life and has allowed the seamless assimilation of many customs, beliefs, and traditions, perhaps accounts for this lack of risk aversion. Synthesis and pluralism have made Indians more acceptable of diversity in the workplace and in everyday life. This sense of synthesis is reflected in racial harmony, primary institutions of family, modes of worship, and faith in democratic institutions. India is largely ethnically homogeneous, and people are generally accepting of religious and gender diversity in the workplace. The ability to cope with uncertainty also comes from a sense of security arising from faith in fate, or belief in *karma*, while at the same time doing one's duty or *dharma* as specific to a particular social position or role. The contradiction also arises from the many meanings of *karma* – a key Hindu philosophy or principle of action, a belief that your present actions will determine your future life rather than the obverse that your present life is determined by your past actions. It's quite an extraordinary contradiction from a generally conservative people who seem to believe in the status quo. The tolerance for uncertainty can be linked to the Hindu belief that the spirit of Brahma or the divine pervades everything, both animate and inanimate.

India scored significantly higher on long term orientation compared to the USA and UK. This dimension describes a society's 'time horizon' and the importance attached to the future versus the past and present. This expansive 'time horizon' is perhaps most powerfully demonstrated in a cyclical notion of time. The word 'Kal', for instance, translates both as tomorrow and yesterday in Hindi. This value can also be attributed to the belief in *karma* that actions in the past and present affect the future. There are other ways long term orientation manifests itself in everyday behavior. First, age and experience have greater value in India when compared to the West and actions are evaluated from their impact in the present and future point of view. A person's seniority can impact the extent of influence a person can have as a leader. Second, managers tend to stay with one job for a longer period of time and are willing to wait for the rewards of experience to come to them. However, both of these values are changing in recent times.

## Political History of India and its Impact on Leadership

The final factor that impacts the psyche, the myths and the values of a nation's people is the political history of a country. Each country's history is unique and leaves its distinct influence on the people and their values.

Two aspects are notable when we consider the political history of India. The first is the 300 years of British colonial rule and its impact on the language and thinking of the average Indian, and the second is the diversity in terms of language, culture and practices and its impact on myths in the past and present, and leadership practice.

British colonialism in India is remarkable for catalyzing a number of processes of change, but most of all for bringing about an intellectual revolution. Britain brought to India a European definition of history, philosophy, science, and language and introduced an educational system that was inspired by Western philosophy and ideals. Leadership is a product of history and educational system in a country (Nachtigal, 2006). The interpretation of myths is also influenced by the education and intellectual evolution of a people.

English education was voluntarily chosen by the Indian intelligentsia as strategic means of upward mobility and this choice empowered them in a multitude of ways. The Europeanization of the imagination provided a valuable resource for the elite that enabled Indians to relate to Western language and culture. The elite were able to merge their English learning with a learning of Indian languages and world views. Kumar (2007) argues that the educated Indian was comfortable with plural intellectual worlds and he/she was able to speak multiple languages, have access to varying notions of truth, and to share cultural meanings between the so-called 'east' and the 'west'. It was normal for the Indian to be comfortable with the values of their grandmothers as well as that of the formal curriculum of their schools that were imitated from the British institutions.

The second aspect of India is it is a conglomeration of multiple languages and cultures that are distinct. Consequently, one cannot focus on an overall pattern of values among the people within the country. The recognition of diversity and its assimilation into their behavior and thinking have made Indians unique. In a sense India is a study in contradictions. On the one hand, Indians have recognized that their success in political or economic ventures, and the legitimacy of their ventures, depended on their ability to attract the support of a variety of ethnic and social groups. This forced those in leadership positions to be more tolerant, and co-opt the opinions of others in less powerful positions. On the other hand, the notion of democracy or a voice for every individual which evolved gradually and naturally in the Western world, is a concept that is still struggling to take hold in the Indian system. The less powerful do not assert their rights and are more likely to buy into the ideas of those in power. This has resulted in the nurturing, more paternalistic leadership style that is a default mode of leading.

## OVERVIEW OF INDIAN LEADERS

In this section, we present profiles of four very influential Indian leaders from very diverse backgrounds, both current and past. These leaders are corporate chieftains, who have created management systems, and are considered thought and action leaders who have broadly impacted their respective organizations in significant ways. We examine them in the context of religion, culture, history, and the myths prevalent in India.

The four leaders we examine here are Narayana Murthy, the founder and head of Infosys, Ratan Tata, the current Chairman of Tata industries, Verghese Kurian, the first Chairman of Gujarat Co-operative Milk Marketing Federation, who provided a model of rural development not only for India, but for the world community, and finally, Vikram Sarabhai, the father of the Indian space program.

Narayana Murthy is one of the co-founders and the first CEO and Chairman of the Indian IT outsourcing company Infosys. Founded in 1981, Infosys was the first Indian company to be listed on the US stock exchange (Nasdaq) in 1999. In 2007, Infosys had over 50 000 employees and over $2 billion in revenues. The company has been voted 'the best employer in India' two years in a row in a survey conducted by Hewitt Associates. In 2006 Narayana Murthy was voted as the most admired CEO in India for the fifth year in a row. Several factors make Infosys stand out, but the most significant one has been its founder CEO and Chairman, Narayana Murthy. His ethics, values and leadership style have shaped the company's reputation, growth and performance. Narayana Murthy asserts that 'I have always believed that leadership does not exist in a vacuum, you need lots of good people to lead ... you need people who have the same or higher level of passion, energy and aspiraton.' He is one of the first Indian leaders who willingly shared the wealth he created with his employees, and at least 400 Infosys employees are dollar millionaires today. His leadership style embodies the nurturing style of Rama. He also believes in being extremely tolerant toward diversity: 'I want Infosys to be a place where people of different genders, nationalities, races, and religious beliefs work together in an environment of intense competition but utmost harmony, courtesy, and dignity to add more and more value to our customers day after day.' Despite all the accolades and the praise he has received, Narayana Murthy remains a simple, humble and caring father figure for the employees of Infosys (Wikipedia, 2007).

Ratan Tata, the Chairman of Tata industries is the second Indian leader we showcase here. When Ratan Tata took over as the Chairman in 1991, the Tata conglomerate resembled an opaque jungle of companies. He rebuilt, tore down, expanded, and forged a powerful holding company that has interests now in seven areas including – steel, automobile production, information technology, telecommunications, and energy. He re-hauled the calcified bureaucratic culture of the Tata companies, and raised the conglomerate's ownership stake in all the Tata companies to 26 percent. He took tough decisions when he got Tata Steel to shed half its 78 000 employees between 1994 and 2005 and changed the firm's relationship with its employees from paternalistic to practical. Some of his leadership decisions embody the pragmatism that Krishna displayed.

Though the business carries his name, he only draws a salary from Tata Sons. Ratan Tata takes personal modesty very seriously and what really excites him is his ability to combine the philanthropic heritage of the Tata group with modern business sense. He has clearly developed a global footprint for the Tata companies by the aggressive acquisitions of Tetley Tea (UK), Daewoo Commercial vehicles (Korean company) and Corus Steel (UK) (Media Reports, Tata Sons, 2007). Through his development of a now much hyped low cost people's car, 'Nano' Ratan Tata reinforces his legacy of commitment to the common man while at the same time recognizing the explosive profit potential in the growing segment of the upwardly mobile in India. Ratan Tata is a leader who has tried to be competitive in the new era of globalization while continuing to maintain the hallowed legacy of benevolent paternalism of its founder Jamshetji Tata.

Verghese Kurien is often called the 'father of the white revolution' in India. He revolutionized the way dairy products were produced and marketed through Anand Milk Producers Union Limited. He attended university in the US, returned to India and dedicated his professional life to empowering the Indian farmer through cooperatives where dairy farmers could own and manage profitable agri-business enterprises with their produce, however small it may be. As a man he is considered self-centered and authoritarian, but thoroughly professional (Singhi, 2007). He is a great strategist who had the unique ability to communicate with multiple stakeholders – farmers, the scientific world, consumers and the international community to transform the power of the farmers. Kurien used his Western education by transferring the Western concept of organization, and provided a model of rural development for India and the world community. He got the farmers to buy into his philosophy of marketing their products and helped create powerful brands to sell their products. Kurien was able to recruit the farmers by inspiring them through the vision of a cooperative that helps the farmers to help themselves. It is largely credit to Kurien's work that India is the largest producer of milk in the world today.

The final leader that we examine in this section is Vikram Sarabhai who many consider as the father of the Indian space program. Sarabhai was much more than a highly talented scientist. He was a dreamer, creator and innovator. He was a scion of a wealthy business family but was also a great believer in equality. He believed that: 'we have to be constantly alert to see that our long-inherited feudal reflexes do not seep back into our veins' (Parthasarathy, 2007). He motivated people with his positive attitude, created scientific institutions and programs because of his vision and foresight.

Sarabhai set up the first rocket launching station at Thumba and India launched its first space rocket under his leadership. He launched the Satellite Instructional Television Experiment which was the result of a negotiation between Sarabhai and NASA of USA (Parthasarathy, 2003). He also initiated the space project which is now a reality with the launching of many satellites. Sarabhai's vision still drives India's ambitious space program and continues to inspire Indians in the fields of science and technology. If leadership is a 'process of influencing the activities of an organized group in its efforts toward goal setting and goal achievement' (Stogdill, 1950) then Kurien and Sarabhai are examples of leaders who exemplify the ability to accomplish ambitious goals with their respective groups.

When analyzing these leaders, we can ask the question: are there unique personality characteristics that set these people apart and distinguish them as leaders or was it the situation and the circumstances that surrounded them that caused them to emerge as leaders? This is the ongoing debate between the trait theories of leadership (Boyatzis, 1982; Conger and Kanungo, 1988; Kirkpatrick and Locke, 1991) and situational theories of leadership (Fiedler, 1967; House and Mitchell, 1974).

The research evidence shows that traits do matter. Six traits on which leaders differ from non-leaders include drive or ambition, the desire to lead, honesty and integrity, self-confidence, cognitive ability and knowledge of the field or business (Stogdill, 1950; Kirkpatrick and Locke, 1991). Many of the traits discussed here are evident in the four leaders discussed above. Drive or ambition is particularly evident in Narayana Murthy and Verghese Kurian both of whom founded their respective organizations. Ratan Tata and Vikram Sarabhai, because of the family background and inherited position, displayed tremendous self-confidence. All four leaders displayed honesty and integrity and had a commanding knowledge of the fields they worked in.

To a large extent, the success of these men can be attributed to the specific circumstance of the organizations that they led. The unique situation of the organization and its external environment raised unique issues that needed to be managed. Consequently, the evaluation of success in a leadership situation is also a function of the situation. For example, Ratan Tata took over the reins of Tata Sons when Indian policy toward industry was being liberalized and the management had greater decision making power in the context of their companies. The CEO of Infosys founded the company when the power of the internet was beginning to be unleashed and the notion of outsourcing was rapidly gaining popularity. Verghese Kurien came upon the scene when the farmers were ready to be organized and there was social awareness in the country about the relevance and importance of cooperatives. In the case of Vikram Sarabhai, India had political leaders who were interested in science and technological progress, and he focused the resources and talent at his disposal to achieve greatness.

Like the immediate situation, the country (India), its myths, its culture, its politics and history create a larger context for leaders and what contributes to leadership effectiveness. Of the four leaders mentioned here, three of them came from relatively affluent backgrounds, were schooled in American Universities and came back to India to assume positions of leadership in their respective organizations. Like the mythical gods of yore, Rama and Krishna, all four of these leaders displayed nurturing qualities and pragmatism in their leadership styles. Narayana Murthy, the CEO of Infosys was exemplified for his humility; Ratan Tata of Tata Sons and Verghese Kurien for their strong sense of ethics and commitment to the welfare of the underprivileged, and Vikram Sarabhai for his visionary qualities and dynamism.

## GLOBAL IMPLICATIONS

What kind of manager or leader have the myths, cultural context and political history of India helped to create? What values have evolved and become institutionalized because of the unique context of the country? How are these leadership qualities different from values in the West? We would argue that there are four distinct values that can be showcased.

### The Ability to Adapt and Assimilate

Its troubled history, being an economically underdeveloped nation for most of the last century, has created among Indians a strong need to go out and seek opportunities and adapt to new and diverse conditions. Thomas Friedman (2005) points out that the educated Indian cannot only compete, but out-compete in the world of technology because of his or her ability to quickly understand and adapt to the current needs of new markets – see Commentary box.

---

## COMMENTARY BOX

### President of a Large Indian Engineering Company

In home grown companies such as ours the leadership styles are moving from paternalistic to participative especially with higher levels of international travel, and exposure to the company 'owners', and increased level and quality of education to the second generations in their family.

### CEO of a Consulting Company

In India, a very high premium is placed on knowledge and therefore education. Knowledge itself is considered power and the symbol of status. Brahmins enjoyed the highest status in Indian society and their profession was to acquire and impart the knowledge. The emphasis on gaining knowledge creates a very strong achievement orientation with a competitive spirit. On hindsight, I feel this is what is responsible for putting India in such an admirable position on the world map despite the serious problems of corruption and a humongous population.

---

The educated elite in India have been products of a formal British educational system and have also imbibed the traditional languages, myths, narratives, values and ethics. In a sense, they are optimally suited to benefit from globalization in that they can relate to the global aspect of business and are yet uniquely local and Indian. A familiarity with the English language and exposure to Western systems make it easier for the Indian manager to adapt to Western systems, than it is for the Western manager to adapt to India. Globalization has necessitated that Indian and Western organizations adapt to the other country's value systems. Current dependencies in the power structure demand greater adaptability on the part of Indian managers as they look for business and additional resources from the West. But in the course of time, the nature of dependency of this relationship is likely to shift and Western managers will recognize the importance of seeing the world from a more polycentric frame.

### Benevolent Paternalism as the Overriding Leadership Value

Many studies (Singh and Bhandarkar, 1990; Virmani and Guptan, 1991) have confirmed benevolent paternalism passed down from myth as a predominant leadership value. The role of *karta* as a father figure who is nurturing, caring, dependable, sacrificing, and yet demanding and authoritative, seems to be expected of Indian leaders. The leader evokes feelings of security, trust, and dependability in creating a familial culture (Sinha, 1980) and 'collectivism' which is strong in the Indian psyche.

Subordinates in India seem to push leaders further towards paternalism. They seem to expect it, relish it, and are motivated by a leader who behaves as a benevolent father figure. The genesis of this relationship probably goes back to the early socialization process which makes even adults in India strive for the father's approval (Ramanujan, 1989). The father as the family head is respected and obeyed; he helps, reprimands and encourages self-sacrificing behavior.

As we know, as families grow, the father grows differentially fond of different family members. A similar phenomenon is also evidenced in organizations (Pandey, 1989). There is a feeling that employees who are close to the 'men who matter' rise faster in organizations (Sinha, 2004). The leader often encourages certain subordinates to get close to him. The smart subordinates place themselves in positions where the leader might turn to them. Once they get to the leader, the leaders extend favors to them. This can be traced back to the *Bhagvada Gita* where subordinates are treated differentially based on their skills and abilities. The leaders start believing in their protégé and the protégé reciprocates by loyalty.

Some of these qualities are distinct to Asian cultures, while some of the leadership qualities are common to many cultures. The acceptance of authority and the style of 'benevolent paternalism' is effective in cultures like India which accept a high power distance. In Western cultures, the assertion of individualism, the ability to push one's ideas in a rational, logical fashion, are valued more and rewarded appropriately. However, the importance of personal relationships in career success is perhaps common across cultures. As leaders manage people, personal relationships that the leader and subordinates build play a large role in the success of the leaders and the subordinates.

## The Emphasis on Spirituality versus Materialism and Economic Rationality

The underlying spiritual context in India and Western nations (USA) is different. Here, we use the USA as our point of comparison. Religion and myths in India emphasize the notion of 'nishakamakarma' which is a perspective that emphasizes action without attachment to the fruits thereof (Chakraborty, 1991). A leader who behaves in accordance with this perspective is generally grounded in wisdom and a state of equanimity. This perspective is in stark contrast to the current Western 'results orientation' which emphasizes materialism, growth and competition (Pruzan, 2004). Closely related to the concept of 'nishakarma' are the concepts of 'selflessness' and 'non-attachment'.

A useful synonym which illuminates the paradoxical nature of the Indian perspective in this context is 'detached involvement'. The underlying idea is that instead of plying our egos and appraising activities by the resultant payoffs, and being elated when desires are fulfilled and disappointed when they are not, there is an alternate way to perform action. Leaders can act without being attached to fruits of their efforts. This also results in Indian leaders perhaps being a little more fatalistic in their action where they believe that they cannot control their destinies.

But both the Indian perspective and the Western perspective are changing because of their respective positions in the economic cycle of development. As Indian businesses grow, because of globalization, and technology developments, Indian managers and leaders are being influenced by Western business practices and are beginning to deify materialism, and becoming more competitive. As Western economies mature, their leaders are becoming more conscious of the larger responsibilities of business to their multiple stakeholders. In a sense globalization is providing an opportunity to assimilate different values and gradually realize a more balanced view of competition and the organization's role in a larger context for both India and the West.

## The Emphasis on Duty in India versus Rights in the West

The Indian approach to leadership and all action is grounded in the concept of 'relationship to others'. This complements the notion of 'servant leadership' (Greenleaf, 1977). The notion of servant leadership, although popularized in the West, is grounded in the Indian idea of duty and leadership. The Western focus is on freedom and the right to do what an individual can do. In the Indian context, the leader typically searches for his or her duty in relation to one's position in life and tries to behave in accordance with that duty, which is his/her *dharma*. In keeping with 'benevolent paternalism' the duty may be toward one's subordinates or toward doing what the leader believes is right for the organization.

In the Western context, individuals are conscious of their rights as individuals and employees. Consequently, leaders within organizations respect the employees for their ideas, contribution and what they bring to the organization. Yet, this ingrained need to protect one's right also creates a certain distance between the employee and the organization and the employee and the leader. The difference in orientation results in differences in perspective toward loyalty and also creates differences in the tenure of employees in organizations.

*Asia and the Pacific Rim*

**Blind Spots of Indian Leaders**

Indian leaders have been criticized for certain traits and qualities that they do not possess. It has often been said that they lack the aggressive, killer instinct. This is perhaps a corollary to the philosophy of 'detached involvement'. The lack of drive and results orientation tend to move the locus of control outside the individual, and more leaders in the Indian context tend to leave situations and problems to sort themselves out.

The concepts of individualism, creativity, innovation and speedy implementation are relatively new to the Indian psyche. The Indian economy has been protected and the government followed a licensing model where many of the key decisions were externally imposed on organizations. With the recent liberalization of government policy, and the globalization of commerce, Indian businesses are recognizing the importance of speedy decision making, innovation and results orientation and how they relate to survival, growth and organizational performance.

Finally, a culture that was until now more focused on the collective, and one that stressed family values, seniority and loyalty, is assimilating the Western values of individualism and respect for individual rights. Employees are becoming more aware of their skills and the demand for labor is creating greater mobility and a pressure on wages. Organizations across different countries are gradually assimilating values that are different from their own but relevant because of globalization. The eclectic organization with changing leadership values is gradually evolving to take its place in a world that is smaller and increasingly more inter-connected.

## REFERENCES

Adler, N. (1983), Cross-cultural management research: The ostrich and the trend. *Academy of Management Review*, **8** (2), 226–32.

Boyatzis, R. (1982), *The Competent Manager*, New York: Wiley and Sons.

Chakraborty, S. K. (1991), *Management by Values: Towards Cultural Congruence*, New Delhi: Oxford University Press.

Chakraborty, S. K. (1995), *Ethics in Management: Vedantic Perspectives*, New Delhi: Oxford University Press.

Choudhary, A. (2006), *Manya Connect Home: The Mystique of Krishna*, Vol 6.

Conger, J. A. and Kanungo, R. N. (1987), Toward a behavioral theory of charismatic leadership in organizational settings, *Academy of Management Review*, **12**, 637–47.

Cummings, L. L. and Schmidt, S. M. (1972), Managerial attitudes of Greeks: The roles of culture and industrialization, *Administrative Science Quarterly*, **17** (2), 265–72.

Damrosch, David *et al.* (eds) (2008), *The Longman Anthology of World Literature*, New York: Pearson Longman.

De Rue, L. (1994), Redefining myth and religion. Introduction to a conversation, *Zygon®* **29** (3), 315–20.

Eliot, T. S. (1948), *Notes Toward a Definition of Culture*, London: Harcourt Publishers.

Engardio, P. (2007), The Last Rajah: India's Ratan Tata aims to transform his once stodgy conglomerate into a global powerhouse, *Business Week*, 2 August.

Engardio, P. and McGregor, J. (2006), Karma capitalism: a special report, *Business Week*, 30 October.

Fiedler, F. E. (1967), *A Theory of Leadership Effectiveness*, New York: McGraw Hill.

Freidman, T. L. (2005), *The World is Flat: A Brief History of the Twenty-first Century*, New York: Farrar, Straus and Giroux.

Greenleaf, R. K. (1977), *Servant Leadership: A Journey to the Nature of Legitimate Power and Greatness*, Mahwah, NJ: Paulist Press.

Guha, R. (1997), *Dominance and Hegemony: History and Power in Colonial India*, Cambridge, MA: Harvard.

Hofstede, G. (1980), *Culture's Consequences: International Differences in Work Related Values*, Beverly Hills, CA: Sage Publications.

House, R. J. and Mitchell, T. R. (1974), Path-goal theory of leadership, *Journal of Contemporary Business*, **3**, 81–97.

Indolink: The Best of Both Worlds: www.indolink.com

Kirkpatrick, S. A. and Locke, E. A. (1991), Leadership: do traits matter?, *Academy of Management Executive*, **5** (2), 48–60.

Kumar, N. (2007), Leadership in a flat world: The past, present and the future of India, *Leadership Review*, **7**, 1–12.

Nachtigal, J. (2006), The uninformed American public: How they follow, *Illumine*, MMVI, **4**, 10.

Pandey, S. N. (1989), *Human Side of Tata Steel*, New Delhi: McGraw Hill.

Panikkar, K. M. (1953), *Asia and Western Dominance*, London: George Allen and Unwin.

Parthasarathy, R. (2003), Vikram Sarabhai (1919–1971): Architect of Indian Space, *The Hindu*, 3 April.

Parthasarathy, R. (2007), 100 people who shaped India, *India Today*.

Pruzan, P. (2004), Spirituality as the context of leadership, in L. Zsolnai (ed.) *Spirituality: East and West of Spirituality and Ethics in Management*, Dordrecht: Kluwer Academic Publishers.

Ramanujam, A. K. (1989), Is there an Indian way of thinking? An informal essay, *Contributions to Indian Sociology*, **25**, 41–58.

Rao, R. (1938), *Kanthapura*, London: George Allen and Unwin.

Rossi, I. and O'Higgins, E. (1980), The development of theories of culture, in I. Rossi (ed.), *People in Culture*, New York: Praeger, pp. 31–78.

Sekhar, R. C. (2001), Trends in ethics and styles of leadership in India, *Business Ethics: A European Review*, **10**, 360–3.

Singh, P. and Bhandarkar, A. (1990), *Corporate Success and Transformational Leadership*, New Delhi: Wiley Eastern.

Singhi, P. M. (2007), 100 people who shaped India, *India Today*.

Sinha, D. (2004), Pluralism and cultural conflict in India, www.crvp.org/book/series03

Sinha, J. B. P. (1980), *The Nurturant Task Leader*, New Delhi: Concept.

Sinha, J. B. P. (2004), *The Cultural Context of Leadership and Power*, Thousand Oaks, CA: Sage Publications.

Smircich, L. (1983a), Concepts of culture and organizational analysis, *Administrative Science Quarterly*, **28**, 339–58.

Smircich, L. (1983b), Organizations as shared meanings, in L. R. Pondy, P. Frost, G. Morgan, and T. Dandridge (eds), *Organizational Symbolism*, Greenwich, CT: JAI Press.

Srinivas, M. N. (1957), Caste in modern India, *The Journal of Asian Studies*, **16** (4), 529–48.

Stogdill, R. M. (1950), Leadership, membership and organization, *Psychological Bulletin*, **47**, 1–14.

Verma, J. R. (1997), Corporate governance in India: disciplining the dominant shareholder, *IIMB Management Review* (http://www.iimb.ernet.in/review.

Virmani, B. R. and Guptan, S. V. (1991), *Indian Management*, New Delhi: Vision Books.

# 18. Cultural mythology and global leadership in Russia

## Stanislav V. Shekshnia, Sheila M. Puffer and Daniel J. McCarthy

## INTRODUCTION

Almost a quarter of a century ago, the first author of this chapter entered a Moscow food store to start his first real job as an assistant manager. His memories of that six-month stint had virtually disappeared except for one story told to him on his first day. A middle-aged worker said that every new manager would hear it on the first day in the store. The anecdote was about a bright, young woman who became the general manager of a prestigious store very early in her career. One morning, an older worker knocked on her office door and asked for a glass of vodka to cure his hangover. Outraged by such an inappropriate request, the manager sent him off. Two hours later, he was back with the same plea: 'Give me a drink or I will die.' The answer was quick: 'If someone like you dies, the rest of us will be relieved.' One hour later, she called for the man to unload a truck, and when he did not answer she went down to confront him. He was sitting still at a table and did not respond. Angrily, the manager shook the worker's shoulder and realized that he was dead. The next day, she resigned and never again worked in food stores, one of the most attractive occupations in a hungry Soviet Union. Even for a 19-year-old, the story's message was clear – workers and alcohol were things to be taken seriously. The incident illustrates the important role that alcohol plays in the workplace as a cultural tradition in Russian society and how those traditions and values have become incorporated in the country's mythology. That early exposure to organizational mythology was the stimulus for the first author's interest in the subject, and led to his collecting and interpreting Russian organizational myths over the years.

Erich Fromm noted that in developed societies, the ruling minority creates its own mythology to try to convince the majority to accept its leadership, values, and objectives (Fromm, 1951). The mythology reflects the country's culture and is used to legitimatize the leadership in the eyes of that majority. And this has also been the case in Russia. Its leaders have traditionally used stories, including supernatural events or characters, to explain to followers the nature of the universe and humanity. Russian leaders have traditionally used such stories, tales, songs and jokes – mythology in a broad sense – as methods of influence and education. Current Russian business leaders have continued this tradition and created their own leadership folklore, which combines traditional themes with new ones reflecting business realities of the twenty-first century.

This chapter first covers traditional Protoslavic folklore and its relationship with Russia's leadership mythology, followed by state-sponsored myths of the nineteenth and twentieth centuries and their influence on Russian leadership. These sections provide background for current Russian leadership myths, which incorporate aspects from the past as well as from the present business and political environments. The next section deals with corporate leadership myths that have developed during the first two decades of the country's transition to a market economy. The chapter concludes with implications for leaders, and those who aspire to leadership or are involved in leadership development, of Russia's tradition of myths and leadership.

## OVERVIEW OF RUSSIAN MYTHOLOGY

Russian leadership mythology has its roots in Protoslavic myths, of which there is no written account (Golan, 1992). However, scholars agree that the principal hero of Protoslavic mythology is Perun (Golosovker, 1987; Klein, 2004). Perun is a heavenly god of thunder and lightning, fiery and dry, who rules the living world from his citadel high above, on the highest branch of the World Tree. Perun is a giver of rain for farmers, and the god of war and weapons (Rybakov, 1994). He looks like an old man, but changes his appearance at different times. Perun should be feared, prayed for, cajoled with sacrifices and gifts, and obeyed (Ivanov and Toporov, 1974). The Perun myth depicts important leadership attributes that have survived through centuries of Russian leadership tradition, including high power distance (lives on top of a tree, made from a different material, should be obeyed), brutality and aggression (fighting with thunder and fire, destroying enemies), and the ability to produce miracles (fire and rain).

Another part of the myth is that Perun dies every year when the sun reaches its highest point in the sky. Ancient Slavs celebrated the death of this feared god with dances, games, and meals, kicked effigies of Perun, and set them floating down rivers. Other gods then take the place of Perun until December when he is welcomed back with new festivities (Klein, 2004). This aspect of the myth depicts another important part of the Russian national character – duality, which translates into followers' specific behavior toward leaders. Leaders have divine status and command obedience and loyalty, but only to a point. When a stronger or more successful leader emerges, old loyalties are quickly forgotten and new ones are born. To maintain the loyalty of supporters, leaders must continue winning (producing new miracles), or keep competing leaders at bay (quickly destroy potential contenders).

Medieval Russian folklore continued the tradition of a god-like hero, but added important attributes to the profile of an ideal leader (Sedov, 1982). One of the most popular Russian fairy tales recounts the story of Ilya Muromets (Afanasev, 1957). A farmer's son from Karacharovo village near Murom, Ilya Muromets was gravely ill and was near motionless until age 33. Cured by an old singer, Ilya acquired enormous strength, and his mythical life began. He went to the Russian capital, Kiev, to serve Prince Vladimir, the Red Sun. On his way he defeated, by dint of sheer force, various enemies including Solovey-Razboynik (the Nightingale Robber), a monster who lived in a forest and killed people with his whistle. Ilya became a favorite knight of the Prince by performing heroic deeds like defending Kiev from nomads and defeating other knights in bloody duels.

Other folk mythical heroes similar to Ilya include Mikula Selianinovich, a farmer who became a mighty warrior, and Ivan Tsarevich, the youngest son of the tsar-catching magical fire-bird, who defeated supernatural enemies (Afanasev, 1957). Unlike in Protoslavic mythology, heroes during this period became human beings, but with links to supernatural forces. They all performed miracles with their hands, but with supernatural help, and had special blessings from above, which other humans lacked. Russian folklore reinforces the idea of the supernatural in leaders, while adding new attributes.

First, folk heroes are deeply rooted in the Russian land. Some are physically connected with the earth, which serves as their principal source of strength, and when uprooted, they lose their strength. Clearly, the earth symbolizes tradition, and successful leaders must respect tradition and act accordingly. Second, although heroes are extremely strong and effective, they are not sophisticated, and their principal attributes are sheer physical power, assistance from supernatural forces, will and determination, and occasionally personal cunning. They all become warriors at some point, fighting ferociously, always defeating and often humiliating their enemies. Showing mercy is not part of their character. Enemies are strangers, either foreigners or non-human creatures who try to take advantage of others in unfortunate circumstances. These enemies are always inferior to the heroes (Putilov, 1971; Zelenin, 1991). Third, folkloric heroes are benevolent. They protect and defend the weak and poor, as well as the motherland, which is also portrayed as weak and poor and surrounded by cowardly enemies. The mighty knights are the only hope of the motherland and its people. Most folkloric heroes have humble backgrounds, and become famous and powerful through some supernatural event. Luck, and nothing else, brings major breakthroughs.

In sum, these three characteristics of Russian folkloric heroes not only create an image of an effective leader, but also provide advice to followers seeking to benefit from the leader's protection and service. They must obey the leader and rely on him for thinking and setting the direction. They must also subordinate their personal egos and accept less-than-good treatment in exchange for protection from the leader who possesses supernatural powers. Finally, they must not try to play by the leader's rules, since such behavior could have negative consequences: leaders have their own rules.

**State-Sponsored Myths and Leadership Models**

From the early nineteenth century, the centralized Russian state took on the role of creating, modifying, and communicating myths to support the monarch's absolute power, continuous territorial expansion to the west and east, the special role of the Russian state as the Third Rome, and protection of the Slavic people and Orthodox Christians. Some of the country's best talents, including writers Alexander Pushkin and Vassily Zhukovski, painters Victor Vasnetsov and Nikolay Reirich, and composers Peter Tchaikovsky and Nikolay Rimsky-Korsakov, participated, perhaps unconsciously, in the creation of this new ethos, based to a large extent on traditional Russian folk-lore.

One of the most powerful and influential myths of that era was of Oleg the Visionary, a tenth-century Russian king. Little is known about the real Oleg, who is believed to have been of Norwegian origin and ruled in Novgorod and later in Kiev, although some historians question his existence (Kliuchevskii, 1989). The mythical Oleg is credited with exceptional abilities and deeds. He possessed unusual foresight, intelligence, energy, and physical power. He was a skillful warrior, talented strategist, canny statesman and great patriot. Oleg created the first Russian centralized state with Kiev as its capital, expanded the Russian territory by conquering neighboring tribes, and marched on Constantinople where he nailed his shield to the main gate as the symbol of Russia's power. The mythical king was known as being brutal toward his enemies, fair with his subjects, and was considered to be religious, a man of the people, and sentimental. Oleg died a mythical death while visiting the remains of his favorite horse and being bitten by a snake hidden in the horse's skull (Pushkin, 1950; Sedov, 1982).

Parents at all levels of nineteenth-century Russian society used the Oleg myth to educate their children and shape their leadership. The myth reinforced exceptional qualities – the ability to produce miracles, exhibit patriotism, hatred, and brutality toward enemies or strangers, and promote the philosophy that ends justify the means. It also glorified war as a major leadership arena (Likhachev, 1989; Vernadskii, 1996). The impact of the Oleg myth, along with other leadership myths, was huge. Millions of young Russian men chose the military as a career even though the nobility was exempt from military service; they led troops into the Caucasus mountains, Central Asian steppes and deserts, and Manchuria. They did so in a decisive and authoritarian way, showed little mercy to enemies, and died without questioning their superiors' orders. They believed in Russia's special destiny, were ready to give their lives to that cause and for personal glory, and sacrificed the lives of their subordinates to achieve these goals. This leadership mentality dominated the nineteenth century and survived into the next, contributing to great losses suffered in World War I, the 1917 October Revolution, and the ensuing civil war.

When the Bolsheviks took power in 1917, they dethroned heroes of the old regime, both real and mythical, and Oleg the Visionary was declared an invention of tsarist propaganda (Black, 1962). Yet, the new regime soon began to create its own myths, including those about leaders (Pipes, 1954; Black, 1962). In the Soviet Union, with its uniform ideology, centralized State, and all-powerful brainwashing apparatus, State-sponsored mythology reached its peak. All methods of communication were employed – poetry, prose, visual arts, newspapers and word of mouth. Like nowhere else, with the possible exception of Nazi Germany, the Soviet government used new technologies such as cinematography, photography, and later radio and television, to create and spread new myths (Golomshtok, 1994). The epoch of 'romantic totalitarianism' produced many leadership myths, but the one about Stalin was by far the most influential, surviving to the present and combining many characteristics of traditional Russian myths with features reflecting twentieth-century realities.

The mythical Stalin had humble beginnings, coming from a poor family in Georgia, a poor region on the outskirts of the empire, with bleak prospects. But in a near-supernatural course of events, he discovered the 'right' ideology – Marxism – became enlightened, and started on his path of liberating the world from exploiters. The rest was straightforward. Using his exceptional intelligence, will, and endurance, he produced a series of miracles such as procuring cash for the underground Bolshevik party, escaping from the tsarist police, defending encircled Tsaritsin (later named Stalingrad) against the massively superior White Guard forces, eradicating bourgeois elements from the Communist Party, industrializing Russia, winning wars, 'liberating' Eastern Europe from capitalism, and other such 'heroic' deeds (Ginzburg, 1990). His miracles were portrayed as changing the world, improving the lives of poor, hard-working people, and making the lives of the rich and selfish miserable (Gefter, 1989).

Although the myth about Stalin was orchestrated by Stalin himself and his entourage, as all myths do, it took on a life of its own and millions of people perpetuated and embellished it. In 1939, at a Moscow exhibition commemorating Stalin's 60th birthday, thousands of people submitted art work depicting the great leader. These included 5-meter-tall statues of him made by factory workers, and school children's pencil drawings depicting him working late at night to protect sleeping children (German, 2000).

## BRIDGING FOLK AND STATE MYTHS

The image of the mythical Stalin is crucial in understanding what the mid-twentieth-century Russian population perceived as their ideal leader. First, the mythical Stalin shares many characteristics of Russian folkloric heroes: an almost divine nature, the ability to perform miracles, and exhibiting patriotism and care for the weak and poor (Gefter, 1989). Stalin is a father of Russian people: he provides guidance, sets the rules, and protects his children. Unlike mothers, he is not sentimental. His love is deep below the surface, and he can be severe with his children if they misbehave (Ginzburg, 1990). His right to lead is divine: one cannot choose a father, and therefore should not challenge him since children have a moral obligation to follow their parents. According to a popular song of 1939:

> We carry your name with us everywhere,
> In days of struggle and times of trial,
> And we follow you on any exploit,
> You are our banner of victory, our Stalin!
> (translation by the authors)

Stalin is seen as caring about the long-term interests of his children and thus may make them suffer today to benefit in the future. He is an adult while everyone else is a child. He knows things children do not know, and will never know. He is cast from a different mold, yet still speaks the language of his children. He simplifies the world for his people, and thanks to him, they always know what is right and wrong (Ginzburg, 1990). As the father, the mythical Stalin sets the rules and alters them as the situation changes, and no rules are permanent except one – obedience to the leader. He has the supreme right to judge, and if he declares something black, it becomes black until he calls it white.

Stalin's 'family' (the Russian people) is unique and blessed with a divine mission – to liberate the workers of the world. Anything that helps advance this cause is good. He fights enemies of working people, but can also have tactical alliances with them. When a war starts, the enemy is shown no mercy (Conquest, 1991; Gorlizki and Khlevniuk, 2004). Blessed with its great cause, Soviet Russia is surrounded with enemies, but Stalin is vigilant, and demands that everyone be vigilant and merciless to the foes. The mythical Stalin is a simple, and even ascetic, person, devoting his life to the service of his people. He has no hobbies, no family life, and no weaknesses (Ginzburg, 1990; Brackman, 2001). In addition to traditional, although often hyperbolized leadership attributes, the mythical Stalin has some modern features. First, he is a scholar and not only embraces, but produces knowledge, and advances philosophy, political economy, sociology, and even linguistics. He is a sage, not simply a ruthless warrior or lucky adventurer (Golomshtok, 1994). The mythical Stalin is also a teacher, who takes time to explain things to his students, correct their mistakes, and encourage their achievements. Second, Stalin not only works hard at times like the old Russian mythical heroes, but never stops working. He never sleeps, never parties, never takes a vacation. He is a man of work (Brackman, 2001). Third, there is a global dimension to his leadership: Stalin is the father of all working people, not only Russians. He is a savior of humankind, a leader of the universe (Gorlizki and Khlevniuk, 2004). His myth was spread through all means, from scientific publications to songs of Kazakh *akyns* (folk poets), as well as art and political propaganda (Brackman, 2001). All had a tremendous impact on the country, as well as on the leadership practices in all areas of Russian life, including the economy (Mawdsley, 2003).

When the real Stalin died in 1953, the Russian people experienced a powerful shock. People were lost because their father, who was immortal, had passed away (Gefter, 1989). Their great wish 'Ты живи и здравствуй, наш Отец Родной!' ('Stay alive and healthy, our Father!') did not materialize. Losing Stalin, they had lost everything – a family member, a leader, a protector, a role model. The second shock came when Khrushchev and his supporters tried to demystify Stalin at the twentieth congress of the Communist Party in 1956 (Gorlizki and Khlevniuk, 2004). Even half a century later, Stalin's myth was still alive (Gefter, 1989). Yet, the mythical Stalin had lost most of his modernist features, such as scholarly wisdom or a global dimension, but had preserved the more traditional ones of a patriot, a street-smart, effective leader with an autocratic and ruthless style, and a skillful politician with a situational approach to ethics.

Stalin's leadership myth had a major impact on leadership practices in Russian enterprises of the 1950s through the 1980s. The famous 'red directors' (Granick, 1961) internalized Stalin's school of leadership, and borrowed heavily from the mythical Stalin. They were focused on their enterprises, practiced centralized decision making and personal accountability for their followers, believed in science and scientific progress; were autocratic, and when needed, brutal and merciless. At the same time, they felt responsible toward their subordinates, going well beyond factory walls. The father-children model worked well in these environments. Praise was scarce, criticism harsh, but protection was always there unless a child committed a moral crime against the father (Gorlizki and Khlevniuk, 2004).

Red directors had flexible ethical principles, except for their loyalty to their enterprises. They worked hard, knew every detail, and fought vigorously for their enterprises, expecting the same from their workers. They demonstrated personal modesty, and carefully hid any excesses in their personal lives (Granick, 1961; Prokhorov, 2002). This leadership style and its variations helped create modern Soviet industry – giant metallurgical combines and aluminum smelters, petrochemical and auto plants, oil and gas pipelines, and large pulp and paper mills. Yet, that style turned out to be ineffective in the highly unstructured conditions of the early market economy of the early 1990s, and most red directors lost out to a new breed of Russian entrepreneurs (Fey *et al.*, 2001; Prokhorov, 2002; Kets de Vries *et al.*, 2004).

All the heroes of the leadership myths described earlier are male, a clear indication of male-dominated Russian society throughout history. While prominent women have emerged, none to our knowledge has been elevated to mythological status. These include Baba Yaga, a witch with magical powers in Russian folktales, Catherine the Great, the nineteenth-century Russian empress, Valentina Tereshkova, the first female cosmonaut, and Ekaterina Furtseva, Khrushchev's minister of culture. And numerous women have achieved prominence and success in the new market economy (Zolotov, 2007; Walker, 2007), but none has yet been elevated to mythological status. Women aspiring to leadership positions must be decisive and authoritative, character-istics typically associated with men (Prokhorov, 2002; Klein, 2004), while still displaying traditional feminine qualities such as nurturing and compassion (Puffer, 1994).

## OVERVIEW OF RUSSIAN LEADERSHIP

Entering the twenty-first century, Russia was in deep crisis – the empire it had nurtured for five centuries had collapsed. Its territory shrank to that of the seventeenth century, the ideology it believed in for seven decades had bank-rupted the country and its people, the leaders it worshiped had been dethroned and discredited (Solnick, 1998). Society badly needed new meaning, new values, and new role models. Wild Russian capitalism (Kets de Vries, 2000) immediately produced its own answer in the form of greed, the unlimited power of money, a lack of moral limitations, and new heroes in leather jack-ets – gangsters (Shevtsova, 1999). The Russian elite, initially paralyzed, even-tually became dissatisfied and began its own search for values and heroes. Following tradition, the answer was found in leaders – the newly elected pres-ident, Vladimir Putin, and the legendary Peter the Great who ruled in the early eighteenth century. During the early 2000s, myths arose in the country about both leaders.

In 2003, St Petersburg celebrated its 300th anniversary. The symbolic date became an opportunity to bring center stage a positive role model – the mythical Peter the Great. President Putin called the city's founder, Peter the Great, a 'great tsar', 'a great reformer', and 'a great Russian leader'. According to opinion polls, ordinary Russians agreed with their president. Peter has been consistently ranked first in polls asking: 'Who is the greatest Russian leader of all time?' (*Peter the Great: Pro and Contra*, 2001). Mythical Peter combines many attributes of the Russian leadership tradition with contemporary Russian ideas on what a good leader should be. He was a great patriot and successful warrior who gained for Russia about a million square kilometers of new territories in the west and east, changing its geopolitical situation by making it part of Europe. He equipped Russia with two mandatory attributes of a European power – a regular army and navy – and in doing so made Russia a leading European power (Kliuchevskii, 1989).

Peter also cleansed the State apparatus of conservative and lazy boyars – representatives of the old nobility – and replaced them with dynamic young people from other social strata. He strengthened centralized power and subjugated all State enemies (Platonov, 2001). Blessed with exceptional physical power and endurance, Peter led with an iron will and never regarded human cost as a limiting factor. Straightforward and accessible, he provided direction to the masses and was admired by them (Massie, 1981).

He exhibited traditional leadership attributes like an imposing physical presence, being over two meters tall, working 18 hours a day, tearing apart iron horse shoes and coins with his bare hands, military and naval strategic savvy, and great vision. He seemed to perform miracles that no one else could, including leading the building of St Petersburg. He showed patriotism, cared for the weak and poor, was decisive, dedicated, down-to-earth, and led with an authoritarian style. Mythical Peter laid the foundations for Russian mining and manufacturing industries by establishing over 300 industrial mines, mills and factories. He modernized all areas of the nation's life – education, industry, trade and family life. He traveled abroad and learned from the rest of the world, and made others follow his example. His myth creates new attributes that reflect today's realities – the ability to produce economic results, conduct relations with foreign countries, and learn from them.

It is of little relevance what the real Peter was like as a leader and a person. Modern Russian society is not interested in his complex, neurotic, narcissistic personality with a strong antisocial disposition, described by some as paranoid (Platonov, 2001; Kets de Vries and Shekshnia, 2006), nor in his true abilities. He was said to be of average intelligence, demonstrating exceptional energy and tenacity, and an authentic leadership style that was highly opportunistic, authoritarian, brutal and somewhat erratic (Richmond, 1996). Suspicious of all Russians and paranoid toward the old elite, Peter often acted out of fear, often lost his temper, and committed atrocities. Having an extremely low opinion of his compatriots' abilities, especially lower classes, Peter pushed rather than persuaded, pulling his followers along with him, and was responsible for hundreds of thousands of deaths during his reign (Brikner, 2002). Peter the Great has become a myth that current Russian leaders use to promote the type of leadership they believe is right for the country – patriotic and traditional at the core, but open to useful techniques and ideas from elsewhere, aggressive in pursuing agendas, and assertive and decisive.

Against the backdrop of the mythical Peter the Great, the early 2000s have witnessed another myth in the making, that of Vladimir Putin who has been cast as the greatest political leader of the new Russia. In 2007, he was constantly described on television as being a great leader, wise and all power-ful, and always thinking about creating a democratic society beyond what mere mortals would dare believe (Pankin, 2007). Attentive observers might gain insights into his leadership style by watching him on TV, analyzing his speeches, reading the book, *First Person*, based on interviews with him, and reflecting on his childhood (Putin, 2000). Such analysis might reveal an inse-cure personality with a controlling disposition, and a nature that some have viewed as paranoid (Kets de Vries and Shekshnia, 2006). Such a combination can produce a mixture of leadership styles, conducive to monitoring internal operations and scanning the environment. In the long term, too much control and monitoring can become highly dysfunctional, creating a toxic environ-ment that talented people will try to escape from (Hogan *et al.*, 1997; Kets de Vries, 2000). Leaders with this personality make-up can be rigid, judgmental, uncomfortable expressing emotions, quick to take offense, and unforgiving of perceived insults (Shapiro, 1965; Jack, 2004; Politkovskaya, 2004; Kets de Vries and Shekshnia, 2006).

But that description is not the mythical Putin presented to the Russian people. The State-controlled mass media, high government officials, func-tionaries of his United Russia party, and loyal artists have carefully created an image of the president that fits their idea of effective leadership. Putin's portrait can be found in most officials' offices, and pop songs extol his disci-pline. Cafés, ice creams, and tomatoes are named after him (Jack, 2004). His face is on T-shirts, carpets, and *matryoshka* dolls. He is the hero of a children's textbook in which he is depicted as a jet pilot, who does not smoke, and loves his family. Millions of citizens, perhaps unconsciously, participate in this creative myth-making by passing on the image to their children, relatives, and friends, often embellishing the legend. Opinion polls consistently show that the majority of Russians trust their president, approve of his actions, and want him to remain in power (Baker and Glasser, 2006).

The mythical Putin shares many characteristics of other mythical Russian leaders. He is viewed as a committed patriot closely tied to the motherland, ready to fight for its interests and dignity. He is kind to the Russian people yet firm toward enemies, be they Georgians, Ukrainians, Americans or Chinese. The world is full of danger, and only a vigilant leader can secure Russia's interests in such a world (Politkovskaya, 2004).

The mythical Putin is also capable of producing miracles. The Russian economy grew rapidly during his presidency, pensions, salaries of government workers, and real incomes increased, Russia's status as an international power was regained, and the army regained respect (Baker and Glasser, 2006). His style is viewed as pragmatic, results-oriented, straightforward, and effective. He does not waste time on intellectual discussions, getting straight to the point. He appears to be in control, keeps a cool head, and is businesslike and direct. He speaks the language of everyday citizens and appears to care about their well-being. Mythical Putin is one of the people, but is the leader of the Russian nation, and is blessed with a 'divine mission'. Like other mythical heroes, the mythical Putin does not make mistakes. If something does not work, it is the fault of cowardly enemies, incompetent aides, or unfortunate circumstances (Baker and Glasser, 2006). Thanks to his superhuman status, the leader is beyond criticism and does not need any improvement (Politkovskaya, 2004).

Beyond traditional leadership attributes, the mythical Putin has some modern features that make him more human, and therefore easier to relate to. He is a sports fanatic, lives a healthy lifestyle, loves his family and protects its privacy, cares for pets, and maintains relationships with old friends. He dresses well and attends sporting events and pop concerts. In short, a modern Russian leader must have a human side, and even some minor weaknesses. Although the Putin leadership myth is still in the making, it has already had a huge impact on how Russian society functions (Jack, 2004; Baker and Glasser, 2006).

## Corporate Leadership Myths

The corporate sector that was transitioning in the 1990s from the centralized Soviet system to a market-oriented economy was quick to create its own myths. One of the first Russian companies to gain prominence in the West was cellular operator VimpelCom, one of the first Russian firms to list shares on the New York Stock Exchange as early as 1996. The true and not-so-true stories about the founder and CEO Dmitrii Zimin, known in the company as the Zimin legends, form a core of corporate mythology and explain what makes a good leader in VimpelCom's environment.

One of the most popular stories is about Zimin sleeping in his office rather than going home after late meetings. It reinforces what Zimin always preached – total commitment to the company and hard work. Another story depicts

Zimin as a liberal, enlightened leader, who has a habit of walking around his company, drinking tea and even cognac with rank-and-file employees, and discussing art, world affairs, and science. It reinforces leadership attributes of intelligence, accessibility, and uniqueness. Another anecdote depicts Zimin being told that the construction manager had stolen from the company, and responding: 'They always steal in construction, and at least he is a modest thief.' The message is clear that it is OK to steal sometimes, or commit other minor offenses, as long as you are modest and loyal to the boss.

Another well-known Russian company, which entered a joint venture with a Western global giant, also produced its own leadership mythology. In one story, one of the cofounders threw a heavy ash tray at a consultant from a top-tier company who was not clear in his presentation. Such managerial behavior is common enough to have been addressed in a North American study of toxic emotions at work (Frost, 2003). The consulting company withdrew the injured employee, but continued its work as if nothing extraordinary had happened. The story demonstrates that effective leaders can be tough, decisive, abrasive, and even violent. They live by their own rules which they expect to be accepted by others, including managers of international companies.

In another corporate myth, the 'hero' arranged a corporate lawyer's release from prison. Here we see a leader who can perform 'miracles', does not let his people down, and plays by his own rules. In a third widely told story, the founder, accompanied by armed guards, held off two busloads of gunmen trying to take control of his company's production facility, following a court decision in a corporate battle, and defended it until a favorable ruling was obtained. The moral of this story is that the leader can produce 'miracles' by being courageous, firm, and at times, violent.

These examples show that corporate myths vary and reflect different styles and values of their leaders. Some common themes emerge, many of which resonate with traditional Russian leadership myths, while others reflect specific realities of the current Russian business environment. Many contemporary corporate leaders have innately understood the importance of incorporating myths into their repertoire of leadership techniques. The myths demonstrate fundamental elements of leadership from traditional mythology, often refining or supplementing them with attributes needed in the contemporary business environment.

## RUSSIAN MYTHOLOGY-BASED LEADERSHIP THEMES

Five themes that are relevant for leadership in today's Russia can be derived from Russian mythology-based leadership and are described below.

## Delivering Extraordinary Results

As in the traditional myths, today's leaders are expected to produce things that other mortals are not capable of, and if one wants to be a legitimate leader, one should learn and practice this magic art. An example is provided in the Commentary box about an owner of a Russian consulting company.

---

### COMMENTARY BOX

#### Leader of a Russian Consulting Company

They [employees] tell all kinds of stories about me. I decided to try to understand if there was any substance to them, and it turned out that they were about miracles. They sincerely believed that I can do things that nobody else could. So I took notice, and from time to time I produce something special, like an interview on the front page of *Kommersant* [the leading Russian business daily], secure an exceptionally large contract, or even have a meeting with a US President. After one such event, I can do nothing for months and the employees still admire me and are ready to die for me.

---

### Demonstrating Superior Ability

Related to the art of making miracles is a myth of Russian business leaders possessing superior qualities or abilities to make them stand out from the crowd. This could be anything from exceptional calculating skills ('he multiplies four-digit numbers in his head' – a myth about a CEO of a mining company) to an unparalleled attractiveness to women ('no woman can resist him' – a myth about a CEO of a metallurgical conglomerate). The leaders may never use such characteristics for business purposes, but the mere thought of having them puts such leaders in a category of super humans, thus giving them a 'divine' right to lead others.

### Exempt From the Rules

Being cast from a different mold, business leaders play by different rules. A popular myth in a retail company with a culture of strict discipline and long hours is that its founder-chairman works only four hours a day. He has explained: 'I put in at least 80 hours a week, but I do not spend most of it in the office. If my employees think that I am a genius, who can do everything in a couple of hours a day, I am fine with that. If it makes them work harder, even better.' The rules for leaders, which they set themselves, do not apply to the rank-and-file, who have to play by different ones. And, extending into business ethics, a company may have a written or unwritten code of conduct which is mandatory for everybody, but leaders are exempt from it and are free to act according to their own instincts.

## Being a Caregiver to the Common People

Another theme in contemporary corporate leadership mythology resonates strongly with Russian tradition – the leader as a caretaker of his/her followers. A very popular myth at VimpelCom is that after the country's 1998 financial crisis, Dr Zimin refused to draw a salary, but kept everyone else's compensation unchanged. A Russian leader may be rough, authoritarian, and even violent, but should not forget his fatherly role – to provide overall direction, explain the rules, and help and protect those in one's care in the face of great need or danger. This characteristic is a deeply rooted Russian cultural tradition, which in one form or another, is omnipresent in today's business life.

## Acting Assertively

'If you want to survive, you need to establish yourself here' is the first phrase a new manager hears at one of the most aggressive private equity firms in Russia. Then he/she hears a myth about the company's founder, who while negotiating the most important deal in the firm's history, announced to the opposing side that he would not move from the office until the deal was signed. After ten hours of negotiations, the exhausted hosts begged for mercy, but the entrepreneur was firm. Those representing the other side tried everything – proposed to re-start early the next morning, offered wine, brandy, and food, and even went to sleep in their chairs, but the entrepreneur was unyielding. After 18 hours of sitting firm, he got his deal.

In some corporate mythologies, such as VimpelCom's, the leaders combine assertiveness with flexibility, while in others like in the ash tray-throwing example it is intensified by aggressiveness and even violence. Yet it is an important attribute of leadership myths in virtually every successful Russian company. Although major themes of corporate leadership mythology resonate with traditional Russian and State-sponsored leadership myths, the corporate myth is not static. Important attributes of mythical business leaders of the 1990s, such as ruthlessness and selfishness, are no longer condoned. In the next decade we should expect a further evolution of Russian corporate leadership myths that reflect the challenges that business leaders face at that time.

The changes will be largely affected by the direction that Russian society and the economy take over the next several years (McCarthy *et al.*, 2005).

## GLOBAL IMPLICATIONS

Those who would do business with Russian corporate leaders can benefit from learning about mythical Russian leadership as well as contemporary corporate folklore, since current leaders, consciously or not, often draw on Russian mythology. Russian business leaders see themselves as possessing unique qualities, even producing 'miracles', and relish accomplishments that support this myth. They may present themselves as being larger than life, speaking in an eloquent fashion, and presenting an imposing or authoritative figure. Yet, Russian leaders may also demonstrate a paternal role, showing care and support for their employees. They are often viewed as having a mandate from their employees that supports whatever actions they take.

Thus, when dealing with Russian business leaders, it is important to recognize that they often enjoy mythological status within their own enterprises, and that people matter more to them than written rules and agreements. Members of their in-group are often given preferential treatment, an important factor in understanding the dynamics of a negotiating session and sensing the roles of various players. The senior executive always has the power, regardless of what others in his entourage may say. Finally, Russian corporate leaders expect special treatment from others, including other senior executives with whom they conduct business. Such deference is not based sheerly on ego, but also on their perceived mythological status within their organizations. This status requires that their image be recognized and respected, particularly in the presence of their employees or other business leaders. So although the behavior of Russian corporate leaders can sometimes be viewed as brash and high-handed, an understanding of their 'mythological' status can serve as a guide for interpreting such behavior in a more culturally grounded context.

## MYTHS AND RUSSIAN LEADERSHIP –
## A CENTURIES-LONG CYCLE

Myths create leaders, and leaders create new myths, which in turn create new leaders. For centuries, this cycle has proven to be a driving force in Russian history, contributing substantially to an underpinning of the Russian leadership style. It has produced such salient attributes as divine (exceptional) qualities and therefore high distance between leaders and followers, as well as the ability to deliver miracles (extraordinary results) at virtually any cost, having responsibility to God (superiors) rather than to their followers.

Consciously or subconsciously, successful Russian leaders have recognized myths as effective instruments for leading and reinforcing their influence. During the nineteenth and especially the twentieth centuries, leadership mythology became institutionalized as a state-sponsored activity, which reached an unprecedented scale and had an enormous impact on Russian society. Yet individual leaders have also created their own myths, skillfully using them to promote their personalities and agendas. Clearly, Russia has been extremely rich in the quantity, variety and pervasiveness of leadership myths, which have taken the form of stories, anecdotes, jokes, books and movies. In the current business environment, leaders of newly created private companies have continued this tradition, and a rich business leadership mythology has emerged over the past two decades.

Corporate leaders actively use myths to influence employee behavior, reinforce their authority, and select and develop future leaders. The myths they create are also intended to enhance their leadership image among numerous external constituencies including customers, suppliers, business partners, investors, government officials, and even the general public. Russian history has shown that myths can be a powerful instrument in enhancing a leader's image and power. However, when used indiscriminately, corporate myths can be counterproductive and may perpetuate outmoded behaviors and attributes unsuited to the country's rapidly changing environment. To avoid such negative outcomes, business leaders and those responsible for leadership development must recognize the importance of leadership myths, but must use them carefully when reinforcing certain leadership attributes. Effectively managing corporate mythology has undoubtedly considerable potential to shape leadership and leadership development in Russia.

# REFERENCES

Afanasev, A. N. (1957), Народные Русские Сказк *(Russian Folk Tales)*, Vols. 1–3, Moscow: Goslitizdat.

Baker, P. and Glasser, S. (2006), *Kremlin Rising: Vladimir Putin's Russia and the End of Revolution*, New York: Scribner.

Black, C. E. (1962), *Rewriting Russian History: Soviet Interpretation of Russia's Past*, New York: Vintage Books.

Brackman, R. (2001), *The Secret File of Joseph Stalin*, New York: Routledge.

Brikner, A. (2002), История Петра Великого *(History of Peter the Great)*, Moscow: ACT.

Conquest, R. (1991), *The Great Terror: A Reassessment*, Oxford: Oxford University Press.

Fey, C. F., Adaeva, M. and Vikovskaya, A. (2001), Developing a model of leadership styles: What works best in Russia, *International Business Review*, **10**, 615–43.

Fromm, E. (1951), *The Forgotten Language: An Introduction to the Understanding of Dreams, Fairy Tales and Myths*, New York: Rinehart.

Frost, P. J. (2003), *Toxic Emotions at Work: How Compassionate Managers Handle Pain and Conflict*, Boston, MA: Harvard Business School Press.

Gefter, M. (1989), От анти-Сталина к не-Сталину: непройденны путь *(From Anti-Stalin to Non-Stalin: The Path Not Taken)*, Moscow: Progress.

German, M. I. (2000), Модернизм. Искусство первой половины XX века *(Modernism: Art of the First Half of the 20th Century)*, St Petersburg: Azbuka-Klassika.

Ginzburg, E. S. (1990),Крутой Маршрут: Хроника Культа Личности' *(Steep Road: Chronicle of the Cult of Personality)*, Moscow: Sovetskii Pisatel.

Golan, A. (1992), Миф и символ *(Myths and Symbols)*, Moscow: Russlit.

Golomshtok, I. V. (1994), Тоталитарное искусство *(Totalitarian Art)*, Moscow: Galart.

Golosovker, Ia. E. (1987),Логика мифа *(The Logic of Myths)*, Moscow: Nauka.

Gorlizki, Y. and Khlevniuk, O. (2004), *Cold Peace*, Oxford: Oxford University Press.

Granick, D. (1961), *The Red Executive*, New York: Doubleday Anchor.

Hogan, R. T., Johnson, J. and Briggs, R. (eds) (1997), *Handbook of Personality Psychology*, New York: Morgan Kaufmann.

Ivanov, V. V. and Toporov, V. N. (1974), Исследования в области славянских древностей *(Research on Slavic Antiquity)*, Moscow: Nauka.

Jack, A. (2004), *Inside Putin's Russia*, London: Granta Books.

Kets de Vries, M. F. R. (2000), Journey into the 'Wild East': Leadership style and organizational practices in Russia, *Organizational Dynamics*, **28** (4), 67–81.

Kets de Vries, M. F. R. (2001), *The Leadership Mystique*, London: Pearson Education.

Kets de Vries, M. F. R. and Shekshnia, S. (2006), Vladimir Putin, CEO of Russia Inc., *Harvard Business Review Russia*, **66–78**, January–February.

Kets de Vries, M. F. R., Shekshnia, S., Korotov, K. and Florent-Treacy, E. (2004), *The New Russian Business Leaders*, Cheltenham, and Northampton, MA: Edward Elgar.

Klein, L. S. (2004), Воскрешение Перуна *(The Revival of Perun)*, St Petersburg: Eurasia.

Kliuchevskii, V. O. (1989), Сочинения в 9 томах *(Works in 9 Volumes)*, Vol. 4, Russian History, Part IV, Moscow: Mysl.

Likhachev, D. S. (1989), Заметки и наблюдения: Из записных книжек разных лет· *(Notes and Observations: From Notebooks Over the Years)*, Leningrad: Sovetskii Pisatel.

Massie, R. K. (1981), *Peter the Great: His Life and World*, New York: Knopf.

Mawdsley, E. (2003), *Stalin's Years: Soviet Union in 1929-1953*, Manchester: Manchester University Press.

McCarthy, D. J., Puffer, S. M., Vikhanski, O. S. and Naumov, A. I. (2005), Russian managers in the New Europe: Need for a new management style, *Organizational Dynamics*, **34** (3), 231–46.

Pankin, A. (2007), A democratic personality cult, *Moscow Times*, 30 October, 10.

Петр Великий: Pro et Contra *(Peter the Great: Pro et Contra)* (2001), St Petersburg: Russian Christian Humanitarian Institute.

Pipes, R. (1954), *The Formation of the Soviet Union: Communism and Nationalism*, 1917–1923, Cambridge, MA: Harvard University Press.

Platonov, S. (2001), Петр Великий: личность и свершения. (Peter the Great: Personality and Deeds), in S. Platonov Под шапкой Мономаха *(Under The Monomach's Hat*, Moscow: Progress-Traditsiia.

Politkovskaya, A. (2004), *Putin's Russia*, London: Harvill Press.

Prokhorov, A. P. (2002), Русская модель управления (*A Russian Model of Management*), Moscow: Expert Magazine.

Puffer, S. M. (1994), Women managers in the former USSR: A case of 'Too much equality'? in N. J. Adler and D. N. Izraeli (eds.), *Competitive Frontiers: Women Managers in a Global Economy*, Cambridge, MA: Blackwell, pp. 263–85.

Pushkin, A. S. (1950), Собрание Сочинений в 6 Томах (*Collected Works in 6 Volumes*), Moscow: Gosizdatelstvo Khudozhestvennoy Literatury.

Putilov, B. N. (1971), Русский и Южнославянский Героический Эпос (*Russian and Southern Slavic Heroic Epics*), Moscow: Nauka.

Putin, V. V. (2000), *First Person: An Astonishingly Frank Self-Portrait by Russia's President*, New York: Public Affairs.

Richmond, Y. (1996), *From Nyet to Da: Understanding the Russians*, Yarmouth, ME: Intercultural Press.

Rybakov, B. A. (1994), Язычество древних славян (*Paganism of the Ancient Slavs*), Moscow: Nauka.

Sedov, V. V. (1982), Восточные славяне в 7-13 вв (*Eastern Slavs of the 7–13th Centuries*), Moscow: Nauka.

Shapiro, D. (1965), *Neurotic Style*, New York: Basic Books.

Shevtsova, L. (1999), *Yeltsin's Russia: Myths and Reality*, Washington, DC: Carnegie Endowment for International Peace.

Solnick, S. (1998), *Stealing the State: Control and Collapse in Soviet Institutions*, Cambridge, MA: Harvard University Press.

Vernadskii, G. V. (1996), История России. Древняя Русь (*History of Russia: Ancient Rus*), Tver-Moscow: LEAN-Agraf.

Walker, S. (2007), Still seeking equality: Feminism takes a different form in Russia than in the West, *Russia Profile*, **2** (4), March, 22–23.

Zelenin, D. K. (1991), Восточнославянская этнография (*Eastern Slavic Ethnography*), Moscow: Nauka.

Zolotov, A. J. (2007), The queen of chocolate, *Russia Profile*, **24**, March, 30–2.

# 19. Cultural mythology and global leadership in Japan

## Tomoatsu Shibata and Mitsuru Kodama

### INTRODUCTION

Certain conditions which characterized Japan as a nation as well as its climate contributed to the formation of an inherent Japanese culture and consciousness. There are views and analyses from two research streams used to explain the backbone of Japanese consciousness. The first is Shinto as described in the Kojiki and Nihonshoki. Prior to its establishment as a nation state (predating the period of Shotoku Taishi), Japan had hardly ever been exposed to outside influences due to its geographical isolation as an island nation. In that environment, a localized religion which celebrated the worship of ancestral gods and which eventually developed into Shinto was establishing solid foundations. The second stream was Buddhism which was officially introduced to Japan in 538. Shotoku Taishi (574–622) embraced Buddhism at a young age and after becoming regent, incorporated the teachings of Buddha into a constitution (Seventeen Article Constitution) as a framework for governing the state, thereby establishing for the first time a basic foundation for a Japanese state. This milestone had a significant influence in the establishment of the inherent consciousness and culture of the Japanese people thereafter.

This initiative was interpreted by some as an effort by Shotoku Taishi to integrate Shinto and Buddhism (the syncretization of Shinto with Buddhism) to maintain the stability of the Japanese state. In the next section, the authors will present general observations on the relevance of Shinto and Buddhism and the Japanese consciousness.

### SHINTO AND BUDDHIST TEACHINGS

In his examination of the basic structure of Japanese mythology in the Kojiki, Kawai (2003) indicated that the 'knowledge of mythology' is important in the lives of human beings and refers to the structure of Japanese mythology as the 'hollow equilibrium structure'. According to him, the starting point of the concept of the hollow equilibrium structure lies in the 'overall harmony' of the human world. The 'overall harmony' accepts new ideas and contradictions, and allows each individual element to coexist in harmony within the whole. Rather than the integration of the whole under a central authority or principles based on logical compliance, however, overall harmony refers to an esthetic sense of harmony where the balance of the whole is skillfully achieved.

Although this view may at first appear to be based on dialectical thinking, it is not a Western model of dialectical logic (the processes of Being, Nothing, and Becoming according to Hegel) but instead is similar to Eastern dialectical thinking which attaches importance on the 'middle way', which psychologist Richard E. Nisbett (2003) asserts and which the authors shall refer to as the 'harmonized dialectic.'

At the same time, Takazawa (1996) refers to the existence of the 'logic of harmony' as a unique and independent sense of order in Japanese culture. According to him, this logic of harmony was emphasized in a semi-subconscious manner and served to maintain order based on the ideals of Shinto for a long period of time prior to the introduction of Confucianism and Buddhism in Japan. Furthermore, the logic of harmony, with its enshrinement of the principle 'harmony is to be valued' in Article 1 of Shotoku Taishi's Seventeen Article Constitution, had a significant impact on the formation of the Japanese State. The logic of harmony therefore became the cornerstone in the building of a society based on oneness in body and spirit and the development of mutual trust between human beings and the resonance of value (Kodama, 2001).

The second stream is the influence of Buddhism. During the reign of Emperor Tenmu in the late seventh century, the conflict between Japan's ancient Shinto and the foreign religion of Buddhism was also reflected in the political authority of that period. At the same time, as mentioned earlier, Shotoku Taishi had placed emphasis on the worship of Buddhism in the Seventeen Article Constitution in a conscious attempt to include Japanese Buddhism. However, it is understood that the Japanese people of that period did not necessarily embrace Buddhist ideas in their entirety but incorporated those aspects of Buddhism which could be accommodated within the scope of the inherent views of the Japanese people which were rooted in Japan's ancient Shinto. This attempt to maintain harmony with Shinto while accommodating Buddhist ideas is believed to have spawned the development of a Japanese type of Buddhism. After 'Buddhism' of this nature went through a process of permeation, a Japanese form of Buddhism eventually took root in Japan and gave rise to an era when Buddhist culture and thought flourished.

One of the most important concepts in this Buddhism is the established view of 'nothingness and self-renunciation'. Nothingness and self-renunciation mean not having fixed ideas about ways of thinking and acting.

Maintaining and adhering to one's views result in bias and rigidity, ruling out the possibility of further progress and development in one's life. It is a way of thinking based on the premise that because human beings have flexibility and mobility, they are able to experience progress and development (for example, Mizuno, 1971). Buddhism takes the view that when this idea of nothingness and self-renunciation is firmly established within a person, it naturally leads to the 'way of practice'. In Buddhism, the principle of practice is expressed in the words the 'middle way'. Based on the idea of nothingness and self-renunciation mentioned above, Buddhism places importance on actions that are guided by a person's practice of the 'middle way', which means steering away from bias toward the extreme left or right, but at the same time accepting the merits of both and compensating for the shortcomings of each (for example, Masutani, 1971).

Buddhism in a broad sense is philosophical anthropology (for example, Mizuno, 1971) and the ideals of this Buddhism share many common areas with the concept of 'practical wisdom' ('practical knowledge') (Kodama, 2007b: 185–9) in Aristotle's Nichomachean Ethics (Aristotle, 1980). Furthermore, they also bear many similarities to the harmonized dialectic of Shinto, which means a sense of balance as stated above.

Shinto and Buddhism, as mentioned above, form the backbone of Japanese thinking and Japanese culture, and also gave rise to a style of work which is characteristic of Japanese companies. The logic of harmony in Shinto was seminal to the development of team work, the concept of community and commitment, which characterize Japanese companies.

Furthermore, overall harmony and harmonized dialectical thinking created new business models (for example, the mobile telephone business and game business) which extend across different specialist fields of knowledge and industrial areas. Moreover, they also created a flexible organizational structure that was autonomous and decentralized, and therefore suited to realizing new business models (for example, Kodama, 2007a, 2007b). The ideals of Buddhism also enhanced the quality of activities which led to innovation in the work place such as concepts of work site priority (Genba-shugi) and Kairyo and Kaizen, which are based on practical knowledge characteristic of the Japanese people.

## OVERVIEW OF JAPANESE MYTHOLOGY

Shinto and Buddhism, which underlie the consciousness of the Japanese people, were the springhead that created the ideals particular to Japanese companies and their corporate culture. Furthermore, in traditional corporations which were established by Japanese founders (for example, Matsushita

Electric, Sony, Honda, Toyota, Fanuc, and so on), the stories of their founders' entrepreneurship and innovative spirit were to be carried on as tradition and shared by successive business managers and staff as their unique corporate myths.

In fact, Japanese companies which are achieving excellent results have devoted a significant amount of energy to spreading their own corporate culture and values based on the philosophy of their founders. For example, companies that have maintained high global competitiveness such as Toyota and Honda in the automotive industry, Canon and Matsushita in the electronics industry, and Fanuc in the field of factory automation (FA) possess corporate philosophies and values created by their founders which have been passed on as myths and stories over generations and have become pervasive among employees at every level within the organization.

Sharing the organizational culture and values of a company created systems and rules particular to that company and this practice firmly established the ways of thinking, views and patterns of behavior unique to that company to its employees. For example, Toyota has values such as 'wisdom and improvement' and 'respect for humanity'. From these values, patterns of thinking and behavior evolved such as the notion that 'water can be wrung even from a dry towel if one applies wisdom' or the idea 'to become a blank sheet of paper and observe production spots without preconceived ideas'. In addition, when considering an object, one should 'ask "why" five times over' and 'never be satisfied with one success but aim for higher goals through continuous improvement'. At Honda too, various patterns of thinking and behavior are pervasive among staff such as the three principles to 'go to the work site, know the actual products and conditions, and be realistic'. Staff are also asked to 'respect theory, ideas and time' and to question 'What is it for, what is the concept and what are the specifications?' In this way, the culture and values inherent in a company create inherent systems and rules as well as an inherent employee style (mold), which in turn takes root within the organization. Needless to say, inherent values, culture and style are elements which companies should create independently. However, among these patterns, there must be an assumption that there are common elements in the way of thinking among Japanese companies. These are represented by concepts such as commitment, team work, workplace principles and community, and are reasons in support of what Drucker (2001) refers to as 'collective-style corporations' in describing Japanese companies.

## OVERVIEW OF JAPANESE LEADERSHIP

Next, from the standpoint of 'Shinto' and 'Buddhism' in the first section, this section will examine the type of leadership the management leaders of elite Japanese companies employed to make myths and stories pervasive within companies and to create, establish and reform their inherent organizational cultures. This chapter refers to this leadership style which elite Japanese companies possess and use to create and transform corporate myths as 'innovative leadership' (Kodama, 2007b).

As mentioned above, the logic of harmony in Shinto develops trust-building and resonance of value among staff including management leaders and is an important element in inducing team work and commitment to the company. The leadership element required for this will be referred to here as 'resonating leadership'. Resonating leadership is a way of thinking and conduct observed among employees and management leaders alike in many Japanese companies.

The element of leadership which induces innovation activities based on practical knowledge, also a fundamental principle of Buddhism, will be referred to here as 'practical knowledge leadership'. Practical knowledge leadership is often observed in the development and production sites of high-tech products in industries such as the automobile, machine tools and consumer electronics industries, which are fields where Japan is currently performing very well.

The two aspects of resonating leadership and practical knowledge leadership will be referred to here as 'value-based leadership'.

In addition, overall harmony and the harmonized dialectic as well as management philosophy based on the middle-way of Buddhism will be referred to as 'dialectical leadership,' which has the two aspects of 'strategic leadership' and 'creative leadership'.

The element of dialectical leadership is thinking centering on management leadership which is observed in particular at development sites in advanced high-tech industries in Japan such as Toyota, Canon and Fanuc, and this is an organizational capability for simultaneously pursuing and integrating contradictory ideas such as 'efficiency and creativity' and 'planning and emergence' continuously. The concept which consolidates value-based leadership and dialectical leadership will be innovative leadership mentioned above. The following section will refer to the respective elements of these types of leadership.

### 'Value-based Leadership'

Resonating leadership, one aspect of value-based leadership, is the management leaders' ability to establish 'resonance of value' and 'trust' (Kodama, 2007b). The resonance of value and trust are gradually formed as employees mutually assert their subjectivity and values in the course of dialectical dialog

(Kodama, 2007b) and discuss strategic visions and the strategic goals. A deep dialectical dialog enables the sharing of strategic visions and goals among employees including the top management. However, in reality, individual interpretations of the visions and goals differ significantly from one individual to the next. When this occurs, as in the case of Honda which was explained earlier, the management leaders pose the question 'why' and keep repeating fundamental questions such as 'What is the reason for doing this?', thereby making it necessary to share and establish this system among staff. Therefore, a sense of unity among staff regarding the formulation and implementation of the corporate strategies is generated by arriving at a mutual understanding of the differences of interpretation of individuals and by sharing values and their resonance. In this chapter, this is referred to as the 'resonating leadership' of management leaders.

The second aspect of value-based leadership is practical knowledge leadership, leadership which enables management leaders and staff to practice 'what' and 'how' to create new values through the resonance of value and mutual trust among the staff. This is leadership for sharing high-quality practical knowledge (Lave, 1998; Hutchins, 1991; Brown and Duguid, 1998; Cook and Brown, 1999; Boland and Tenkasi, 1995; Tsoukas, 1997; Spender, 1992; Orr, 1996; Schon, 1983, 1987; Wenger, 1998) among staff including management leaders for putting into practice optimal decision-making and processes by staff. In this chapter, this is referred to as 'practical knowledge leadership' of management leaders.

'Resonating leadership' and 'practical knowledge leadership' together are given the generic name 'value-based leadership' in the sense that they generate knowledge as new value in the organization. Put another way, this value-based leadership can perhaps be viewed as 'the organizational capability where management leaders form resonance of value and mutual trust and discover appropriate decision-making and optimal actions based on practical knowledge to create new knowledge for implementing individual, specific strategies'.

**'Dialectical Leadership'**

Another important form of leadership for reforming the organizational culture and acquiring new organizational capability is dialectical leadership. Dialectical leadership has the aspect of leaders and staff implementing strategies as a science in an attempt to formulate and implement the corporate strategies analytically and rationalistically, and a second aspect of leaders and staff implementing strategies as a craft and art in attempts to create and implement the corporate strategies creatively and intuitively. This chapter will now take up the issue of satisfying both efficiency and creativity as an example and examine it in relation to dialectical leadership which is demonstrated for that purpose.

There are two important aspects in dialectical leadership. The first is the aspect of strategic leadership for formulating and implementing both the short-term business plan (including immediately pressing issues) and the long-term business plan (road map) aimed at rationalistically and analytically improving productivity and efficiency of the company as goals. The second is the aspect of creative leadership (Kodama, 2005) for promoting creative ideas and behavior which are independently disseminated for achieving new business creation. In dialectical leadership, both strategic leadership and creative leadership are essential.

For example, when Toyota workers are faced with a discrepancy, they do not adopt an 'either or' attitude but pursue the problem from a 'both and' stance. As a result of this perspective, Toyota is not only able to pursue quality and cost efficiency uncompromisingly, but is also able to successfully produce creative cars like Lexus which possess 'elegance' and 'depth' (Osono, 2004). At Honda and Canon (Kodama, 2007c), at Fujitsu, a typical company in the field of ICT (Kodama, 2005) and at NTT DoCoMo (Kodama, 2007a), dialectical leadership is the starting point for the realization of innovation. The source of dialectical leadership which is peculiar to Japanese companies exists in the dialectical dialogue among staff including the top management. The dialectical dialogue enables the sharing of deep thoughts and sentiments among staff including the top management. In the time and space where the dialectical dialogue transpires, a process of 'how will we create it?' is asked rather than the conventional syllogistic approach of 'does it or does it not exist?' In other words, the dialectical dialogue makes use of the productivity of contradiction by delving into the content (meaning). Open thinking among staff including the leaders therefore becomes significant. In concrete terms, it is important to recognize the compatibility of self-assertion and modesty among members. It also becomes important that staff become aware that they personally make errors and that they use confrontations with others as the medium for developing themselves to a higher level.

In the Commentary box, corporate myth, organizational culture and leadership are examined by taking a look at the example of Fanuc, a typical blue-chip firm in Japan (see p. 353).

## FANUC, SUPPORTING JAPANESE MANUFACTURING INDUSTRIES

Since 1982 the Japanese machine tool industry has been an industry boasting the world's largest production in terms of volume and has strong international competitiveness. Since its founding to the present day, Fanuc has consistently had a close to 50 percent share of the market worldwide and at the same time maintained extremely high ordinary profit level, reaching as high as 30 percent. Fanuc started out as an in-house venture of Fujitsu and became independent as a separate enterprise in 1972. Since then, Dr Seiuemon Inaba has been involved in the management of Fanuc as an actual founder of the business. A notable characteristic of Fanuc is its speedy ability to get things done through concerted efforts by staff in carrying out business decisions made by Inaba. What makes this highly developed organizational ability to get things done possible is the company's bureaucratic system in executing top-down processes effectively and the sharing of visions and ideas on a company-wide level (Shibata and Kodama, 2007).

**Vision Sharing and Resonating Leadership**

Since Fanuc separated and became independent from Fujitsu, Inaba has devoted significant efforts to finding ways of sharing the corporate visions and ideas with all staff of the company. Then, Dr Inaba is very skillful at using symbols for sharing visions. Symbols allow for various interpretations depending on the persons viewing them and depending on their view of the world and the life. Symbols also spark the imagination. Inaba had a profound understanding of the effect symbols have and attempted to steer the consciousness of company staff in the same direction by actively using the power of the symbols. The following examples demonstrate how Inaba utilized symbols for demonstrating the resonating leadership.

To begin with, the Fanuc company emblem contains five vectors facing in the same direction. These vectors stand for the five current product groups of Fanuc, which are NCs, robots, servo motors, injection molding machines and wire-cut electric discharge machines, and they symbolize that the company's business is developing with all divisions moving in the same, single direction and sharing the same purpose. Inaba emphasizes the importance of bringing together the vectors of all staff of the company and, to drum this into the consciousness of all staff of the company, used the five vectors as symbols.

Second, in the foyer of the main office there is a painting of a tree known as the *Keyaki tree* (Japanese zelkova tree). Inaba's ideals, expectations and hopes for Fanuc are said to be encapsulated in this painting. His great expectations for young engineers in particular are said to be contained in it.

These two visions and ideals have been passed on to Fanuc staff today as Inaba myths. They include the meaning of 'new value creation in society with technology at the core' and, as mentioned earlier, also the meaning that demonstrating 'resonating leadership' is required of Fanuc's management leaders. This indicates how much attention Inaba paid to sharing visions and ideas among the staff in demonstrating resonating leadership at Fanuc. A sophisticated organizational driving force demonstrated by Fanuc's management leaders through their resonating leadership is possible only when there is pervasive sharing of the visions and ideas which have been handed down as the myth.

## Practical Knowledge Leadership

On the wall in the foyer of Fanuc's research laboratory there is a clock which operates ten times faster than normal speed. This clock is placed there to raise a pervasive awareness among staff of the importance of speed in research and development. To emphasize the importance of timing, Inaba often makes reference to the Battle of Stalingrad between the Soviet and German armies in 1943. The German army completed the development of the Tiger tank, which was the state-of-the-art tank at the time and outfitted with powerful destructive and defensive capabilities. However, by the time its development was completed, the battle was already over and ended in the defeat of the German army. No matter how advanced a developed product may be, there is no use for it if it has missed its timing. The purpose of the clock on the foyer wall of Fanuc's research laboratory that measures time at ten-fold the pace of normal clocks is to raise awareness among engineers of the importance of timing and speed. Through the clock, Inaba is driving home the point that engineers should not view the progress of their work in terms of 'clock time' alone but should tackle their work with an awareness of the importance of what he calls 'timely time'. Timely time is a concept of time which the engineers themselves consciously redefine on their own, and has the connotation of emergent and extemporaneous time. In this chapter 'timely time' is referred to as 'emergent time' (Kodama, 2008). Following this notion of emergent time, engineers undertake product development and product marketing based on emergent ideas and extemporaneous action.

At Fanuc, there is also a policy whereby management leaders with positions in top management as well as division and section managers are required to be involved in work at the work site for a certain percentage of their working time apart from their own management duties. This is to encourage management leaders in the development division to engage in work which they develop on their own outside of their management duties.

Rooted in experience, this principle is also Inaba's mantra which asserts that unless managers are involved in the front line of work at the work site all the time and unless they are fully conversant with details and actual conditions of the work site, they will not be able to manage their subordinates. As part of their training, engineers are also required to experience the field of sales work through first hand experience. The main point in doing so is to drive home the point that the formulation and implementation of strategies should not be separated. The mindset that managers of headquarters and administrative departments are apt to fall into is one which has the illusion or misunderstanding that strategy formulation is a manager's work and that the work of strategy implementation is the role of staff at the work site. Formulation and implementation of the strategy are parts of an integrated whole and must be promoted by management leaders dynamically through an ongoing process of trial and error (Kodama, 2007a, 2007c).

In this way, the management leaders of Fanuc demonstrate practical knowledge leadership and implement in emergent time strategies underpinned by knowledge accumulated on a daily basis. Furthermore, their engineers hone their daily practical knowledge and accumulate it as an organization and, through the smooth interaction between the work place and the market, they create products in a rapid and timely manner.

### Synthesis of Paradox and Dialectical Leadership

Fanuc is a company which has placed technical development at the core of its business and has accordingly devoted relentless efforts to strengthening its technological development expertise (Shibata *et al.*, 2005). Fanuc's three principles, which are displayed in the foyer of its research lab, are: 1. RELIABILITY UP (Enhance the reliability of products), 2. COST CUT (Produce at a cost that is cheaper than any other product) and 3. WENIGER TEILE (Design products with fewer parts). Staff involved in research and development see these principles every time they pass through the foyer in the morning and in the evening. Fanuc's basic policy toward technical development is condensed in these principles.

A viewpoint of particular importance in the three principles mentioned above is the third principle of WENIGER TEILE. This principle is a German term created by Inaba as a symbol, so to speak, meaning to create a design that enables production using a small number of parts. While Fanuc places priority on both reliability and cost at the time of product development, the notions of increasing reliability and cutting costs are generally considered to be at odds with each other. This is because increases in costs cannot ordinarily be avoided when efforts are being made to enhance reliability. The notion of 'designing products with fewer parts' as a design process for achieving this task is a concept established by Inaba, and Fanuc has tried to firmly build this process of design into work procedures at its research laboratory. There is no doubt that a product design based on a smaller number of parts reduces the complicated relationship of interdependence of parts and, therefore, most likely does contribute to both increased reliability and reduced costs.

This is simply dialectical leadership aimed at achieving both efficiency and creativity, which seem contradictory at first glance. No matter how many times top management repeatedly talk of enhancing reliability and cutting costs, unless this contradiction is resolved at the actual behavioral level, it is difficult for staff to implement it at the work site. The fact that a vision for enhancing reliability and cost reduction became embodied at the level of an action agenda of 'design with a smaller number of parts' and that it became embedded inside the organization as the corporate vision, mission, and, furthermore, as the strategy goal, are perhaps key points in gaining an insight into Fanuc's sustained capability in technical development.

The above observations illustrate how at Fanuc the ideas, business philosophy and corporate mission of Inaba, the founder of the company, pervaded the company as corporate myths and stories and resulted in the formation of a unique organizational culture. Furthermore, the corporate culture, which is unique to Fanuc and which is imbedded in the management leaders at each management level including the top management, and the management leaders' innovative leadership ('value-based leadership' and 'dialectical leadership'), which is rooted in this corporate culture, are generating initiatives in support of Fanuc's sustained technological innovation – see Commentary box.

---

## COMMENTARY BOX

### Dr Seiuemon Inaba, Founder of Fanuc

If we undertake our work under one clear principle which is understood by all staff in a strict sense, we are unlikely to compromise or neglect our duties easily, nor should [we] become absorbed in our own personal prestige and turn to dishonest acts. [The] painting [of the Keyaki tree, which hangs in the foyer of his company's main office] is an expression of my expectations for Fanuc, which, though small in size, I hope will grow massive and robust, and that in five to ten years new technologies will grow from its thick trunk. My request is that all staff will take pride in such a Fanuc and help nurture its growth. (from Inaba, 2003)

---

## GLOBAL IMPLICATIONS

As the authors have discussed, Japanese mythology and Buddhism had a powerful impact on the formation of corporate culture and on the leadership of management leaders. In practice, it is the top leaders of the organization (CEO and executives) who create a company's unique corporate culture and fulfill the role of promoting the sharing of values among employees. At the same time, it must be recognized that fulfilling this role depends to a large extent on their power to create a myth and the quality of their leadership.

Shein (1985) argued that the essence of top management leadership was not to provide management for the sake of achieving goals but for creating the organizational culture, for managing it, and even destroying it. Furthermore, Selznick (1957) placed emphasis on the importance of the mythical power of leaders. To promote the sharing of culture and values in an organization, he argued that the use of myths and stories was an effective way of uplifting the morale of the employees and in speaking of the company's particular vision and strategic objectives. In addition to promoting the establishment and sharing of the corporate vision, myths and stories play a role in creating a consensus in decision-making in strategy formulation and implementation in the course of daily corporate activities.

One point which requires attention here is that although stories such as these, which have been passed down as corporate myths, must be perpetuated as oral tradition within the company as the source of values and culture, the actual corporate systems and rules must change with the times and the market and undergo dynamic transformation. However, when the systems and rules become inseparable and associated with the myths which originally created them, there is a tendency to regard them as something inviolable. When the systems and rules are created by the founders themselves, there is a tendency for them to be associated with the strong charismatic characteristics attached to the founders in the myths, thus making it difficult to reform existing systems and rules. For example, Matsushita Electric, which is considered a typical company with Japanese-style management, posted an enormous deficit in excess of 400 billion yen for the first time since its establishment in 2001. One of the causes for this was the obsolete business division system within the company which was established by the founder of the company, Konosuke Matsushita. Despite suffering from systemic fatigue in an age of digitalization and network systematization and becoming somewhat dysfunctional, the system became inseparable from the myth of the company founder and, therefore, nobody was able to undertake its reform. Without a doubt, Matsushita's business division system had in the past been a driving force in the development of Matsushita Electric but the system was not able to respond to the changes in the market of recent years.

Despite its flaws, the business division system, which was merely a system that had become linked with the myth of the company founder and incorporated in the myth as being inviolable, had to wait until the arrival of Kunio Nakamura for reform to take place. Assuming the position of president in June 2000, Nakamura dismantled the business division system and reorganized it into a more broad-based system of 14 separate business areas. Openly declaring within the company that it was okay to dismantle any aspect of the company save the philosophy of the company founder, Nakamura promoted reform through a *modus operandi* of 'demolition, creation and leaping forward' and succeeded in achieving a V-shaped recovery in 2002 (Kodama, 2007a, 2007c). In fact, Nakamura did away with all systems, rules and work structures which had become entrenched within the organization by force of habit and which were no longer in tune with the times and he formulated new systems and rules. As the above illustrates, corporate myths may become the source of corporate value but they may also become the source of inhibiting reform.

At the same time, in the shakeup of IBM (Gerstner, 2002) and Nissan Motor Company (Ghosn, 2002), unlike the case of Matsushita Electric, the intervention of top management from outside (for example, Sull, 1999; Siggelkow, 2001) consciously dismantled the corporate culture and organizational identity (for example, Thornton, 2002) and brought about a recovery in corporate results. The organizational identity can generate in the members of the organization a deep attachment to their work and commitment (Kogut, 2000) and can also become the source of the corporate competitive edge. However, in situations where the market and technology are undergoing dramatic changes, there is a possibility that the organizational identity will conversely lead to weakness (Walsh, 1995). An excessive bias toward an organizational identity rooted in corporate myth may entrench the mental model of the organization and restrict the way in which the organizational members respond to change (for example, Brown and Starkey, 2000). Furthermore, the corporation may slip into a state of core rigidity (Leonard-Barton, 1995).

In Japan, the culture of harmony in Japanese mythology and the pragmatism of Buddhism created a corporate competitive edge through team work and commitment, and a unique style in work practices. It also established within the organization an excellent attitude toward improving the work place as seen in *Kairyo* and *Kaizen* as well as an innovative spirit. However, an entrenched culture of harmony excludes heterogeneous ways of thinking, and the company's work style becomes entrenched in the work style of the business processes. As a result, there is a possibility that the mental model of the organizational members will become homogeneous and will lead to an aversion to new business processes and technologies (such as IT) among the organizational members.

To respond to changes in the environment flexibly as in the cases of Matsushita Electric, Nissan and IBM mentioned above, companies (especially large corporations) are inevitably confronted with the need to review their corporate organizational identity as the situation dictates.

For Matsushita Electric, it was a case of 'creation from destruction'; for IBM, it meant dismantling the corporate culture and making the transition from products to services, and for Nissan, it was the dismantling of the mental model of the employees. Therefore, for a company to respond flexibly to changes in the environment, a dialectical examination of its present and future business and the innovative leadership of management leaders who possess practical competence based on practical knowledge will be vital. This is also a universal proposition applicable to all eras and countries.

## PRACTICAL APPLICATION

This chapter examined insights from a new viewpoint of leadership looking at the relevance of myths and corporate founders through Japanese cases. Innovative leadership examined in this chapter was required not only of the top management team but also of the management leaders at the various management levels. It is difficult for a company to achieve corporate reforms and innovation by merely having a charismatic leader or through the demonstration of innovative leadership by the top management team alone. In a company it is important for each level of the organization (top level, middle level) to fulfill its respective role. It is also important to nurture management leaders who demonstrate innovative ideas and performance through practice in order to establish a management system where many management leaders are able to demonstrate their ability. One important element in establishing this management system is the promotion of management based on a sense of values rooted in 'Shinto' and 'Buddhist teaching' described in the first section of the chapter. At the same time, it is important to embed deep in the hearts of the members of each organization the corporate philosophy and corporate vision based on the ideas of the corporate founders as the corporate myths and stories, and, in that way, to create, maintain and transform the unique organizational culture.

However, as indicated in Section 3, in response to changes in the environment, a continuous review of the organizational identity based on the established corporate culture is also an element for maintaining ongoing competitive superiority.

As a future topic, this paper will take up the concept of innovative leadership presented in this article and focus on the issue as to whether it can be applied to companies in other countries. It is, of course, assumed that the leadership styles of management leaders are affected by the environment, type of business, business style and traditional organizational culture and are dependent on factors such as the ideas, corporate philosophy and sense of value of the top management. At the same time, however, it is a fact that Japanese elite companies achieved successful outcomes by implementing 'business management based on a sense of values' and 'dialectical management' in the past.

There are many journalists who make the comment that Japanese young people's sense of values has changed in recent years. However, many Japanese (including young Japanese) consciously (or unconsciously) place importance on Japanese mythology and the Buddhist way of thinking. They also learn about concepts such as the 'spirit of harmony' and 'universal harmony', which are based on these, from an early stage in their education and they learn about these ideas repeatedly in various situations including training for new employees when they join a company. This traditional characteristic of Japanese companies as learning organizations has enabled high-tech industries such as the automobile, FA and electronics industries to lead the world in their fields.

# REFERENCES

Aristotle (350BCE/1980), *The Nicomachean Ethics*, translated with an introduction by David Ross, Oxford: Oxford University Press.

Boland, J. and Tenkasi, R. (1995), Perspective making and perspective taking: Implications for organizational learning, *Organization Science*, 9 (3), 605–22.

Brown, A. D. and Starkey, K. (2000), Organizational identity and learning: A psycho-dynamic perspective, *Academy of Management Review*, **251**, 102–20.

Brown, J. S. and Duguid, P. (1998), Organizing knowledge, *California Management Review*, **40** (3), 90–111.

Cook, S. and Brown. J. (1999), Bridging epistemologies: The generative dance between organizational knowledge and organizational knowing, *Organization Science*, **102**, 381–400.

Drucker, P. (2001), *Management Challenges for the 21st Century*, New York: Harper Business.

Gerstner, V. L. (2002), *Who says Elephants can't Dance? Inside IBM's Historic Turnaround*, New York: Janklow and Nesbit Associates,.

Ghosn, C. (2002), Saving the business without losing the company, *Harvard Business Review*, **80** (1), 37–42.

Hutchins, E. (1991), Organizing work by adaptation, *Organization Science*, **2** (1), 14–39.

Inaba, U. (2003), *Yellow Robot in Japanese*, Nikkan Kogyo, Tokyo, Japan.

Kawai, H. (2003), *Mythology and Japanese Mind in Japanese*, Iwanami, Tokyo, Japan.

Kodama, M. (2001), Creating new business through strategic community management, *International Journal of Human Resource Management*, **11** (6), 1062–82.

Kodama, M. (2005), Knowledge creation through networked strategic communities – Case studies in new product development, *Long Range Planning*, **38** (1), 27–49.

Kodama, M. (2007a), *The Strategic Community-Based Firm*, London: Palgrave Macmillan.

Kodama, M. (2007b), *Knowledge Innovation – Strategic Management As Practice*, Cheltenham: Edward Elgar Publishing.

Kodama, M. (2007c), *Project-Based Organization In The Knowledge-Based Society*, London: Imperial College Press.

Kodama, M. (2008), *New Knowledge Creation Through ICT Dynamic Capability:*

*Creating Knowledge Communities Using Broadband*, Charlotte, NC: Information Age Publishing.

Kogut, B. (2000), The network of knowledge: Generative rules and the emergence of structure, *Strategic Management Journal*, **21**, 405–25.

Lake, J. (1998), *Cognition in Practice*, Cambridge, UK: Cambridge University Press.

Leonard-Barton, D. (1995), *Wellsprings of Knowledge: Building and Sustaining the Sources of Innovation*, Boston, MA: Harvard Business School Press.

Masutani, F. (1971), *Buddhism in Japanese*, Chikuma Shobo, Tokyo, Japan.

Mizuno, H. (1971), *Basics of Buddhism in Japanese*, Syujyunnsya, Tokyo, Japan.

Nisbett, R. (2003), *The Geography of Thought*, New York: The Free Press.

Orr (1996), *Talking about Machines: An Ethnography of a Modern Job*, Ithaca, NY: ILP Press.

Osono, E. (2004), The strategy-making process as dialogue, in H. Takeuchi and I. Nonaka (eds), *Hitotsubashi on Knowledge Management*, Singapore: John Wiley and Sons Asia, pp. 47–86.

Schein, E. H. (1985), *Organizational Culture and Leadership*, San Francisco: Jossey-Bass.

Schon, A. (1983), *The Reflective Practitioner*, New York: Basic Books.

Schon, A. (1987), *Educating the Reflective Practitioner*, San Francisco: Jossey-Bass.

Selznick, P. (1957), *Leadership in Administration*, Philadelphia, PA: Harper and Row.

Shibata, T. and Kodama, M. (2007), Knowledge integration through networked strategic communities – Cases of Japan, *Business Strategy Series*, **86**, 394–400.

Shibata, T., Yano, M. and Kodama, F. (2005), Empirical analysis of evolution of product architecture: Fanuc numerical controllers from 1962 to 1997, *Research Policy*, **34** (1), 13–31.

Siggelkow, N. (2001), Change in the presence of fit: The rise, the fall and the renaissance of Liz Claiborne, *Academy of Management Journal*, **44** (4), 838–57.

Spender, J.C. (1992), Knowledge management: Putting your technology strategy on track, in T. M. Khalil and B. A. Bayraktar (eds), *Management of Technology*, Vol. 3, Norcross, GA: Industrial Engineering and Management Press, pp. 404–13.

Sull, D. N. (1999), The dynamics of standing still: Firestone Tire and Rubber and the radical revolution, *Business History Review*, **73** (Autumn), 430–64.

Takazawa, H. (1996), *What is Wa for Japanese in Japanese*, Tokyo: Hakuto Syobo.

Thornton, P. (2002), The rise of the corporation in a craft industry: Conflict and conformity on institutional logic, *Academy of Management Journal*, **451**, 81–101.

Tsoukas, H. (1997), Forms of knowledge and forms of life in organizational contexts, in R. China (ed.), *The Realm of Organization*, London: Routledge.

Walsh, J. P. (1995), Managerial and organizational cognition: Notes from a trip down memory lane, *Organization Science*, **63**, 280–321.

Wenger, E. C. (1998), *Community of Practice: Learning, Meaning and Identity*, Cambridge: Cambridge University Press.

# 20. Cultural mythology and global leadership in Australia

## David Lamond

## INTRODUCTION

The central thesis advanced by Hofstede (2001, 2005) and Trompenaars (1994; Trompenaars and Hampden-Turner, 1997) is that nationality-based cultural differences influence differences in work values, beliefs and orientations held by organizational members in different countries. In their GLOBE study of 62 societies, House *et al.* (2004) demonstrated that these differences are reflected also in the leadership styles of the middle managers they surveyed. Subsequent studies (see, for example, Braithwaite *et al.*, 2007; Kakabadse and Kakabadse, 2007) reinforce the view that differences in leadership styles are informed, at least in part, by the culture in which the leader is embedded. As Borgelt and Falk (2007: 127) point out, leadership exists, not in a vacuum, but in a particular socio-culturally and chronologically situated context. Indeed, they maintain that, even in thinking about leadership, we bring our socio-culturally derived preconceptions to bear.

The GLOBE study described leadership as 'the ability of an individual to influence, motivate, and enable others to contribute toward the effectiveness and success of the organizations of which they are members' (House *et al.*, 2004: 56). We can think of leadership styles then as how an individual influences, motivates and enables others. The purpose of this chapter is to consider managerial leadership styles in Australia and how Australian myths and legends may have shaped them.

In *Doing Leadership Differently*, Sinclair (2005) identifies Australian leadership values as heroism, physical and emotional toughness, and self-reliance, all the hallmarks of the traditional picture of the 'bronzed Aussie', a suntanned, rugged individual much like Banjo Patterson's man from Snowy River:

> He sent the flint-stones flying, but the pony kept his feet,
> He cleared the fallen timber in his stride,
> And the man from Snowy River never shifted in his seat –
> It was grand to see that mountain horseman ride.
> (A.B. 'Banjo' Patterson, The Man from Snowy River)

International readers might be more familiar with this rugged individual in the form of the latter-day character of Crocodile Dundee, appearing in the film of the same name, which is the most successful Australian film of all time. Indeed, Australia is well-known for this 'macho' culture, which extends into management and the company boardroom and is an essential element of the executive culture (Sinclair, 1994). Given the limits of a book chapter, I proceed from this point of departure and concentrate the discussion on this form of 'heroic masculinity' (Sinclair, 2005: 37), but there is space later devoted to the problematic nature of this characterization and the blind spots that it has produced for managerial leadership in Australia.

## OVERVIEW OF AUSTRALIAN MYTHS – BUSHIES, MATES AND ANZACS

The modern mainstream culture of Australia is a Western culture, drawing primarily from the Anglo-Celtic cultures of the waves of convicts and settlers who began arriving in 1788. Blainey (1966) explores the whys and hows of this settlement in *Tyranny of Distance*.

Having 'discovered Australia' in 1770, through naval captain James Cook's detour on Her Majesty's Bark *Endeavour*, and then lost its alternative penal colony following the American Revolution of 1776, England had decided to use the great southern land to rid itself of its surplus convicts. The sheer distance made it an ideal location and large numbers of convicts were transported to Sydney Cove and Hobart, while those who continued to offend were sent to Norfolk Island and Port Macquarie, further up the east coast. Along with the forced transportation, were waves of migration and settlement based on whales, sheep and gold, with the east coast occupied by sheep farmers ('squatters') who simply put their sheep on the land instead of buying it, and hired convict labour to tend their herds.

This geographical isolation (see Blainey's (1966) *Tyranny of Distance*), together with the harsh climate (see poet Dorothea Mackellar's (1904/1997) 'sunburnt country') and the sparseness of the population, created a context of significant hardship for the bushies (the early settlers and the convicts who worked for them), that was later reflected in the poetry of Henry Lawson and Banjo Patterson (Page, 2002). Indeed, Lawson cemented the concept of mateship in the way he extolled the virtues of those people who were prepared to stand with and support others in the midst of that hardship and adversity (Page, 2002: 193), as *per* this sample verse from his poem, *Sez You*:

> When you're camping in the mulga, and the rain is falling slow,
> While you nurse your rheumatism 'neath a patch of calico;

Short of tucker or tobacco, short of sugar or of tea,
And the scrubs are dark and dismal, and the plains are like a sea;
Don't give up and be down-hearted – to the soul of man be true!
Grin! if you've a mate to grin for, grin and jest and don't look blue;
For it can't go on for ever, and – 'I'll rise some day', says you.
(Lawson, 1900)

The notion of mateship and its attendant qualities were reinforced in the early twentieth century when Australian troops (the majority of whom were bushies and mates) were engaged in World War I, when the term *ANZAC* was first used. Devised by a signaller in Egypt as a useful acronym for 'Australian and New Zealand Army Corps', 'ANZAC' has been a part of Australian thought, language, and life since the Gallipoli Peninsula landing on 25 April 1915 (AWM, 1997). Used at first to signify a man who had served on Gallipoli, the term was popularized by war correspondent Charles Bean and grew to have broader application, with the 'ANZAC legend' referring to the representation of the way Australians in war, think, speak and write of their war experience (AWM, 1997). Bean's (1946/1997) reflection on the meaning of ANZAC is often quoted:

> By dawn on December 20th ANZAC had faded into a dim blue line lost amid other hills on the horizon as the ships took their human freight to Imbros, Lemnos and Egypt. But ANZAC stood, and still stands, for reckless valour in a good cause, for enterprise, resourcefulness, fidelity, comradeship, and endurance that will never own defeat.

It still echoes today in commentaries such as those by Burke (2006), who observes that the 'comradeship, courage and sacrifice: others before self' that constitutes the Spirit of ANZAC, 'is a feeling that burns in the heart of every Australian and New Zealand countryman'. Indeed, it is unusual for any public commentary on the ANZAC experience not to include a concomitant reference to the value of mateship, a desirable defining quality to which individuals should aspire (Page, 2002: 194). So much so that in 2003, as Prime Minister of the day, the Right Honourable John Howard sought to have the following phrase inserted in a proposed Preamble to the Australian Constitution:

> Australians are free to be proud of their country and heritage, free to realise themselves as individuals, and free to pursue their hopes and ideals. We value excellence as well as fairness, independence as dearly as mateship. (Parliamentary Library, 2000)

It is not surprising perhaps, that one of Australia's heroes, seen to embody all that is best in mateship and the ANZAC spirit is surgeon Sir Edward 'Weary' Dunlop.

### Sir Edward 'Weary' Dunlop (1907–1993)

Sir Edward 'Weary' Dunlop was a surgeon in the Australian Army during World War II. He is legendary for his care of soldiers taken prisoner by the Japanese. His nickname might have been 'Weary' but his nature certainly wasn't. Even in the most horrific conditions Weary found energy to fight for the wellbeing and often, the lives of these men.

Weary grew up in Benalla, in Victoria, where he preferred to play sport than to study. As an older sportsman, he played with Australia's national rugby team, The Wallabies, and was a champion boxer. He studied medicine at Melbourne University and, soon after graduation, he sailed to London as a ship's surgeon. When World War II broke out, Weary 'just couldn't get into the army quick enough'.

When the Japanese attacked the island of Java, in Indonesia, Weary was sent there to help treat the casualties but, just two weeks after his arrival, Japanese troops captured the town where Weary was living. The prisoners were taken by ship from Singapore to Burma, and then crammed into train carriages for a five day horror ride into Thailand.

The Japanese wanted to build a 421 kilometre long railway from west Thailand into Burma, a job requiring physical strength and good tools – the prisoners had neither: 'I'd see these fellas off at the crack of dawn, just carrying their rice for the day, and then they would drag in any time up until midnight, some of them on their hands and knees'.

As a commander, Weary had the awful job of deciding who was fit enough to work. As a surgeon, he was also the one who patched the men up after their hours of hard labour. Standing nearly two metres tall, Weary had to stoop as he operated on patients beneath kerosene lamps: 'Weary was never sitting down. He was always on his feet, and his feet were terrible with ulcers. He had all these complaints too, you know. The germs didn't leave him alone.'

Weary argued with his captors about making sick men work: 'I'd have all sorts of conspiracies. I'd tell the fellas to start to march, but collapse and I'll grab you'. Former prisoner of war, Bill Griffiths is among the many who owe their lives to Weary. The Japanese planned to kill him. What use is a disabled man, it was argued. Weary stepped in front of the bayonets and refused to move until Bill's life was spared.

A habit of keeping track of the war via a hidden wireless also landed Weary in the firing line: 'I got handcuffed around a tree, my tummy exposed to four bayonets and a countdown. Things were pretty grim.' Weary ended up being tortured instead ... but the experience only made him more defiant.

Weary's work as a surgeon continued after the war, in Australia and parts of Asia, and in 1969, he was recognized for his contribution to medicine with a knighthood. Weary's compassionate nature enabled him to forgive and even meet, some of his former enemies.

In 1993, ten days short of his 86th birthday, Sir Edward 'Weary' Dunlop died. More than 10 000 people lined the streets of Melbourne for the state funeral of the man they called 'The Surgeon of the Railway'.

'I have a conviction that it's only when you are put at full stretch that you can realise your full potential.' If ever anyone lived life at full stretch, it was Weary. (Adapted from Anon, 2007.)

Even a cursory examination of Weary Dunlop's profile shows up the heroism, physical and emotional toughness, and self-reliance that Sinclair (2005) identified as central to Australian leadership values. But are these values reflected in Australian managerial leadership styles? The next section considers what is known about Australian leadership and management skills.

## OVERVIEW OF AUSTRALIAN LEADERSHIP

Much has been written about Australian managerial leadership – the Australian Government spent three years and four million Australian dollars to produce the Karpin Report on leadership and management skills, a multivolume report which incorporated an extensive research agenda (Commonwealth of Australia, 1995a; 1995b). One area given considerable attention in the report was that related to the 'soft skills' of Australian managers, as they engaged in the activity of 'getting things done through other people' (managing). Here we review some of the Karpin Report's findings and recommendations regarding Australian managers' 'soft skills', and then examine some of the subsequent literature that has expressed concern about the slow progress being made in this area.

The Karpin Report was produced in response to the Charter of the Industry Task Force on Leadership and Management Skills (Chaired by David Karpin) to 'advise on measures to strengthen management development and business leadership within Australian enterprises. It was asked to identify effective management practices in a range of areas, to raise awareness of the need for improved leadership and management skills and to foster enterprise commitment to management development' (Commonwealth of Australia, 1995a: 4).

The report identified as one of the seven themes to emerge from the research programme, 'the need for enhanced "people" skills' (Commonwealth of Australia, 1995a: 25). By people, or 'soft', skills, the report meant 'the ability to communicate, the ability to motivate, the ability to lead and delegate, and the ability to negotiate' (Commonwealth of Australia, 1995a: 25). The view that Australian managers had poor people skills was shared by 91 Australian management experts (Commonwealth of Australia, 1995a: 67–8) and 502 Asian managers (Commonwealth of Australia, 1995a: 68). The Task Force recognized the need to achieve 'best practice management development' (Commonwealth of Australia, 1995a: 151) and to 'reform management education' (Commonwealth of Australia, 1995a: 152*ff*), so as to promote the development of people skills and close the gap perceived to exist between the level of skills possessed by Australian managers and the skill level considered as 'world best practice' (see Commonwealth of Australia, 1995a: 172–4). It went on to point to managers as having primary responsibility for their own learning and development, while enterprises have primary responsibility for 'providing management development to encourage learning and self development by all managers' (Commonwealth of Australia, 1995a: 266).

Subsequent commentators have pointed to the slow progress that has been made in implementing the kind of approach recommended by the Karpin Report (see, for example, Edwards *et al.*, 1997; Fisher and Dowling, 1999). At the same time research by Kane *et al.* (1999) has identified management attitudes as a key factor in determining the success of people management strategies. To the extent that the Australian managers they surveyed gave low priority to people management issues and were focused on the short term, Kane, *et al.* (1999) were able to specify some of the barriers to this progress. Jones and Jackson (2000) examined the attitudes of Australian managers towards managing people and the managers' perceptions of their organizations. They found that Australian business continued to demonstrate a 'command and control' focus and that, while they perceived themselves as more humanistic, Australian managers are also less egalitarian than one might anticipate.

These findings, in turn, point to important individual and organizational factors that might vitiate the impact of any 'soft skills' training as recommended by Karpin, and raise questions about the extent to which Australian managers' leadership behaviour reflects the leadership values previously outlined. A study by Lamond (2001) suggests that there are characteristics of Australian managers, and of the organizational contexts within which they operate, that have contributed to the apparent difficulty in bridging the 'people skills' gap.

**Individual Characteristics**

One reason why the Australian managers surveyed by Kane *et al.* (1999) gave low priority to people management issues, may be found in their personalities. Personality-based explanations of behaviour are many and long-standing, going back as far as Plato and Aristotle (Statt, 1994: 168). One explanatory model, based on psychological types, is that of Carl Jung (1921/1971). A study of 228 Australian managers in 1980 found the group to be heavily populated by individuals who make decisions using a Thinking (T) preference and who put emphasis on order (the Judging (J) preference) (Myers and McCaulley, 1985: 39–40). Myers and McCaulley (1985: 39) commented on the high percentage (62 per cent) of what they referred to as 'tough-minded TJs' in this sample. A subsequent study of 523 Australian managers by Lamond (2001) showed that, not only was there a similar proportion of the tough-minded TJs (61 per cent), but also the female respondents were as tough-minded as the males. Here certainly, is the emotional toughness lauded by the poets and popular writers, exhibited by both male and female managers, not just in their behaviour but as part of their individual make-ups.

## Organizational Culture

March (1994: 71) has observed that '[o]rganizations shape individual action both by providing the content of identities and rules and by providing appropriate cues for invoking them'. Culture, in turn, has been described as one of the most powerful and stable forces operating in organizations (Schein, 1990), and has been linked to a variety of measures of organizational success (see, for example, Bluedorn and Lundgren, 1993; Denison, 1984). While management scholars fail to agree on a definition of organizational culture (Howard, 1998), the overriding similarity in the organizational culture literature is in the reference to a shared value system (Rousseau, 1990; see also O'Reilly *et al.*, 1991: 492; Schein, 1990).

Quinn (1988) characterizes organizations as complex, dynamic and contradictory systems in which managers must fulfil many competing expectations, and has identified four cultures or models of organizing, varying along two dimensions in terms of the extent to which they favour flexibility over control, and an internal focus over an external focus (Quinn, 1988: 47–8):

the *human relations* culture (flexibility/internal focus) is broadly orientated toward human commitment, typically valuing human resources, training, cohesion and staff morale;

the *open systems* culture (flexibility/external focus) is orientated towards expansion and adaptation to the external environment, valuing adaptability, readiness, growth, resource acquisition and external support;

the *internal process* culture (internal focus/control orientation) is orientated toward consolidation and continuity, and values information management, communication and stability;

the *rational goal* model (external focus/control orientation) aims to maximise output and values productivity, efficiency, planning and goal setting.

Noting March's (1994) observation regarding the influence of organizations on individual behaviour, it would be reasonable to expect that those organizations which evince a human relations culture are more likely to provide an environment wherein the Karpin recommendations concerning management development would be played out. The CVM has been applied to a number of organizational cultures in Australia (Colyer, 2000; Lamond, 2003; Vilkinas and Cartan, 2006; Wyse and Vilkinas, 2004) and can be used to inform a taxonomy of organizational cultures.

Given that all four competing values coexist in organizations, with some values more dominant than others, it is just not the scores on each CVI subscale, but the combination of the four subscale scores that is important. Lamond (2003) identified eight clusters, derived from the combination of subscale scores and the relative influences of the four approaches suggested by the mean scores, as follows (the reference high/low is in relation to the mean for the subscale as a whole and in relation to each of the other subscale mean scores):

- Weak: (20 per cent) lowest mean scores on every subscale except IP (second lowest); suggests a poorly defined culture.
- Pragmatic: (16 per cent) low on OS and RG, just above average on HR and average on IP; suggests a reactive organization, with systems in place doing what it needs to do.
- Strong: (8 per cent) highest mean scores on both IP and RG, with second highest scores in HR and OS; suggests an organization strongly emphasizing all four approaches.
- Bureaucratic: (13 per cent) low on HR, OS and RG, but high on IP; suggests an organization emphasizing bureaucratic processes for control.
- Millennial: (8 per cent) highest mean scores on OS and HR and second highest score on RG, with lowest score on IP; suggests the 'ideal organization' according to contemporary management literature, emphasizing innovation, people and striving for success – the millennial organization.
- Ad Hocracy: (15 per cent) low on HR, IP and RG and only above average for OS; suggests an organization focused on the 'next chance', with less purpose and fewer processes.
- Adaptive: (10 per cent) very high scores on HR and IP, with above average on OS and RG; suggests an organization with an external focus, translating goals into people focused policies and practices.
- Entrepreneurial: (12 per cent) very high scores on OS and high on RG, with above average on HR and low on IP; suggests externally focused organization, striving to achieve without being held back by restrictive internal processes.

Taken together, these clusters indicate that only those organizations whose cultures can be classified as Strong, Millennial or Adaptive (26 per cent of the total) have mean scores on the HR subscale that are consistent with the approach that is broadly orientated towards human commitment, with its valuing of people, training, cohesion and staff morale. In other words, Australian organizations have not developed the kinds of cultures that are conducive to the developmental environment envisaged in the Karpin Report. Further, even if the organizational context supported the development of 'soft skills', it seems that the individual managers, being 'tough-minded TJs' in the main, would not be interested.

## GLOBAL IMPLICATIONS

Certainly, 'Weary' Dunlop's life reflects the heroism, physical and emotional toughness, and self-reliance that Sinclair (2005) identified as Australian leadership values. Following the line introduced at the beginning of the chapter, it would be reasonable to expect to see the range of qualities exhibited by 'Weary' to be played out in the behaviour of Australian managers. Yet the evidence of recent research on Australian managers (see Lamond, 2003) suggests that, while emotional toughness is reflected in the individuals employed in managerial leadership positions in Australian firms, the caring, supportive side is absent – see Commentary box. Some reasons why this may be so, in terms of individual and organizational characteristics have been proposed. But I have not told the entire story to this point.

---

## COMMENTARY BOX

### Rupert Murdoch

I'm a catalyst for change ... You can't be an outsider and be successful over 30 years without leaving a certain amount of scar tissue around the place ... You can't build a strong corporation with a lot of committees and a board that has to be consulted every turn. You have to be able to make decisions on your own.

### Kerry Packer, Australia's Richest Man Before he Died

(Genghis Khan) wasn't very lovable but he was bloody efficient.

---

## Janet Holmes à Court, One of Australia's Richest Women

The company was quite hierarchical. I often think it was like a pyramid with Robert (husband Robert Holmes à Court) at the top and lots of us paying homage to him. I try to turn the pyramid upside down so that I'm at the bottom and bubbling away and encouraging people and energising them so that they are all empowered so that they can do what they need to do, now that's the dream ... We have to shift our emphasis from economic efficiency and materialism towards a sustainable quality of life and to healing of our society, of our people and our ecological systems.

## Jackie Huggins, Aboriginal Leader and Co-Chair of Reconciliation Australia

It's a very Aboriginal thing to do, to give younger people greater responsibilities within the community as they become able to take those responsibilities on. It is a culturally appropriate transfer of roles that involves respect in both directions ... from the younger to the older and the older to the younger.

(from http://www.woopidoo.com/business_quotes/)

### Indigenous Australians and Managerial Leadership

Australia the nation is a little over 100 years old (the Commonwealth of Australia was brought into being on 1 January 1901), following European settlement beginning in 1788. Australia the continent, on the other hand, has been inhabited for more than 40 000 years by its indigenous Aboriginal and Torres Strait Islander people (Australian Museum, 2004). Before 1788 there were over 600 languages spoken throughout Australia by an estimated population of 750 000 people (Australian Museum, 2004), embedded in a variety of cultural milieux that, nonetheless, shared in common many of their mythological heroes as well as the Dreaming (the process of the world being called into being and the ability to see with eternal vision), where people are very much part of the land, and associated with particular places (http//en. wikipedia.org/wiki/Australian_Aboriginal_Culture).

Today Indigenous people constitute just 2.3 per cent of the Australian population at the 2006 census (ABS, 2007), as a result of the impact of cities and towns on populations and the effects of removal of people from traditional lands, following successive government policies of annihilation and then assimilation. It was not until 1966, following a country-wide referendum, that Aboriginal people were recognized as Australian citizens rather than Australian fauna. Aboriginal narratives over the last 200 years reflect a different experience of the same Australian space – invasion, exploitation and resistance (see Austin-Broos, 1994; Beckett, 1994). Gebhardt's (2003) 'Kimberley Killings' is a chilling poetic reminder of:

> gunshot
> Running round the etched edges,
> And the necklace chains rattling.

## Women in Management in Australia

It has often been claimed that, of all OECD country workforces, Australia's is the most gender segregated (see Wallace, 2000). Further, despite 30 years of considerable legislative, policy and social change in the equity area, surveys of senior management and the boards of the nation's top companies show that women have not attained leadership positions in any significant numbers in Australia (Still, 2006). It is not surprising then, that most literature and research on women in management concentrates on the reason for the low proportion of women in senior management (Rindfleish, 2000).

Women were not visible in a management context until relatively recently, with considerations of leadership being informed by, *inter alia*, the 'great man' theory (Jogulu and Wood, 2006). At the same time, one of the obvious exclusionary characteristics of the mateship concept is that women are not included in most understandings of mateship and what it means to be a mate (Page, 2002: 195). That being said, senior management women in Australia are divided in their support of legislative initiatives such as Equal Employment Opportunity and Affirmative Action and also in their propensity to assist the advancement of other women in their workplaces (Rindfleish, 2000). Indeed, while the majority of women in the most senior ranks of management in the Australian private sector identify the need for change, they have not used their senior management role as a means of challenging gendered structures (Rindfleish and Sheridan, 2003).

## Where To From Here?

So it is that, to date, constructions of managerial leadership in Australia have been derived from notions of heroic masculinity that, in turn, reflect a culture that has valued the heroes of the bush and of war. Whether this celebration of the bronzed Aussie will continue in an increasingly heterogeneous, multicultural society, is yet to be seen. Indeed, fully 30 per cent of the Australian population at the 2006 census self-identified as being from a non-English speaking background (ABS, 2007), and that adds yet another dimension to the discussion here. Several ways forward have already been suggested.

Both Smith (2000) and Sinclair (2000) have pointed to the perceptible masculine ethos in management education, which can disadvantage female and male students in different ways, and the need for greater awareness of gender issues as a basis of enabling future managers to recognize and harness gender diversity in the workplace. Meanwhile, Fitzgerald (2003) notes the growing body of literature on cultural diversity and leadership that conceptualizes and constructs theories that value and recognize indigenous ways of knowing, acting and leading. Significantly, the literature seeks to document ways in which leadership is experienced and exercised within a multicultural framework.

In the more recent spirit of reconciliation, the acts of acknowledgement of country and welcome to country at formal events recognize the unique position of Aboriginal people in Australian culture and history (see NSW Premier's Department, 2004). Acknowledgement of country is a way that non-Aboriginal people show respect for Aboriginal heritage and the ongoing relationship of the traditional owners of an area with the land. In the same spirit, this chapter recognized, albeit all too briefly, the unique position of Aboriginal culture in Australia. The contemporary global context requires those wishing to engage with Australia to look past the 'Crocodile Dundees' and see the women and men from a multiplicity of backgrounds, including their own, if they are to do so effectively. Equally, as Australian leaders engage with the world, they need to recognize that not everyone is, or wants to be, a 'mate'.

Finally, as Sinclair (2005: 175) suggests, 'Until we unravel and expose the links between being a leader and enacting a particular form of manliness, then, in gender and racial terms, leadership will remain the domain of a homogeneous elite'. Still, there is cause for optimism as the dialogue continues, and so I conclude this chapter in the same spirit as that of the final lines proffered by Oodgeroo Noonuccal (1994) in her *Song of Hope*:

To our father's fathers
The pain, the sorrow;
To our children's children
The glad tomorrow.

## REFERENCES

Anon (2007), Digger History: an unofficial history of the Australian and New Zealand Armed Forces, http://www.diggerhistory.info/pages-heroes/weary-dunlop.htm. Accessed 27 June 2007.

Austin-Broos, D. (1994), Narratives of the encounter at Ntaria, *Oceania*, **65** (2), 131–50.

Australian Bureau of Statistics ABS (2007), *2006 Census QuickStats*: Australia. Web site http://www.censusdata.abs.gov.au. Accessed 26 June 2007.

Australian Museum (2004), The oldest living culture, http://www.dreamtime.net.au/ indigenous/culture.ofm#oldest. Accessed 3 July.

Australian War Memorial AWM (1997), The Anzac Spirit, http://www.awm.gov.au/ encyclopedia/anzac/spirit.htm. Accessed 28 June 2007.

Bean, C. E. W. (1946), ANZAC to Amiens. Canberra: Australian War Memorial, Cited in Australian War Memorial AWM (1997), The Anzac Spirit. http://www.awm. gov.au/encyclopedia/anzac/spirit.htm. Accessed 28 June 2007.

Beckett, J. (1994), Aboriginal histories, aboriginal myths: an introduction, *Oceania*, **65** (2), 97–116.

Blainey, G. (1966), *Tyranny of Distance: How Distance Shaped Australia's History*, Melbourne, Vic.: Sun Books.

Bluedorn, A. C. and Lundgren, E. F. (1993), A culture-match perspective for strategic change, *Research in Organizational Change and Development*, **7**, 137–9.

Borgelt, K. and Falk, I. (2007), The leadership/management conundrum: innovation or risk management?, *Leadership and Organization Development Journal*, **28** (2), 122–36.

Boyle, G. J. (1995), Myers-Briggs Type Indicator MBTI.: some psychometric limitations, *Australian Psychologist*, **30** (1), 71–4.

Braithwaite, J., Westbrook, M. T. and Mallock, N. A. (2007), Pressures exerted on managers by their superior and peer managers: Australian-Singaporean comparisons, *Journal of Managerial Psychology*, **22** (3), 227–56.

Burke, A. (2006), The Spirit of Anzac, http://www.anzacday.org.au/spirit/spirit2.html. Accessed 28 June 2007.

Chatman, J. A. and Jehn, K. A. (1994), Assessing the relationship between industry characteristics and organizational culture: How different can you be?, *Academy of Management Journal*, **37**, 522–53.

Colyer, S. (2000), Organizational culture in selected Western Australian sport organizations, *Journal of Sport Management*, **14**, 321–41.

Commonwealth of Australia (1995a), *Report of the Industry Task Force on Leadership and Management Skills*, Chair: David Karpin, Canberra: Australian Government Printing Service.

Commonwealth of Australia (1995b), *Report of the Industry Task Force on Leadership and Management Skills: Research Report Volumes 1 and 2*, Chair: David Karpin, Canberra: Australian Government Printing Service.

Consulting Psychologists Press (1994), *1994 Catalogue*, Palo Alto, CA.

Denison, D. R. (1984), Bringing corporate culture to the bottom line, *Organizational Dynamics*, **13** (2), 4–22.

Edwards, R. W., O'Reilly, H. and Schuwalow, P. (1997), Global personnel skills: A dilemma for the Karpin Committee and others, *Asia Pacific Journal of Human Resources*, **35** (3), 80–9.

Fisher, C. and Dowling, P. J. (1999), Support for an HR approach in Australia: the perspective of senior HR managers, *Asia Pacific Journal of Human Resources*, **37** (1), 1–19.

Fitzgerald, T. (2003), Changing the deafening silence of indigenous women's voices in educational leadership, *Journal of Educational Administration*, **41** (1), 9–23.

Gardner, W. L. and Martinko, M. J. (1996), Using the Myers-Briggs Type Indicator to study managers: A literature review and research agenda, *Journal of Management*, **22** (1), 45–83.

Gebhardt, P. (2003), *Their Stories Our History*, Wahroonga, NSW: Helicon Press.

Hofstede, G. (2005), *Cultures and Organizations: Software of the Mind* (2nd edn), New York: McGraw-Hill.

Hofstede, G. (2001), *Culture's Consequences: Comparing Values, Behaviors, Institutions and Organizations across Nations* (2nd edn), Thousand Oaks, CA: Sage.

House, R. J., Hanges, P. J., Javidan, M., Dorfman, P. W. and Gupta, V. (2004), *Culture, Leadership, and Organizations: The GLOBE Study of 62 Societies*, Thousand Oaks, CA: Sage.

Howard, L. W. (1998), Validating the competing values model as a representation of organizational cultures, *International Journal of Organizational Analysis*, **6** (3), 231–50.

Jogulu, U. D. and Wood, G. J. (2006), The role of leadership theory in raising the profile of women in management, *Equal Opportunities International*, **25** (4), 236–50.

Jonas, H. S., Fry, R. E. and Srivastva, S. (1989), The person of the CEO: Understanding the executive experience, *Academy of Management Executive*, **3** (3), 205–15.

Jones, J. T. and Jackson, T. (2000), *Managing People and Organizational Change in Australian Organizations*, School of Commerce Research Paper No 16, The Flinders University of South Australia, 9 November.

Jung, C. G. (1971), *Psychological Types*, London: Routledge and Kegan Paul, originally published 1921.

Kakabadse, N. K. and Kakabadse, A. P. (2007), Chairman of the board: demographics effects on role pursuit, *Journal of Management Development*, **26** (2), 169–92.

Kane, B., Crawford, J. and Grant, D. (1999), Barriers to effective HRM, *International Journal of Manpower*, **20** (8), 494–515.

Kotter, J. P. (1982), *The General Managers*, New York: The Free Press.

Lamond, D. A. (2003), The value of Quinn's Competing Values Model in an Australian context, *Journal of Managerial Psychology*, **18** (1), 46–59.

Lamond, D. A. (2001), Developing Australian managers' 'soft' skills: A forlorn hope?, *Proceedings of the Australian and New Zealand Academy of Management Conference*, Auckland, New Zealand, 5–7 December.

Lawson, H. (1900), 'In the days when the world was wide and other verses' (2nd edn), http://www.gutenberg.org/dirs/etext95/dwwww11.txt. Accessed 27 June 2007.

Mackellar, D. (1904/1997), http://oldpoetry.com/opoem/21197-Dorothea-Mackeller-My-Country. Accessed 26 June 2007.

March, J. G. (1994), *A Primer on Decision Making*, New York: Free Press.

Margerison, C. J. and Lewis, R. (1981), Mapping managerial styles, *International Journal of Manpower*, **21**, 2–24.

Mintzberg, H. (1973), *The Nature of Managerial Work*, New York: Harper and Row.

Myers, I. B. and McCaulley, M. H. (1985), *Manual: A Guide to the Development and Use of the Myers-Briggs Type Indicator*, Marwal, CA: Consulting Psychologists Press.

Myers, I. B., McCaulley, M. H., Quenk, N. L. and Hammer, A. L. (1998), *MBTI Manual: A Guide to the Development and Use of the Myers-Briggs Type Indicator* (3rd edn), Palo Alto, CA: Consulting Psychologists Press.

Noonuccal, O. (1994), Song of Hope, in Jensen, D. and Granger, M. (eds.) *Top Lines from Australian Contemporary Poets,* Sydney: Phoenix Education.

NSW Premier's Department (2004), Aboriginal cultural protocols and practices policy, www.premiers.nsw.gov.au/our_library/protocol/AboriginalCulturalProtocolsand PracticesPolicy2004.doc. Accessed 3 July 2007.

O'Reilly, C. A., Chatman, J. and Caldwell, D. E. (1991), People and organizational culture: A profile comparison approach to assessing person-organization fit, *Academy of Management Journal*, **34**, 487–516.

Page, J. S. (2002), Is mateship a virtue?, *Australian Journal of Social Issues*, **37** (2), 193–200.

Parliamentary Library PL (2000), Bills Digest No. 32 1999-2000 Constitution Alteration Preamble, 1999, http://www.aph.gov.au/Library/pubs/bd/1999-2000/2000bd032.htm#Purpose. Accessed 26 June 2007.

Quinn, R. E. (1988), *Beyond Rational Management: Mastering the Paradoxes and Competing Demands of High Performance*, San Francisco, CA: Jossey-Bass.

Rindfleish, J. (2000), Senior management women in Australia: diverse perspectives, *Women in Management Review*, **15** (4), 172–83.

Rindfleish, J. and Sheridan, A. (2003), No change from within: senior women managers' response to gendered organizational structures, *Women in Management Review*, **18** (6), 299–310.

Rousseau, D. M. (1990), Assessing organizational culture: The case for multiple methods, in B. Schneider (ed.) *Organizational Climate and Culture*, San Francisco, CA: Jossey-Bass, 153–92.

Schein, E. H. (1990), Organizational culture, *American Psychologist*, **45** (2), 109–19.

Sinclair, A. (2005), *Doing Leadership Differently: Gender, Power and Sexuality in a Changing Business Culture*, revised edition, Carlton, Vic.: Melbourne University Press.

Sinclair, A. (2000), Teaching managers about masculinities: Are you kidding? *Management Learning*, **31** (1), 83–101.

Sinclair, A. (1994), *Trials at the Top: Chief Executives Talk about Men and Women and the Australian Executive Culture*, Parkville, Vic.: The Australia Centre, University of Melbourne.

Smith, C. R. (2000), Notes from the field: gender issues in the management curriculum: a survey of student experiences, *Gender, Work and Organization*, **7** (3), 158–67.

Statt, D. A. (1994), *Psychology and the World of Work*, London: Macmillan.

Still, L. V. (2006), Where are the women in leadership in Australia?, *Women in Management Review*, **21** (3), 180–94.

Trompenaars, F. (1994), *Riding the Waves of Culture: Understanding Cultural Diversity in Global Business*, Burr Ridge, IL: Irwin.

Trompenaars, F. and Hampden-Turner, C. (1997), *Riding the Waves of Culture. Understanding Cultural Diversity in Business*, London: Nicholas Brealey Publishing.

Vilkinas, T. and Cartan, G. (2006), The integrated competing values framework: its spatial configuration, *Journal of Management Development*, **25** (6), 505–21.

Wallace, M. (2000), Workplace training initiatives: implications for women in the Australian workforce, *Journal of European Industrial Training*, **24** (5), 268–74.

Wyse, A. and Vilkinas, T. (2004), Executive leadership roles in the Australian Public Service, *Women in Management Review*, **19** (4), 205–11.

# Index

12 labours of Herakles 119
Aboriginal languages in Canada 52
Aboriginal people, recognition 370
Abraham's argument with God 272
absence of caring support, Australia 367
adventurer and work 98
Africa 17–19
  Ananci stories 65
  challenge to colonialism 227
  culture, importance of 220
  leadership failure 225–6
  magical beliefs 13, 65, 66, 68–70
  worldview of ancestors 212–13
Aga Khan, leader of Shia Ismaili
  Muslims 57
Agamemnon 115–18
  and leadership 116–17
age and experience in India 313
age and seniority in leadership 217
aggressive, assertive leadership, Russia
  334, 338
aid agencies, Western, in Africa 221
AIDS pandemic, Africa 61
Akhilleus (Achilles), leader and hero
  118–20
alcohol and workers, Russia 325
Alexander the Great 257
Allianz insurance group, Germany 137
ambiguity in Brazilian leadership 102
American Film Institute (AFI), 'heroes'
  32
Americanization in Israel 282
American War of Independence 187
Ananci (Anansi), mythical African
  spider 13, 68, 70–71, 73
Anand Milk Producers Union Limited
  316
ancestors as custodians of culture 210
ancestor veneration Africa 209–19
  important to Africans 222–3
  Zulus 213–18
ancestor worship myth 210–18

Ancient Egypt 257
Anglo-Celtic heritage of England 146
Anglo-Saxons 147
animal sacrifices for ancestors 213
anti-heroism sentiment, Canada 57
'ANZAC' (Australia and New Zealand
  Army Corps) 361
Aquaman 35, 36
Arab-Israeli conflict 262, 275, 278
Arab leadership, decision-making 243
Arap Moi, Daniel, Kenya 228
Arawak people 66
Arctic, Canada 51
Arctic Circle 12
Argentina 12, 13, 79–91
  leadership 83–5
aristocratic behaviour of Hanseatic
  merchants 131
Aristotle, Nichomachean Ethics 345
Arthur, warrior and king 150–54
  and Knights of Roundtable 148, 149
'Asar', sky gods, Sweden 167
Asia, Pacific 19–22
assassination
  of Charles IV, French king 179
  of Yitzhak Rabin 277
Australia 21–2, 359–70
  age of continent and nation 368
  leadership values 359
  management, heroic masculinity
    369–70
  managers, 'soft skills', lack of 363,
    366–7
Austria 134
Authentic Leadership Questionnaire
  (ALQ) 238
authoritarian leadership style 75–6
  of Ben-Gurion 275–6
  China 300
  Egypt 266
authority of God 273
authority, hierarchical 102

automobile industries, Japan 347, 348
autonomous leadership 160
autonomy in Sweden 174
Avalokitesvara, India 293

bachelor status as non-adult, Africa 210
Barbados 66, 67
Batman 35, 36
Battle of Hastings, 1066 146
Becket, Thomas 157
Becoming, Buddhism 344
Begin, Menachem, Prime Minister, Israel
    262
    authoritarian leader 276
    orator 276
behavioural rigidity 140
Being, Buddhism 344
Bell, Alexander Graham, inventor of
    telephone 55
bending rules in Brazil (*jeitinho*) 94
benevolence of folk heroes, 327–8
benevolent leadership, Kenya 235
benevolent paternalism, India 319–20
Ben-Gurion, David 275–6
Beowulf hero15, 149
Berton, Pierre, *The Last Spike* 51
*Bhagavad Gita* 20
    preaching of duty 308, 309
*bhakti*, ideology of subordination 309,
    310
Bible (Old Testament) 271
Biblical 'superheroes' 42
birth, time of 290
Blackberry wireless email device 55
Boccaccio, Giovanni, on rules for
    Arthur's Knights 152–3
Bolsheviks, 1917 329
Bondar, Roberta, Canadian astronaut 60
Boudicca (Boadicea), Iceni war leader
    158
Brahma, creator 308
brainwashing in Soviet Union 329
Brandenburg electorate 130
Brazil 12, 93–105
    conflict avoidance 105
    *jeitinho* and football 101
    leadership 99–103
    myths of 14
    traditional or modern society 94
British abolishment of slave trade 67

British and traditional education, India
    319
British colonial rule
    India 306, 314
    Kenya 231
British Empire 145
British North America Act 1867 50, 53
British protectorate, Kenya 226–7
brutality of Poland's captors 189
brutality towards strangers, Russian
    myth 328
Buber, Martin 273
Buddha 293–5
    influence on corporate culture 353–4
    in Japan 343, 344
    teachings 21
bureaucracy as burden 199, 201
Bush, George W., US President 4
business contracts, Hanseatic 132
Business Fit International 73–4
business leaders
    China 296–8
    Egypt 263
    English 158
    Israel 278–80
    modern Poland 196–7
business schools recruitment, Sweden
    171
business stereotypes, Germany 134

Calvinistic approach to work 132, 137
Camp David Peace Agreement 262
Canada 12
    character and leadership 58–9
    cultural mythology 12–13, 49–62
    global leadership 49–62
    leadership qualities 54–8, 61–2
    'Seven Wonders' 54
    social experiment 54
Canada-US Free Trade Agreement 56
Canadian Broadcasting Corporation
    (CBC) 52
Canadian Pacific Railway 50
Canon company, Japan 349
Captain America 35, 36–7
Caribbean islands 12, 13, 65–77
    leadership system 69–74
    mythology 68–71
Caribs in Caribbean 66
Carnival and 'real world', Brazil 95–6,
    101

cartoons depicting Mohammed 3
caste system, India 311
Castro, Fidel, revolutionary forces 82
Catholic Church, veneration of saints
    211, 219
cattle in Maasai culture 229
Celtic gods in England 150
change in Iran 253
charisma 136
    of leaders 80, 81–2, 105, 135
Charlemagne 155
    King Arthur as rival 151
Chaucer, Geoffrey, *Canterbury Tales*
    153, 154
Che' Guevara, Ernesto 13, 81–2, 86
Check Point Software Technologies Ltd
    279
Cheung Kong Holdings 297–8
Cheung Yan, business leader 298–9
*chi* (energy) 290
China 289–303
    Communist regime 9
    culture 19–20
    immigrants to Caribbean 67
    leadership 294–9
    mythologies 290–94
    political systems 289
Chinese cosmology 289–90
Chinese Cultural Revolution 10
Chinese medicine 291
Chinese workers on Canadian railways
    52
chivalric codes of conduct 152
chivalry, age of 148
'chosen people' Jewish theme 270
Christian beliefs 65, 66
Christianity 13, 146, 150, 167
    in Caribbean 68–9
    in King Arthur's time 150–51
    in Sweden 178–9
Christianization in Africa 220
*chutzpa* 272
Ciboney people 66
circumcision 229
Cleopatra VII, queen of ancient Egypt
    260–61
Clytemnestra *see* Klytaimnestra
coffee 52
collaboration
    Germany 135
    Sweden 171–2

collective bargaining in industry 133
collective culture, stronger in Greeks
    123
collective identity for Israel 277
'collective-style corporations', Japan 346
collectivism 23, 89, 100, 104
    in China 294
    in Egypt 267
    in England, low 158
    in India 310, 320
    in leadership 74
colonial despotism 231
colonial expansion 147
colonial heritage 71
colonialism in Africa 220, 225
color problem in Caribbean 67
Columbus, Christopher 66
comic book heroes 12, 33, 34, 41
Commonwealth Caribbean 65
communication
    in Canada 50
    in leadership 174
    in Swedish management 175, 181
communism 16
    China 289, 296
    fall of, in Poland 202
    occupation of Poland 192
competence of Polish workers 195–6
competitive ability of India 318
concubines buried alive, China 291
conflict averse society, Brazil 97
conflict avoidance, Sweden 171–2
Confucian primary values 20, 294, 297
    in Japan 344
consensus decision making, Sweden 172,
    181–2
consideration in leadership 136
consultative environment 267
Contrastive Rhetoric 90
convicts to Australia 360
corporate competitive edge 355
corporate culture clashes 197–9
Corporate Governance 132
corporate leadership myths, Soviet
    system 335–6, 339
corruption under communism 194
Corus Steel (UK) 316
cosmology, China 295
cosmopolitan leaders 139
cotton as cash crop, Egypt 261

courage of leaders 247
courage of Odysseus 121
creation by group 176
creative leadership, Japan 349
Credit Suisse First Boston, Zurich 60
Creole dialect 67
Creole religions 68
Crocodile Dundee, rugged character,
    Australia 360
cross-cultural blunders 4
cross-cultural communication 221
Crusaders, from Europe 261
cultural awareness 140
cultural differences, appreciation of 41,
    140
cultural diversity need, Australia 370
cultural evolution 26
cultural gaffes 4, 5
cultural mythology 2, 5–21
    the Americas 12–14
    for global leaders 24. 25
    in United States 31–46
Cultural Revolution, China 289, 296
culture and leadership 232
    early England 150
    India 310–13
cultures, reciprocation of 25–6
cunning of Odysseus 120, 121
Curie, Maria and Pierre187
curling, ice sport 52–3
customer service, high quality 5
customs, respect for 222

Daewoo Commercial vehicles (Korea)
    316
Dalai Lama, invitation by Angela Merkel
    136
Dallaire, General Roméo 61
Daniel in the lions' den, bravery 273
Danish newspaper, *Jyllands-Posten* 3
dates, choice of 290
dead become ancestors, Africa 210, 212
death 294
    of Eva Perón 81
death penalty, abolition in Prussia 131
death threats from Muslims 3
deaths of ancestors, Africa 211
Debora, prophet in Bible 272
decentralization in Sweden 172–3
decision processes and social interaction
    101–2

defense industry, Israel 278
delegation from managers, Sweden 173
democratic system in Poland 192
democratization
    of Caribbean 67–8
    in Germany 128, 130, 132–3, 137–8
destruction of cultural artefacts, China
    289
development, sustainable 162
*dharma* 321
'dialectical leadership' Japan 347,
    348–9, 352–3
Diaspora 270
discourse patterns, differences 90
diversity in Canada 57
divine status of Russian leaders 326
*Domesday Book* for taxation 146
Douglas, Tommy, 'Father of Medicare'
    58
Drake, Sir Francis,
    'Drake's Drum' 149, 157, 163
    explorations 157
    national hero 156
Dreaming, Australia 368
Dunlop, Sir Edward 'Weary', Australian
    surgeon 362–3, 367
Dutch colonies 66
duty and rights, India and West 321

earth roots of folklore heroes, Russia
    327–8
economic development
    and cultural change 232
    Kenya 228
    Prussia 130
economic virtues 132
educated elite in India 319
egalitarianism 58, 180
    Australian lack of 364
    in Sweden 172
'ego-massaging' 87
Egypt 257–68
    gods and goddesses 258
    leadership 18–19, 260–64
        cultural values 265
Egyptian Revolution 1952 261
Eight Elders, China 296
Eight Immortals, China 292–3, 296
El Sadat, Muhammad Anwar, President
    of Egypt 262
    assassination 262

Eliot, T.S., on myths as religious beliefs 307
Elizabeth I of England 145
    shrewd leader 158
Elizabeth II, servant leader 158
Emaar Properties 59
emotional expression, Brazil 102
emotional toughness, Australia 365, 367
employee empowerment, Kenya 236–7
'employee family' 312
employee participation 85
ends justifying means, Russia 328
energy in environment 290
England (Britannia) 15–16, 145–63
    leadership qualities 159–60
        global implications of 161
    nation 153
    Scandinavia and 147
English education in India 314
English history as superpower 161
English in Canada 49, 53
English nationalism 154
Englishness, ideal 154
Ennead, Nine Gods of Heliopolis 257
entrepreneurial activity, Israel 282, 283
environmental protection, Merkel's view 136
equal rights for minorities, Israel 282
Eriksson, Sven-Göran 180
Estruga, Manuel, Exiros SA 87
ethical behaviour 273
ethnic groups in Kenya 229
Europa, Phoenician princess 14
Europe 14–17
European conquest of Caribbean 66
Europeanization of imagination 314
external environment, Australia 365

fairness and justice 246–7
faith and knowledge 273
family
    background emphasis 123–4
    leadership aspect 253–4
family in Brazil 98–9
family name, Chinese 290
family relations, empire building 259
family values, China 299–301
Fantastic Four 35, 37
Fanuc, machine tools, Japan 349–520
farmer as warrior, Russian myth 327

farmer helper 169
Farouk I, King of Egypt 261
fatalism of Indians 321
father figure
    for Iranian leadership 249, 252
    India 320
    in Infosys 315
father of Russian people, Stalin 330, 331
fatwa from Omar Abdel-Rahman 262
fecundity in African culture 212
feminist myth 275
*feng shui* (wind and water) 290
Ferdowsi, Abol-Qassem, Shahnameh 243–5
fetish priests, Africa 213
feudal China 289
'few against many' myth 270, 281, 283
filial piety, China 299, 300, 301
film heroes in United States 33, 34
Finnish expatriates on leadership 135–6
First and Second World Wars 128
First Nation people
    Canada 49, 53
    diversity of 51
First World War 145
flexibility for progress, Buddhism 345
folk music, Canadian 52
folk revival for tourism, China 303
folk tales 177–8
    of King Arthur 148
folklore 127
    Russia 20–21, 327
    United States 31
followers, recognition of needs by leader 310
football
    in Brazilian culture 101
    and cordial man, Brazil 101
forceful relationships 87–8
'foreign is better' myth, Brazil 99
forest laws of Normans 155, 163
forgiveness of leaders 247
francophone culture in Canada 50
Frederick the Great, absolute monarch 130–31
Frederick William I and II, kings 130
freedom of speech 3
free market system, American 198
Freja, Norse goddess 168
French colonies 66

French in Canada 49, 53
French romance literature 150
Frigga, Norse goddess 168
frost giants, Ymer and Bure 167
fur trade, Canada 50

G8 summit 4
Gandhi, Mahatma, modern day Rama
    306–7
gaucho in Argentine folklore 13, 82–3
gender
    awareness, Australia 370
    diversity in workplace 313
    egalitarianism, South Asia 243
    roles in England 159
General Motors (GM) 59–60
genes, English, from Northern Europe
    147
genocide in Rwanda 61
Geoffrey of Monmouth, *Historia Regum
    Britannicae* 148, 150, 151
Geofizyka Torun 196
German Empire, and Prussian kings 130
German epics 150
German Federal Armed Forces 133
Germanic ancestors of English 149
German leadership behaviour 136
German style management 140
Germany 127–41
    leadership in Germany 133–9
    mythology 15, 140
ghetto revolts 274
Giants, Norse mythology 170
Global Centre for Pluralism, Ottawa 57
global cultures, understanding 221
global investment 274–5
globalization
    and balance 321
    of business 139
    Israel and 281
global leadership 1–5, 10–11, 24–5
    and cultural mythology 25
    need for 10, 11
    United States 31–46
Global Leadership and Organizational
    Behaviour
    Effectiveness (GLOBE) 2004 85–6,
        88, 123, 125, 134–5, 359
    Egypt 265
    England 158
    Iran 243

global orientation of Egypt 261
global power 145
glorification of war, Russia 328
God
    belief in 273
    as *Inkosi Yezulu,* for Zulus 210
    and man encounters, I-thou 273
    as *Nyame,* for Ashantis 210
    as *Quamata,* for Xhosa 210
'God of the Sky', Zulus 216, 218
god of war, Russia 326
Goddess of Longevity and Immortality,
    China 292
godfather in Brazil 102
gods as flawed leaders 124, 125
golden age of Chinese inventions 291
good fortune 290
Great Wall of China 291
Greece 111–26
    gods and famous men 14–15
    leadership 112
Greek gods, leadership capricious 118
Gretsky, Wayne, ice hockey player 57
*guanxi,* trust and face, Chinese 301
Gujarat Co-operative Milk Marketing
    Federation 315, 318
Guyana 66

Haier Corporation, China 296–7
Halevi, Yehudah 273
Hamburg, city of 131, 132
Han, dominant group, China 289
Hanseatic League 15, 131, 133
Hatshepsut, queen of ancient Egypt 260
headman and priest of Kraal 214
health care in Canada 58
He-Halutz movement, Russia 274
Hejnal Mariacki (Hymn to Mary) 188
Hektor, killed by Akhilleus 120
Hellenistic period 257
Henry V, egalitarian leader 156
Hera, a wife of Zeus 118–19
Herakles, (Hercules), leader and hero
    118–20
heroes in Greek mythology , flawed 113
'heroic masculinity' Australia 360, 363
Heschel, Abraham 273
Hesiod, *Theogony* 115
hierarchical leadership 71–4, 300
hierarchical order, elimination of 135

hierarchical power 294
hierarchical society, Brazil 94
hierarchy for social order 245–6
high-tech business, Israeli economy 275, 278
Hinduism, majority religion in India 20, 307–8
history, respect for 204
Hofstede cultural value model 72, 73
holism concept 94
Holmes à Court, Janet, economic efficiency 368
Holocaust 274
Holy Roman Empire of German nation 128
home and street behavior, Brazil 96–7
Homer's *Odyssey* 114
homogeneity 153
Honda company, Japan 346, 349
Honour of Hanseatic merchants 128, 131–2, 137
Horus, son of Isis 259
Horvitz, Eli, leader of Teva 279, 281
hostile environment 281
Hudson's Bay Company 49–50
Huggins, Jackie, Aboriginal leader 368
human capital 281
humane altruism, South Asia 243
humane rule of emperors, China 295
human nature, nuanced view 178
human relations culture 365
human resource development (HRD) 238
human rights
    Canada 55
    importance 191
    Merkel's view 136
humanity in leadership 217
humility of leaders 246
Hutchison Whampoa Limited 297–8
hygiene standards, McDonalds 4

IBM shakeup, Japan 355
ice hockey players, Canada 52
image recognition for Russian leaders 339
immigration into Israel 275
imperial China 289
imperialism 161
Inaba, Dr Seiuemon, Fanuc company 350, 352–3

inclusive society, Canada 50, 55
income distribution, inequality 102
Incredible Hulk 35, 38
India 306–22
    cultural mythology 20
    political history 313–14
Indian farmer, empowerment of 316
Indian immigrants to Caribbean 67
Indians in Trinidad 66
Indian space program 316–17
indigenous people of Australia, treatment 368–9
individual competition 98
individual employers' rights 321
individualism 23, 94
    in England, high 158
    in Greece 123
    in India 310
    in leadership 74
    in society 100
individuals, mythicals symbols 79–80
Indo-European mythology 183
informal relationships in business 283
Infosys, IT company, India 315, 318
'inscrutability' and Chinese myth 303
instability in Argentina 88–9
institutional collectivism 243
integrity
    Greek leadership 124
    and honesty in Shahnameh 246
intellectual revolution in India 314
internal process culture, Australia 365
international and western influences to Egypt 264
international business opportunities 6
international ventures 197
Inuit in Canada 55
    culture preservation 51, 53
invincibility of Siegfried (Nibelungenlied) 129
Iphigenia, sacrificed 117
Iran 242–55
    charismatic change-agents as leaders 254
    Indo-European ethnic roots 242
    mythology of 18
    South Asian 243
Iranian leadership themes 251–4
Iscar, metal cutting tools, Israel 279
Isis, Egyptian goddess 258–9

Islamic literature 265
Isle of Avalon, mythical place 151
Israel 270–83
  Biblical stories and history 19
  borders 281
  national identity 274
  political leadership 275–7
Israel-Egypt Peace Treaty 262
Israeli comments on leadership 280
Israeli-Palestine conflicts 278
Ivan Tsarevich, 327

Janosik, Jerzy, Slovak Robin Hood
    188–9
Japan 21, 343–57
Japanese corporations 345–6
Japanese prisoners building railway
    (WW2) 362
*jeitinho* (bending of rules) 102
'Jewish Genius' myth 274–5, 281
Jewish heroism 273–4
Jewish immigrants to Israel 276
Jewish religion and nationality 276
Jewish resistance, armed 274
Jews, Hebrew-speaking 271
Judaism and myth 271–5
Judeo-Christian ethic in United States 42
Judging (J) preference, Australia 365
justice 272
  of Greek gods 125
  guiding principle 281, 282, 283
  of Zeus 115–16

Kaplan, Robert, on rhetorical style 90
*karma*, Hindu philosophy 313
Karpin Report on leadership, Australia
    363
Kenya 225–39
  leadership in 17–18
    authentic in Kenya 233–99
    transformational 232–9
    tribal 231
Kenya African National Union (KANU)
    228
Kenyan independence 228
Kenyatta, Jomo, Prime Minister 228
Kikuyu, Kenya 18, 229
Kikuyu prophet, warnings of colonial
    invasion 230
kindness of leaders 247

King Arthur 15–16
  as national hero 155
King Boleslaw and Knights, Poland 188
King David, Bible 272
King Hussein 277
kingship, ideal of 150
kings in Sweden 179
kin networks, extended 94
kinship ties for business heads 214–15
Klytaimnestra, wife of Agamemnon
    117–18
knighthood, qualities of 153–4
knight, iconic figure 153
Knights of the Round Table 151, 152
Knossos, Crete, palace complexes 114
knowledge
  as power, India 319
  seeking for, in leaders 248
  thirst for, among Norse gods 177
Kosciusko Insurrection 189
Kosciuszko, Tadeusz 187
Kraals (small villages), Africa 214–15
Krakus, legendary Polish prince 188
Krishna, Hindu religious deity 306,
    308–10
  leadership qualities of 309
Kuan Yin, Goddess of Mercy and
    Compassion 293–4
Kurian, Verghese, rural development,
    India 315, 316, 318
Kwazulu Natal, South Africa 214

laissez-faire, low ranking 136
Lake Victoria, Kenya 230
land, inhospitable, Canada 49, 50
language translations, awkward 4
Latin America 83
  personalism 93
Lautman, Dov, textile business 279, 282
Lawson, Henry, Australian poetry
    360–61
leaders
  ancestral veneration of 213
  characteristics needed 317
  heroes of Shahnameh, Iran 245, 251
  as *primus inter pares* 176, 180
  role in Brazil 103
leadership 6, 37
  and cultural mythology 22–3
  definition of 134

humane 160
people-based, *ubuntu* 217
post-heroic, 41, 42
practices 1, 2, to 21
qualities 44
self-protective 159–60
strong 203
team-oriented 160
leadership role
Cleopatra's reign 264
Saladin's rule 264
legends 127
of England 147
Lewis, Stephen, UNICEF work 56
light in dark forest 169
Lightfoot, Gordon, *Canadian Railroad Trilogy* 52
linguistic differences in Canada 53
literacy boosting, Kenya 228
Live Nation, Beverley Hills 59
local conditions 7
Local Native Councils, Kenya 227
'logic of harmony' Shinto, Japan 344, 345, 347
long term orientation, India 310
long term views in leadership 302
loss of face 104
loyalty 310
to authority 246

Maasai, pastoral society, Kenya 229
*Mabinogion* (Welsh chronicle) 150
Maccabees, freedom fights 273
MacDonald, Sir John A., Prime Minister, Canada 55
machine tool industry, Japan 349–50
*machismo*, Latin American 84
macho culture, Australia 360
images 21
Macri, Mauricio, Mayor of Buenos Aires 84–5, 86
magic spells 69
*Magna Carta*, England 145
*Mahabharata*, epic poem 308
Mahatma Gandhi 20
Mahmood Ahmadi-Nejad, President of Iran 250
Maimonides on belief 273
male ancestors 215
male and female values, India 312

male-dominated Russian society 332
Malory, Sir Thomas, *Morte'd'Arthur* 153
management
best practices 196
coercive, in Egypt 266
leadership 199
Australia 363–7
in Poland under Soviets 200–201
managerial style of Mauricio Macri 84
managers on work site, Japan 351–2
Mandela, Nelson, compassionate leadership of 217
Mao Zedong 303
Mapai, Israel 275
marital status as adulthood, Africa 210
Masada mythical narratives 273
Masai of Kenya 18
masculine and feminine in work leaders 100–101
masculine values in India, US, and UK 312
masculinity in England 158–9
materialism
and competition 321
in West 320
mateship
Australia 361
exclusion of women 369
Matsushita Electric, deficit 354–6
Mau Mau uprising, Kenya 227–8
McDonalds restaurants 7
mediating role of Angela Merkel 136
Meir, Golda, Prime Minister of Israel 276
female leader 273
mentoring in leadership 238
Merkel, Angela, German Chancellor 4, 15, 135–6
Mesquita, Luiz, Argentina 87
Miao Shan 293–4
*see also* Kuan Yin
microcultures in Kenya 232
Middle East 17–19
'middle way' of Buddhism 345
Midgård, Oden in 168, 177
migration, forced, in Poland 191
militarism and obedience, negative for Prussia 131
military government 130

military leaders
  Germany 133
  Israel 278, 282
  Russia 329
miracle performer, Stalin 330
'miracle working' Russian leaders 337,
  339
Mirabilis, Israeli IT firm 279
misfortunes of sickness 294
Mithras, cult of 150
  rival of Isis 259
mixture of races in Brazil 93
modernity and industrialization 179–80
Modern Project 178–9
modesty in Swedish culture 172
Mohamed Al-Fayed, Harrods owner,
  comment 266
Mohammad Ali Pasha, Ottoman officer
  261
Monkey King, Ming dynasty 293
monotheistic religions 271
Moody-Stewart, Sir Mark, Chairman,
  Anglo-American 161–2
morality in Chinese culture 295
Moses 42
  as leader 272
motherhood, signified by Isis 258, 260
motherly figure, Golda Meir 275
motivation of individuals 359
Mount Olympus 114
Muhammad Hosni Mubarak, President
  of Egypt 262
  comment 266
Mulroney, Brian, PM of Canada 56
multiculturalism in Canada 50, 59
Multifactor Leadership Questionnaire
  (MLQ) 238
multinational businesses
  American 198
  Egypt 265
  India 306
multiple cultures 3, 4, 5
multiple language speaking, India 314
Murdoch, Rupert, sole decision maker
  367
Murthy, Narayana, Infosys, India 315,
  318
Muslim Conquest 257
Muslim conquest of Egypt 261
'Muspelhem' hot realm, Sweden 167

myth
  cordial man, Brazil 98–9
  equality versus hierarchy 95–6
  religion and 306
  worker in Brazil 97–8
mythical deities, for fortune 290
mythology
  of ancient Egypt, and present 263–4
  cultural 7–9, 22
  of Iran, Shahnameh 245
myths
  about leaders 79
  ancient Greece 111–12
  ban under Mao 303
  in Chinese culture 302–3
  defining Canada 53
  definition of 271
  half-truths 209
  need for 270
  power of 1, 2, 3
  as taboo, China 289
  universal 148
  use of, in modern Russia 340

names of deities, Chinese 290
Napoleonic invasion of Egypt 257
Nasser, Gamal Abdel, first president,
  Egypt 261–2
  comment 266
  pan-Arab agenda 261
national culture
  influence of 136
  in work situations 100
national identity, 19th century Britain
  155
National Socialists in Germany (Nazis)
  128
  dictatorial 132
  invasion of Poland 189
  Jewish rebellion against 274
nationalism 153
nationalities in China 289
Nation's Anthem 189–90
nation with enemies 270
natural resources
  of Africa 225
  scarce 270
naval power, English 147
Nazis *see* National Socialists
Negev desert, settlement in 276

Nelson, Admiral Lord Horatio,
    popularity 157
nepotism 94, 102, 215
    in Chinese business 300, 301
    in Egyptian business 264
Netherlands 135
niche strategy 36
Nichomachean Ethics, Aristotle 345
Niebelungenlied, medieval saga 128–30
'Nifelhem' frozen world, Sweden 167
Nine Dragons Paper (Holdings) Limited
    298–9
Nissan Motor Company shakeup, Japan
    355, 356
Nobel Peace Prize 56, 262
Norse creator gods 167
Norse influence of myth in England 148
Norse mythology 16
    influence of 176–7
    pre-Christian 166–7
nothingness, Buddhism 334–5
nurturing towards subordinates 312

Obeah 13, 68–9
obedience to leader, Russia 327–8
occupation of Poland 191
October War 1973 262
Oden, god of war 168
Odysseus (Ulysses). King of Ithaca 15,
    120–22
old age 294
Oleg the Visionary, creation of Russian
    state 328, 329
Olympic Games, 2008, China 191
Onassis, Aristotle, inspiration from
    Odysseus 122
one party state, Kenya 228
open systems culture, Australian 365
opportunistic culture of Greece 125
oral agreements, Hanseatic 132
organizational culture
    Australian 365–7
    Japan 346, 354
organizational skills in Sweden 174–5
orientation, long term, India, 313
Orthodox Christians, Russia 328
Osiris
    bringer of enlightenment 259, 260
    god of the dead 258–9
    god of the resurrection 259, 260

leadership qualities 264
Osman Ahmed Osman, Aswan Dam
    262–3
Ottoman Turks 257
outlaw of medieval England 155
'overall harmony' of human world 344,
    345

Packer, Kerry, on Ghengis Khan 367
Pagani, Luis, Arcor, Argentine
    multinational 85, 86
Pahlavi dynasty 249–50
Palestine Liberation Organization 262
Palmerston, Henry John Temple, 3rd
    Viscount 145
paper company in China 298–9
participation in leadership 57–8, 135,
    160, 173, 181
partitioning of Poland 189, 194
passivity, under Soviet rule, Poland 194
paternalistic leadership 60, 61, 62, 235
    benevolent 243, 310, 311
    Brazilian 99, 103
    Russian 338, 339
patience of leaders 247
patriarchal families 98–9
patriarchal leadership, Germany 137
patriarchy versus team-based 136
patriotic symbol, Captain America 36–7
patriotism 128, 248
    for Iran 250
    in Soviet Union 330
Patroklos, friend of Akhilleus 120
Patterson, Banjo, Australian poetry 359,
    360
peaceful nation, Canada 53, 54
Pearson, Lester, Prime Minister of
    Canada 56
people management, low priority,
    Australia 363–4, 367
Perón, Evita, Argentina 13, 80–81, 86
Persian (Farsi)-speaking world 244
Persian Empire 500 BC 243
personal ambitions of Greek gods 117
personal interaction in business life 89,
    93
personalism in Brazil 94–5, 104
personalities of Herakles and Akhilleus
    120
Perus, god of thunder 326

Peter the Great, Russia
   myth of 332, 333
   real person 333–4
Pharaohs 258–60
physical geography of Canada 49
'pioneer' myth 281, 283
plagues of God 273
plantation agriculture 93
pluralist society, Canada 57
Po Si Ju Campaign, China 289
Poland 16–17, 187–204
   economy crisis 195
   modern economic power 203–4
   partitioning of 189, 194
   passivity, under Soviet rule 194
   resistance to German occupation 190
   rich culture 204
Polish intelligentsia 193
Polish management mythology 202
Polish mythology 188–96
Polish nationalism 192
political elite, Israel 275
poor people and mythical kings 95–6
popular culture in United States 33, 34
Portuguese character traits 98
Portuguese colonial legacy, Brazil 93
power and wisdom 129
power based on age, family, China 295
power concentration in family firms 312
power distance 73, 75–6, 100
   Argentina 88
   Brazil, high 102
   Caribbean countries 71, 73–4
   China, high, 294–5, 300
   England, low 158–9
   Greece 113
   India, high 310–11, 320
   Iran 243
   Israel, low 283
   Russia, high 326
power distance cultures 72, 104
'power of action', Swedish management
   171
power of ancestors 212, 214
power, limited, of Greek gods 115–17
practical knowledge leadership, Japan
   345, 347–8, 351–2
pragmatism 177
   in Swedish leadership 175
pride

of Greek leaders 123
of Hanseatic merchants 132
Prime Minister of Canada 45
problem solving ingenuity 294, 301
products with fewer parts (Weniger
   Teile) 352–3
professionalism in Germany 140
Protestantism 146
ProtoSlavic folklore 326, 327
Prudential Financial, Canada 58
Prussian Virtues, fundamentalist beliefs
   128, 130–31, 133, 137
psychoanalysis in Argentina 85
psychological state, belief as 273
punishment of living by ancestors 212
Putin, Vladimir, Russian president 332,
   333
   image for the people 334–5
   myth and reality of 334–5

Qin dynasty 289
Qin Shi, Emperor of China 291
qualities for Iranian leaders 254–5
Québec Act 1774 50
Québec terrorism 56
Queen Elizabeth I 145, 153, 158
Queen Elizabeth II 158

Rabin, Yitzhak 276–7
   assassination of 275
   Six Days War 281
racist attitudes to Africans 219
Ra, Egyptian god 257–9
Rafael, weapon systems 278
rags-to-riches stories, China 297, 300
railways in Canadian mythology 51–2
rain-giver 326
Rama, Hindu religious deity 306,
   308–10
   leadership qualities of 309
*Ramayana*, epic poem 308
Rapino, Michael, Live Nation 59
rational goal model 365
rebirth of Iran, importance of 252
recognition of Iranian culture 254
reform, necessity for a company 354–5
regional power stuggles 59
relational culture, Brazil 103–5
religion and state, separation in Iran 250
religious beliefs 127

religious diversity in workplace 313
religious folklore, Iran 243
religious tolerance, Prussia 130–31
religious traditions 42
republican China 289
Research in Motion, Canada 55, 57
resettlement in Poland 194
resistance in Israeli identity 274
'resonating leadership' Japan 347, 348
'Respect for humanity' Japan 346
Rhodes, Cecil, on the English 163
Richard I, King of England, and Saladin
   261
rifles 230
risk aversion, lack of, India 313
risk-taking behavior 267
   in Polish business 199
rites in Brazil 97
rituals 127
   participative, Brazil 103
   spear of Zulus 215
Robin Hood (Robert Hode) 15–16, 148,
   155; as national hero
   and misuse of authority 157
role models 32
Roman Catholicism in Poland 187
Romance language communication
   90–91
Romans in Britain 149–50
romanticism in Germany 128
Rousseau, Jean-Jacques, influence on
   Sweden 178
rules
   authority of 100
   leaders' exemption from 337–8
'ruling minorities' mythology 325
rural development, India 316, 318
Russia 325–40
   collapse in 21st century 332
   leadership in 20–21
   Third Rome 328
Russian fairy tale, Ilya Muromets 327
Russian leadership mythology 326–40
Rwanda, massacre in 61

sacred stories 127
sacrifice of ox 216
Sadat, Anwar
   charismatic leader 265
   comment by 266

Salah-al-Din Yusuf ibn Ayyub 261
Sarabhai, Vikram, Indian space program
   315, 316–18
Satan, Set (Seth, Egyptian god) as model
   for 258
Satellite Instructional Television
   Experiment 317
scientific research, Prussia 130
Scott, Sir Walter, *Ivanhoe* 156
Second World War 133, 137
   developments after 140
self-analysis in Argentina 85
self-assertion in leadership 349
self-awareness 233
self-definition of Canadians 54
self-made woman, China 298–9
   Confucian principles in 295
self-management, China 294;
self-reliance in leadership, Australia 359
'self-renunciation' Buddhism 334–5
separation from Muslim-Arab nations
   251
'servant leadership' 321
servant-caretaker model of leader 265
Set (Seth), Egyptian god 258
settlers in England 146
Seventeen Article Constitution 344
Shahnameh (Book of Kings), Iranian
   mythology 18, 243–50
Shakespeare, William
   *Henry IV* 157
   *Henry V* 156, 157
sheep farming, Australia 360
Shinto teachings 21
   Japan 343–5
Shiva, Hindu deity, destroyer 308
Shotoku Taishi 343, 344
Shwed, Gil, high tech IT companies 279,
   282
Siegfried, at court of Burgundian kings
   129
silence of Swedes 176
   in leadership 181
silkworm cultivation, China 291
Sir Li Ka-Shing, business leader 297–8
Six Days War 262, 275, 277
slave labor 98
   Brazil 102
slave trade 66–7
Slavic people, protection of 328

'Smok', mythical Polish dragon 188
'social capital' in Egypt 267
social disequilibrium 98
social individualism, Sweden 171
socialism in Israel 277–8
socialization
    Germany 138
    Poland under Soviets 200
social learning theory 9
social networks, Chinese 301
social practices, corrupt 94
Sodom and Gomorrah 272
olidarity movement, Poland 195, 202
Solomon, son of David 272
'Son of Heaven' China 291
*Song of Roland* 154–5
South Africa 209–23
    Zulus 17
Soviet industry, modern 332
Soviet propaganda, Polish resistance
    190–91
space and climate in Canada 52–3
Spanish Armada 156
Spanish colonists of Caribbean 66
Spenser, Sir Edmund, *The Faerie
    Queene* 153
Spiderman 35, 38
'spirit of harmony' Buddhism 357
spirits, belief in 69
spirituality in India 320
St George, patron saint of England
    156–7
St Lucia 73–4
Stalin
    death 331
    leadership myth 329–31
    and Marxism
start-up business ventures 274–5
state-sponsored mythology, Soviet 329
stereotypes 140
    of military leaders 133
Sufism 265
sugarcane 66–7
    Brazil 102
Sunni Muslim 261
superheroes of United States mythology
    31–41
    changes in 43, 44, 45
'superheroes', not Greek 112
superhuman status of Vladimir Putin,
    Russia 335

superior abilities of Russian leaders 327,
    337
Superman in United States 34, 35,38–9
supervision as distrust 174
Suzuki, David, on climate change 57
Sweden 16, 166–84
    leadership 16, 170–76
    mythology 166–70
Switzerland 135
symbols
    of good fortune 295
    use of in Japan 350

Taliesin, Welsh bard 150
Taoism 291, 295
    eight as numeric basis 292
Tata companies, India 315–18
    paternalistic attitude 312
Tata, Ratan, Tata industries 315–18
team-based orientation 135, 138
team building, effective 86
teamwork 37, 176–7
    in Japanese companies 345
    in Sweden 171–72
technology 8
Tel-Hay hero 274
Tenmu, Emperor 344
terracotta warriors of Xian, burial site
    291
terrorist networks, global 43
Tetley Tea (UK) acquisitions by India
    316
Thinking (T) preference, Australia 365
third estate in Chaucer's England 154
Third Reich 128, 133
'time horizon', India 313
timing and speed, research and
    development 351
'Tomte', Swedish gnome, elf 169
Torah rabbinical students 274
Tor, thunder and lightning god 168
toughness in leadership, Australia 359
tourism industry, China 303
Toyota company, Japan 346, 349
traditional medicine 215
tragedy of Greek leaders 124
trains 230
Trans Canada Highway 50
transformational leadership 56
    German 135

transnational competence 3, 4, 5
tree-like growth of company, Japan 353
trickery against those in power 71, 73, 75–6
Trinidad 66, 67
trolls 170
Troy
    expedition against 117
    war against 120, 121
Trudeau, Pierre, Prime Minister of Canada 56
Trumpeldor, Yosef, self-sacrifice 274
trust-building, Japan 347
Tusk, Donald, Polish Prime Minister 191
Tutankhamun, descendant of Hatshepsut 260

uncertainty avoidance
    England 158
    India 310, 313
unification of Egypt 264
United States 12, 31–46
    flag, American reverence for 4
    leadership style 31
'universal harmony', Buddhism 357

valour of Greek leaders 123
value system, non-egalitarian, India 311
'value-based leadership' Japan 347–8
Vaner and Asar, god clans, Sweden 177
'Vaner', fertility gods, Sweden 167
VectorSeis technology 196
veneration of ancestors 213, 215
Vice and Virtue 119
VimpelCom, Russia 335
violence
    of Greek heroes 118–20
    in Russian leadership 336
virtue (moral duty) 309
Vishnu, preserver 308
visionary leadership, Iran 243
vision in Greek leadership 124
Voltaire, and Age of Enlightenment 178
Voodoo 13, 68, 69
Vorstand (executives group) 132
vulnerable spot of Siegfried 129

Wagner, Richard, 'Der Ring des Nibelungen' 129
Walesa, Lech, Poland 17, 202–3

Wales and the Welsh 146
war experience of Australians 361
war heroes in management 369–70
War Measures Act 1970 56
War of Independence 1948 277
Warring States period, China 290
warriors
    as folk heroes, Russia 327–8
    mythical leaders in England 147
Warsaw Ghetto 274
Warsaw Uprising, 1944 16, 189, 190
Washington, George, President of United States 34
WASP (White Anglo-Saxon Protestant) 147
Water Sprite, Nordic folktales 169
wealth creation of Jews, in finance 274
Wertheimer, Stef, established Iscar company 279, 281
Western approaches to Chinese mythology 294
Western culture
    Australia 360
    imposition of 220
    India, influence of 321
    Israel national culture as 270
    management, contrast with Egyptian 266
    style of democracy, Kenya 228
    systems of education, India 306
    theories of leadership 234
William I, Duke of Normandy 145–6
'Will'o the Wisp', Swedish 169
winter sports 52
wisdom and fairness, King Arthur 151
women
    Canadian leadership 60
    definition of royal lineage, Egypt 260
    English myth 158
    famous in Russia 332
    leaders, rare in Bible 272–3
    management, Australia 369
    Norse mythology 166
    power of, in Sweden 177
    respect for 155
women's votes in Argentina 81
Wonder Woman 35, 39
wooden horse of Troy 121
Wood-nymph, Sweden 169–70
work environment in Poland 198

worker attitudes, poor 76
workers and managers 76
Workers' Riots 1956, Poland 193
work ethic of Osman Ahmed Osman
  262–3
working class in Poland, empowering of
  193
'world best practice' management skills
  364
World Trade Center 43
World Tree 326
  *see also* Yggdrasil
worship of deities, suppression of 9
writers on Odysseus 121–22
writing system standardization, China
  291

Xiwang Mu, Queen Mother of West,
  China 291–2

X-Men 35, 39–40

Yellow Emperor, Huang Di, China 9, 10,
  20, 290–91
  myth, shift of meaning 303
'yes' and no' in Chinese business
  302
Yggdrasil, world tree 168, 183
Ymir, Norse frost giant 176
Yom Kippur war 1973 274–6, 278

Zeus 115–18
Zhang Ruimin, business leader 296–7
Zimin, Dmitrii, VimpelCom 335–6
Zionists
  freedom fights 273
  vision 279
Zoroastrian teachings 244, 254
Zulus of South Africa 210